COMPUTER VISION

COMPUTER SCIENCE, TECHNOLOGY AND APPLICATIONS

Additional books in this series can be found on Nova's website
under the Series tab.

Additional E-books in this series can be found on Nova's website
under the E-books tab.

COMPUTER SCIENCE, TECHNOLOGY AND APPLICATIONS

COMPUTER VISION

SOTA R. YOSHIDA
EDITOR

Nova Science Publishers, Inc.

New York

For permission to use material from this book please contact us:
Telephone 631-231-7269; Fax 631-231-8175
Web Site: http://www.novapublishers.com

NOTICE TO THE READER

The Publisher has taken reasonable care in the preparation of this book, but makes no expressed or implied warranty of any kind and assumes no responsibility for any errors or omissions. No liability is assumed for incidental or consequential damages in connection with or arising out of information contained in this book. The Publisher shall not be liable for any special, consequential, or exemplary damages resulting, in whole or in part, from the readers' use of, or reliance upon, this material. Any parts of this book based on government reports are so indicated and copyright is claimed for those parts to the extent applicable to compilations of such works.

Independent verification should be sought for any data, advice or recommendations contained in this book. In addition, no responsibility is assumed by the publisher for any injury and/or damage to persons or property arising from any methods, products, instructions, ideas or otherwise contained in this publication.

This publication is designed to provide accurate and authoritative information with regard to the subject matter covered herein. It is sold with the clear understanding that the Publisher is not engaged in rendering legal or any other professional services. If legal or any other expert assistance is required, the services of a competent person should be sought. FROM A DECLARATION OF PARTICIPANTS JOINTLY ADOPTED BY A COMMITTEE OF THE AMERICAN BAR ASSOCIATION AND A COMMITTEE OF PUBLISHERS.

Additional color graphics may be available in the e-book version of this book.

Library of Congress Cataloging-in-Publication Data

Computer vision / editor, Sota R. Yoshida.
    p. cm.
 Includes bibliographical references and index.
 ISBN 978-1-61209-399-4 (hardcover)
 1. Computer vision. I. Yoshida, Sota R.
 TA1634.C647 2011
 006.3'7--dc22
                        2010054279

Published by Nova Science Publishers, Inc. † New York

CONTENTS

Preface   vii

Chapter 1   Some Applications of Computer Vision Systems
                  in Micromechanics   1
                  E. Kussul, 0. Makeyev, T. Baidyk, A. Martín-Gonzalez
                  and G. Toledo-Ramirez

Chapter 2   A Survey of Face Recognition by the Genetic Algorithm   41
                  Fengzhi Dai , Yutaka Fujihara and Naoki Kushida

Chapter 3   The Attentive Co-Pilot: Robust Driver Assistance Relying
                  on Human-Like Signal Processing Principles   57
                  Thomas Paul Michalke1 and Robert Kastner

Chapter 4   Traffic Monitoring: A Practical Implementation
                  of a Real-Time Open Air Computer Vision System   187
                  Tomas Rodrıguez

Chapter 5   Algebraic Topology for Computer Vision   239
                  Daniel Freedman and Chao Chen

Chapter 6   Spectral Imaging Versus Non-Spectral Imaging   269
                  Ismail Bogrekci

Chapter 7   Least Squares Fitting of Quadratic Curves and Surfaces   285
                  N. Chernov and H. Ma

Chapter 8   Ontology Based Image and Video Analysis   303
                  Christopher Town

Chapter 9   Computer Vision by Laser Metrology and Algorithms
                  of Artificial Intelligence   329
                  J. A. Muñoz-Rodríguez

Index   363

PREFACE

Computer vision is the science and technology of machines that see, where seeing in this case means that the machine is able to extract information from an image that is necessary to solve some task. This new book presents topical research in the study of computer vision, including computer vision systems in micromechanics; genetic algorithm-based face recognition; algebraic topology for computer vision and computer vision by laser metrology and algorithms of artificial intelligence

Chapter 1- For general purpose image recognition systems the authors developed three neural classifiers: LIRA, PCNC, and Pairwise Coding Classifier. The authors tested the neural classifiers in various tasks of image recognition in the area of micro mechanics. The first task was the texture recognition problem. Different methods of mechanical metal treatment give different surface textures. It was made the computer vision system for recognition of 4 different types of workpiece treatment: milled surface, polished with sandpaper, turned with lathe, and polished with file. The LIRA classifier was used to solve this problem. 20 samples of each texture were prepared for the experiments. Some randomly selected samples were used for classifier training, and other samples were used for testing. In the case of 10 training samples 99.8% recognition rate was obtained. The second task was connected with recognition of the shape of small screws. When small screws are manufactured on computer numerical control (CNC) machine tool the cylinder part of the screw is turned with one cutter and the thread is made with another cutter. The mutual position of the cutters sometimes is not aligned precisely. In this case the shape of the thread will be incorrect. The recognition of the thread shape gives the information about mutual position of the cutters. This information allows us to correct the cutter positions. The authors tested the LIRA classifier in the task of thread shape recognition. The recognition rate of 98.9% was obtained. The cost of micromechanical devices will depend not only on the cost of manufacture of components but also on the cost of the device assembly. So, the assembly automation is very important. Many assembly procedures can be made with the aid of computer vision systems. Earlier the authors proved the LIRA classifier to obtain adaptive feedback in the pin-hole alignment task. Now they consider the problem of component selection from the depository, detection of their orientation and transportation to the assembly device. This is the third task that the authors describe in this chapter. This system will include the micromanipulator and camera, and will permit us to work with different micromechanical components without the development of new mechanical feeders. The manipulator using computer vision system must recognize the types of components, their position (coordinates) and their orientation. To solve this problem special program was written and tested. The authors will describe the image data base and the recognition results obtained in this task.

Chapter 2- Computer vision and recognition is playing an increasing important role in the modern intelligent control. Object detection is the first and the most important step in object recognition. Traditionally, special objects can be detected and recognized by the template matching method, but the recognition speed has always been a problem. Also for recognition by the neural network, training the data is always time consumption. In this chapter, the genetic algorithm-based face recognition system is proposed. The genetic algorithm (GA) has been considered as a robust and global searching method. Here, the chromosomes generated by GA contain information (parameters) of the image, and the genetic operators are used to obtain the best match between the original image and the face of interest. The parameters are the coordinate (x, y) of the center of the face in the original image, the rate of scale and the angle θ of rotation. The purpose of this chapter is to summarize the GA-based method for face detection and recognition. Finally, the experimental results, and a comparison with the traditional template matching method, and some other considerations, are also given.

Chapter 3- Increasingly complex driver assistance functionalities are combined in today's vehicles.Typically, these functionalities run as independent modules bringing own sensors,

processing devices, and actuators. In general, no information fusion, i.e., cross talk between modules, takes place as a consequence of unsolved questions in system design that come along with high system complexity. However, information fusion of available sensors and processing modules could lead to a new quality of driver assistance functionalities in terms of performance and robustness. Additionally, the growing number of driver assistance functionalities in today's vehicles will cause problems regarding the limited number of interaction channels to inform the driver of potential dangers - the so-called human machine interface (HMI). Already today, in specific traffic scenarios a contradicting HMI access of different driver assistance functionalities cannot be avoided. Furthermore, typical driver assistance functionalities on the market are based on highly specialized and optimized algorithms that show sound performance for a restricted number of clearly defined scenarios only. Also, the combinationof several of these rigid systems as a means to reach the long-term goal of autonomous driving will not lead to robust system performance, taken the immense variety of traffic situations into account. As opposed to that, the following contribution presents a flexible, biologically inspired driver assistance system that adapts its modules and data exchange between modules online depending on the task. More specifically, the morphology of the brain as well as brain-like signal processing principles are mimicked in order to increase the robustness and flexibility of the system. Thereby, authors aimed at reaching a generic system structure, that supports several system tasks by modulating and parameterizing its system modules (e.g., detect fast objects, redetect once tracked and later lost objects, predict object trajectories, locate cars on the road, detect traffic signs). Put differently, authors main research focus is on the design of general mechanisms that lead to a certain observable behavior without being explicitly designed for this behavior. Following that paradigm, a tunable attention sub-system was developed that allows the pre-filtering of the visual environment for task-relevant information in order to provide the driver with assistance in dangerous situations. In order to include information of the scene context into the system, a robust unmarked road detection module as well as an approach for assessing the general type of environment (highway, country road, inner-city) is included into the system.

The realized driver assistance system is tested online and in real-time on a prototype car. The gathered results prove the applicability of the developed biologically inspired driver assistance system in real-world scenarios. Extensive system evaluation shows that different system properties are in close compliance with measurements gathered in psychophysical studies of humans. Based on these results, it can be stated that the realized advanced driver assistance system closely models important human information processing principles allowing the usage of the system as Attentional Co-Pilot for human drivers.

Chapter 4- Open air is a challenging environment where few computer vision applications succeed. The reasons behind these difficulties must be found in the uncontrolled nature of open air applications. Computer vision is a passive technology. Typically a camera mounted on a mast observes the scene while using "clever" algorithms to interpret the images. However, doing this interpretation is no easy task since almost any type of moving or static object may appear in scene. Also, there are many circumstances which are not under direct control of the system: illumination changes caused by passing clouds, movements of the sun or day / night transitions; presence of shadows and moving artificial lights; camera artifacts resulting from blooming or smearing; overreaction of camera compensation devices; occlusions; vibrations of the camera; weather elements, such as: rain, snow or fog; etc.

All these circumstances combined turns computer vision in open scenarios into a formidable task. Only those applications working under very constrained conditions and with very concrete objectives will have any opportunity to succeed. In this chapter the authors present a computer vision based traffic monitoring system able to detect individual vehicles in real-time. Our fully integrated system first obtains the main traffic variables of the vehicles: counting, speed and category; and then computes a complete set of statistical variables. The objective is to investigate alternative solutions to some of the difficulties impeding existing traffic systems achieve balanced accuracy in every condition; most notably: day and night transitions, moving shadows, heavy vehicles, occlusions, slow traffic and congestions.

Chapter 5- Algebraic topology is generally considered one of the purest subfields of mathematics.However, over the last decade two interesting new lines of research have emerged, one focusing on algorithms for algebraic topology, and the other on applications of algebraic topology in engineering and science. Amongst the new areas in which the techniques have been applied are computer vision and image processing. In this paper, the authors survey the results of these endeavours. Because algebraic topology is an area of mathematics with which most computer vision practitioners have no experience, the authors review the machinery behind the theories of homology and persistent homology; our review emphasizes intuitive explanations. In terms of applications to computer vision, authors focus on four illustrative problems: shape signatures, natural image statistics, image denoising, and segmentation. Our hope is that this review will stimulate interest on the part of computer vision researchers to both use and extend the tools of this new field.

Chapter 6- Conventional approaches to Computer Vision harvested many opportunities for different disciplines and resulted in many applications and practices into our life. However, spectral imaging is promising many more looking into the future. Before author discuss what the difference between spectral and non-spectral imaging is, the authors shall define what the spectral and non-spectral imaging are at the beginning of this chapter. Later on, image acquisition tools and techniques will be discussed. Following on, the focus is intended to cover image processing techniques for spectral and non-spectral. Finally, the chapter is focused to discuss the advantages and disadvantages of spectral and non-spectral imaging.

Chapter 7- In computer vision one often fits ellipses and other conics to observed points on a plane or ellipsoids/quadrics to spacial point clouds. The most accurate and robust fit

is obtained by minimizing geometric (orthogonal) distances, but this problem has no closed form solution and most known algorithms are prohibitively slow. Authors revisit this issue based on recent advances by S. J. Ahn, D. Eberly, and our own. Ahn has sorted out various approaches and identified the most efficient one. Eberly has developed a fast method of projecting points onto ellipses/ellipsoids (and gave a proof of its convergence). Authors extend Eberly's projection algorithm to other conics, as well as quadrics in space. They also demonstrate that Eberly's projection method combined with Ahn's most efficient approach (and using Taubin's algebraic fit for initialization) makes a highly efficient fitting scheme working well for all quadratic curves and surfaces.

Chapter 8- This chapter shows how ontologies can be used as the basis for an effective computational and representational framework for computer vision. A particular focus is on the role of ontologies as a means of representing structured prior information and integrating different kinds of information in an inference framework. Ontologies are presented as an effective means of relating semantic descriptors to their parametric representations in terms of the underlying data primitives. The efficacy of the proposed approach is demonstrated through the development and analysis of solutions to a range of challenging visual analysis tasks. Firstly, author consider the problem of content based image retrieval (CBIR) Author present a CBIR system that allows users to search image databases using an ontological query language. Queries are parsed using a probabilistic grammar and Bayesian networks to map high level concepts onto low level image descriptors, thereby bridging the semantic gap between users and the retrieval system. Author then extend the notion of ontological languages to video event detection. It is shown how effective high-level state and event recognition mechanisms can be learned from a set of annotated training sequences by incorporating syntactic and semantic constraints represented by an ontology.

Chapter 9- The authors present a review of our algorithms for computer vision based on laser metrology and artificial intelligence. This chapter includes laser metrology, image processing, contouring by neural networks, modelling of mobile setup and vision parameters. To achieve the computer vision, the object shape is reconstructed by a laser metrology method. To carry it out, the object is scanned by a laser line. Based on the deformation of the laser line, a network provides object dimension. The behavior of the laser line is obtained by image processing. The modelling of the relationship between the laser line and the object shape is performed b approximation networks. The architecture of the networks is built using data of images of a laser line projected on objects, whose dimensions are known. The approach of the neural networks is to perform the contouring without measurements on the optical setup. Also, the network provides the camera parameters and the setup parameters. Thus, the performance and accuracy are improved. It is because the errors of the measurement are not passed to the contouring system. To describe the accuracy a root mean square of error is calculated using data produced by the networks and data provided by a contact method. This technique is tested with real objects and its experimental results are presented.

In: Computer Vision
Editor: Sota R. Yoshida

Chapter 1

SOME APPLICATIONS OF COMPUTER VISION SYSTEMS IN MICROMECHANICS

*E. Kussul[1], O. Makeyev[2], T. Baidyk[1], A. Martín-Gonzalez[3]
and G. Toledo-Ramirez[4]**

[1]CCADET, Universidad Nacional Autónoma de México (UNAM), México
[2]Department of Electrical and Computer Engineering
Clarkson University, Potsdam, NY, USA
[3]Computer Aided Medical Procedures,
Technische Universitaet Muenchen (TUM), Germany
[4]Institute for Industrial Automation and Software Engineering,
Stuttgart University, Germany

ABSTRACT

For general purpose image recognition systems we developed three neural classifiers: LIRA, PCNC, and Pairwise Coding Classifier. We tested the neural classifiers in various tasks of image recognition in the area of micro mechanics. The first task was the texture recognition problem. Different methods of mechanical metal treatment give different surface textures. It was made the computer vision system for recognition of 4 different types of workpiece treatment: milled surface, polished with sandpaper, turned with lathe, and polished with file. The LIRA classifier was used to solve this problem. 20 samples of each texture were prepared for the experiments. Some randomly selected samples were used for classifier training, and other samples were used for testing. In the case of 10 training samples 99.8% recognition rate was obtained. The second task was connected with recognition of the shape of small screws. When small screws are manufactured on computer numerical control (CNC) machine tool the cylinder part of the screw is turned with one cutter and the thread is made with another cutter. The mutual position of the cutters sometimes is not aligned precisely. In this case the shape of the thread will be incorrect. The recognition of the thread shape gives the information about

---

∗ ekussul@servidor.unam.mx; makeyevo@clarkson.edu; tbaidyk@servidor.unam.mx; anabel.martin@hotmail.com; toledo@ias.uni-stuttgart.de

mutual position of the cutters. This information allows us to correct the cutter positions. We tested the LIRA classifier in the task of thread shape recognition. The recognition rate of 98.9% was obtained. The cost of micromechanical devices will depend not only on the cost of manufacture of components but also on the cost of the device assembly. So, the assembly automation is very important. Many assembly procedures can be made with the aid of computer vision systems. Earlier we proved the LIRA classifier to obtain adaptive feedback in the pin-hole alignment task. Now we consider the problem of component selection from the depository, detection of their orientation and transportation to the assembly device. This is the third task that we describe in this chapter. This system will include the micromanipulator and camera, and will permit us to work with different micromechanical components without the development of new mechanical feeders. The manipulator using computer vision system must recognize the types of components, their position (coordinates) and their orientation. To solve this problem special program was written and tested. We will describe the image data base and the recognition results obtained in this task.

I. TEXTURE RECOGNITION TASK

1.1 Introduction

The main approaches to microdevice production are the technology of Micro Electromechanical Systems (MEMS) [12, 17] and Microequipment Technology (MET) [1, 5, 9, 13]. To get the best of these technologies it is important to have advanced image recognition systems.

Texture recognition systems are widely used in industrial inspection, for example, in textile industry for detection of fabric defects [4], in electronic industry for inspection of the surfaces of magnetic disks [6], in decorative and construction industry for inspection of polished granite and ceramic tiles [16], etc.

Numerous approaches were developed to solve the texture recognition problem. Many statistical texture descriptors are based on a generation of co-occurrence matrices. In [6] the texture co-occurrence of n-th rank was proposed. The matrix contains statistics of the pixel under investigation and its surrounding. Another approach was proposed in [16]. The authors proposed the Coordinated Cluster Representation (CCR) as a technique of texture feature extraction. The underlying principle of the CCR is to extract a spatial correlation between pixel intensities using the distribution function of the occurrence of texture units. Experiments with one-layer texture classifier in the CCR feature space prove this approach to be very promising. Leung et al. [11] proposed textons (representative texture elements) for texture description and recognition. The vocabulary of textons corresponds to the characteristic features of the image. There are many works on applying neural networks in texture recognition problem [7, 14].

In this chapter we propose the LIRA neural classifier [1] for metal surface texture recognition. Four types of metal surfaces after mechanical treatment were used to test the proposed texture recognition system.

Different lighting conditions and viewing angles affect the grayscale properties of an image due to such effects as shading, shadowing, local occlusions, etc. The real metal surface images that it is necessary to recognize in industry have all these problems and what is more there are some problems specific for industrial environment, for example, metal surface can have dust on it.

The reason to choose a system based on neural network architecture for the current task was that such systems have already proved their efficacy in texture recognition due to significant properties of adaptability and robustness to texture variety [8].

We have chosen the LIRA neural classifier because we have already applied it in the flat image recognition problem in microdevice assembly and the results were very promising [1]. We have also tested it in handwritten digit recognition task and its recognition rate on the MNIST database was 99.45% [1] that is among the best results obtained on this database.

1.2 Metal surface texture recognition

The task of metal surface texture recognition is important to automate the assembly processes in micromechanics [9]. To assembly a device it is necessary to recognize the position and orientation of the work pieces to be assembled [1]. It is useful to identify the surface of a work piece to recognize its position and orientation. For example, let the shaft have two polished cylinder surfaces for bearings, one of them milled with grooves for dowel joint, and the other one turned with the lathe. It will be easier to obtain the orientation of the shaft if we can recognize both types of the surface textures.

There are works on fast detection and classification of defects of mechanically treated metal surfaces [7, 14]. In [14] a back propagation neural network based approach to surface inspection of rolling bearing metal rings is proposed. In [7] a Genetic Algorithm (GA) based approach to finding and quantitative evaluation of minor flaws of metal surfaces of the multi-plate clutch is proposed. In both cases preprocessing of the initial images of the metal surfaces is needed. In [14] the brightness histogram serves as an input to the neural network. In [7] model-based matching technique is used and the correlation between the initial image and the surface-strip model is used as a fitness function of the GA.

The only work on texture classification of mechanically treated metal surfaces that we know is [3]. The authors propose to use a vibration-induced tactile sensor that they called Dynamic Touch Sensor (DTS) combined with one-layer Rosenblatt perceptron [15]. The DTS produces signals based on the vibration induced by a sensor needle sliding across the metal surface with fixed velocity and pressure. The motion path of the sensor is a part of a circle of approximately 100 degrees. Such motion path permits to capture information about surface in both directions in one sweep; however, system is very sensitive to the changes in texture position and orientation. Spectral energy of the sensor was used as an input to the neural classifier. Metal surfaces were characterized by two characteristics: surface type and surface roughness. Surface roughness is a measure of the average height of the surface irregularities given in microinches. In texture recognition system testing six types of surfaces and six values of surface roughness were used. The obtained recognition rate varied from 74.16% in recognition of two types of metal surfaces with roughness of 8 microinches to 100% in recognition of three types of metal surfaces with roughness of 250 microinches. In our experiments we achieved the recognition rate of 99.7% in recognition of four types of metal surfaces with roughness of the order of 1 microinch. Not to mention that our approach doesn't require the use of a complex mechanical sensor and is robust to the changes in texture orientation and position.

To test our texture recognition system we created our own image database of metal surface images. Four texture classes correspond to metal surfaces after: milling, polishing with sandpaper, turning with lathe and polishing with file (Figure 1). 20 grayscale images of 220x220 pixels were taken for each class. We randomly divide these 20 images into the training and test sets. It can be seen that different lighting conditions affect greatly the grayscale properties of the images. The textures may also be arbitrarily oriented and not centered perfectly. Metal surfaces may have minor defects and dust on it. All this image properties correspond to the conditions of the real industrial environment and make the texture recognition task more complicated. Two out of four texture classes that correspond to polishing with sandpaper and to polishing with file sometimes can be hardly distinguished with the naked eye (Figure 1, columns *b* and *d*).

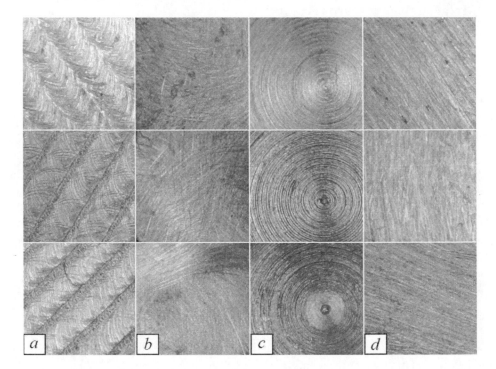

Figure 1. Examples of metal surfaces after (columns): a) milling, b) polishing with sandpaper, c) turning with lathe, d) polishing with file.

On the first stage of our experiments with this image database we worked with texture recognition system based on the Random Subspace (RSC) neural classifier [2]. The best recognition rate of 80% was obtained in recognition of three classes of metal surfaces. The class that corresponds to metal surface after polishing with file was excluded because of its similarity with the class that corresponds to metal surface after polishing with sandpaper. The numbers of images in training and test sets were 3 and 17 correspondingly. The use of the LIRA neural classifier in our texture recognition system resulted in recognition rate of 83.39% in recognition of four classes of metal surfaces with only 2 images in training set and 18 images in test set.

1.3 The LIRA neural classifier

The LIRA (Limited Receptive Area) [1] neural classifier was developed on the basis of the Rosenblatt perceptron [15]. The three-layer Rosenblatt perceptron consists of the sensor S-layer, associative A-layer and the reaction R-layer. The first S-layer corresponds to the retina. In technical terms it corresponds to the input image. The second A-layer corresponds to the feature extraction subsystem. The third R-layer represents the system's output. Each neuron of this layer corresponds to one of the output classes.

The associative layer A is connected to the sensor layer S with the randomly selected, non-trainable connections. The weights of these connections can be equal either to 1 (positive connection) or to -1 (negative connection). The set of these connections can be considered as a feature extractor.

A-layer consists of 2-state neurons; their outputs can be equal either to 1 (active state) or to 0 (non-active state). Each neuron of the A-layer is connected to all the neurons of the R-layer. The weights of these connections are modified during the perceptron training.

We have made four major modifications in the original perceptron structure. These modifications concern random procedure of arrangement of the S-layer connections, the adaptation of the classifier to grayscale image recognition, the training procedure and the rule of winner selection.

We propose two variants of the LIRA neural classifier: LIRA_binary and LIRA_grayscale. The first one is meant for the recognition of binary (black and white) images and the second one for the recognition of grayscale images. The structure of the LIRA_grayscale neural classifier is presented in Figure 2.

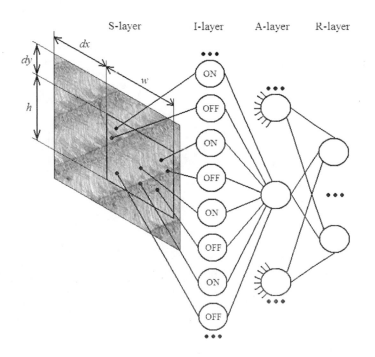

Figure 2. The structure of the LIRA_grayscale neural classifier.

The one-layer perceptron has very good convergence, but it demands the linear separability of the classes in the parametric space. To obtain linear separability it is necessary to transform the initial parametric space represented by pixel brightness to the parametric space of larger dimension. In our case the connections between the S-layer and the A-layer transform initial $(W_S \cdot H_S)$ - D space (W_S and H_S stand for width and height of the S-layer) into N-dimension space represented by binary code vector. In our experiments $W_S = H_S = 220$ and N varied from 64,000 to 512,000. Such transformation improves the linear separability. The coding procedure used in the LIRA classifier is the following.

1.3.1. Image coding

Each input image defines the activities of the A-layer neurons in one-to-one correspondence. The binary vector that corresponds to the associative neuron activities is termed the image binary code $A = (a_1, ..., a_N)$, where N is the number of the A-layer neurons. The procedure that transforms the input image into the binary vector A is termed the image coding.

We connect each A-layer neuron to S-layer neurons randomly selected not from the entire S-layer, but from the window $h \cdot w$ that is located in the S-layer (Figure 2).

The distances dx and dy are random numbers selected from the ranges: dx from $[0, W_S - w)$ and dy from $[0, H_S - h)$. We create the associative neuron masks that represent the positions of connections of each A-layer neuron with neurons of the window $h \cdot w$. The procedure of random selection of connections is used to design the mask of A-layer neuron. This procedure starts with the selection of the upper left corner of the window $h \cdot w$ in which all connections of the associative neuron are located.

The following formulas are used:

$$dx_i = random_i\,(W_S - w), \tag{1}$$
$$dy_i = random_i\,(H_S - h),$$

where i is the position of a neuron in associative layer A, $random_i(z)$ is a random number that is uniformly distributed in the range $[0, z)$. After that position of each connection within the window $h \cdot w$ is defined by the pair of numbers:

$$x_{ij} = random_{ij}(w), \tag{2}$$
$$y_{ij} = random_{ij}(h),$$

where j is the number of the connection with the retina.

Absolute coordinates of the connection on the retina are defined by the pair of the numbers:

$$X_{ij} = x_{ij} + dx_i, \tag{3}$$
$$Y_{ij} = y_{ij} + dy_i.$$

In case of the LIRA_binary neural classifier A-layer neurons are connected to S-layer neurons directly (Figure 3). In this case S-layer consists of 2-state neurons; their outputs can be equal either to 1 (active state) or to 0 (non-active state). The weights of connections between the S-layer and the A-layer are randomly selected and are equal either to 1 (positive connection) or to -1 (negative connection). For example, in Figure 3 four connections, two positive (marked with arrows) and two negative (marked with circles), are chosen within the window $h \cdot w$. The i-th neuron of the A-layer is active ($a_i = 1$) only if all the positive connections with retina correspond to active neurons of the S-layer and all negative connections correspond to non-active neurons and is non-active ($a_i = 0$) in the opposite case.

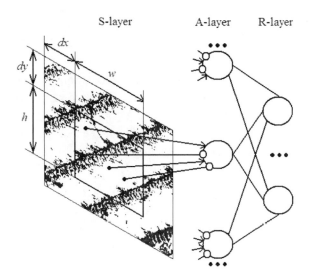

Figure 3. The structure of the LIRA_binary neural classifier.

To adapt the LIRA neural classifier for grayscale image recognition we have added the additional 2-state neuron layer between the S-layer and the A-layer. We term it the I-layer (intermediate layer, see Figure 2).

The input of each I-layer neuron is connected to one neuron of the S-layer and the output is connected to the input of one neuron of the A-layer. All the I-layer neurons connected to one A-layer neuron form the group of this A-layer neuron. The number of neurons in one group corresponds to the number of positive and negative connections between one neuron of the A-layer and the retina in the LIRA_binary structure. There are two types of I-layer neurons: ON-neurons and OFF-neurons. The output of the ON-neuron i is equal to 1 if its input value is larger than the threshold θ_i and it is equal to 0 in the opposite case. The output of the OFF-neuron j is equal to 1 if its input value is smaller than the threshold θ_j and it is equal to 0 in the opposite case. The number of ON-neurons in each group corresponds to the number of the positive connections of one A-layer neuron in the LIRA_binary structure. The number of OFF-neurons in each group corresponds to the number of the negative connections. For example, in Figure 2, the group of eight I-layer neurons, four ON-neurons and four OFF-neurons, corresponds to one A-layer neuron. The rule of connection arrangement between the retina and one group of the I-layer is the same as the rule of mask design for one A-layer neuron in the LIRA_binary structure. The thresholds θ_i and θ_j are selected randomly from the range $[0, \eta \cdot b_{max}]$, where b_{max} is maximal brightness of the image pixels, η is the parameter selected experimentally from the range $[0, 1]$. The i-th neuron of the A-layer is active ($a_i = 1$) only if outputs of all the neurons of its I-layer group are equal to 1 and is non-active ($a_i = 0$) in the opposite case.

Taking into account the small number of active neurons it is convenient to represent the binary code vector not explicitly but as a list of numbers of active neurons. Let, for example, the vector A be:

$$A = 00010000100000010000.$$

The corresponding list of the numbers of active neurons will be 4, 9, and 16. Such compact representation of code vector permits faster calculations in training procedure. Thus, after execution of the coding procedure every image has a corresponding list of numbers of active neurons.

The LIRA_binary neural classifier can be used for the recognition of grayscale images after transforming them to binary form, for example, by the following procedure:

$$\theta = \frac{2 \cdot (\sum\limits_{i=1}^{W_S} \sum\limits_{j=1}^{H_S} b_{ij})}{W_S \cdot H_S}, \tag{4}$$

$$s_{ij} = \begin{cases} 1, if\ b_{ij} > \theta, \\ 0, if\ b_{ij} \leq \theta, \end{cases} \tag{5}$$

where θ is the threshold value, b_{ij} is the brightness of the grayscale image pixel with coordinates (i, j), s_{ij} is the brightness of the resulting binary image pixel with coordinates (i, j). However, experiments performed on the MNIST grayscale image database [1] have shown that the recognition rate obtained with the LIRA_grayscale neural classifier on original grayscale images was better than the one obtained with the LIRA_binary neural classifier on the transformed binary images. That is why taking into account that our current image database is grayscale we worked with the LIRA_grayscale neural classifier.

The training and recognition procedures are the same for both LIRA_binary and LIRA_grayscale neural classifiers. The training procedure is the following.

1.3.2 Training procedure

Before starting the training procedure the weights of all connections between neurons of the A-layer and the R-layer are set to 0. As distinct from the Rosenblatt perceptron our LIRA neural classifier has only non-negative connections between the A-layer and the R-layer.

The first stage. The training procedure starts with the presentation of the first image to the LIRA neural classifier. The image is coded and the R-layer neuron excitations E_i are computed. E_i is defined as:

$$E_i = \sum_{j=1}^{N} a_j \cdot w_{ji},$$

(6)

where E_i is the excitation of the i-th neuron of the R-layer, a_j is the output signal (0 or 1) of the j-th neuron of the A-layer, w_{ji} is the weight of the connection between the j-th neuron of the A-layer and the i-th neuron of the R-layer.

The second stage. Robustness of the recognition is one of the important requirements the classifier must satisfy. After calculation of the neuron excitations of the R-layer, the correct class c of the image under recognition is read. The excitation E_c of the corresponding neuron of the R-layer is recalculated according to the formula:

$$E_c{}^* = E_c \cdot (1 - T_E),$$

(7)

where $0 \le T_E \le 1$ determines the reserve of excitation the neuron that corresponds to the correct class must have. In our experiments the value T_E varied from 0.1 to 0.5.

After that we select the neuron with the largest excitation. This winner neuron represents the recognized class.

The third stage. Let us denote the winner neuron number as j keeping the number of the neuron that corresponds to the correct class denoted as c. If $j = c$ then nothing is to be done. If $j \ne c$ then following modification of weights is to be done:

$$w_{ic}(t+1) = w_{ic}(t) + a_i,$$

(8)

$$w_{ij}(t+1) = w_{ij}(t) - a_i,$$

(9)

$$\text{if}\,(w_{ij}(t+1) < 0) \text{ then } w_{ij}(t+1) = 0,$$

where $w_{ij}(t)$ and $w_{ij}(t+1)$ are the weights of the connection between the i-th neuron of the A-layer and the j-th neuron of the R-layer before and after modification, a_i is the output signal (0 or 1) of the i-th neuron of the A-layer.

The training process is carried out iteratively. After all the images from the training set have been presented the total number of training errors is calculated. If this number is larger than one percent of the total number of images then the next training cycle is performed, otherwise training process is stopped. The training process is also stopped if the number of performed training cycles is more than a predetermined value.

It is obvious that in every new training cycle the image coding procedure is repeated and gives the same results as in previous cycles. Therefore in our experiments we performed the coding procedure only once and saved the lists of active neuron numbers for each image on the hard drive. Later, during the training procedure, we used not the images, but the corresponding lists of active neurons. Due to this approach, the training process was accelerated approximately by an order of magnitude.

It is known [10] that the performance of the recognition systems can be improved with implementation of distortions of the input image during the training process. In our experiments we used different combinations of horizontal, vertical and bias image shifts, skewing and rotation.

1.3.3 Recognition procedure

In our LIRA neural classifier we use image distortions not only in training but also in recognition process. There is an essential difference between implementation of distortions for training and recognition. In the training process each distortion of the initial image is considered as an independent new image. In the recognition process it is necessary to introduce a rule of decision-making in order to be able to make a decision about a class of the image under recognition based on the mutual information about this image and all its distortions. The rule of decision-making that we have used consists in calculation of the R-layer neuron excitations for all the distortions sequentially:

$$E_i = \sum_{k=0}^{d} \sum_{j=1}^{N} a_{kj} \cdot w_{ji},$$ (10)

where E_i is the excitation of the i-th neuron of the R-layer, a_{kj} is the output signal (0 or 1) of the j-th neuron of the A-layer for the k-th distortion of the initial image, w_{ji} is the weight of the connection between the j-th neuron of the A-layer and the i-th neuron of the R-layer, d is the number of applied distortions (case $k = 0$ corresponds to the initial image).

After that we select the neuron with the largest excitation. This winner neuron represents the recognized class.

1.4 Results

To test our texture recognition system we created our own image database of mechanically treated metal surfaces (see Section 2 for details). We work with four texture classes that correspond to metal surfaces after: milling, polishing with sandpaper, turning with lathe and polishing with file. 20 grayscale images of (220 x 220) pixels were taken for each class. We randomly divide these 20 images into the training and test sets for the LIRA_grayscale neural classifier. The number of images in training set varied from 2 to 10.

All experiments were performed on a Pentium 4, 3.06 GHz computer with 1.00 GB RAM.

We carried out a large amount of preliminary experiments first to estimate the performance of our classifier and to tune the parameter values. On the basis of these preliminary experiments we selected the best set of parameter values and carried out final experiments to obtain the maximal recognition rate. In preliminary experiments the following parameter values were set: window $h \cdot w$ width $w = 10$, height $h = 10$, parameter that determines the reserve of excitation the neuron that corresponds to the correct class must have $T_E = 0.3$. The following distortions were chosen for the final experiments: 8 distortions for training including 1 pixel horizontal, vertical and bias image shifts and 4 distortions for recognition including 1 pixel horizontal and vertical image shifts. The number of training cycles was equal to 30.

The numbers of ON-neurons and OFF-neurons in the *I*-layer neuron group that corresponded to one *A*-layer neuron were chosen in order to keep the ratio between the number of active neurons K and the total number of associative neurons N within the limits of $K = c \cdot \sqrt{N}$, where c is the constant selected experimentally from the range [1, 5]. This ratio corresponds to neurophysiological data. The number of active neurons in the cerebral cortex is hundreds times less than the total number of neurons. For example, for the total number of associative neurons $N = 512,000$ we selected three ON-neurons and five OFF-neurons.

In each experiment we performed 50 runs to obtain statistically reliable results. That is, the total number of recognized images was calculated as number of images in test set for one run multiplied by 50. New mask of connections between the *S*-layer and the *A*-layer and new division into the training and test sets were created for the each run.

In the first stage of final experiments we changed the total number of associative neurons N from 64,000 to 512,000. The results are presented in Table 1. Taking into account that the amount of time needed for 50 runs of coding and classifier's training and recognition with $N = 512,000$ is approximately 3 h and 20 min (4 min for one run) we can conclude that such computational time is justified by the increase in the recognition rate. That is why we used $N = 512,000$ in all the posterior experiments.

Table 1. Dependency of the recognition rate on the total number of associative neurons

Total number of associative neurons	Number of errors / Total number of recognized images	% of correct recognition
64,000	20 / 2000	99
128,000	13 / 2000	99.35
256,000	8 / 2000	99.6
512,000	6 / 2000	99.7

In the second stage of final experiments we performed experiments with different combinations of distortions for training and recognition. The results are presented in Table 2. It can be seen that distortions used in training process have great impact on the recognition rate that is no wonder if to take into account that the use of distortions for training allows to increase the size of training set 9 times. Distortions used in recognition process also have significant positive impact on the recognition rate.

Table 2. Dependency of the recognition rate on the distortions

Distortions		Number of errors / Total number of recognized images	% of correct recognition
Training	Recognition		
-	-	1299 / 2000	35.05
-	+	1273 / 2000	36.35
+	-	14 / 2000	99.3
+	+	6 / 2000	99.7

In the third stage of final experiments we performed experiments with different numbers of images in the training and test sets. The results are presented in Table 3. The note tr./t. reflects how many images were used for training (tr.) and how many for testing (t.). It can be seen that even in case of using only 2 images for training and 18 for recognition the LIRA_grayscale neural classifier gives a good recognition rate of 83.39%.

Table 3. Dependency of the recognition rate on the number of images in training set

tr./t.	Number of errors / Total number of recognized images	% of correct recognition
2/18	598 / 3600	83.39
4/16	174 / 3200	94.56
6/14	34 / 2800	98.78
8/12	8 / 2400	99.67
10/10	6 / 2000	99.7

1.5 Discussion

The LIRA neural classifier was tested in the task of texture recognition of mechanically treated metal surfaces. This classifier does not use floating point or multiplication operations. This property combined with the classifier's parallel structure allows its implementation in low cost, high speed electronic devices. Sufficiently fast convergence of the training process and very promising recognition rate of 99.7% were obtained on the specially created image database (see Section 2 for details). There are quite a few methods that perform well when the features used for the recognition are obtained from a training set image that has the same orientation, position and lighting conditions as the test image; but as soon as orientation or position or lighting conditions of the test image is changed with respect to the one in the training set the same methods will perform poorly. The usefulness of methods that are not robust to such changes is very limited and that is the reason for developing of our texture classification system that works well independently of the particular orientation, position and lighting conditions. In this regard the results obtained in experiments are very promising.

1.6. Conclusion

This chapter continues the series of works on automation of micro assembly processes [1, 9].

The LIRA neural classifier is proposed for texture recognition of mechanically treated metal surfaces. It can be used in systems that have to recognize position and orientation of complex work pieces in the task of assembly of micromechanical devices as well as in surface quality inspection systems. The performance of the proposed classifier was tested on specially created image database in recognition of four texture types that correspond to metal surfaces after: milling, polishing with sandpaper, turning with lathe and polishing with file. The promising recognition rate of 99.7% was obtained.

II. TASK OF SHAPE RECOGNITION OF SMALL SCREWS

We propose a neural network based vision system for attending micro pieces manufacturing process in micromechanics. The system permits us to recognize the shape of micro pieces (screws of 3 mm diameter) in order to get information for controlling and improving the manufacturing process. The neural classifier used for the shape recognition task is termed Limited Receptive Area Grayscale (LIRA Grayscale). The developed vision system has a recognition rate of 98.90%. This work is motivated by the idea of obtaining an automated control system for micro machines. This chapter contains a detailed description of the model and learning rules, and discusses future perspectives.

2.1 Introduction

Shape recognition is a major problem in image understanding and computer vision. In the area of micromechanics, shape recognition is an important task that is related to many micro factory processes such as micro device assembly task [1], micro piece manufacturing process [18], among others [2, 19].

The micro factory concept was proposed in Japan in 1990 at the Mechanical Engineering Laboratory (MEL) with the developing of a desktop machining micro factory [13]. The micro factory consists of machine tools such as a lathe, a milling machine and a press machine; and assembly machines such as a transfer arm and a two-fingered hand. This portable micro factory has external dimensions of 625 × 490 × 380 mm. The purpose of the micro factory concept is to build very small production units saving space and energy and characterized by a high level of flexibility.

In 1996, the Micro Equipment Technology (MET) was proposed [20]. In Mexico, scientists from the Center of Applied Sciences and Technological Development (CCADET), UNAM developed and applied this technology [9]. The main idea of this method is to create successive generations of micro equipment, in which the micro equipment sizes of each generation have smaller sizes than the ones of the previous generations. Each generation produces the micro machine tools of its next generation. This approach would allow to use low cost components for each micro equipment generation and to create micro factories capable to produce low cost micro devices. The disadvantage of this micro equipment is the poor precision of their processes. So we suggest the construction of micro factories composed with micro machine tools with automated control of their process in order to have autonomous and precision systems. Therefore, it is necessary to develop such control systems that improve its precision.

One of the main problems in such micro factories is the automation on the base of vision systems. There are different approaches to construct a computer vision system for these purposes [21-23].

One of the mechanical micro components produced by micro machine tools (i.e., micro lathe) is the screw. These are necessary components to construct micro equipment. The problem related on producing these micro pieces is that some of these could have shape defects. These errors are related to the microscrew cutter tool position (Figure 4). Because of the micro machine small size it is impossible to use ordinary instruments (on a large scale) for control processes. It is necessary to create a vision system that controls automatically the manufacturing process of these work pieces by means of a shape recognition process. High-quality micro pieces will be achieved in this case.

Our purpose is to develop a vision system based on an artificial neuronal network (LIRA_grayscale) to attend micro screws manufacturing process. The system's target will be the recognition of the shape of the micro work pieces. Thus, the information obtained can be used to make the appropriate manufacturing corrections (i.e., relocate the cutter position) in case of error detection. The vision system proposed in this chapter can be used with micro machines tools of MET technology for improving their performance and precision.

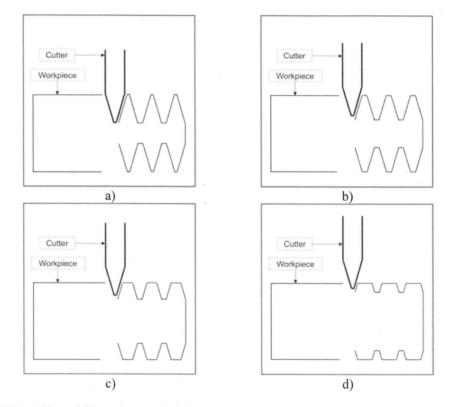

Figure 4. The position of the cutting tool relatively to the work piece: (a) cutting tool located 0.1 mm below the correct position, (b) cutting tool located at the correct position, (c) cutting tool located 0.1 mm above the correct position, (d) cutting tool located 0.2 mm above the correct position.

2.2 Neural Classifier LIRA_grayscale

Progress of neuroscience and information technologies give us opportunity to develop not only recognition system based on neural networks but makes possible actual implementation of old ideas to enable individual human being informational individuality with ability of autonomous existence ("life") in computers [24]. The artificial neural networks as one of the mechanisms can be realized with different methods, for example, through computer simulation [1], [2], [18], [19] or neuro-holographic processing [25]. One of the interesting approaches is a vector presentation of associative memory [26]. We will describe the special type of neural classifiers [1], [27].

The neural classifier LIRA (Limited Receptive Area), based on Rosenblatt's perceptron principles, was tested on micro device assembly tasks and handwritten digit recognition showing good results [1, 27]. We adapted LIRA for classifying microscrew grayscale images after the manufacturing process. The resulting neural network was termed LIRA_grayscale [27], [28].

2.2.1 Architecture

LIRA_grayscale consists of four layers: input layer (S), intermediate layer (I), associative layer (A) and output layer (R). The neural classifier architecture is presented in Figure 5. The input layer neurons correspond to every image pixel having outputs in range [0, 255], where 0 and 255 indicate the minimum (black) and maximum (white) brightness pixel value. This layer has $W \times H$ neurons, where W and H correspond to the image width and height. The S-layer is connected to A-layer through I-layer by means of a random procedure we will describe later, and the resulting connections are non-trainable ones.

The intermediate layer adapts LIRA_grayscale for handling grayscale images. This layer is located between S-layer and A-layer. The I-layer contains N groups of neurons, where N corresponds to the total number of neurons in the associative layer A. There are two types of neurons in I-layer: ON-neurons and OFF-neurons. According to the brain mechanisms for vision presented in [29], ON-neurons react with the presence of a stimulus and OFF-neurons with the absence of it. These neurons have two-state output values {0, 1}, where 1 indicates a neuron active state.

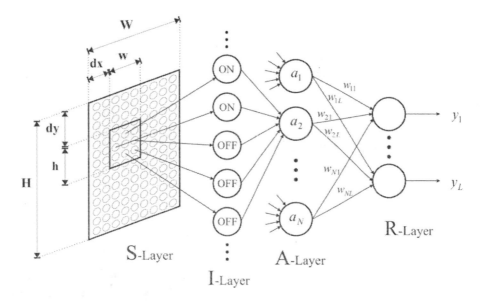

Figure 5. LIRA_grayscale detailed architecture.

The associative layer corresponds to an image feature extractor containing neurons with two-state outputs {0, 1}. The A-layer is fully connected to R-layer, where the weights of these connections will be modified during the training process. The output layer consists of linear neurons and the number of neurons in this layer corresponds to the number of classes to recognize. The R-layer is the system's output.

2.2.2 Layer interconnections and neuron activation

The procedure to connect the input layer S with the associative layer A through the I-layer is as follows. Let N be the number of associative neurons. For each associative neuron a_k, where $k = 1, ..., N$, we randomly select a rectangular area (called window) of $h \times w$ neurons in S-layer, as in Figure 5. From this window we randomly choose m neurons (points) that will be randomly divided into two sets, one of p positive points and one of n negative points, where $p + n = m$. A positive point is defined as an S-layer neuron connected to an ON-neuron of I-layer and a negative point as an S-layer neuron connected to an OFF-neuron of I-layer. Every positive and negative point from this window will be connected to an ON-neuron and OFF-neuron of I-layer that has no previous connections, respectively, forming a new neurons group k in I-layer, and each one of these neurons in this group will have a threshold T_{mk} randomly selected from the range [0, 255]. This group k of m neurons of intermediate layer will be connected to the a_k neuron. This connection process will be done only once before training.

Let x_{ij} be an S-layer input neuron. The output of an ON-neuron will be equal to 1 (active state) if its input value is larger than a threshold T_{pk} and will be equal to 0 otherwise, i.e.,

$$\varphi_{on}(x_{ij}) = \begin{cases} 1, x_{ij} \geq T_{pk} \\ 0, x_{ij} < T_{pk} \end{cases} \tag{11}$$

The output of an OFF-neuron will be equal to 1 (active state) if its input value is smaller than a threshold T_{nk} and will be equal to 0 otherwise, i.e.,

$$\varphi_{off}(x_{ij}) = \begin{cases} 1, x_{ij} \leq T_{nk} \\ 0, x_{ij} > T_{nk} \end{cases} \tag{12}$$

An associative neuron will have output equal to 1 (active state) if all ON-neurons and OFF-neurons connected to it are active, otherwise the output will be 0. Each associative neuron acts like one image feature, which output shows if this feature exists or is absent in the image.

2.2.3 Learning method

The neural network we propose uses a supervised learning method that implements a winner selection scheme. This scheme consists of applying to the simple rule of winner selection the following modification: let y_g be the winner neuron output, let y_c be its nearest competitor neuron output, if

$$\frac{y_g - y_c}{y_g} < T_e \tag{13}$$

the competitor is now considered the winner, where T_e is a constant termed the winner neuron superfluous excitation parameter. This modification was proposed in order to improve the recognition process, eliminating the possibilities of selecting a winner neuron by chance.

The learning process consists of three stages described next.

2.2.3.1. Initial phase.

The training procedure begins with the presentation of the image to the neural network input layer. The image features are extracted and coded through I-layer and A-layer, respectively. The R-layer neuron output y_i is computed, as

$$y_i = \sum_{k=1}^{N} w_{ki} \cdot a_k \qquad (14)$$

where y_i is the output (excitation) of the i-th neuron of the R-layer, a_k is the output signal (0 or 1) of k-th neuron of A-layer, w_{ki} is the weight of the connection between k-th neuron of A-layer and i-th neuron of R-layer.

2.2.3.2. Winner selection scheme.

After calculating all the outputs of R-layer neurons, the neuron output y_r, corresponding to the neuron real class, is modified by the factor $(1 - T_e)$, i.e.,

$$y_r = y_r \cdot (1 - T_e) \qquad (15)$$

After this, the neuron having maximum excitation is selected as the winner neuron g.

2.2.3.3. Weights adaptation.

Once we have obtained the winner neuron (recognized class by LIRA_grayscale), if the neuron r (real class neuron) is the same as the neuron g (winner class neuron), the connection weights remain unchanged; but if $r \neq g$ then

$$\forall k, w_{kr}(t+1) = w_{kr}(t) + a_k$$
$$\forall k, w_{kg}(t+1) = w_{kg}(t) - a_k$$

if

$$(w_{kg}(t+1) < 0) \rightarrow w_{kg}(t+1) = 0$$

where $w_{ki}(t)$ is the connection weight between k-th neuron of A-layer and i-th neuron of R-layer before reinforcement, $w_{ki}(t+1)$ is the same weight connection after reinforcement, a_k is the output signal of k-th neuron of A-layer.

This process will be repeated until a convergence criterion is reached, in our case, until the maximum number of training cycles (epochs) is attained or the recognition error equals zero. A test phase is then carried out, in which unknown test images are presented to the network to establish the extent to which the network has learned the task in hand.

2.2.4. Improvements in learning process

The image features extracted and coded in the first two layers are the same for every epoch of the training procedure. Therefore, in our experiments we performed the coding procedure only once and saved the lists of active associative neuron indexes for each image on the hard drive. Later, during the training procedure, we used not the images but the corresponding lists of active A-layer neurons. Due to this approach, the training process was accelerated approximately by an order of magnitude.

Reference [10] shows that the performance of the recognition systems can be improved by implementing distortions to the input image during training process. In our experiments we used different image transformations by combining horizontal and vertical displacements and rotations.

2.3 Results

To test the performance of the neural classifier LIRA_grayscale we create an image database with 440 grayscale images of 40 microscrews of 3 mm diameter (11 images in different positions per microscrew) with resolution of 320×280 in BMP format (Figure 6). We worked with four different microscrew classes; therefore we had 110 microscrew images per class.

In class 0 the micro screws were manufactured with a cutter position of 0.1 mm below the cutter correct position, for class 1 the micro screws were manufactured with the cutter correct position, for classes 2 and 3 the micro screws were manufactured with a cutter position of 0.1 mm and 0.2 mm above the correct one, respectively (see Figure 6). The total number of images from the database was randomly divided to form the training and test sets for the neural classifier. We carried out preliminary experiments to estimate the neural classifier performance and for tuning its parameters. On the basis of these experiments we selected the best set of parameter values and carried out final experiments in order to obtain the maximal recognition rate. The following parameters were set: associative neurons $N = 512\ 000$, the winner neuron superfluous excitation parameter T_e was set to 0.3, a window size of 20×20 with 4 positive and 3 negative points. To select the number of ON-neurons and OFF-neurons from I-layer corresponding to one associative neuron in A-layer we were based on that the active neuron number K in A-layer must be many times less than the whole associative neuron number N of this layer, i.e.,

$$K = c \cdot \sqrt{N}$$

where c is a constant experimentally selected from the range [1, 13]. This relation corresponds to neurophysiologic facts: the active neurons in the cerebral cortex is hundreds times smaller than the total number of neurons.

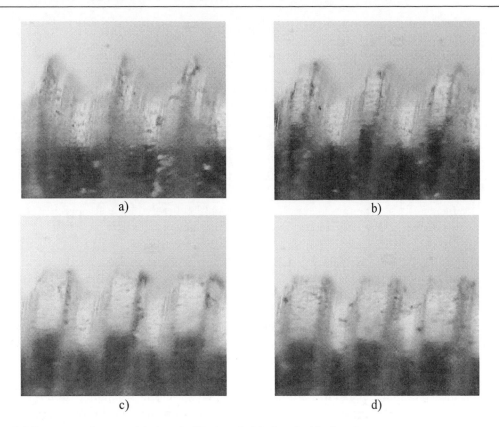

Figure 6. Micro screw images: (a) class 0, (b) class 1, (c) class 2, (d) class 3.

Three main experiments were done for evaluating the system. In order to obtain statistically reliable results we execute 30 runs for each experiment. Thus, the total number of images to recognize was calculated as the number of test images for one run multiplied by 30 and the recognition errors number was calculated as the sum of the misrecognized images per run.

In the first experiment we chose images from six micro screws per class for training and the last four for testing, from a total of 10 micro screws per class (Table 4). Since we varied the image transformations number we had three different numbers of training images related with it (i.e., 0, 4, and 8). The second experiment consists of images from seven micro screws per class for training and three for testing (Table 5). In the last experiment we selected images from eight micro screws per class for training and the last two for testing (Table 6).

Table 4. Recognition rates 6 / 4

Image Distortions	Training Images / Test Images	Recognition Errors Number / Images to Recognize	Recognition Rate (%)
0	264 / 176	88 / 5280	98.33
4	1320 / 176	86 / 5280	98.37
8	2376 / 176	84 / 5280	98.41

Table 5. Recognition rates 7 / 3

Image Distortions	Training Images / Test Images	Recognition Errors Number / Images to Recognize	Recognition Rate (%)
0	308 / 132	57 / 3960	98.56
4	1540 / 132	56 / 3960	98.59
8	2772 / 132	52 / 3960	98.69

Table 6. Recognition rates 8 / 2

Image Distortions	Training Images / Test Images	Recognition Errors Number / Images to Recognize	Recognition Rate (%)
0	352 / 88	34 / 2640	98.71
4	1760 / 88	33 / 2640	98.75
8	3168 / 88	29 / 2640	98.90

It can be seen that the training sample size is an important parameter because as the number of training images increases also the recognition rate increases. For example, in Table 4 with 264 training images it obtains 98.33% of recognition rate and in Table 6 with 352 training images it obtains 98.71%, this is 0.38% more exactitude.

On the other hand, image transformations help on increasing the recognition rate too. For example, in Table 5 as the number of image transformations increments, the recognition rate improves.

In addition, we compared our results with the classifier based on ensembles of extremely randomized decision trees for image classification [30] which was evaluated on different publicly available object recognition databases (MNIST, ORL, COIL-100, etc.) and had promising results. We tested this classifier the same way as ours and with 3168 training images and 88 test images it gave 44 recognition errors from a total of 2640 images to recognize, and therefore the recognition rate of 98.33%. The process time for this classifier was 10 minutes while LIRA_grayscale performed the same task in two minutes.

2.4 Conclusion

The neural classifier LIRA_grayscale for shape recognition of microscrew images for manufacturing process was developed. It was trained and tested with a database containing images of 40 micro screws of four classes, where every class is related to the definite cutter position. The recognition rate for the training phase was 100% and for the test phase, in the best case, the recognition rate was of 98.90%. These results are acceptable, nevertheless is necessary to improve the classification precision.

Finally, we want to notice that the major advantage of this neural classifier LIRA_grayscale is its universality. It was not constructed for a particular shape recognition problem but that can be adapted and be implemented in different image recognition problems.

III. TASK OF MICRO WORK PIECE RECOGNITION WITH LIRA NEURAL CLASSIFIER

The aim of this section is to describe a technical vision system for automation of micro manufacturing and micro assembly processes. One of the principal problems is connected with the recognition of work pieces and detection of their positions. For this purpose we use neural classifier named limited receptive area (LIRA_grayscale). This classifier was developed for wide range of image recognition tasks. Special software was designed. We describe some experiments and results of application of LIRA in the recognition of micro work pieces and their positions for automated handling system. The best recognition rate obtained was 94%.

3.1 Introduction

The miniaturization of products coupled with development of new technologies [31], [32] has enabled us to develop equipment and instruments of small dimensions [20], [33]. Our aim is to create fully automated desktop microfactory. With help of this microfactory it is possible to create smaller and smaller microfactories. We consider different generations of micro-factories, each of them corresponds to a microfactory of certain dimensions. The proposed technology is MicroEquipment Technology (MET) [20]. In development of each generation new problems will appear, but a lot of useful products can be produced. We are developing this technology at the Centre of Applied Science and Technological Development (CCADET) of National Autonomous University of Mexico (UNAM) [9], [33].

The most important areas of microtechnology applications are: automotive industry, medical engineering, electronics, security systems, vision systems, environmental control, traffic control, communication networks and aerospace technology.

The potential market for microproducts was estimated in more than 30 billions euros in 2002 [34]. Micromanufacturing and microassembly processes automation is fundamental goal to achieve good performance of corresponding equipment [5], [13]. It is important to apply computer vision methods in automation. One essential part of an automated microfactory is a system for work pieces handling. We are working out a fully automated work pieces handling system. The goal of this system is to recognize one random-located work piece in work area, to define its coordinates, to take it with manipulator and to transport it to another place. This system has to be flexible. This means, the system must be able to handle work pieces of different dimensions and shapes.

The scheme of the proposed system is presented in Figure 7.

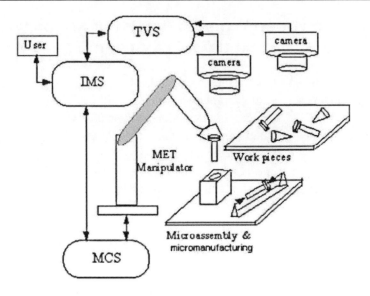

Figure 7. The scheme of automatic work piece handling system.

This system is composed of two cameras, one manipulator and three subsystems: manipulator control subsystem (MCS), technical vision subsystem (TVS) and intelligent manipulation subsystem (IMS). The manipulator has special characteristics for mini–micro handling abilities. It will have six degrees of freedom. We use general purpose, low cost, commercial CCD cameras. They serve as an input to the TVS. The main purpose of this system is to process the data from the cameras for recognize work pieces and their positions. This is the main topic of this section. The IMS controls the whole system. This means it gives the instructions to manipulator, processes the data from the TVS, and communicates between both and with the user. The user can be a person or another system.

We begin to work with the system that contains one camera and the TVS. TVS is based on the method of micro work piece recognition and their position detection. For this purpose we adapted the neural classifier LIRA_grayscale [35]. In work piece recognition task we obtained the recognition rate of more than 90%. In position detection task we obtained coordinates of recognized work pieces.

3.2 State of the art and related works

Object recognition problem and different methods to solve this task are presented in [36], [37]. There are many approaches and methods to resolve the object recognition problem. Very often the first step of these methods is to extract contours from the image. We want to analyze four methods based on contour images applied to objects of 2D, these methods are: pattern matching, principal component analysis, graph matching and generalized Hough transform [38].

3.2.1. Pattern matching method

The square differences between an image I and a template image T are summed pixel wise:

$$r(x, y) = \sum_{i \in T} \sum_{j \in T} (I(x + i, y + j) - T(i, j))^2 \tag{16}$$

If the resulting sum is larger than experimentally obtained threshold, the object template T is found in I. This method is time and memory consuming and it does not handle brightness changes or scaling on image.

3.2.2. Principal components analysis method

This is a correlation based technique. The application of this technique has the learning phase and the application phase. The image is stored in a vector. To reduce the computation time this vector is transformed to a smaller dimension vector with a vector transformation T. This vector is chosen to maximize the variation of the transformed image vectors. In the application phase, an image to be processed is transformed with vector T and after that the correlation with the database images is found [39]. This method has detection stability and detection correctness but it is time consuming and it works only if the object can be differentiated from the background.

3.2.3. Graph matching method

The idea is to analyze orthogonal line segments that cross certain points of the object contour. The search of image features is performed along these lines. The similar features are used to compare a model with a given image for object recognition. Any feature can be implemented in this method (colour, brightness, texture or others). This method demands memory, but time is reduced. Under specific conditions this method can work with partially hidden, scaled or rotated objects. This method does not work with images that have several objects. It is hard to recognize small objects too.

3.2.4. Generalized Hough transform (GHT)

The contours are approximated by a set of points taken in the object contour. Every point of the object contour is described in terms of some reference point inside the contour. The contour image can be obtained by the application of a Laplacian-of-Gauss filter. Partially hidden, scaled or rotated objects can be recognized. This method is not memory consuming but it is time consuming and it does not work with small objects on images.

The super quadrics technique is used for object recognition and modeling. The super quadrics consist of a parametric descriptive family of shapes. In the $2D$ case it is defined as:

$$\overline{X}(\theta) = \begin{pmatrix} a_1 \cos \theta^{\varepsilon} \\ a_2 \sin \theta^{\varepsilon} \end{pmatrix} \tag{17}$$

where $\overline{X}$ is a $2D$ vector that describes an image object contour; q is the orientation angle; 3 is the shape parameter; a_1 and a_2 are the size parameters [40]. This function describes a large set of simple geometrical figures like circles, rectangles, etc and more complicated ones like ellipses. Combining these basic shapes, super quadrics can be used for modeling of a lot of objects. Super quadrics object recognition is used in $3D$ recognition [41]. Super quadrics are invariant to object size and orientation. Super quadrics technique has a lot of problems in complex shape object recognition, i.e. in the recognition of the natural objects.

For object recognition the neural networks are used [35], [42], [43]. Adaptive learning, flexibility and recognition in real time are very useful characteristics of neural networks for object recognition tasks. There are some works on object recognition for robot handling or manufacturing systems that use neural networks as their basic recognition technique [42]–[44]. J. Radjenovic and H. Detter use image after a preprocessing stage as input to the neural classifier. The best recognition rate obtained was 97.7% for three classes of objects. The time for preprocessing stage was 1.2 and 0.4 s for recognition. Mitzias and Mertzios [43] use in their work a multineural classifier approach. It consists of three neural networks working in parallel. A different preprocessing stage is used for each one of the classifiers. So, each classifier works with different characteristics of the image to be processed like brightness, textures or contours. To examine the method they used nine irregular flat objects with a hole. This approach requires too much time or too much computer resources to achieve real time recognition.

Preprocessing stage is widely used for image preparation to the specific recognition technique. Several preprocessing techniques are used, according to the specific recognition method and the characteristics of the base images. The most frequently used techniques are: edge detection, part segmentation, feature extraction methods, calculation of geometrical parameters. The preprocessing stage takes a lot of computing resources and time with respect to the total computer time for object recognition tasks.

Micromanufacturing and microassembly technologies need the automation of handling and machining systems. The system for assembly has been proposed by Mardanov et al. [45]. The proposed assembly station has logical modules and common information paths to be easily integrated into the whole automated assembly system.

We selected neural network based approach because it was successfully applied to different problems of image recognition. For example, in handwritten digit recognition this approach has shown the best results. The recognition rate of 99.6% was reported for the MNIST database in the paper [46]. As far as we know this is the best result for this database. We tested our LIRA neural classifier on the MNIST database and obtained the recognition rate of 99.45% [27]. We also tested the LIRA neural classifier in micro assembly problem [1], [35], [44]. We have applied it to the recognition of mutual pin-hole position. For this purpose image database of 441 images was created. We collected the images for different positions of pin with steps of 0.1 mm along X and Y axes. We used one web camera and four light sources that gave us pin shadows. These shadows together with pin and hole permit us to recognize the mutual $3D$ pin-hole position. The output of LIRA classifier in that case was the coordinates (X, Y). We obtained the recognition rate of 99.5% for X coordinate and of 89.9% for Y coordinate with the precision 0.1 mm. It is a rather high quality of recognition [1].

After obtaining these encouraging results we decided to apply LIRA neural classifier for micro work piece recognition. We describe our method based on a neural classifier LIRA that is robust, fast and includes a grey scale image preprocessing stage.

3.3 Technical Vision Subsystem (TVS)

The aim of the TVS is to recognize microobjects and their positions. It has three internal subsystems: interface, object finder that searches for certain work pieces and defines their position and orientation, and the camera controller that controls the camera and its data flow (Figure 8).

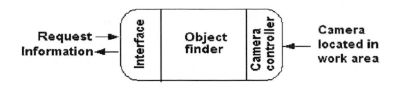

Figure 8. The structure of the TVS.

The task of TVS is to find the object on the image. In Figure 9 the coordinates x, y and the orientation angle θ of the required work piece are presented. The task is to find a work piece, its coordinates, and orientation with an acceptable performance.

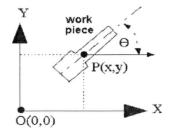

Figure 9. Example of the object with coordinates x, y and the orientation angle θ.

TVS is developed as a part of an automated general purpose micromechanical system. To test TVS we chose different types of work pieces that are presented in Figure 10.

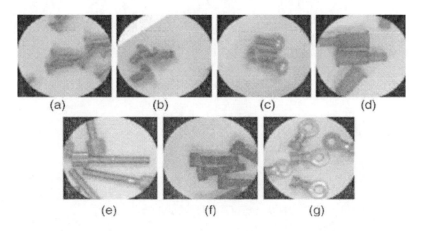

Figure 10. Seven different types of work pieces: (a) tube base, (b) cone head screw, (c) round head screw, (d) cone, (e) stator axis, (f) Allen screw, (g) wire terminal.

We work with seven classes of objects: tube base, cone head screw, round head screw, cone, stator axis, Allen screw and wire terminal. These work pieces sometimes have dirty surfaces, insufficient illumination, and heterogeneous brightness; sometimes they are surrounded by shadows that complicate the recognition task. Every work piece has to be recognized by the TVS from a set of random distributed work pieces. Further we will describe the preprocessing of images. In the next section we will describe the proposed method of image recognition.

3.4. Neural classifier

3.4.1. The structure

The neural classifier that we use is based on the principles of the random subspace classifier (RSC) and modified Rossenblatt Perceptron [15]. We term this neural classifier as limited receptive area grey scale or simply LIRA_grayscale. This classifier was proposed and tested in [27] with good results in handwritten digit recognition. This neural classifier we want to adapt to resolve new task. Let us describe the LIRA_grayscale structure (Figure 11).

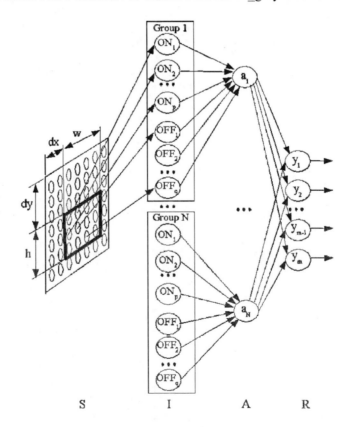

Figure 11. LIRA_ grayscale structure for work pieces recognition.

The LIRA_grayscale neural classifier is an artificial neural network with four layers: Input layer (*S*), Layer of groups (*I*), Associative layer (*A*), Output layer (*R*). *S* layer corresponds to the input image to be classified. In this layer, called retina, each neuron corresponds to the brightness of each pixel of the image to be processed; therefore, the output range of these neurons is $[0, B]$, where 0 corresponds to null brightness (black) and B equals to the highest brightness. This layer has $W \times H$ neurons, where W and H are, respectively, the width and the height of the image to be classified. The group layer or I layer contains N neuron groups, each group i contains p ON-neurons and q OFF-neurons. Each ON-neuron is active if $x_{ij} > T_{ONij}$, each OFF-neuron is active if $x_{ij} < T_{OFFij}$, where x_{ij} is the input of the corresponding neuron (the brightness of corresponding pixel in the S layer), T_{ONij} is the ON-neuron threshold and T_{OFFij} is the OFF-neuron threshold. Each neuron threshold is randomly selected within $[0, B \times h]$, where h is a constant selected experimentally from $(0,1]$. The neurons of the group are randomly connected with the neurons of S layer located in a rectangular window $(w \times h)$ defined on S layer. Values dx and dy are selected randomly from $[0, W - w]$ to $[0, H - h]$, respectively. Parameters w and h are very important for performance of the neural classifier, and should be chosen experimentally. Connections between S layer and I layer cannot be modified in the training process.

The A layer contains N neurons; each neuron has $(p + q)$ inputs connected to the outputs of corresponding group. The A layer neuron is active if, and only if all its inputs are active, the neuron output equals 1 if it is active and equals 0 if it is not. The connections between layers I and A can not be modified in the training process. All A layer neurons are connected to each R layer neuron. The weights of these connections are modified in the training process. The output from R layer neuron i is calculated with the following equation

$$ y_i = \sum_{j=0}^{N} w_{ji} a_j , \tag{18} $$

where w_{ji} is the connection weight between A layer neuron j and R layer neuron i and a_j is the output of the A layer neuron. When an image is assigned to the classifier input we calculate the activity of A layer neurons and present the activity as a binary vector A. This calculation we term 'image coding' and the vector A we term 'image code'. We store the image codes of training set on the hard drive for not to repeat the coding process in each training cycle.

3.4.2. Training process

At the start of training process we set all the weights of the connections between the layers A and R equal to zero. The process begins with an image input to the classifier. The image is coded and presented to the classifier to be recognized, and the output of the classifier is calculated. To make the training robust, after calculation of the R layer outputs, the correct class corresponding to the input image is read. Its output y_i is modified according to the equation

$$ y_i = y_i(1 - T_E) , \tag{19} $$

where T_E is a constant termed additional excitation of the winner neuron. After that, the neuron from layer R with the highest output value, called the winner, is detected. This neuron represents the recognized class for the given input y_w be the winner neuron output and y_c the output of the neuron that really represents the correct class. If $y_w = y_c$ nothing to be done.

If $y_w \neq y_c$,then

$$(\forall j)w_{jc}(t+1) = w_{jc}(t) + a_j \, , \qquad\qquad (20)$$

$$(\forall j)w_{jw}(t+1) = w_{jw}(t) - a_j \, , \qquad\qquad (21)$$

$$(\forall j)w_{jw}(t+1) < 0 \Rightarrow w_{jw}(t+1) = 0 \, , \qquad\qquad (22)$$

where $w_{jc}(t)$ is the corresponding weight of the connection between the A layer neuron j and the correct R layer neuron c before modification and $w_{jc}(t+1)$ is the weight after modification; $w_{jw}(t)$ is the corresponding weight of A layer neuron j with the winner neuron of R layer before modification and $w_{jw}(t+1)$ is the weight after modification; a_j is the output value of A layer neuron j. The training process of the neural classifier is an iterative process. First all images from the training set are coded. After this, each training cycle deals with the image codes but not with the initial images. It allows us to save computer time. The training process stops after fixed number of cycles or when the amount of errors in the training cycle is lower than a predefined value.

3.4.3. Distortions

The training image set can be enlarged by adding new images obtained by application of distortions to the original images. In our investigation, we applied rotational distortions. Each image was rotated in clockwise and counter clockwise directions forming the pairs of new images.

3.5 Software and databases

3.5.1. The developed software

We developed object oriented software called OptikRNA for several tasks. With this software we realize the LIRA neural classifier, create databases for classifier training and testing. In Figure 12 the structure of OptikRNA is presented. This software has three principal modules: Optik, RNA and RNA interface. Optik functions help the user to create work piece database for the neural classifier training and test, to define characteristics of work pieces and to perform some basic preprocessing procedures. RNA module contains the LIRA neural classifier. The entire RNA module functions and the communications between user and databases are made by RNA interface module. The RNA interface module searches for certain work piece on the image and defines its position.

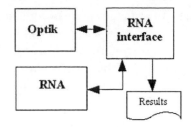

Figure 12. Block diagram of the OptikRNA software.

The user defines the properties like height or width for each type of work piece in Optik module. This information is stored in the system. Source image contains several random located work pieces. The user marks each work piece approximately in the centre of its major axis. Then Optik module normalizes image of each work piece. These normalized images are stored creating the database. RNA module implements the LIRA neural classifier. This module communicates with other modules and with the user only by RNA interface module. RNA interface module is developed to manage the neural classifiers and the available databases, to train and test the classifier, and to look for certain work piece in a source OptikRNA software was tested and results are presented in this section.

3.5.2. Databases

We use two databases in our experiments. The first and smaller database that contains 150 images was used for initial experiments with LIRA classifier and parameter tuning. The second and larger database that contains 320 images was used for verify the results and for practical recognition and position finder experiments.

3.5.3. Chosen work pieces

For our experiments, we chose seven different types of work pieces (Figure 10). The chosen work pieces are of different size (between 28.8 and 4.2 mm.) and shapes but not all of them. The work pieces geometry has circular parts. There are three classes of work pieces that are very similar (Figure 10 a–c).

3.5.4. Databases description

Both databases were created with the help of specially designed software. This software was applied to several initial images that contained large sets of work pieces. Every image was taken by a low resolution CCD camera. A top view of work pieces without special illumination was used. By the software, the user marks the centre of the major axis of the work pieces on the images. Then, the software extracts and normalizes images for database creation. Normalization means that every database image is grey scale with 256 levels, has size of (150 x 150) pixels, work pieces on the image are centered and have fixed orientation (its major axis is coincided with axis X). A circular window algorithm is used to make image rotations easier. In the process of the image database creation, the work pieces on the images are not isolated (they are heaped up), so the images can contain some work pieces in addition to the normalized one.

The first database contains 30 images for each of five different work piece classes, 15 images for the training set and other 15 images for the test set. The first four classes correspond to different types of work pieces and the fifth one to the work piece absence in the centre of the image (Figure 13).

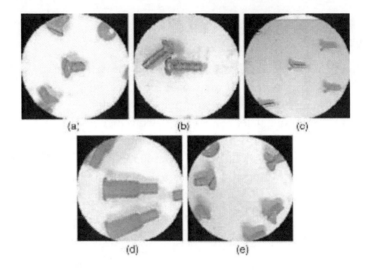

Figure 13. Examples of five image classes from database I used in parameter tuning of the classifier: (a) screw I, (b) screw II, (c) tube base, (d) cone, and (e) no work piece in central point of image.

The second database contains 40 images for each of the eight different classes of work pieces, 20 images for the training set and 20 images for the test set. The eight classes consist of seven different types of work pieces (Figure 14) and the eighth class corresponding to the absence of work piece in the centre of the image. The images for the training and test set were randomly selected.

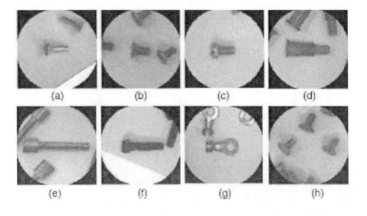

Figure 14. Examples of eight different classes from database II used for LIRA neural classifier training and test: (a) tube base, (b) cone head screw, c) round head screw, (d) cone, (e) stator axis, (f) Allen screw, (g) wire terminal, and (h) no work piece in the central point of image.

The training set of images can be enlarged with distortions applied to the original set. The images have low resolution, heterogeneous brightness and some of them have the shadows. In addition, sometimes a background is not homogenious. Such characteristics present real conditions and make the recognition problem more complicated. We trained and tested the classifier on normalized images from our databases. Due to random selection of work pieces from database to training and test sets the obtained results are statistically reliable.

3. 6. Experiments and results

We tuned the classifier parameters with several experiments on database I. For the LIRA neural classifier we find the parameters (for example, w and h for LIRA window, number of training cycles and number of neurons of A layer) to achieve the best recognition rate. Several experiments were made for this purpose. We did the similar experiments with contour images of work pieces too. Final experiments were made on database II to recognize the work piece positions.

3.6.1. Work piece recognition with grey scale images
We tested several parameter combinations. In the first group of experiments we did not use distortions of training images. We show the results of this group of experiments in Table 7. The best result was achieved in experiment with a window of 15 x 15 pixels, 175 000 neurons in A layer, four ON-neurons and three OFF-neurons in each group, classifier parameter h equal to 1.0 and training parameter T_E equal to 0.15. For these parameters the percentage of active neurons in A layer was 0.164%. In this experiment percentage of correct recognitions was 94%. For experiments of this group the best performance was reached with 40 training cycles. The training time for 75 images was less than 1.5 min.

Table 7. The experiments for the parameter tuning (database I).

Number of experiments:	1	2	3	4	5	6	7	8	9
Window size (w x h)	12x12	15x15	15x15	10x10	13x13	17x17	15x15	15x15	10x10
Experimental classifier constant (η)	0.8	1.0	1.0	1.0	1.0	1.0	1.0	1.0	1.0
Number of neurons in layer A (N) (thousands)	175	175	175	175	175	175	175	200	200
Number of ON-neurons by group (p)	3	3	4	4	4	5	4	4	4
Number of OFF-neurons by group (q)	4	4	3	3	3	3	3	3	3
Active neurons (%)	0.06	0.09	0.16	0.12	0.13	0.08	0.17	0.17	0.15
Recognition rate (%)	68	89	94	93	85	88	93	89	89

3.6.2. Experiments with distortions
The experiments of the second group were performed with distortions of the training images. The purpose was to improve classifier recognition of work pieces with different

orientations. The results of these experiments are presented in Table 8. The best result was obtained in experiment with six distortions (+ 15°, +10°, +5v, -5°, -10°, -15°).

Table 8.Experiments with distortions

Experiment number	1	2	3	4
Distortions number	6	10	10	16
Step(°)	5	10	3	3
Distortions angles	± 5, 10, 15	± 10, 20, 30, 40, 50	± 3, 6, 9, 12, 15	± 3, 6, 9, 12, 15, 18, 21, 24
Training cycles	80	10	60	80
Recognition rate (%)	92	68	88	90

The training time in case of 16 distortions of the training images was approximately 16 min. The recognition time of any normalized image from any database was less than 0.4 s.

3.6.3. Work piece recognition in contour images

We made the same experiments with the images that were preprocessed. We extracted the contours of the images using a filter based algorithm. The LIRA classifier, in this case, demonstrated poor results, only 12% of correct recognition.

3.6.4. Experiments with database II and position recognition

We found the best parameters for the LIRA_grayscale classifier on the database I. After that we trained the classifier with images from database II without adding distortions. In this case we achieved the best result of 90%. Six classes of images (round head screw, cone, stator axis, allen screw, wire terminal and no work piece in the central point of image) where recognized with a recognition rate of 100%. The images from the other two classes (tube base and cone head screw) were recognized with several errors. These work pieces are very similar in size and shape. Examples of badly recognized images are shown in Figure 15.

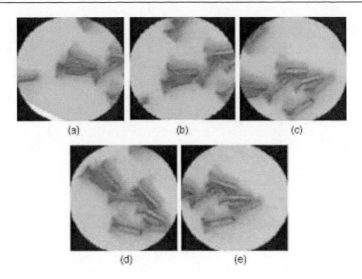

Figure 15. Examples of the images from database II, which were not recognized by the system.

3.6.5. Position recognition

The TVS goal is not only to recognize the work piece but to find the position of this work piece to handle it with a manipulator. For this task, the point from a work piece to be found is the centre of its major axis.

We applied the position algorithm to find certain work piece in a given image after the classifier training with the eight classes from the database II (Figure 14). The algorithm begins with the window (w x h) moving across the whole image. This movement is performed from the centre of the initial image (x_0, y_0) in the form of clockwise snail and serves to find a specific work piece (Figure 16).

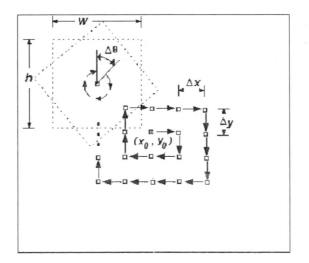

Figure 16. The scheme of the window movement (spiral trajectory).

The little square is the centre of the window. The vertical and horizontal steps of this movement are Δx and Δy, respectively. At each position the centre of the window is rotated by an angular step $\Delta \theta$ (Figure 16). For each angular position the system searches for the requested work piece. The window continues to rotate until something is recognized or a complete revolution is made. The window centre moves until something is recognized or image limits are achieved. If a work piece is recognized the system store the coordinates c, Δy, $\Delta \theta$ and finish the recognition task. The user is able to indicate the window displacement parameters (Δy, Δy, $\Delta \theta$) for investigation goals.

In Figure 17 we show two examples of recognized images.

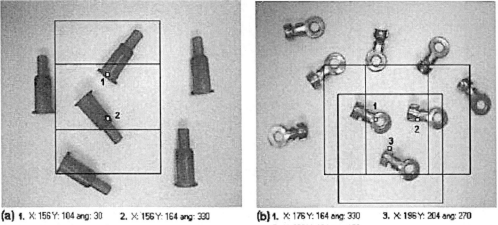

(a) 1. X: 156 Y: 104 ang: 30   2. X: 156 Y: 164 ang: 330   (b) 1. X: 176 Y: 164 ang: 330   3. X: 196 Y: 204 ang: 270
                                                               2. X: 236 Y: 164 ang: 150

Figure 17. Work piece position recognition.

The image contains two recognized cones (cones 1, 2 in the Figure 17(a)). In Figure 17(b) image contains three recognized wire terminals (1, 2, 3). The little white square in this figure represents the position where the request work piece was recognized and the big square represents the search window attached to this position. At the bottom of the images you can read the position coordinates and orientation found by the system for each recognized work piece. The LIRA classifier is a flexible method, this means, the system recognizes a work piece out of its centre, but sufficiently near of the work piece body.

Sometimes the system can recognize one work piece several times. In Figure 18 is shown multiple recognition of one work piece (case 1 and 3). In some cases this happens because the system is able to find a work piece far away of its centre point, for example marks 2, 3 in Figure 18(a) and 1, 7 in Figure 18(b). In other cases, it happens because the window movement step (q_x, q_y, q_q) is too large, for example mark 1 in Figure 18(a) and marks 2, −5, 8, 9 in Figure 18(b). Marks 4 (Figure 18(a)) and 6 (Figure 18(b)) have sufficient accuracy for a manipulator work.

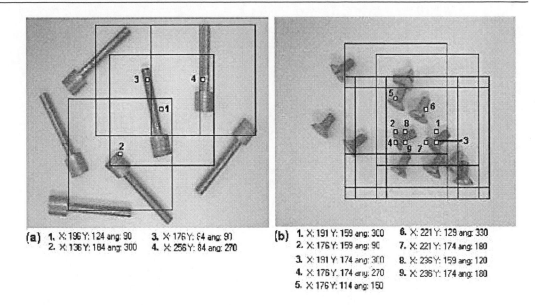

(a) 1. X: 196 Y: 124 ang: 90   3. X: 176 Y: 84 ang: 90
      2. X: 136 Y: 184 ang: 300   4. X: 256 Y: 84 ang: 270

(b) 1. X: 191 Y: 159 ang: 300   6. X: 221 Y: 129 ang: 330
      2. X: 176 Y: 159 ang: 90   7. X: 221 Y: 174 ang: 180
      3. X: 191 Y: 174 ang: 300   8. X: 236 Y: 159 ang: 120
      4. X: 176 Y: 174 ang: 270   9. X: 236 Y: 174 ang: 180
      5. X: 176 Y: 114 ang: 150

Figure 18. Work piece position recognition with redundancy.

Two examples of images with work pieces that contact each other are presented in Figure 19. In Figure 19(a) the system found three work pieces, though these objects are far from the image centre. In Figure 19(b) the system has redundancy. In this case, it can filter the best recognized work piece by taking the higest value of neural network output, this means, the best recognized work piece in this case corresponds to mark. We faced with two specific recognition problems. The first problem is to avoid work piece recognition redundancy and the second problem is to improve the accuracy of the work piece finder. The obtained results are sufficiently good, but the searching method should be improved. All these experiments were realized with an Intel Pentium 4, 2.66 GHz personal computer with 512 MB RAM

3.7 Discussion

LIRA classifier was adapted to recognize the micro work pieces of different classes. It demonstrates sufficiently good results in object recognition even if the images are of low quality and have the different illumination. The best results were obtained with normalized images. Two classes (tube base and cone head screw, Figure 14(a) and (b)) were recognized with errors. In the future it is necessary to improve the recognition of the work piece centre, and to add more images to databases.

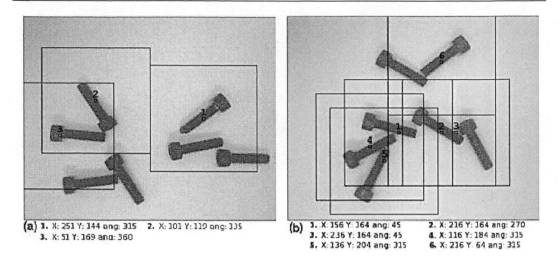

(a) 1. X: 251 Y: 144 ang: 315   2. X: 101 Y: 119 ang: 135
3. X: 51 Y: 169 ang: 360

(b) 1. X: 156 Y: 164 ang: 45   2. X: 216 Y: 164 ang: 270
3. X: 236 Y: 164 ang: 45   4. X: 116 Y: 184 ang: 315
5. X: 136 Y: 204 ang: 315   6. X: 216 Y: 64 ang: 315

Figure 19. Work pieces position recognition with contact.

3.8 Conclusion

LIRA_grayscale neural classifier was adapted for work piece recognition. It was trained and tested in recognition of five and eight classes. Every class corresponds to a work piece type, except one that corresponds to the absence of work piece, so the system can recognize the case when there is no work piece. In the experiments with five classes we used 20 samples for each class and for eight classes we used 40 samples for each class. Images of a tube base, a cone head screw, a round head screw, a cone, a stator axis, an allen screw and a wire terminal were used to test our system. For five classes, the best recognition rate of 94% was obtained (without distortions) and of 92% with distortions of initial images of training set. For eight classes the recognition rate was 90%. The results are acceptable. Nevertheless it is necessary to improve the accuracy of work piece position detection. The LIRA_grayscale classifier has good performance in work piece recognition with the images of low quality. It has also good perspectives for piece position finding. The training and recognition computer time is rather small. The time for recognition of any sample of any database was less than 0.4 s.

ACKNOWLEDGMENT

This invetidation was supported partially by projects CONACYT50231, PAPIIT IN110510-3, PAPIIT IN119610 and project of ICyTDF 330/2009.

E.Kussul and T.Baidyk thank DGAPA, UNAM for sabbatical grant.

The information presented in this chapter was initially published with "Neurocomputing", "Image and Vision Computing", and "Optical Memory & Neural Networks (Information Optics)".

The part of information is reprinted from Neurocomputing, Makeyev et al: Limited receptive area neural classifier for texture recognition of mechanically treated metal surfaces,

Issue 7-9, Vol. 71, March 2008, pp. 1413-1421 with the authors' right from Elsevier to prepare other derivative works, to extend the journal article into book-length form.

The part of information is reprinted from Optical Memory & Neural Networks (Information Optics), Martin-Gonzalez et al: Improved Neural Classifier for Microscrew Shape Recognition, Allerton Press, Vol. 19, No. 3, 2010, pp. 220-226 with the authors' right from Allerton Press to use the materials from the published article in a book written by the author (co-authors).

The part of information is reprinted from Image and Vision Computing, Toledo-Ramírez et al: Neural classifier for micro work pieces recognition Vol.24, Issue 8, 2006, pp.827-836 with permission from Elsevier.

We have invited researchers interested in classifier investigations to use our databases: http://gengis.dialetheia.net/workpiecesDBs. This data base was prepared by Dr. Gengis Khang Toledo-Ramirez.

REFERENCES

Baidyk, T.; Kussul, E.; Makeyev, O.; Caballero, A.; Ruiz, L.; Carrera, G.; Velasco, G., Flat image recognition in the process of microdevice assembly, *Pattern RecognLett* 2004, Vol. 25, No. 1, 107-118.

Baidyk, T.; Kussul, E.; Makeyev, O., Texture recognition with random subspace neural classifier, *WSEAS Transactions on Circuits and Systems* 2005, Vol. 4, No. 4, 319-325.

Brenner, D.; Principe, J.C.; Doty, K.L., Neural network classification of metal surface properties using a dynamic touch sensor, in: *Proc. IJCNN'91 International Joint Conference on Neural Networks*; Publisher: IEEE, Seattle, 1991 Vol.1, pp. 189-194.

Chi-ho Chan; Grantham K.H. Pang, Fabric defect detection by Fourier analysis, *IEEE T IndAppl* 2000, Vol. 36, No. 5, 1267-1276.

Friedrich, C.R.; Vasile, M.J. Development of the micromilling process for high- aspect-ratio micro structures, *J Microelectromech S.* 1996, Vol.5, 33-38.

Hepplewhite, L.; Stonham, T.J., Surface inspection using texture recognition, in: *Proc. IAPR'94 12th International Conference on Pattern Recognition*, 1994, Vol. 1; Publisher: IEEE, Jerusalem, pp. 589-591.

Jianing Zhu, M. Minami, Finding and quantitative evaluation of minute flaws on metal surface using hairline, in: Proc. IECON'04 30th Annual Conference of IEEE Industrial Electronics Society, 2004, Vol. 2;Publisher: IEEE, Busan,pp. 1240-1245.

Kraaijveld, M.A., An experimental comparison of nonparametric classifiers for time-constrained classification tasks, in: *Proc. ICPR'98 14th International Conference on Pattern Recognition*, 1998, Vol. 1; Publisher: IEEE, Brisbane, pp. 428-435.

Kussul, E.; Baidyk,T.; Ruiz-Huerta, L.; Caballero, A.; Velasco, G.; Kasatkina, L. Development of micromachine tool prototypes for microfactories, *J MicromechMicroeng* 2002, Vol. 12, 795-813.

LeCun, Y.; Bottou, L.; Bengio, Y.; Haffner, P., Gradient-based learning applied to document recognition, *P IEEE* 1998, Vol. 86, No11, 2278-2344.

Leung, T.; Malik, J., Representing and recognizing the visual appearance of materials using three-dimensional textons, *Int J Comput Vision* 2001, Vol. 43, No. 1, 29-44.

Madni, A.M.; Wan, L.A., Micro electro mechanical systems (MEMS): an overview of current state-of-the art, in: *Proc IEEE Aerospace Conference*, 1998, Vol. 1; Publisher: IEEE, Snowmass, pp. 421-427.

Naotake Ooyama; Shigeru Kokaji; Makoto Tanaka; et al, Desktop machining microfactory, in: *Proc. IWMF'00 2nd International Workshop on Microfactories*, 2000; Publisher: FSRM, Fribourg, pp. 14-17.

Neubauer C., Fast detection and classification of defects on treated metal surfaces using a backpropagation neural network, *Neural Networks* 1991, Vol. 2, pp. 1148-1153.

Rosenblatt, F. *Principles of neurodynamics*,Publisher: New York, Spartan books, 1962.

Sanchez-Yanez, R.; Kurmyshev, E.; Fernandez, A., One-class texture classifier in the CCR feature space, *Pattern RecognLett* 2003, Vol. 24, pp. 1503-1511.

Trimmer, W.S. (ed.), *Micromechanics and MEMS. Classical and seminal papers to 1990*; Publisher: IEEE Press, New York, 1997.

Baidyk, T.; Kussul, E., Neural network based vision system for micro workpieces manufacturing, *WSEAS Transactions on Systems*, April 2004, Vol. 3, No. 2, pp. 483-488.

Toledo-Ramírez, G.K.; Kussul, E.; Baidyk, T., Neural classifier for micro work pieces recognition, *Image and Vision Computing*, 2006, Vol. 24, No. 8, pp. 827-836.

Kussul, E.; Rachkovskij, D.; Baidyk, T.; Talayev, S., Micromechanical engineering: A basis for the low cost manufacturing of mechanical microdevices using microequipment, *Journal of Micromechanics and Microengineering*, December 1996, Vol. 6, No. 4, pp. 410-425.

Wu, Q. M. J.; Lee, M.F.R.; de Silva, C.W., Intelligent 3–D sensing in automated manufacturing processes, *Proceedings of the IEEE/ASME International Conference on Advanced Intelligent Mechatronics*, 2001, pp. 366-370.

Lee, S.J.; Kim, K.; Kim, D.H.; Park J.O.; Park, G.T., Recognizing and tracking of 3–D shaped micro parts using multiple visions for micromanipulation, *IEEE International Symposium on Micromechatronics and Human Science*, 2001, pp. 203-210.

Kim, J.Y.; Cho, H. S., A vision based error-corrective algorithm for flexible parts assembly, *Proceedings of the IEEE International Symposium on Assembly and Task Planning*, 1999, pp. 205-210.

Dunin-Barkovskii, V.L., On neuroscience, *Optical Memory & Neural Networks,* 2007, Vol. 16, No. 1, pp. 47-50 .

Mikaelyan, A. L. Neuro-holographic processing methods and availability of neural nanostructure development, *Information Technology and Computer Systems*, No.1, pp. 9-19, 2004.

Kryzhanovsky, B.V.; Litinskii, L.B., The vector models of associative memory, *Neuroinformatics-2003, MIFI Session*, 2003, Moscow, Russia, pp.72-85.

Kussul, E.; Baidyk, T., Improved method of handwritten digit recognition tested on MNIST database, *Image and Vision Computing*, October 2004, Vol. 22, No. 12, pp. 971-981.

Martín, A.; Baidyk, T., Neural classifier for microscrew shape recognition in micromechanics, *CLEI - IFIP WCC AI*, August 2006, pp. 10.

Hubel, D.H.; Wiesel, T.N., *Brain mechanisms of vision.* Scientific American, 241:150-162, 1979.

Marée, R.; Geurts, P.; Piater, J.; Wehenkel, L., Random subwindows for robust image classification, *Proc. IEEE International Conference on Computer Vision and Pattern Recognition (CVPR)*, 2005, Vol.1, pp. 34-40.

Ofeifer, T.; Dussler, G. Process observation for the assembly of hybrid microsystems, *IEEE International Sysposium on Micromechatronics and Human Science* 2002,pp. 117–123.

Bleuler, H.; Clavel, R.; Brequet, J-M.; Langen, H.; Pernette, E., Issues in precision motion control and microhandling, in: *Proceedings of the 2000 IEEE International Conference on Robotics & Automation*, USA, 2000, pp. 959–964.

Kussul, E.; Baidyk, T.; Ruiz, L.; Caballero, A.; Velasco, G., Development of Low Cost Microequipment, in: *International Symposium on Micromechatronics and Human Science*, Nagoya Japan, October 2002, Vol. 20–23, pp. 125–134.

Detter, H.; Popovic, G., Industrial demands on micromechanical products, *IEEE International Conference on Microelectronics NIS*, Serbia, 2000, pp. 61–67.

Baidyk, T.;   Kussul, E., Application of neural classifier for flat image recognition in the process of microdevice assembly, in: *Proceedings of the IEEE International Join Conference on Neural Networks*, Hawaii, USA, 2002, Vol. 1 pp. 160–164.

Jain, R.; Schunck, B.G.; Kasturi, R. *Machine Vision*, Publisher: McGraw Hill, New York, U.S.A., 1995.

Faugeras, O. *Three-Dimensional Computer Vision*, Publisher: MIT Press, Cambridge, New York, 1993.

Ehrenmann, M.; Ambela, D.; Steinhaus, P.; Dillman, R., A comparison of four fast vision based object recognition methods for programming by demonstration applications, *IEEE International Conference on Robotics & Automation*, San Francisco, CA, USA, 2000, pp. 1862–1867.

Steinhaus, P. Prinzipiellekomponenten-analyse versus multimediale filterhistogramme, Master Thesis, Universitat Karlsruhe (TH), Germany, July, 1997

Bennamoun,M.; Boashash, B. A structural description based vision system for automatic object recognition, *IEEE Transactions on Systems Man and Cybernetics* Part B (Cybernetics) 1997, Vol. 27, No.6,pp. 893–906.

Sun-Ho,L.; Hyun-Ki, H.; Jong-Soo, C., Assembly part recognition using part-based superquadrics model, *IEEE TENCON*1999, pp. 479–482.

Detter, H.; Radjenovic, M.J., Recognition of thin, flat microelectromechanical structures for automation of the assembly process, *Journal of Intelligent Manufacturing* 1997, Vol. 8, No. 3, pp. 191–201.

Mitzias, D.A.;Mertzios, B.G., A neural multiclassifier system for object recognition in robotic vision applications, *Measurement* 2004, Vol. 36, pp. 315–330.

Toledo, G.K.; Kussul, E.; Baidyk, T., Neural classifier LIRA for recognition of micro work pieces and their positions in the processes of microassembly and micromanufacturing, *The Seventh All-Ukrainian International Conference on Signal/Image Processing and Pattern Recognition*, UkrObraz2004, Kiev, Ukraine, October 2004, pp. 17–20.

Mardanov,A.; Seyfried, J.; Fatikow, S., An automated assembly system for a microassembly station, *Computer in Industry* 1999, Vol. 38, pp. 93–102.

Simard, P.Y.; Steinkraus, D.; Platt, J.C., Best practices for convolution neural networks applied to visual document analysis, *International Conference on Document Analysis and Recognition* (ICDAR), IEEE Computer Society, Los Alamitos, USA, 2003, pp. 958–962.

In: Computer Vision
Editor: Sota R. Yoshida

ISBN: 978-1-61209-399-4
© 2011 Nova Science Publishers, Inc.

Chapter 2

A SURVEY OF FACE RECOGNITION BY THE GENETIC ALGORITHM

Fengzhi Dai [1] *, Yutaka Fujihara* [2] *and Naoki Kushida* [3]

[1] College of Electronic Information and Automation, Tianjin University of Science and Technology, China
[2] Department of Control Engineering, Matsue College of Technology, Japan
[3] Department of Electronic Mechanical Engineering, Oshima National College of Maritime Technology, Japan

ABSTRACT

Computer vision and recognition is playing an increasing important role in the modern intelligent control. Object detection is the first and the most important step in object recognition. Traditionally, special objects can be detected and recognized by the template matching method, but the recognition speed has always been a problem. Also for recognition by the neural network, training the data is always time consumption. In this chapter, the genetic algorithm-based face recognition system is proposed. The genetic algorithm (GA) has been considered as a robust and global searching method. Here, the chromosomes generated by GA contain information (parameters) of the image, and the genetic operators are used to obtain the best match between the original image and the face of interest. The parameters are the coordinate (x, y) of the center of the face in the original image, the rate of scale and the angle θ of rotation. The purpose of this chapter is to summarize the GA-based method for face detection and recognition. Finally, the experimental results, and a comparison with the traditional template matching method, and some other considerations, are also given.

Keywords: Face detection and recognition, Genetic algorithm, Image processing, Template matching

INTRODUCTION

There are lots of papers and applications are presented on the web, in the conference proceedings or journals about the intelligent control. Among them, image processing and recognition occupy a very large percentage. The higher the degree of intelligence is, the more important the image detection and recognition technology is.

For controlling an intelligent system (the autonomous mobile vehicle, robot, etc), the most important element is the control strategy. But before automatically making the system move, image recognition is needed. For an intelligent control system, it is necessary to acquire information about the external world automatically by sensors, in order to recognize its position and the surrounding situation. A camera is one of the most important sensors for computer vision. That is to say, the intelligent system endeavors to find out what is in an image (the environment of the robot) taken by the camera: traffic signs, obstacles or guidelines, etc.

The reliability and time-response of the object detection and recognition have a major influence on the performance and usability of the whole object recognition system [1]. The template matching method is a practicable and reasonable method for object detection [2], but the recognition speed has always been a problem.

In addition, in order to search for the object (face) of interest in an image, lots of data need to be processed. The genetic algorithm (GA) has been considered to be a robust and global searching method (although it is sometimes said that GA can not be used for finding the global optimization [3]). Here, the chromosomes generated by GA contain information about the image data, and the genetic and evolution operations are used to obtain the best match to the template: searching for the best match is the goal of this method.

This thought emerged from the features of GA, and the need to recognize the faces of special people easily and quickly by an intelligent system. The single concept and feature of image processing and the GA will not be introduced here, because there is already extensive literature on these subjects.

This chapter summarizes the research on GA-based face recognition by the authors of the chapter and other researchers. In the chapter below, the encoding and decoding method of GA and the experimental setting that is used here, the experiment and the analysis, and conclusion are addressed sequentially.

THEORY AND EXPERIMENTAL SETTING

For an image recognition system, firstly, the most interesting part that has special features has to be detected in the original image. This is called object detection. After that, this part will be compared to the template to see if they are similar or not. This is called object recognition. For example, if we want to find a special person in an image, we first have to detect people in the image, and then recognize which one is the person of interest (sometimes these two steps will be executed simultaneously). The whole procedure is shown in Figure 1.

Statistical object recognition involves locating and isolating the targets in an image, and then identifying them by statistical decision theory. One of the oldest techniques of pattern recognition is matching filtering [4], which allows the computation of a measure of the similarity between the original image $f(x, y)$ and a template $h(x, y)$. Define the mean-squared distance

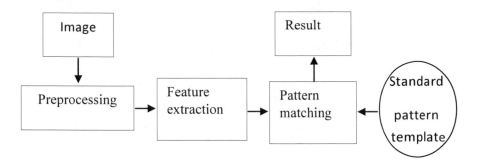

Figure 1. Object recognition system.

$$d^2_{fh} = \iint \{f(x, y) - h(x, y)\}^2 \, dxdy \tag{1}$$

and $R_{fh} = \iint f(x, y)h(x, y)dxdy$ \hfill (2)

If the image and the template are normalized by

$$\iint f^2(x, y)dxdy = \iint h^2(x, y)dxdy \tag{3}$$

then

$$\begin{aligned}
d^2_{fh} &= \iint \{f(x, y) - h(x, y)\}^2 \, dxdy \\
&= \iint \{f^2(x, y) - 2f(x, y)h(x, y) + h^2(x, y)\}dxdy \\
&= 2\iint f^2(x, y)dxdy - 2R_{fh}
\end{aligned} \tag{4}$$

For the right-hand side of Eq.4, the result has two terms. The first term is constant, thus R_{fh} can measure as the least-squared similarity between the original image and the template [5]. If R_{fh} has a large value (which means that d^2_{fh} is small enough), then the image is judged to match the template. If R_{fh} is less than a pre-selected threshold, recognition will either reject the match or create a new pattern, which means that the similarity between the object in the original image and the template is not satisfied.

A. Genetic encoding

As introduced above, Eq.4 is used to match the object between the original image and the template. Since the chromosomes generated by the GA contain information about the image data, the first step is to encode the image data into a binary string [6].

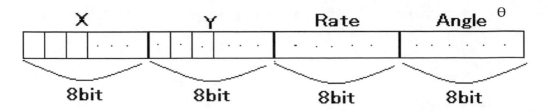

Figure 2. One chromosome contains 4 bytes.

Some important parameters of GA are given in Table 1, and the search field and region are given in Table 2. Table 2 shows that there are 4 image parameters: the center of a face (x, y) in the original image, the rate of scale to satisfy Eq.3, and the rotating angle θ, are encoded into the elements of gene (the meanings of which will be introduced below). Since one parameter uses 8 bits (1 byte), and there are 4 image parameters, thus one chromosome contains 4 bytes shown in Figure 2.

Table 1. Some GA parameters

Source	The original and template images
Generations	Maximum = 300 (the stopping criterion)
Population Size	200
Reproduction (selection)	P_r of the best individuals will be selected to survive. The remained $(1-P_r)$ will be treated by the genetic operators (crossover and mutation)
Crossover	Offspring are produced from parents by exchanging their genes at the crossover point, the ratio is P_c
Mutation	Produce spontaneous random changes in various chromosomes. The general random change method is used at the rate of P_m

Table 2. Settings for the experiment

Image parameter (minimum, maximum)		
x	8 bits	(0, max_x)
y	8 bits	(0, max_y)
$rate$	8 bits	(1.0, 3.0)
θ	8 bits	($-35°$, $35°$)
GA parameters		
P_r	0.6	
P_c	0.5	
P_m	0.01	

B. Genetic algorithm and decoding

The flow chart of the GA is shown in Figure 3. The fitness is defined as

$$\text{fitness} = 1.0 - \frac{\sum_{j=0}^{\text{temp\_y}} \sum_{i=0}^{\text{temp\_x}} | f(x, y, rate, \theta) - \text{temp}(i, j) |}{(\text{temp\_x}) \times (\text{temp\_y}) \times 255}$$

$$(5)$$

In Eq.5, temp(i, j) is the gray level of the coordinate (i, j) in the template image, the width and height of which are temp_x and temp_y. $f(x, y, rate, \Theta)$ gives the gray level in the original image, the coordinate of which are calculated by translation from (x, y), and by changing the scale and the rotation angle Θ from the template. Since the images have 256 gray levels, in Eq.5, division by 255 ensures that the resulting fitness is between 0 and 1.

Based on Eq.5, in the program, the fitness is calculated by the following four steps, and Figure 4 gives the figural example.

(1) The coordinate (i, j) in the template is scaled by the value of parameter *rate*, then the result $f(x, y, rate, \Theta) = f(0, 0, rate, 0) = (i \times rate, j \times rate)$ can be gotten;

(2) The result of step (1) is rotated by the value of parameter Θ, thus $f(x, y, rate, \Theta) = f(0, 0, rate, \Theta)$;

(3) The result of step (2) is translated by the coordinate (x,y) in the original image, then the result $f(x, y, rate, \Theta)$ is calculated;

(4) All the differences between the gray level of the coordinate (i, j) in the template and that of the calculated $f(x, y, rate, \Theta)$ in the original image are summed by Eq.5 to calculate the fitness.

Based on Figure 3, if the value of the fitness is lager than the preset threshold, the search process is over and the result is given, otherwise the loop will be continued.

In order to obtain the true value of the image parameters from the chromosome, decoding is needed. In Eq.6, after decoding from datum of GA, the value of each parameter is standardized. A figural example is given in Figure 5.

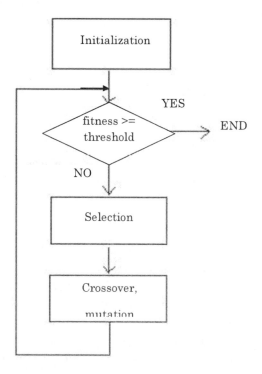

Figure 3. Flow chart of GA.

$$\text{Value} = \text{MIN} + \frac{\text{MAX} - \text{MIN}}{255} \times (\text{datum from GA}) \tag{6}$$

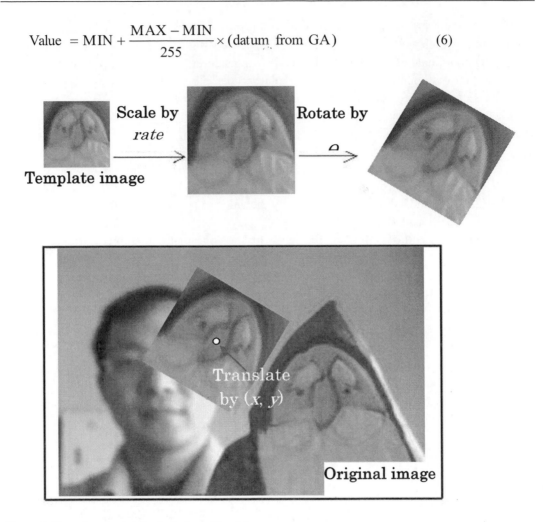

Figure 4. Figural example of calculation of Eq. 5 by program.

C. Experimental setting

The experiment is done by first loading the original and the template images. GA is used to find whether or not there is the object (face) of a template in the original image. If the answer is YES, then in the original image the result gives the coordinate of the center of the object, the rate of scale, and the rotation angle from the template. For comparison, the general template matching method is also presented [7]. The execution time shows the effectiveness of the GA-based recognition method.

Figure 6 and Figure 7 are the original images and the templates for the experiment [8]. The values are the width × height in pixels of the image. In Figure 6, three original images are presented, the content and size of which are different. Figure 6a has two faces (the faces of a person and a toy), Figure 6b shows a face tipped to one side, and the person in Figure 6c wears a hat and the background is more complicated than Figure 6a and b.

	X	Y	rate	angle
datum from GA	89	109	23	43
MIN	0	0	1.0	-35
MAX	320	240	3.0	35

$$Value = MIN + \frac{MAX - MIN}{255} \times (datum\ from\ GA)$$

Value	$0 + \dfrac{320-0}{255} \times 89$	$0 + \dfrac{240-0}{255} \times 109$	$1.0 + \dfrac{3.0-1.0}{255} \times 23$	$-35 + \dfrac{35-(-35)}{255} \times 43$
	112	103	1.180	-23.2

Figure 5. Figural example for decoding.

a) 238 × 170   (b) 185 × 196   (c) 275 × 225

Figure 6. Three original images (max_X max_Y).

62 × 62   60 × 64

(a) Template 1   (b) Template 2

Figure 7. Templates for matching (temp_X x temp_Y).

The two templates in Figure 7 are not extracted only from one image. For normal use, the template should be extracted as the average of several feature images. In Figure 8, the template (a)-0 is generated from (a)-1, (a)-2 and (a)-3, which takes the average value of the gray levels from those three models. The same is also done for the template (b)-0.

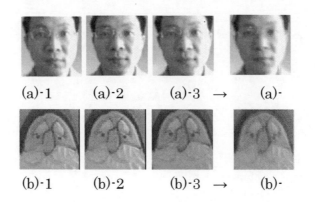

Figure 8. Creation of the template.

EXPERIMENT AND COMPARISON

The maximum number of generation is limited to 300, and the threshold of the matching rate is set to 0.9. That is to say, if within 300 generations the matching rate can reach 0.9, then it is said that the template is found in the original image (the template matches to the original image by the threshold 0.9). Otherwise, the result gives the best match until the training reaches the 300th generation.

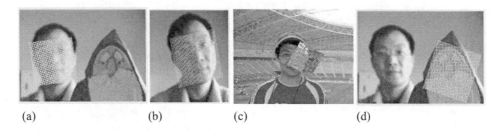

Figure 9. Result of searching by GA.

The results of the GA-based face recognition are given in Figure 9 and Table 3. Figure 9a-c are searched to match to the template Figure 7a, while Figure 9d is matched to Figure 7b.

The result of Table 3(a) means that after the template is scaled by 1.31 times and rotated anticlockwise rotation 7°, it matches the original image (centered by (64,97)) as 91.6591%.

Figure 9a and Figure 9d reach the matching rate 0.9 within 300 generations, while Figure 9b and Figure 9c cannot reach the matching rate 0.9 within 300 generations (the best match is given in Table 3).

In the images of Figure 9a, b, d, we see that the matches to the template are well. The coordinate (x, y), the rate of scale, and the angle of rotation θ have been found correctly. But for Figure 9c, the result is not very satisfactory.

Table 3. Results of recognition by GA

Image in Figure 9	Result
(a)	Original image is Figure 6a, template is Figure 7a.
	The 18th generation gives the result, fitness = 0.916591, time = 2 seconds. $(x, y) = (64, 97)$, rate = 1.31, θ= -7°
(b)	Original image is Figure 6b, template is Figure 7a.
	The 300th generation gives the result, fitness = 0.889581, time = 39 seconds. $(x, y) = (111, 103)$, rate = 1.72, θ= -11°
(c)	Original image is Figure 6c, template is Figure 7a.
	The 300th generation gives the result, fitness = 0.832722, time = 39 seconds. $(x, y) = (165, 120)$, rate = 1.00, θ= 30°
(d)	Original image is Figure 6a, template is Figure 7b.
	The 2nd generation gives the result, fitness = 0.901470, time = 0 second. $(x, y) = (179, 112)$, rate = 1.45, θ= 18°

The reasons are

i. The template Figure 7 cannot represent the face of interest at all times. That is to say, although the person to be recognized in different images is the same, the template cannot give the features for this person at all times (different appearance, etc.), and in all conditions. (The creation of template is shown in Figure 8.)

ii. The algorithm itself has some problems. For example, by using a GA-based recognition method, the settings of the search field (in this chapter, $(x, y$, rate, $\theta)$ is selected), the determination of the genetic operations, and the selection and optimization of the fitness function all have a strong effect on the level of recognition.

For the purpose of comparing the effect of the GA-based algorithm, the result of the general matching method [7] is also presented. From Figure 10, we see that although both the original image (the top-left image) and the template (the top-right image) are simplified by binarization, the search time is 1 min 22s. The recognized result is the bottom-left image in Figure 10. For the general matching method, the search time depends mainly on the location of the object of interest in the original image.

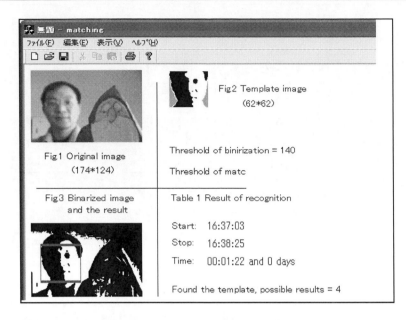

Figure 10. Result by the general matching method.

Figure 11 and Figure 12 are the template and original images for another experiment [9].

The genetic operations and GA parameters are presented in Table 1 and Table 4. The fitness is defined in Eq.5. The result of the GA-based face recognition is given in Figure 13 and Table 5. The result shows that it reaches the matching rate 0.904 at the 116th generation. The result of the general matching method is shown in Figure 14.

Table 4. Settings for the experiment

Parameters	Length	Region
x	8 bits	$(0, Max\_x)$
y	8 bits	$(0, Max\_y)$
$rate$	8 bits	$(1.0, 3.0)$
θ	8 bits	$(-35°, 35°)$
P_r	0.6	
P_c	0.2	
P_m	0.02	

Figure 11. Template for matching (size: temp_X x temp_y = 32x32).

Figure 12. The original image (size 320x240).

Figure 13. Result of the GA-based recognition.

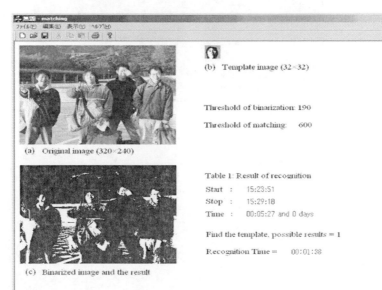

Figure 14. Result for the general matching method.

Table 5. Results of recognition by GA

Fitness	0.904
Generation	116
Time [sec]	10
(x, y)	(145, 77)
Rate	1.118
Angle Θ [deg]	3.431

Based on the genetic operations and GA parameters presented in Table 1 and Table 4, another experiment has been done. Figure 15 and Figure 16 are the template and original images [10]. The result of the GA-based face recognition is given in Figure 17 and Table 6. The result of the general matching method is shown in Figure 18.

Figure 15. Template for matching (size: temp_X x temp_Y).

320×240

Figure 16. The original image (size: max_x, max_y).

Table 6. Results of recognition by GA

Fitness	0.944
Generation	112
Time [sec]	5
(x, y)	(112, 107)
Rate	1.02
Angle Θ [deg]	2.24

CONCLUSION

In this chapter, the GA-based image recognition method is tested, and a comparison with the general matching method is presented.

As we know, GA starts with an initial set of random solutions called population. Each individual in the population is called a chromosome, and represents a solution to the problem. By stochastic search techniques based on the mechanism of nature selection and natural genetics, genetic operations (crossover and mutation) and evolution operation (selecting or rejecting) are used to search for the best solution [11].

Figure 17. Result of the GA-based recognition.

Figure 18. Result for the general matching method.

In this chapter, the chromosomes generated by GA contain information about the image, and we use the genetic operators to obtain the best match between the original image and the template. The parameters are the coordinate (x, y) of the center of the face in the original image, the rate of scale, and the angle of rotation θ.

In fact, translation, scale and rotation are the three main invariant moments in the field of pattern recognition [12]. However, for face recognition, the facial features are difficult to be extracted and calculated by the general pattern recognition theory and method [13]. Even these three main invariant moments will not be invariant because the facial expression is changed in different images.

Thus, recognition only gives the best matching result by an upper predetermined threshold [14]. Both the GA-based method and the general template matching method are presented here, and the comparison with the traditional pattern matching method shows that the recognition is satisfactory, although under some conditions the result is not very good (Figure 9c).

Based on the results of experiments, further work will emphasize [15]

    i.   Optimizing the fields of chromosomes,
    ii.   Improving the fitness function by adding some terms to it.

This work is important and necessary in order to improve the GA-based face recognition system.

ACKNOWLEDGMENT

This work was sponsored in part by the Scientific Research Foundation of Tianjin University of Science and Technology (China) for the Introduced Talented Scholars, No. 20100408.

REFERENCES

[1]   M. Sugisaka; X. Fan. Development of a face recognition system for the life robot. Proc. of the Seventh Int. Symp. on Artificial Life and Robotics. 2002, Vol. 2, pp 538-541.

[2]   K. Castleman. Digital image processing; Original edition published by Prentice Hall, Inc., a Simon & Schuster Company, Press of Tsinghua University, China, 1998.

[3]   H. Iba. Foundation of genetic algorithm – solution of mystic GA (in Japanese); Omu Press, 1994.

[4]   K. Deguchi; I. Takahashi. Image-based simultaneous control of robot and target object motion by direct-image-interpretation. Proc. the 1999 IEEE/RSJ International Conf. of Intelligent Robot and System. 1999, Vol. 1, pp 375-380.

[5]   B. Jaehne. Digital image processing - concepts, algorithms, and scientific applications. The Third Edition, Springer-Verlag, 1995.

[6]   T. Agui; T. Nagao. Introduction to image processing using programming language C (in Japanese). Shoko-do press, 2000.

[7]   Ishidate (2010). Ishidate's Studying Room of Visual C++ (in Japanese), http://homepage3.nifty.com/ishidate/vcpp.htm

[8]   F. Dai; T. Kodani; Y. Fujihara. Research on a face recognition system by the genetic algorithm. J. of Artificial Life and Robotics. 2007, Vol. 11, Number 1, pp 67-70.

[9]   F. Dai; Y. Fujihara. Research on object recognition by genetic algorithm. Proc. of 8th Int. Conf. on Industrial Management. 2006, pp 907-912.

[10] F. Dai; T. Adachi; Y. Fujihara; H. Zhao. Fundamental research on face recognition by genetic algorithm. Proc. of 12th Int. Symp. on Artificial Life and Robotics. 2007, pp 639- 642.

[11] M. Gen; R. Cheng. Genetic algorithms and engineering design. A wiley-Interscience Publication, New York, 1997.

[12] T. Agui; T. Nagao. Image processing and recognition (in Japanese). Syokoudou Press, 1992.

[13] H. Takimoto; T. Mitsukura ; M. Fukumi; et al. A design of face detection system based on the feature extraction method. Proc. of 12th Symp. on Fuzzy, Artificial Intelligence, Neural Networks and Computational Intelligence, 2002, pp 409-410.

[14] Kresimir Delac; Mislav Grgic. Face recognition. I-Tech Education and Publishing, Vienna, Austria, 2007.

[15] D. Goldberg. Genetic algorithm in search, optimization, and machine learning. Addison-Wesley Publishing Company, Inc., 1989.

In: Computer Vision
Editor: Sota R. Yoshida

ISBN: 978-1-61209-399-4
© 2011 Nova Science Publishers, Inc.

Chapter 3

THE ATTENTIVE CO-PILOT: ROBUST DRIVER ASSISTANCE RELYING ON HUMAN-LIKE SIGNAL PROCESSING PRINCIPLES

Thomas Paul Michalke[1,*]*and Robert Kastner*[2]
[1]Daimler AG, Research and Advanced Engineering, Germany
[2]Darmstadt University of Technology, Institute for Automatic Control, Germany

Abstract

Increasingly complex driver assistance functionalities are combined in today's vehicles. Typically, these functionalities run as independent modules bringing own sensors, processing devices, and actuators. In general, no information fusion, i.e., cross talk between modules, takes place as a consequence of unsolved questions in system design that come along with high system complexity. However, information fusion of available sensors and processing modules could lead to a new quality of driver assistance functionalities in terms of performance and robustness. Additionally, the growing number of driver assistance functionalities in today's vehicles will cause problems regarding the limited number of interaction channels to inform the driver of potential dangers - the so-called human machine interface (HMI).

Already today, in specific traffic scenarios a contradicting HMI access of different driver assistance functionalities cannot be avoided. Furthermore, typical driver assistance functionalities on the market are based on highly specialized and optimized algorithms that show sound performance for a restricted number of clearly defined scenarios only. Also, the combination of several of these rigid systems as a means to reach the long-term goal of autonomous driving will not lead to robust system performance, taken the immense variety of traffic situations into account. As opposed to that, the following contribution presents a flexible, biologically inspired driver assistance system that adapts its modules and data exchange between modules online depending on the task. More specifically, the morphology of the brain as well as brain-like signal processing principles are mimicked in order to increase the robustness and flexibility

---

*E-mail address: thomas_paul.michalke@daimler.com
[1]The presented results have been obtained while carrying out research as part of a Ph.D. program at Darmstadt University with support from Honda Research Institute Europe GmbH. The author Thomas Paul Michalke now works for Daimler AG (email: thomas_paul.michalke@daimler.com).

of the system. Thereby, we aimed at reaching a generic system structure, that supports several system tasks by modulating and parameterizing its system modules (e.g., detect fast objects, redetect once tracked and later lost objects, predict object trajectories, locate cars on the road, detect traffic signs). Put differently, our main research focus is on the design of general mechanisms that lead to a certain observable behavior without being explicitly designed for this behavior. Following that paradigm, a tunable attention sub-system was developed that allows the pre-filtering of the visual environment for task-relevant information in order to provide the driver with assistance in dangerous situations. In order to include information of the scene context into the system, a robust unmarked road detection module as well as an approach for assessing the general type of environment (highway, country road, inner-city) is included into the system. The realized driver assistance system is tested online and in real-time on a prototype car. The gathered results prove the applicability of the developed biologically inspired driver assistance system in real-world scenarios. Extensive system evaluation shows that different system properties are in close compliance with measurements gathered in psychophysical studies of humans. Based on these results, it can be stated that the realized advanced driver assistance system closely models important human information processing principles allowing the usage of the system as Attentional Co-Pilot for human drivers.

1. Introduction into Advanced Driver Assistance Systems

Among the various possible applications of vision systems, the task of driver assistance is highly interesting as it implicitly contains the challenge of understanding a dynamic scene and is at the same time of great commercial and social importance. The goal of building such intelligent vision systems can be approached from two directions: either searching for the best engineering solution or taking the human as a role model. In the latter case, research results from disciplines like, e.g., psychophysics or neurobiology can be used to guide the vision system design. While it may be argued that the quality of an engineered system in terms of isolated aspects like, e.g., object detection or tracking, is typically sound, the solutions lack the necessary flexibility. Small changes in the task and/or environment often lead to the necessity of redesigning the whole system. Considering the human vision system, nature has managed to realize a highly flexible system capable of adapting to severe changes in the task and/or the environment. Hence one of the main design goals is to implement a system able to accomplish new tasks without adding modules or changing the system's structure. Equally, it was aimed at getting inspiration from the underlying principles of the human vision system and not directly at engineering efforts to attain its measurable abilities.

It is important to note that the focus was not on building a close "psychophysical model" of the human vision system that models all its known aspects as close as possible. Among other things, said psychophysical models are useful for predicting or explaining measurements in psychophysical studies with humans. Different from such a global paradigm, functionality-related findings of the human visual pathway are mimicked in cases known classical approaches do not perform better, are restricted in their flexibility, or perform less robust. Put differently, the contribution aims at realizing a "computational model" of the human vision system that allows robust, real-time operation in a real-world environment (please refer to [1] for a comprehensive discrimination between computational and psychophysical models of the human vision system).

Aiming at going beyond standard industrial computer vision applications, there is an increasing emphasis in the computer vision community on building so-called cognitive vision systems [2] (i.e., systems that work according to or get inspiration from human information processing principles) suitable for solving complex vision tasks. One important principle in cognitive systems is the existence of top-down links in the system, i.e., informational links from stages of higher to lower knowledge integration. Top-down links are believed to be a prerequisite for fast-adapting biological systems living in changing environments (see, e.g., [3]).

Returning to the car domain, constraints like, e.g., lane markings and traffic rules restrict the environmental complexity and ease the driving task considerably. Still, vision-based driver assistance functionalities developed up to now are mainly capable of dealing with simple traffic situations. While this already resulted in specialized commercial products improving driving safety (e.g., the "Honda Intelligent Driver Support System" [4] which helps the driver to stay in the lane and maintain the right distance to the preceding car), the problem of developing a generic vision system for advanced driver assistance, i.e., capable of operating in all kinds of challenging situations, is still unsolved.

One possible way to achieve this goal is to realize a task-dependent perception using top-down links. In this paradigm, the same scene can be decomposed in different ways depending on the current task. A promising approach for decomposing the scene is to use a high-performance attention system that can be modulated in a task-oriented way, i.e., based on the current context. For example, while driving at high speed, the central field of the visual scene becomes more important than the surrounding. Put differently, the envisioned system modulates and parameterizes submodules thereby fulfilling tasks without being explicitly designed for specific tasks of a scenario.

Aiming towards such a task-based vision system, this contribution describes an instance of a vision architecture that is being developed as perceptual front-end of the "Attentive Co-Pilot" - a prototypical, biologically inspired Advanced Driver Assistance System. The proposed vision system provides a framework that enables the task-dependent tuning of visual processes via object-specific weighting of input features of the attention system. The system generates an appropriate system reaction in dangerous situations (e.g., autonomous braking). In major parts, its architecture is inspired by findings in the human visual system and organizes the different functionalities in a similar way. For the analysis of the overall system, a construction site scenario as well as a challenging inner-city traffic scene are evaluated in order to illustrate the performance gain of the top-down approach in complex environments. The overall system achieves real-time performance on a prototype car and is evaluated offline on among other things 10 construction site sequences and online on 60 documented test drives. The obtained results demonstrate the feasibility and benefits of top-down attention and the chosen architectural approach in a complex ADAS. Furthermore, additional sequences of real world traffic scenes are used to evaluate different system modules.

The contribution is organized as follows: In Sect. 2. the here presented ADAS is related to the current research on visual attention systems and existing car vision architectures. Subsequently, Sect. 3. provides an overview of the system architecture. In the following Sections, with the attention system in Sect. 4., the scene classification in Sect. 5., the depth cues in Sect. 6., and the road detection system in Sect. 7. some major sub-modules are described. Evaluation results for the most crucial system modules as well as the overall system performance measured in an experimental setup are given in Sect. 8.. The contribution ends with a summary in Sect. 9. and an outlook on future work in Sect. 10..

2. Related Work Advanced Driver Assistance

Today's Advanced Driver Assistance Systems effectively support the driver in clearly defined traffic situations like keeping the distance to the forward vehicle. For this purpose Radar sensors, Lidar sensors, and cameras are used to extract parameters of the scene, like, e.g., headway distances, relative velocities, and relative position of lane markers ahead. Such approaches resulted in specialized commercial products improving the driving safety (e.g., the "Honda Collision Mitigation Brake System" [5, 6] to help the driver to avoid rear end collisions in case the forward vehicle brakes unexpectedly). Although traffic rules and road infrastructure, like, e.g., lane markings, restrict the complexity of what to sense while driving, perception systems of today's ADAS are capable of recognizing simple traffic situations only. Furthermore, driving in normal traffic scenes can be done mainly in a rather reactive way by staying in the middle of the lane and keeping an appropriate distance.

However, for assisting the driver over the full range of driving tasks less reactive, intelligent systems are required. Different from typical engineering-driven approaches and taking the high quality of signal processing reached in biology into account, one promising way for building such intelligent systems is to take the human as a role model, mimicking known signal processing principles in the human brain.

Recently, the topic of researching intelligent cars is gaining increasingly interest as documented by the DARPA Urban Challenge [7] and the European Information Society 2010 Intelligent Car Initiative [8] as well as several European Projects like, e.g., Safespot or PRe-VENT. The gathered results of such purely engi-neering-driven approaches are somewhat limited.

Turning to the domain of vision systems developed for ADAS, there have been few attempts to incorporate aspects of the human visual system into complete systems. With respect to attention processing, a saliency-based traffic sign detection and recognition system was demonstrated in [9, 10]. In terms of complete vision systems, one of the most prominent examples is a system developed in the group of E. Dickmanns [11]. It uses several active cameras mimicking the active nature of gaze control in the human visual system. However, the processing framework is not closely related to the human visual system. Without a tunable attention system and with TD aspects that are limited to a number of object-specific approaches for classification, no dynamic preselection of image regions is performed. A more biologically inspired approach has been presented by Färber [12]. However, their publication as well as the recently started German Transregional Collaborative Research Centre "Cognitive Automobiles" [13] address mainly human-inspired behavior planning whereas the here presented work focuses more on task-dependent perception aspects.

The only other known vision system approach that attempts to explicitly model aspects of the human visual system is described by [14]. The system is somewhat related to the here presented ADAS. However, different from the here proposed "Attentive Co-Pilot", the approach allows for a simple attention-based decomposition of road scenes only, without incorporating object knowledge or context information. Additionally, the overall system organization is not biologically inspired and hence shows limitations in its flexibility.

In contrast to the here presented ADAS, a tendency of most large-scale research projects like, e.g., the European PreVENT project [15] is the decomposition of the overall functionality into many building blocks and combining these blocks into subsets for solving isolated tasks. While this "divide and conquer" approach does lead to impressive results in specific settings, the challenge of integrating all these functionalities into a coherently working flexible system is not yet solved.

For supporting the driver over the full range of driving tasks in all kinds of challenging situations and going beyond simple reactive behaviors, a more sophisticated task-dependent processing strategy is required. As the major challenge and in order to achieve this target, an adequate organization of perception using a generic vision system has to be found.

When assessing biological vision systems, it can be experienced that these are highly flexible and capable of adapting to severe changes in the task and/or the environment. Hence, one of the basic design goals on the way to achieve an "all-situation" ADAS could be to implement a biologically motivated, cognitive vision system as perceptual front-end of an ADAS, which can handle the wide variety of situations typically encountered when driving a car. Note that only if an ADAS vision system attends to the relevant surrounding traffic and obstacles, it will be fast enough to assist the driver in real-time during all dangerous situations.

As motivated before, for solving this challenge a computational model of the human attention system is suitable for the "how" and "when" of scene decomposition and interpretation. Recently, some authors stress the role of incorporating context into the attention-based scene analysis. For example [16], proposes a combination of a bottom-up saliency map and a top-down context-driven approach. The top-down path uses spatial statistics, which are learned during an offline learning phase, to modulate the bottom-up saliency map. This is different to the here described system, where no offline spatial prior learning phase is required. In the realized online system, context is incorporated in the form of top-down weights that are modified at run time as well as by fusing road information.

3.   The "Attentive Co-Pilot" - System Description

In the following, an overview of the realized biologically inspired ADAS is given, which introduces the whereabouts of the five major system sub-modules.

The proposed overall architecture concept for robust attention-based scene analysis is depicted in Fig. 1. It consists of five major parts: "what" pathway (light blue region in the system graph), "where" pathway (darker brown region), a part executing "static domain-specific tasks" (red region), a part allowing "environmental interaction" (darker blue region), and a "system control module" (lighter brown region). In the following, the intertwinings of these five sub-modules are made clearer.

The distinction between "what" and "where" processing path is somewhat similar to the human visual system where the dorsal and ventral pathway are typically associated with these two functions (see, e.g., [17]). Among other things, the "where" pathway in the human brain is believed to perform the localization and tracking of a small number of

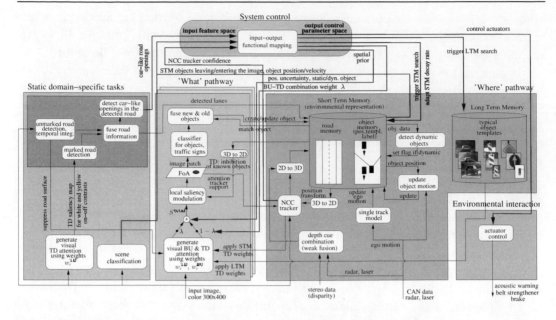

Figure 1. Biologically motivated system structure for active, attention-based scene analysis.

objects. In contrast, the "what" pathway considers the detailed analysis of a single spot in the image. Nevertheless, an ADAS also requires context information in form of the road and its shape as well as scene context from a scene classifier, both generated by the static domain-specific part. Furthermore, for assisting the driver, the system requires interfaces for allowing environmental interaction (i.e., triggering actuators). The system control module relies on numerous internal system percepts as input and numerous system parameters for controlling the system states and behavior. In order to allow a closer understanding of the proposed system a detailed description of its sub-modules is given.

The "what" Pathway

Starting in the "what" pathway the 400x300 color input image is analyzed by calculating the attention map S^{total}. The attention map S^{total} results from a weighted linear combination of $N = 136$ biologically inspired low-resolution (256x256) input feature maps F_i (see Equation (1)). More specifically, for attaining these feature maps the image is filtered using, among others Difference of Gaussian (DoG) and Gabor filter kernels that model the characteristics of neural receptive fields measured in the mammal brain. Furthermore, the RGBY color space [18] is used as attention feature that models the processing of photoreceptors on the retina. All features are computed on 5 scales relying on the well-known principle of image pyramids in order to allow computationally efficient filtering. All feature maps are postprocessed non-linearly in order to suppress noise and boost conspicuous or prominent scene parts (for a detailed description of the named features as well as the mentioned nonlinear processing steps, please refer to Sect. 4.2. and Sect. 4.4.).

The top-down (TD) attention can be tuned (i.e., parameterized) task-dependently to search for specific object classes (e.g., vehicles, signal boards, traffic signs). This is done by applying a TD weight set w_i^{TD} that is computed and adapted online, based on the weight training method shown in Equation (2). In Equation (2) the threshold ϕ is set to

$\phi = K_{conj} Max(F_i)$ with $K_{conj} = (0,1]$ (see Fig. 2a for a visualization of the object training region and the background). The weights w_i^{TD} dynamically boost feature maps that are important for the current task / object class in focus and suppress the rest. The bottom-up (BU) weights w_i^{BU} are set object-unspecifically in order to detect unexpected potentially dangerous scene elements. The central parameter $\lambda \in [0,1]$ (see Equation (1)) determines the relative importance of TD and BU search in the current system state. For more details on the attention system see Sect. 4..

It is important to note that the TD weights (calculated using Equation (2)) are dependent on the features present in the background (rest) of the current image, since the background information is used to differentiate the searched object from the rest of the image [18]. Because of this, it is not sufficient to store the TD weight sets w_i^{TD} of different object classes directly and switch between them during online processing. Instead, all feature maps of objects $F_{i,RoI}$ are stored. To compensate the dependency from background the stored object feature maps are fused with the feature maps of the current image before calculating the TD weights. In plain words, the system takes the current scene characteristics (i.e., its features) into account in order to determine the optimal TD weight set that shows a maximum performance on the current frame. Put differently, the described separation approach in Equation (2) includes the current scene context on a sensory level.

$$S^{total} = \lambda \sum_{i=1}^{N} w_i^{TD} F_i + (1-\lambda) \sum_{i=1}^{N} w_i^{BU} F_i \qquad (1)$$

$$w_i^{TD} = \begin{cases} \dfrac{m_{RoI,i}}{m_{rest,i}} & \forall \dfrac{m_{RoI,i}}{m_{rest,i}} \geq 1 \\[2ex] -\dfrac{m_{rest,i}}{m_{RoI,i}} & \forall \dfrac{m_{RoI,i}}{m_{rest,i}} < 1 \end{cases} \qquad (2)$$

$$\text{with } m_{\{RoI,rest\},i} = \dfrac{\displaystyle\sum_{\forall u,v \in \{RoI,rest\}} F_i(u,v)}{\text{size region } \{RoI,rest\}}$$

$$\text{and } F_i(u,v) = \begin{cases} F_i(u,v) & \forall (u,v), F_i(u,v) \geq \phi \\ 0 & \text{else} \end{cases}$$

Now, the maximum on the current attention map S^{total} is detected and the focus of attention (FoA) is derived by generic region-growing-based segmentation on S^{total}. In the following, only the FoA is classified in full image resolution using a state-of-the-art object classifier that is based on neural nets [19]. This procedure (attention generation, FoA segmentation) models the saccadic eye movements of mammals, where a complex scene is scanned and decomposed by sequential focusing of objects in the central 2-3° foveal retina area of the visual field. The system uses a temporal integration approach to decide on the object class, in order to improve the reliability of the classifier decision. More specifically, all detected objects are tracked and reclassified in the following frames. On each frame a majority decision (voting) on the current and all stored classifier results decides on the object class.

The proposed system incorporates the biologically motivated concept of TD-links. Based on these links information on higher levels of knowledge integration modulate (i.e., parameterize) lower levels of knowledge integration. This brain-like concept improves robustness, increases the relevance of input data for higher system levels, and accelerates the system reaction (see evaluation results in Sect. 8.). The "Attentive Co-Pilot" uses such links for the task-specific modulation of the TD attention (i.e., by adapting system parameters online, as, e.g., the previously described TD-weights w_i^{TD}) and for suppressing the detected road (see Sect. 8.1.5. for a visualization) as context information in all feature maps F_i before fusing them in the overall saliency map S^{total}. Additionally, TD-links are used for the modulation of the attention based on detected car-like holes in the found drivable road segment (see "where" path in Fig. 1). Such car-like holes are detected by searching for car-sized openings in the detected road segment (see module "static domain-specific tasks" path in Fig. 1). To that end, the roadsegment is transformed to the metric bird's eye view (for an example see Fig. 10b) by inverse perspective mapping. On the metric bird's eye view, the non-linearities of the perspective mapping are resolved, which eases the detection of suitable candidates of car-sized openings. In a nutshell, the bird's eye view is the representation of the scene as viewed from above, computed by transforming a monocular camera image taking intrinsic and extrinsic camera parameters into account (refer to [20] for more details).

Especially for the mentioned attention-based traffic sign recognition, a slightly modified classification approach was incorporated. Still, as for all attention search targets the system comprises of two stages, firstly the attention system, which generates the mentioned FoAs with possible traffic sign candidates. Different from the standard case, for traffic signs each FoA is processed by a number of weak classifiers, where each classifier generates a probability value for each traffic sign class. Finally, all probability values for a single traffic sign class are multiplied, resulting in an overall probability for each traffic sign class and region. The weak classifiers were chosen to be highly generic, for being able to easily extend the number of traffic sign classes. So far the parameters of the weak classifiers were analyzed to recognize *Stop*, *Give Way* and *Warning* signs. The proposed approach is an important step towards the simultaneous detection of a number of traffic sign classes in complex environments with varying sizes. For a detailed description please refer to Sect. 4.6..

The "where" Pathway

The next step is the fusion between the newly detected object and the already known ones. The result will be further processed in the "where" pathway and stored in the short term memory (STM). All objects in the STM are then suppressed in the current calculated attention map to enable the system to focus on new objects. The principle of suppressing known objects was proved to exist in the human vision system as well and is termed inhibition of return (IoR), refer to [21] for details.

All known objects are tracked using a 2D tracker that is based on normalized cross correlation (NCC). The tracker gets its anchor (i.e., the currently predicted 2D pixel position where the correlation-based object search on the new image will be started) from a Kalman-filter-based prediction running on the 3D environmental representation taking the ego-motion of the camera vehicle and tracked object into account. The predicted 3D position is transformed to 2D pixel positions (u,v) using a pin hole camera model that contains all intrinsic and extrinsic camera parameters (in detail these are the 3 camera angles θ_X, θ_Y, and θ_Z, the 3 translational camera offsets t_1, t_2, t_3, the horizontal and vertical principal point c_u and c_v, as well as the horizontal and vertical focal length f_u and f_v), refer to Equation (3) and (4) asa well as Fig. 33b for the applied coordinate system.

In case the NCC tracker is able to re-detect the object in 2D pixel coordinates, the 3D position in the representation is updated using 4 different depth cues for the 2D pixel (u,v) to 3D world (X_{obj}, Y_{obj}, Z_{obj}) transformation. More specifically, the system uses stereo data, radar, depth from object knowledge and depth from bird's eye view (see Fig. 37 and Sect. 6. for more details on these cues). The available depth cues are combined using the biologically motivated principle of weak fusion (see [22]). Weak fusion combines the depth sources based on their reliability (i.e., sensor variances). The fusion is realized using an Extended Kalman Filter (EKF) that combines the cues based on dynamically adapted weights depending on the static predefined sensor variances and the available depth sources, as not every cue is available in each time step. The EKF uses a second order process model for its prediction step that models the relevant kinematics of the car (velocity and acceleration).

$$u = -f_u \frac{r_{11}(X\text{-}t_1) + r_{12}(Y\text{-}t_2) + r_{13}(Z\text{-}t_3)}{r_{31}(X\text{-}t_1) + r_{32}(Y\text{-}t_2) + r_{33}(Z\text{-}t_3)} + c_u \tag{3}$$

$$v = -f_v \frac{r_{21}(X\text{-}t_1) + r_{22}(Y\text{-}t_2) + r_{23}(Z\text{-}t_3)}{r_{31}(X\text{-}t_1) + r_{32}(Y\text{-}t_2) + r_{33}(Z\text{-}t_3)} + c_v \tag{4}$$

with

$$
\begin{aligned}
r_{11} &= cos(\theta_Z)cos(\theta_Y) \\
r_{12} &= -sin(\theta_Z)cos(\theta_X) + cos(\theta_Z)sin(\theta_Y)sin(\theta_X) \\
r_{13} &= sin(\theta_Z)sin(\theta_X) + cos(\theta_Z)sin(\theta_Y)cos(\theta_X) \\
r_{21} &= sin(\theta_Z)cos(\theta_Y) \\
r_{22} &= cos(\theta_Z)cos(\theta_X) + sin(\theta_Z)sin(\theta_Y)sin(\theta_X) \\
r_{23} &= -cos(\theta_Z)sin(\theta_X) + sin(\theta_Z)sin(\theta_Y)cos(\theta_X) \\
r_{31} &= -sin(\theta_Y) \\
r_{32} &= cos(\theta_Y)sin(\theta_X) \\
r_{33} &= cos(\theta_Y)cos(\theta_X)
\end{aligned}
$$

Objects that leave the represented surrounding scene or whose Kalman variances are too high (i.e., they received no new measurements for several frames) are deleted from the STM. The concept of appearance-based 2D tracking (analysis of motion in 2D) supported by a 3D representation (interpretation of motion in 3D) was found in humans as well [23]. From a technical point of view, the advantage of this approach is the simple correction of the ego-motion determined from the internal 3D representation. The vehicle ego-motion (translations ΔX_e and ΔZ_e, as well as the change of the yaw angle $\Delta\theta_X$) is determined based on a standard single track model and compensated in the Kalman prediction step (see Equation (5) and (6) for the state vector E and process model A). Therefore, a computationally intensive optical-flow-based motion prediction is no longer needed, as it was done in a previous system implementation [24]. The main reason for the strong object motion in the 2D image is compensated by correcting the ego-motion-based position change of objects, which eases the tracking task considerably.

$$E = \begin{bmatrix} Z_{\text{obj}} & X_{\text{obj}} & v_{Z,\text{obj}} & v_{X,\text{obj}} & 1 \end{bmatrix} \tag{5}$$

$$A = \begin{bmatrix} cos(\Delta\theta_X) & sin(\Delta\theta_X) & T & 0 & \text{-}\Delta Z_e \\ \text{-}sin(\Delta\theta_X) & cos(\Delta\theta_X) & T & 0 & \text{-}\Delta X_e \\ 0 & 0 & cos(\Delta\theta_X) & sin(\Delta\theta_X) & 0 \\ 0 & 0 & \text{-}sin(\Delta\theta_X) & cos(\Delta\theta_X) & 0 \\ 0 & 0 & 0 & 0 & 1 \end{bmatrix} \tag{6}$$

A comparison between the current Kalman-fused 3D object position $P_t = [Z_{\text{obj}}, X_{\text{obj}}]$ and the predicted 3D object position P_t' decides, based on the state variances $\sigma_{P_t'}^2$ and $\sigma_{P_t}^2$, if the tracked object is static or dynamic (see Fig. 2b). P_t' is calculated by an ego-motion-based prediction starting from the stored Kalman fused value P_{t-4}. For the comparison, β_{th} is used as a threshold on the measure $\beta(P_t, P_t')$ defined in Equation (7). The calculated measure is motivated from a statistical parameter test that checks for the equality of two distributions. It showed good performance on various test sequences. If $\beta(P_t, P_t')$ is bigger than β_{th} (i.e., the object is detected to be dynamic) the Kalman filter receives the object ego-motion $v_{Z,\text{obj}} \neq 0$ and $v_{X,\text{obj}} \neq 0$ that is derived from the integrated object position change $D_{\text{obj,ego}_t}$ as measurement.

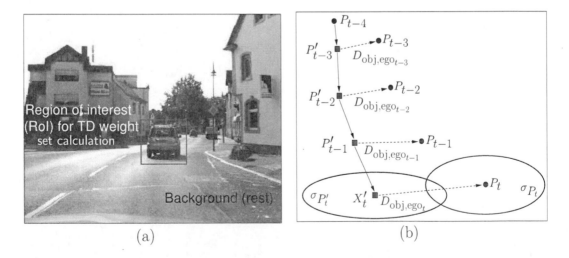

(a)   (b)

Figure 2. (a) Visualization of the object training region (RoI) for TD weight calculation against the background (rest), (b) Prediction of object ego-motion (dots: Kalman tracked object position, squares: ego-motion predicted object position, dashed line: accumulated object ego-motion).

$$\beta(P_t, P_t') = \left| \frac{P_t - P_t'}{\sqrt{\sigma_{P_t}^2 + \sigma_{P_t'}^2}} \right| \tag{7}$$

For all dynamic (i.e., moving) and therefore potentially dangerous objects in the scene an additional attention-based tracker support is realized, in order to solve a typical problem appearance-based trackers suffer from (i.e., a tracker type that relies on the comparison of image patches). Said trackers depend strongly on the quality of the object template (i.e., the image patch the tracker has to relocalize in the current image). In Fig. 3a the functional description of a NCC tracker is visualized. Here, the template is fix, which leads to a decreasing tracking performance. The object gets lost quickly. This is caused by the fact that in the vehicle domain the appearance of tracked objects quickly changes (due to changes in illumination, view angle, or varying scale), which makes an adaptation of the template necessary. A typical approach for template adaptation is shown in Fig. 3b, where the template is reset based on the previous tracking result. Using this procedure incremental errors of the tracker are accumulated. The detected region drifts away from the object and gets finally lost. More advanced approaches for template adaptation exist that adapt the initial template by model-based image transformations in order to compensate the scale variance and change of view angle (see, e.g., [25]). Said methods suffer from noise, still perform rather robustly, but require specific and complex algorithms. In the here presented system, a novel approach for template adaptation is proposed that relies on already system-immanent approaches. As visualized in Fig. 3c based on the previous template and Equ. (2) a TD weight set and a TD saliency map S^{total} is computed for the previous image frame. The maximum of this map marks the new position of the object template used for tracking in the current frame. In other words, the initial template position is derived from the typical feature characteristics present in the previous template. As opposed to Fig. 3b, the template adaptation and object redetection is organized separately, thereby preventing the accumulation of incremental errors.

From a representational point of view, the "where" pathway of the here presented ADAS consists on the one hand of the STM, that stores all properties of sensed objects in a 3D representation and on the other hand of a long term memory (LTM) that stores the generic properties of object classes. The LTM is filled offline with typical patches and corresponding feature maps F_i of specific object classes. Typically, 3-5 object patches are sufficient to allow a robust attention-based object detection. For evaluation purposes cars, reflection posts, and signal boards are used as LTM content, but the ADAS can detect any other object types as well, if the attention and the object recognizer are trained accordingly (see [10] for the attention-based detection and classification of traffic signs). In the default state the system searches for the generic LTM object class "car". This is done by calculating the geometric mean of all TD weight sets of the stored LTM objects that were calculated based on Equation (2). These weights tune the TD attention in the "what" pathway.

As described above, in case the tracker has re-detected the object in the current frame the 3D representation is updated. In case the tracker looses the object the system searches for the lost STM object in the following frames. This is realized by calculating a TD weight set that is specific to the lost STM object using Equation (2). The object O_f found by the STM search is then compared to the searched object O_s by means of the distance measure $\delta(O_f, O_s)$ that is based on the Bhattacharya coefficient(a measure for determining

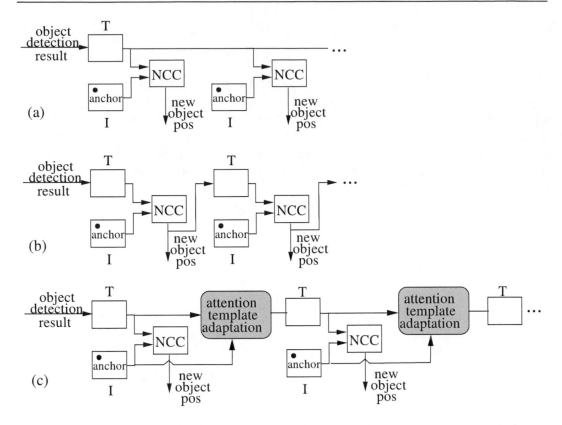

Figure 3. Functional description of appearance-based tracking approaches (with Normalized Cross Correlation NCC, image I, and template T): (a) Fixed template, (b) Continuous template adaptation based on the previous tracking result, (c) Continuous template adaptation based on saliency maximum (TD weight set computed using the previous template).

the similarity between two histograms) calculated on the histograms of all N object feature maps $H_i^{O_f}$ and $H_i^{O_s}$ (see Equation (8)).

$$\delta(O_f, O_s) = \sum_{i=1}^{N} \sqrt{1 - \gamma(H_i^{O_f}, H_i^{O_s})} \tag{8}$$

$$\gamma(H_i^{O_f}, H_i^{O_s}) = \sum_{\forall u,v} \sqrt{H_i^{O_f}(u,v) H_i^{O_s}(u,v)}$$

The LTM and STM object search run in parallel as indicated visually in Fig. 1. Again, it is important to note that the ADAS is not restricted to the detection and tracking of cars, reflection posts, signal boards, and traffic signs. By using different LTM object patches and by offline training of the ADAS object classifier in combination with the generic concept of online tunable TD attention the ADAS is highly dynamic and flexible.

Static Domain-specific Tasks

The third major part of the ADAS handles the domain-specific tasks related to marked and unmarked lane detection. The marked lane detection is based on a standard Hough transform parameterizing a clothoid model, whose input signal is generated by the here presented generic attention system. The TD attention weights used here boost white and yellow structures on a darker background (so called on-off contrast), to which the biological motivated DoG filter (see Sect. 4.2.1.) is selective. The yellow on-off structures are weighted stronger than the white to allow the preferred handling of lane markings in construction sites.

The state-of-the-art unmarked lane detection evaluates a street training region in front of the car and two non-street training regions at the side of the road. The features in the street training region (stereo, edge density, color hue, color saturation) are used to detect the drivable road based on dynamic probability distributions for all cues (see [26] for more details). A temporal integration procedure between the current and past detected road segments based on the bird's eye view is applied (refer to [20] for a comprehensive description of the temporal integration procedure). The procedure is used to increase the completeness of the detected road by decreasing the number of false negative road pixels. Based on a biologically motivated curbstone/elevated road border detection approach the gathered road detection results are post-processed. This allows the correction of some minor false positive errors that are induced by the temporal integration step (see Sect. 7.3. for details). In the final step, a fusion between the detected marked and unmarked road segments is used to derive the currently drivable lanes.

The final part of the static domain specific tasks is the state-of-the-art scene classification. For being able to efficiently tune the generic system modules to the current environment and their challenges the current scene context (e.g., inner-city, country road, highway) has to be known. For classifying the scene image data is required as the only input. The processing is roughly organized as follows: After the preprocessing the resulting image is divided in 16 parts and each part is independently transformed to the frequency domain. In the following, each transformed part is sampled with an array of shifted and oriented Gaussian filters, resulting in an average power spectrum for each of the parts. The final classification step is realized by Hierarchical Principal Component Classification that is trained during an offline learning phase. For more information please refer to Sect. 5..

Environmental Interaction

The system can interact with the world via an actuator control module. Currently the ADAS implementation uses a 3 phase danger handling scheme depending on the distance and relative speed of a recognized obstacle. When an obstacle is detected in front at a rapidly decreasing distance, a visual and acoustic warning is issued and the brakes are prepared. In the second phase, the brakes are engaged with a deceleration of 0.25 g followed by hard braking of 0.6 g in the third phase.

System Control

The system control module realizes a functional mapping of an input feature space of measured internal system-state variables and an output-parameter space for the modulation of the system behavior. In the following, the specific features and parameters are named, the current system uses for control.

Measurement of internal system-state variables (input feature space):

- (i_0) No condition,

- (i_1) Car-like road opening,

- (i_2) NCC tracker confidence (marking a lost object),

- (i_3) STM object leaving/entering the image,

- (i_4) Object position, object velocity.

- (i_5) Object position uncertainty,

- (i_6) Dynamic/static object.

Control parameters to influence/modulate the system behavior (output-parameter space):

- (o_1) Actuator control (autonomous braking, acoustic warning, belt strengthener),

- (o_2) LTM search (for cars, signal boards, ...),

- (o_3) Trigger STM search (lost objects, saliency tracking support),

- (o_4) STM decay rate (number of objects in STM),

- (o_5) BU-TD combination weight λ,

- (o_6) Spatial prior (position, sharpness of degradation).

In the following, instances of the functional mapping are listed that control the multiple parallel "what" pathways, the actuators, as well as the STM data. The functional mapping between input and output is visualized by the symbol $\Rightarrow$. The task represented by each instance is set in parentheses at the end.

- 1. (i_0) $\Rightarrow$ (o_2) LTM search for cars, (o_5) $\lambda = 0.5$ (search for cars),

- 2. (i_2) NCC tracker confidence for a car below threshold $\Rightarrow$ (o_2) Interrupt LTM search, (o_3) redetect lost object using TD attention, (o_6) Set spatial prior, (o_5) $\lambda = 1$ (redetect lost cars),

- 3. (i_0) $\Rightarrow$ (o_2) LTM search for signal boards, (o_5) $\lambda = 0.5$ (search for signal boards),

- 4. (i_2) NCC tracker confidence for a signal board below threshold $\Rightarrow$ (o_2) Interrupt LTM search, (o_3) redetect lost object using TD attention, (o_6) Set spatial prior, (o_5) $\lambda = 1$ (redetect lost signal boards),

- 5. (i_4) Potential collision $\Rightarrow$ (o_1) Trigger danger handling (collision mitigation),

- 6. (i_6) Dynamic object leaving the field of view $\Rightarrow$ (o_5) $\lambda = 0$, (scene exploration, search dynamic objects),

- 7. (i_6) Dynamic object reentering the field of view $\Rightarrow$ (o_5) $\lambda = 1$, (o_4) Number of STM objects = 1, (o_6) Set spatial prior, (o_3) Saliency tracker support (track dynamic object),

- 8. (i_1) Car-like road opening detected $\Rightarrow$ (o_6) Set spatial prior in (o_2) for cars (analyze conspicuous image region).

In the following, with the attention sub-system the generic visual preprocessing module is described.

4. Visual Attention Sub-System

Facilities for controlling and managing traffic are always visually conspicuous. For example, lane markers are white on a typically dark road and traffic signs or traffic lights have bright colors. According to that, in many countries flashy advertisement is prohibited in the proximity of roads. The said examples exploit a key aspect of the human visual processing - the principle of early selection. With vision being the most important sensory modality of humans having the highest information density, the named principle significantly accelerates the processing of vision data. More specifically, the abundance of visual stimuli in the world is prefiltered or preselected early to match the restricted cognitive capacity of the human brain. In plain words, the principle of early selection suppresses sensor data that is not relevant to the current needs or goals of the system causing a colorful, bright traffic sign to visually pop-out in a traffic scenario. For realizing said early selection principle the human disposes of the so-called attention mechanism, which preselects the scene elements.

More specifically, the human vision system filters the high abundance of environmental information by attending to scene elements that either pop out of the scene (i.e., objects that are visually conspicuous) or match the current task best (i.e., objects that are compliant to the current internal state or need/task of the system), while suppressing the rest. For both attention guiding principles psychophysical and neurological evidence exists (see [27, 28]). Following this principle, technical vision systems have been developed that prefilter a scene by decomposing it into its features (see [29]) and recombining these to a saliency map that contains high activation at regions that differ strongly from the surrounding (i.e., bottom-up (BU) attention, see [30]). More recent system implementations additionally include the modulatory influence of task relevance into the saliency (i.e., top-down (TD) attention, see [31] as one of the first and [32, 1] as the most recent and probably most influential approaches). In these systems, instead of scanning the whole scene in search for certain objects in a brute force way, the use of TD attention allows a full scene decomposition despite restraints in computational resources. In principle, the vision input data is serialized with respect to the importance to the current task. Based on this, computationally demanding processing stages located higher in the architecture work on prefiltered data of improved relevance, which saves computation time and allows complex real-time vision applications.

During the vision system design the focus was set on building a computational efficient system implementation for online use on vehicles. The overall system should be flexible, meaning that a new system task should not lead to the necessity of realizing new modules or a structural redesign of the whole system. While getting inspiration from biology, the target was the design of a system that exhibits specific properties without being specifically designed for these properties (e.g., the here presented ADAS is able to locate the horizon edge or detect fast moving objects or red traffic signs without being explicitly designed for these tasks).

The design goals of the introduced TD attention sub-system comprised the development of an object and task-specific tunable saliency map suitable for the real-world scenarios in the car domain.

However, the robustness of biological attention systems is difficult to achieve, given e.g., the high variability of scene content, changes in illumination, and scene dynamics. Most computational attention models do not show real-time capability and are mainly tested in a controlled indoor environment on artificial scenes. Important aspects discriminating real-world scenes from indoor and artificial scenes are the dynamics in the environment (e.g., changing lighting and weather conditions, dynamic scene content) as well as the high scene complexity (e.g., cluttered scenes). Dealing with such scenarios requires a strong system adaptation capability with respect to changes in the environment. Here, the focus was set on five conceptual issues crucial for closing the gap between artificial and natural attention systems operating on real-world scenes. The feasibility of this approach will be shown on vision data from the car domain (see Sect. 8.1.1.). The described TD tunable attention system is used as front-end of the vision system of the previously described advanced driver assistance system, whose architecture is inspired by the human brain.

After elaborating on related approaches in Sect. 4.1. and the attention features in Sect. 4.2., Sect. 4.3. will describe specific challenges for an attention system under real-world conditions. Section 4.4. will describe the ADAS attention sub-system in detail pointing out the solutions to the denoted challenges. Taken these challenges, Sect. 4.5. compares the proposed attention system on a functional level to two other, influential attention approaches from literature. Finally, Sect. 8.1.1. evaluates the attention system as a sub-model of the ADAS.

4.1. Related Work

In the past, the human vision system has been examined in a large number of studies. For example, the psychophysical experiments of [33] impressively showed that the task has a modulating effect on attention. The gathered results were formalized in the concept of inattentional blindness. In the referenced experiments participants did not notice unexpected events (like a black gorilla walking through an indoor scene) when the task (counting ball contacts of a white basketball team) involved features complementary to the unexpected events (see Fig. 4).

Figure 4. Psychophysical study conducted by [33] marking the human visual attention as strong mediator between the world and our perception of the world.

Related to the vehicle domain the task-dependent nature of gazing has also been proven while steering a car. Recently, it was shown by [34] that the performance for dangerous situation detection (a colored motorcycle veering into the vehicle's path) strongly depends on the feature-match between the current distracting visual task and the unexpected obstacle. In another example, the gaze of drivers in a virtual environment was examined [35]. The results show that the performance in detecting stop signs is heavily modulated by context (i.e., top-down) factors and not only by bottom-up visual saliency. Endowing a vision architecture for an intelligent car with similar, task-based attention can result in a gain of performance with minimal additional resource requirements (see gathered results Sect. 8.2.1.).

In most research on human visual attention, the focus is on the bottom-up detection of salient features/objects in a scene (for a review of biologically evident attention features see [29]). A well-known computational model for saliency calculation is the approach by [36] that is used in a number of implemented systems. Recently, this approach has been extended by various researchers to account for task-dependent aspects of visual attention (see, e.g., [37, 38, 39]) by applying dynamic weights to different processing stages. The task is often to find a specific object within a predominantly static indoor scene. A more complete view on a possible architecture for a visual system incorporating task-dependent visual attention is given by [32, 40]. The proposed architecture combines top-down (TD) and bottom-up (BU) influences by using TD weights on the calculated BU features. However, there is no separation between the untuned BU saliency map and the calculated TD saliency maps allowing a weighted combination, which would ensure the preservation of BU influence in all system states. The system is evaluated mainly on static indoor scenes and a few static outdoor scenes. Furthermore, there are only few attention-based vision systems that use a motion feature (see [41, 42]). Given the importance of motion in the human visual perception, modeling the influence of scene dynamics on attention can be seen as a key issue to realize robust human-like vision systems.

In Sect. 4.5., the two related top-down attention systems of [32] and [1] were chosen for a detailed structural and functional comparison, since these impacted the here presented work most.

However, numerous other psychophysical and computational attention models exist (please refer to [43, 44, 1, 45] for a comprehensive overview of the latest developments in attention research and [46] for an overview of related psychophysical studies).

To the author's knowledge, in the car domain so far no task-dependent tunable vision system exists that mimics human attention processes.

4.2. Attention Features

The following section describes the major treats of the developed biologically inspired feature space the ADAS architecture relies on for fulfilling its generic vision tasks. Typical features for biologically motivated vision systems are intensity, orientation, and color (see, e.g. [36, 37]). These features are often preferred because they are so-called basic features. A feature is a basic feature, in case it allows, among other things, an efficient visual search. The efficiency of visual search tasks is assessed by psychophysical studies that determine the reaction time of subjects to visual impulses (see [47] and [29] for a summary). More specifically, a basic feature allows an efficient parallel search, i.e., in a search task with a growing number of distractors the mean search time is constant or only slightly increasing (see Fig. 5). A basic feature allows a clear differentiation against distractors that do not dispose of this feature (i.e., one differentiating feature exists in these so-called feature search tasks).

Additional to the named three features, recent biologically motivated systems also incorporate depth and motion (see, e.g., [48]). Both features are marked as basic features by most researchers (see [29] for an overview). An important property of said basic features and reason for their efficiency in visual search tasks is that they draw or guide attention. The attention principle plays an important role for the here developed ADAS since it will allow solving specific vision tasks in a generic fashion. It will be described in detail in Sect. 4.4.. In a nutshell, the attention features introduced in the following are combined to form a saliency map that is the key aspect and major output of a human-like attention system. This saliency map shows high activation at image regions that contain a high level of information in terms of a specific vision task (top-down driven activation) or because the image regions differ strongly from the rest of the image, meaning that a high local entropy is present (bottom-up driven activation).

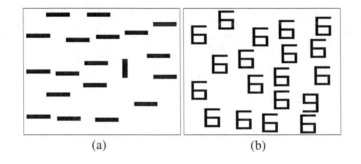

(a)   (b)

Figure 5. Efficient and inefficient visual search tasks: (a) Efficient search: Orientation is a basic feature, (b) Inefficient search: Numeric character differentiation is not a basic feature.

In the following paragraphs, three well-known biologically motivated visual features together with some important conceptional extensions are described. These features are static, i.e., they depend on the current image only (as opposed to dynamic features that also depend on previous images, see [49] for details on these features). These static features will be Difference of Gaussians (DoG) filters for detecting intensity changes, Gabor filters for detecting oriented structures, and RGBY-colors.

With DoG and Gabor, specific filter types and thereby an extensively used image processing method will be motivated by showing the resemblance to the processing in the human brain.

This resemblance is based on the fact that receptive fields of neurons (i.e., their measurable transfer functions, see [50]) are equivalent to filter kernels. Therefore, the signal processing principles in neurons can be described in computational image processing by a convolution, as stated in [51]. Furthermore, in the first stage of the human visual processing the image is sampled with the resolution of photoreceptors on the retina. All this makes the computational image filtering based on convolution with biologically inspired filter kernels to a close approximation of the human visual signal processing. Figure 6 visualizes the neuronal signal processing for a DoG-like receptive field that equals the convolution:

$$I_{\text{filt}}(u,v)=g(u,v)*I(u,v)=\sum_{u'=0}^{U-1}\sum_{v'=0}^{V-1}g(u,v)I(u-u',v-v').\tag{9}$$

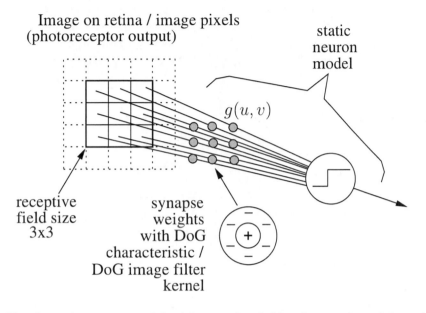

Figure 6. Simple static neuron model with receptive field and synaptic weights $g(u,v)$ that are equivalent to a symmetric filter kernel used in image convolution.

In the following two subsections, the technical equivalents of two basic measured receptive field types are described (DoG and Gabor). After that, with RGBY, a color space is described that mirrors the processing on the retina.

4.2.1. Intensity Feature

In the following, the Difference of Gaussians feature is biologically motivated and a parameterization is derived that allows the implementation of a filter bank for a sparse signal decomposition.

Biological Motivation

In vitro receptive field measurements of ganglion cells in the retina of macaque monkeys have shown a characteristic center-surround behavior [50]. Also measurements of receptive fields of neurons located in early regions of the visual pathway of macaque monkeys have shown a similar characteristic [52]. In other words, the receptive fields are selective to monotonous regions (blobs), which differ from the background in terms of their intensity. An example for such contrast is shown in the lower left image in Fig. 8b. Furthermore, theories and supporting measurements exist, which allow to interpret specific brain regions in the human visual pathway as filter banks that decompose an input image in terms of the existing frequencies [53]. The realized attention system extends this principle to all static and dynamic features.

In the following, the measured center-surround behavior is modeled using a filter kernel of two 2D Gaussian functions that are subtracted (Difference of Gaussians). A parameterization of these Gaussian functions will be provided that will allow the implementation of a low-loss filter bank for said filter kernel.

The Difference of Gaussians (DoG) filter is selective to monotonous regions (blobs) of different sizes (see Fig. 8). The filter kernel is not orientation selective (i.e., isotropic). In its basic form the centre of the DoG filter kernel is excitatory and the lateral region is inhibitory. The discrete DoG filter kernel results from the sampling of a Gaussian curve with a small variance σ_e^2 that is subtracted from a Gaussian curve with a bigger variance σ_i^2 (see also Fig. 7):

$$DoG(u,v) = \frac{1}{2\pi\sigma_i^2}e^{-\frac{u^2+v^2}{2\sigma_i^2}} - \frac{1}{2\pi\sigma_e^2}e^{-\frac{u^2+v^2}{2\sigma_e^2}}. \tag{10}$$

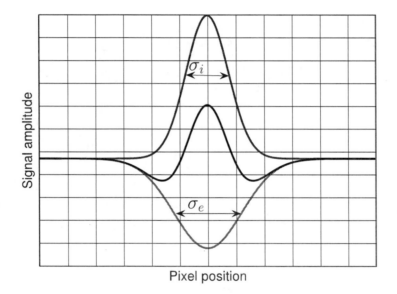

Pixel position

Figure 7. One-dimensional on-off DoG (black) and the two Gaussian functions it is composed of (positive Gaussian function with small standard deviation in blue, negative Gaussian function in red).

On a more qualitative level, the DoG subtracts the mean weighted intensity of a smaller center region from the mean weighted intensity of a bigger surround for each image pixel.

As will become apparent in Sect. 4.4., in order to yield high hit rates in top-down related search (i.e., when searching for a specific object using the saliency map), the features of an attention system need high selectivity to provide as much supporting and inhibiting (i.e., suppressing) maps as possible. At the same time, high efficiency is needed due to constraints in computational resources. An approach fulfilling these demands, is the separation of the DoG filter in on-center (called on-off in the following) and off-center selectivity (off-on) as it is emphasized in [1] (see Fig. 9a and Fig. 9b). Thereby, the attention system can

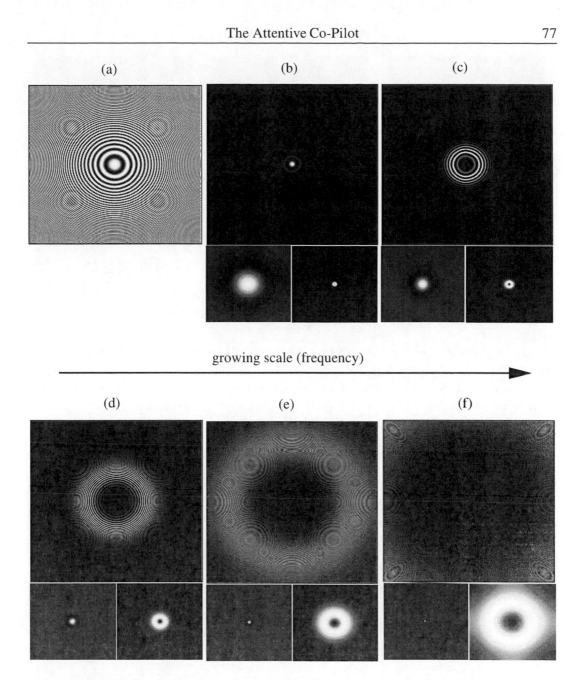

Figure 8. (a) Test image containing all frequencies in all orientations, (b)-(f) Different levels of the DoG filter bank with the filter response for the test image on top, the filter kernel in the image domain at bottom left, and the filter kernel in the frequency domain at bottom right.

differentiate between bright blobs on a dark background and dark blobs on a bright background. To realize such an on-off/off-on separation the DoG filter response is separated into its positive and negative part, which is equivalent to the computationally more demanding independent filtering with the two different filter kernels depicted in the lower left corner of Fig. 9a and Fig. 9b respectively.

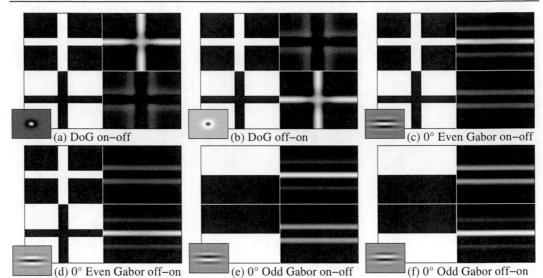

Figure 9. Application of filter kernels on simple test images (negative filter response is cut off). Both the 2 DoG features (a), (b) and the 4 Gabor features (c)-(f) are realized with one filter operation each. Every picture shows on the left the used input test image and on the right the respective filter response for the filter kernel in the bottom left corner.

As described at the beginning of this section, the attention features are computed on different scales allowing a decomposition of the signal into overlapping frequency chunks. In the following, the appropriate parameterization of the DoG kernel is derived, which makes such a decomposition possible.

Parameterization of the DoG Kernel

The parameters σ_i and σ_e in Equ. (10) determine the frequency characteristic of the filter. For efficient filtering a Gaussian pyramid approach that scales the input image is used, while the filter kernel is not changed in size. In order to assure an accurate filtering procedure, the normalized central frequency f_{center} of the band-pass-type DoG filter needs to be 0.25, which equals a period length of 4 pixels and hence a blob of 2x2 pixels or a line of 2 pixels of any orientation. If $f_{center} = 0.25$ it can be assured that a low-loss pyramid-based image filtering can be done.

After some transformations in the frequency domain (see [49] for details), Equ. (11) can be derived.

$$\sigma_i = \frac{1}{\pi f_{center}} \sqrt{\frac{\ln(\gamma_{DoG})}{\gamma_{DoG}^2 - 1}} \tag{11}$$

As described before, f_{center} in Equ. (11) is set to 0.25. Furthermore, e.g., [53] recommends to set the ratio between the inner and outer Gaussian $\gamma_{DoG} = 1.6$, which results in a low-loss signal decomposition with only few redundancies between scales. Thereby all parameters of Equation (10) are determined and hence the DoG kernel is defined.

Discussion

As described in the previous subsection, the separation of the DoG filter response into on-off and off-on contrasts increases the feature space without additional computational costs. In the following, it is qualitatively shown that this approach increases the performance of a marked lane detection system. The approach extends known algorithms for lane marking detection by adding a biologically motivated filter step for preprocessing. More specifically, the DoG filter is used as input feature. Figure 10a shows a typical inner-city scenario with strong shadows on the road. For detecting the lane markings, the view from above (the so-called bird's eye view) is computed (see Fig. 10b), as will be described in Sect. 6.4.. On the bird's eye view, lane marking-like contrasts (bright image regions on a darker background) are detected by the DoG filter after which a clothoid-model-based approach for detecting the markings is used (see, e.g., [54, 55, 56] for related clothoid-based approaches). Figure 10c depicts the DoG filter results without the described on-off/off-on separation. Since lane markings have a typical on-off contrast (white/yellow markings on a darker street), the on-off DoG filter results should be used, since these contain less false-positive activations (Fig. 10d). For example, in [57] the pre-filtered road image still contains the lane-marking-unspecific off-on contrasts (e.g., shadows on the road). Such off-on contrasts are filtered out in the marked street detection approach to improve the road detection performance.

For a quantitative evaluation of the influence of the described on-off DoG separation an implemented lane marking detection system is used. The system gets a DoG-filtered edge image without on-off (please refer to Fig. 10c) and with on-off separation (as shown in Fig. 10d). The gathered results are summarized in Tab. 1. The evaluation reveals the improvement in accuracy of the detected offset (i.e., horizontal position of lane markings) and radius of the road based on manually labeled ground truth (GT) data of 330 highway frames (see Fig. 11 for a visualization of the scenario and the gathered results).

Table 1. Mean relative error of detection results (offset and radius of lane marking model)

Type of input data preprocessing	Mean relative error in offset $MREO = 1/N \sum \frac{GT_{\text{offset}} - \text{offset}}{GT_{\text{offset}}}$	Mean relative error in radius $MRER = 1/N \sum \frac{GT_{\text{radius}} - \text{radius}}{GT_{\text{radius}}}$
Without DoG on-off separation	4.46	80.87
With DoG on-off separation	**4.35**	**72.22**

4.2.2. Orientation Feature

In the following, the Gabor feature for the detection of oriented lines and edges is biologically motivated and a parameterization is derived that allows the implementation of a filter

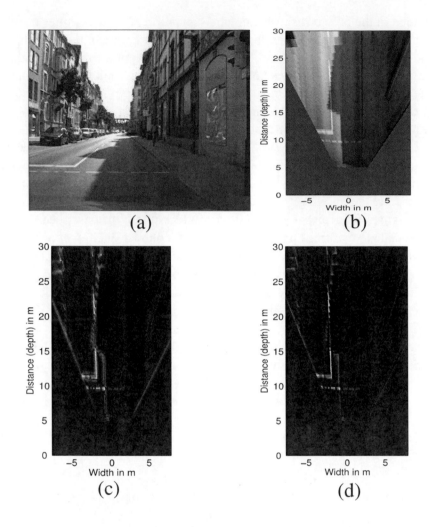

Figure 10. Exemplary performance gain of on-off DoG separation as pre-processing step of a lane marking detection system: (a) Input image, (b) Bird's eye view, (c) DoG result without on-off separation, (d) DoG result with on-off contrasts only (off-on contrasts are filtered out)

bank for a sparse signal decomposition.

Biological Motivation

According to [58], the lower layers of the cortex in cats contain orientation selective neuron populations. Please note that for lines and edges no 360 degree direction, but only 180 degree orientation is defined. The activation of these neuron populations lessens by 50% when the stimulus is rotated by 15-20 degree versus the preferred orientation. According to the spatial frequency theory (refer to [17] for details), these results give biological motivation for a filter bank with an angle selectivity of 30-40 degree. Also a frequency (respectively scale) selectivity of these neuron populations was proven to exist based on

Figure 11. Sample images of the evaluation scene (lane marking detection results visualized).

experiments (see [59]). The receptive fields of these neurons can be described by even and odd Gabor functionals (pairs of quadrature filters), which represent a Gaussian kernel that is modulated by a sine functional with a phase shift of 0 and 90 degree. For a visualization Fig. 12 depicts a one dimensional odd and even Gabor kernel.

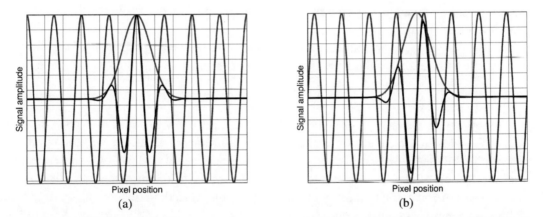

Figure 12. (a) One-dimensional even Gabor function (black), the Gaussian function (blue) and the modulating cosine function (red) it is composed of, (b) One-dimensional odd Gabor function.

Parameterization of the Gabor Kernel

The even Gabor filter kernel, which is selective to lines, equals the real part of $g(x)$ in Equ. (12). The odd Gabor filter kernel, which is selective to edges, equals the imaginary part of $g(x)$ in Equ. (12) with $x = \begin{bmatrix} u \\ v \end{bmatrix}$.

$$g(x) \quad = \frac{1}{2\pi ab} e^{-\frac{1}{2} x^T A x} e^{jk_0^T x} \tag{12}$$

With:

$$k_0 \quad = \begin{bmatrix} |k_0| cos\phi \\ |k_0| sin\phi \end{bmatrix}$$

$$A \quad = RPR^T = \begin{bmatrix} cos\phi & -sin\phi \\ sin\phi & cos\phi \end{bmatrix} \begin{bmatrix} a^{-2} & 0 \\ 0 & b^{-2} \end{bmatrix} \begin{bmatrix} cos\phi & sin\phi \\ -sin\phi & cos\phi \end{bmatrix}$$

The variances a^2 and b^2 influence the size of the underlying Gaussian function in the two image dimensions. According to the biological measurements, the filter kernel will have a modulation orthogonal to the longer principal axis of the Gaussian curve, which requires a^2 being smaller than b^2. The angle ϕ in the rotation matrix R determines the orientation of the filter kernel:

$$\phi \quad = m\Delta\phi \quad \text{and} \quad \Delta\phi = \frac{2\pi}{M} \quad \text{with} \quad m \in [0..M-1]. \tag{13}$$

The wave number vector k_0 determines the 2D period length of the modulated complex oscillation and thereby the selectivity of the kernels in the frequency domain. The value $|k_0|$ determines the line width the filter is selective to. It is important to note that $|k_0|$ is constant for all filter orientations.

The factor γ_{Gabor} is introduced, which is the ratio between the principal axes a and b (i.e., width and height) of the underlying Gaussian curve:

$$\gamma_{Gabor} \quad = \frac{a}{b} \quad \text{with} \quad a < b. \tag{14}$$

In [60] γ_{Gabor} was measured to be between 0.25 and 1.0 with a mean of 0.6 in neuronal receptive fields in the cat cortex. Taken these measurements and Equ. (13) the number of orientation channels M is typically set to a value between 4 and 18. As shown in [52], the application of the same parameter setting for the size of the Gaussian curve on all orientations of a specific frequency channel is possible. Based on this, for γ_{Gabor} in [52] the following generic Equation is derived:

$$\gamma_{Gabor} = \frac{a}{b} = \frac{3sin\left(\frac{\Delta\phi}{2}\right)}{\sqrt{1 - 9\left(cos\frac{\Delta\phi}{2} - 1\right)^2}}. \tag{15}$$

Since the filter bank uses a Gaussian resolution pyramid the filter kernel is also independent of the frequency channel (i.e., scale).

It is now sufficient, to determine the parameter a in Equ. (15), which encodes the overlap in frequency domain between the filter kernels of a specific orientation of two adjacent frequency channels (scales). In [52], a generic formulation for the parameter a is proposed that contains the parameter r, which determines the value at the overlap of two adjacent transfer functions (adjacent in orientation or scale):

$$a = \frac{3\sqrt{-2ln(r)}}{|k_0|}. \tag{16}$$

The parameter r is a value between 0 and 1 and is the ratio between the overlap value and the maximal value of the transfer function. The bigger r the more do adjacent filter kernels overlap in the frequency domain. Setting r=0.5 yields a reversible (non-dissipative and disjoint) signal decomposition compatible to the wavelet theory. This means that during Gabor decomposition of an image and subsequent recombination nothing is lost and no redundancy exists.

Summarizing, the filter bank formulation uses the parameter $\Delta\phi$ defining the number of orientation channels. Furthermore, the overlap value r and the value $|k_0|$ define the frequency selectivity of the filter. A typical value for $|k_0|$ is 0.25, which makes the filter selective to lines with a period length of 4 and hence a line thickness of 2 pixels. The following Fig. 13 depicts a Gabor filter bank with $\Delta\phi = 45$ degree, $r = 0.5$ and $|k_0| = 0.25$.

As stated before, Gabor functions model the receptive field characteristics in early layers of the vision system of mammals. Gabor filters are suited to the local detection of image frequencies since they optimally fulfill the trade-off between a good resolution in frequency and image domain, which represents the "uncertainty principle of quantum mechanics" for image processing. In other words, the time bandwidth product reaches its lower border for Gabor functions, as was shown in [61], which is equivalent to the fact that Gabor filter pairs are optimally localized both in the image and frequency domain. For a very descriptive mathematical formulation of the mentioned facts see [52]. A good localization in the image domain allows small filter kernels and hence minimizes the calculation time for filter operations. Additionally, a good localization in frequency domain allows an efficient use of Gaussian pyramids as well as sparseness in the orientation selective feature maps. An optimized localization in the image domain alone leads to sparse lines in the Gabor filter response (no repeating patterns), but lines of adjacent orientations are amplified as well. An optimized localization in the frequency domain leads to good selectivity regarding the orientation of lines, but the filter response in the image domain shows no isolated line at a certain location, but an unlocalized pattern of lines of the specific orientation.

For summarizing qualitatively, Gabor filters are selective to oriented lines (i.e., contours), when filtering an image with the even part of the Gabor kernel. Furthermore, Gabor filters are selective to oriented edges (i.e., steps), when using the odd part of the Gabor kernel. Additionally, Gabor filters are scale selective (i.e., selective to a certain thickness of lines respectively sharpness of edges).

Conceptional Extensions

Besides the well-known concept of decomposing the Gabor filter response in the odd and even part (i.e., computing the real and imaginary part of the filter response), here, an additional decomposition is done, which is motivated from the DoG filter decomposition. More specifically, the DoG on-off center concept is transferred to the Gabor filter and separate the odd and even Gabor responses into their positive and negative parts (please refer to Fig. 9c-f for a visualization). The proposed decomposition increases the performance of the ADAS attention system. For example, an on-off versus off-on even Gabor separation allows for the efficient separation of specifically oriented white lane markings from shadows on the road. Also, as shown in the following subsection an on-off/off-on separation for odd Gabor allows for the crisp suppression of the sky edge present in most scenes in the car domain.

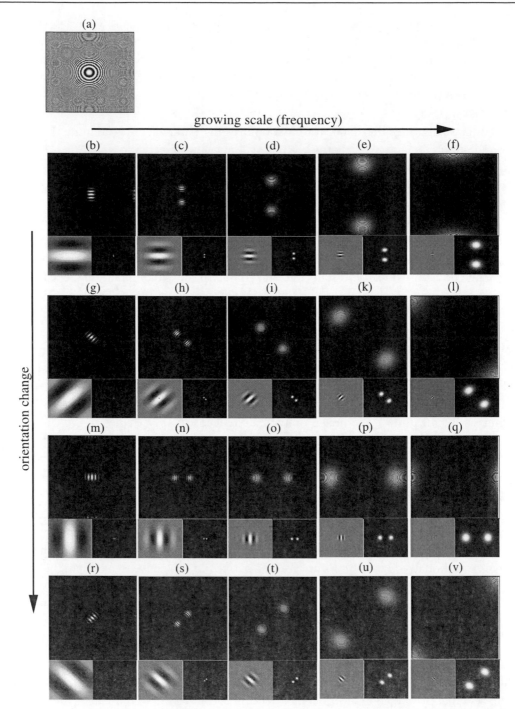

Figure 13. (a) Test image containing all frequencies in all orientations, (b)-(f) Even Gabor (without on-off/off-on separation), orientation 0 degree on 5 scales, on top: filter response to test image, bottom left: filter kernel in image domain, bottom right: filter kernel in frequency domain, (g)-(l) Even Gabor orientation 45 degree, (m)-(q) Even Gabor orientation 90 degree, (r)-(v) Even Gabor orientation 135 degree.

In sum, 4 different Gabor-based feature types are derived from one filtering step (even on-off, odd on-off, even off-on, odd off-on). Each of these 4 Gabor feature types consists of 20 independently weighable sub-feature maps (4 orientations on 5 scales each). Hence, the Gabor filter bank in the used parameterization allows for 80 independent filter responses and hence features.

Discussion

As discussed in the last subsection, a decomposition of the even and odd Gabor feature in their on-off and off-on component is proposed, in order to increase the feature selectivity. In the car domain the search performance is strongly influenced by the horizon edge, which is present in most images of highways and country roads. In the following, this serves as exemplary problem for showing the importance of a high feature selectivity. Typically, the horizon edge is removed by mapping out the sky in the input image, which might not be biologically plausible and is error prone. Instead, the horizon edge is suppressed directly in the attention by weighting the sub-feature maps (the required weighting procedure is described in Equation (2) in Sect. 3.), based on the high selectivity of the attention features. The gain of this approach is depicted in Fig. 14c that shows the diminished influence of the horizon edge on the saliency map of the real-world example in Fig. 14a. For a quantitative evaluation of the performance gain based on attentional sky suppression, refer to Sect. 8.1.1..

For a further qualitative assessment of the gain of on-off/off-on separation see Fig. 15a-d. Here a successful top-down search of the black vehicle is only possible using full separability of the input feature space.

When comparing the properties of Gabor and DoG filters, it is perceivable that a DoG filter response of a specific scale is equivalent to a combination of 4 Gabor filter responses for the 4 orientations of the same scale. Still using both features in an attention system (instead of Gabor alone) is reasonable, because the discrete nature of image filtering will lead to a certain loss in selectivity for combined Gabor feature maps. Supporting the DoG feature in the attention system makes up for these losses.

However, it is important to note that DoG and Gabor filters are not independent, which will play an important role in the normalization process described in Sect. 4.4. (see page 98). Normalization will be done to assure a comparability of all attention features, which is commonly neglected in comparable systems but is important for a robust vision system.

4.2.3. RGBY Color Space

Numerous color spaces are known in image processing (e.g., RGB, HSV, XYZ, Lab). The implemented biologically motivated RGBY color space shows several important advantages. The color space is introduced and assessed in the following.

Biological Motivation

The so-called human search asymmetries, which are measured in psychophysical studies (e.g., an inclined line among vertical lines is detected more easily than a vertical line among inclined lines) were conceptionalized by [62]. The authors propose a theory, which supports that it is easier to detect feature deviations of a non-canonical feature among canonical features than the other way around. The term canonical feature is related to the term

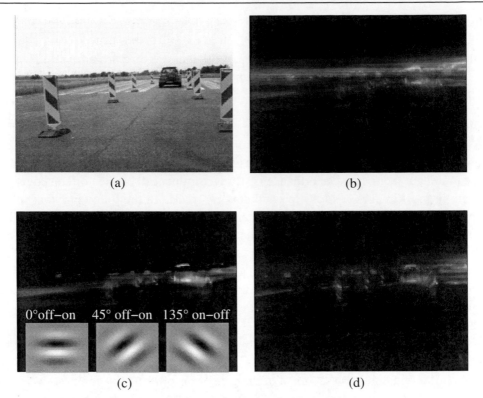

Figure 14. Evaluation of selectivity, (a) Input image, (b) Original bottom-up attention without sky suppression, (c) Modified bottom-up attention with attentional sky suppression (top-down influence), using suppressive odd Gabor filter kernels in low scales, (d) Bottom-up attention with traditional sky suppression.

basic feature (refer to the first paragraph of Sect. 4.2. on page 73 for details on basic features). In short, basic features define specific feature types that guide the attention (e.g., lines, color), whereas a canonical feature defines characteristics of a certain feature parameterization within a basic feature type (e.g., a subset of certain orientations leads to a line feature that is canonical). Hence, canonical features can be understood as feature parameterizations that mimic the way neuron populations are tuned in the human vision system (e.g., lines of 0 degree and 45 degree orientation are canonical). Feature deviations are represented by a combination of canonical features (e.g., a 10 degree line is represented by a combination of 0 degree and 45 degree neurons). Based on measured search asymmetries, such canonical features can be located. The psychophysical tests described in [47] revealed typical search asymmetries for colors, which suggest that a canonical feature parameterization for colors should differentiate between red, green, blue, and yellow. Furthermore, the human morphology in the early visual processing on the retina supports this notion. More specifically, cells exist on the retina that are tuned to red-green and blue-yellow contrasts (so-called color opponents). Both facts give a biological motivation, for preferring RGBY colors to any of the earlier mentioned color spaces.

(a)   (b)

(c)   (d)

Figure 15. Evaluation of the gain of on-off/off-on decomposition and usage of DoG as feature, (a) Shady input image with top-down search target black car, (b) Bottom-up attention, (c) Top-down attention, without on-off feature separation (overall attention is negative, maximum is not on the car, search is not successful), (d) Top-down attention, with on-off feature separation, only positive values are displayed, search is successful.

Computation of RGBY Colors

A very basic and thereby computationally efficient approach to compute RGBY colors was proposed by [36] (the so-called color opponent approach from the Neuromorphic Vision Toolkit of Itti):

$$R \quad = R - \frac{G+B}{2} \tag{17}$$

$$G \quad = G - \frac{R+B}{2} \tag{18}$$

$$B \quad = B - \frac{R+G}{2} \tag{19}$$

$$Y \quad = \frac{R+G}{2} - \frac{|R-G|}{2} - B. \tag{20}$$

Drawbacks of this approach are the missing white balance and missing uniformity in the resulting color maps. A color space is uniform, in case the distance between adjacent colors is equal over the whole color space (as related to the human color perception, i.e., the human ability to distinguish between colors). Uniform color spaces hence numerically represent colors very similar to the human color perception.

A more complex approach for computing RGBY colors is described in the following. The basic idea is based on the work of [1]. This more complex approach has a number of important advantages, namely its incorporated white balance and uniformity. Since the computational demands are moderate enough, the said RGBY approach is included into the feature space of the introduced attention system.

RGBY colors are based on the Lab color space. The Lab color space like the Luv color space was defined in 1976 by the CIE (Commision Internationale d'Eclairage) as a more accurate model of the human color perception. Both color spaces are uniform. The well-known HSV (Hue, Saturation, Value) and XYZ (X and Z contain color information, Y luminance information) are examples for non-uniform color spaces. In the uniform Lab color space "L" holds luminance information, "a" represents the red-green contrast and "b" the blue-yellow contrast. Since the L-channel is independent from the color information the Lab shows a certain extend of invariance against changes in illumination (similar to the HSV color space). A basic illumination invariance is very important for the proposed attention system. At the end of this subsection, the illumination variance properties of RGB and RGBY color space will be compared for a color-based detection of signal boards in twilight. The Lab color space is computed based on the following Equations:

$$L \quad = 116 \left(\frac{Y}{Y_n} \right)^{1/3} - 16 \tag{21}$$

$$a \quad = 500 \left[\left(\frac{X}{X_n} \right)^{1/3} - \left(\frac{Y}{Y_n} \right)^{1/3} \right] \tag{22}$$

$$b \quad = 200 \left[\left(\frac{Y}{Y_n} \right)^{1/3} - \left(\frac{Z}{Z_n} \right)^{1/3} \right]. \tag{23}$$

With default values for a full spectrum light source:

$$X_n \quad = 242.4$$
$$Y_n \quad = 255.0$$
$$Z_n \quad = 277.7$$

It depends on the XYZ color space:

$$\begin{bmatrix} X \\ Y \\ Z \end{bmatrix} = \begin{bmatrix} 0.490 & 0.310 & 0.200 \\ 0.177 & 0.812 & 0.011 \\ 0.000 & 0.010 & 0.990 \end{bmatrix} \begin{bmatrix} R \\ G \\ B \end{bmatrix}. \tag{24}$$

The XYZ color space incorporates a white balance mechanism based on the reference values X_n, Y_n, and Z_n, which are the XYZ values of a white reference patch in the image [63]. A white balance is necessary in order to adapt the perceived colors to the current spectrum of the current light source. More specifically, the sensed colors have to be shifted and biased depending on the spectrum of the current light source. More qualitatively, this mechanism assures that the human can recognize a bright yellow cab in full spectrum noon light as well as in reddish evening light.

The CIE XYZ was initially developed in order to better match the characteristics of monitors based on RGB color information. The elements of the XYZ-transformation matrix have to be selected dependent on the monitor type. In the here proposed system, the transformation matrix proposed in [64] is used.

To compute RGBY, [1] proposes the Euclidian distance between the Lab color pixels of the image to the four Lab reference colors ($a_{ref,R}=0$ and $b_{ref,R}=127$ for red, $a_{ref,G}=127$ and $b_{ref,G}=127$ for green, $a_{ref,Y}=127$ and $b_{ref,Y}=0$ for yellow and $a_{ref,B}=127$ and $b_{ref,B}=127$ for blue). Exemplarily, Equ. (25) to (27) show the computation of the R color map of RGBY space that has to be applied pixel-wise over the whole image:

$$P_{ref,R} = (a_{ref,R}, b_{ref,R}) = (0, 127) \tag{25}$$

$$R_{final} = dist(P_{Lab} - P_{ref,R}) = \|(a,b) - (a_{ref,R}, b_{ref,R})\| \tag{26}$$

$$= \sqrt{(a - a_{ref,R})^2 + (b - b_{ref,R})^2}. \tag{27}$$

Based on this, 4 color maps will result that contain only non-negative values (see [1]). For a numerical representation of the interdependencies between RGBY and RGB see Tab. 2.

Table 2. Numerical interdependencies between RGB and RGBY

Reference color	RGB color space			RGBY color space (without normalization)			
	red	green	blue	red	green	blue	yellow
RGB red	255	0	0	217.7	81.9	100.0	210
RGB green	0	255	0	92.7	228.8	96.7	227.2
RGB blue	0	0	255	232.7	118.0	247.9	81.5
RGB yellow	255	255	0	141.6	176.1	39.0	222.5

However, there is a drawback in the approach of [1], which makes the resulting color maps inappropriate for their usage in the here proposed attention system. The problem is that the so computed color maps are not independent. More specifically, the R map is equal to the inverted G map and the B map is equal the inverted Y map, which means that only 2 independent color maps exist. Thereby selectivity is lost. Furthermore, for example the R map holds zeros at image positions of pure green, whereas for an attention system zero value in the red and green color map should define the intermediate value between red and green.

Therefore, in the following, a rescaling is proposed, which will lead to four independent RGBY color maps. Furthermore, it will be shown that the on-off/off-on separation for RGBY colors is system-immanent and therefore already included. Additionally, so-called double color opponent maps are proposed that are selective to color contrasts. Furthermore, exemplarily their importance for the attention is shown.

Conceptional Extensions

In order to allow a more suitable decomposition of color maps, the approach of

Equ. (27) is adapted leading to the following equations:

$$R_{\text{tmp}} = \sqrt{(a - a_{\text{ref},R})^2 + (b - b_{\text{ref},R})^2}/R_{\max} - 0.536 \tag{28}$$

$$G_{\text{tmp}} = \sqrt{(a - a_{\text{ref},G})^2 + (b - b_{\text{ref},G})^2}/G_{\max} - 0.555 \tag{29}$$

$$B_{\text{tmp}} = \sqrt{(a - a_{\text{ref},B})^2 + (b - b_{\text{ref},B})^2}/B_{\max} - 0.512 \tag{30}$$

$$Y_{\text{tmp}} = \sqrt{(a - a_{\text{ref},Y})^2 + (b - b_{\text{ref},Y})^2}/Y_{\max} - 0.559 \tag{31}$$

With: $R_{\max} = 232.7$, $G_{\max} = 228.8$, $B_{\max} = 247.9$, $Y_{\max} = 227.2$

$$R_{\text{final}} = \begin{cases} 2R_{\text{tmp}} & \forall \quad R_{\text{tmp}} > 0 \\ 0 & \forall \quad R_{\text{tmp}} \leq 0 \end{cases} \tag{32}$$

$$G_{\text{final}} = \begin{cases} 2G_{\text{tmp}} & \forall \quad G_{\text{tmp}} > 0 \\ 0 & \forall \quad G_{\text{tmp}} \leq 0 \end{cases} \tag{33}$$

$$B_{\text{final}} = \begin{cases} 2B_{\text{tmp}} & \forall \quad B_{\text{tmp}} > 0 \\ 0 & \forall \quad B_{\text{tmp}} \leq 0 \end{cases} \tag{34}$$

$$Y_{\text{final}} = \begin{cases} 2Y_{\text{tmp}} & \forall \quad Y_{\text{tmp}} > 0 \\ 0 & \forall \quad Y_{\text{tmp}} \leq 0 \end{cases}. \tag{35}$$

As the equations show, a normalization is done prior to the decomposition in four independent color channels. The received RGBY color maps do not contain redundancies after the proposed decomposition procedure.

As a result, four normalized independent RGBY color maps are received. An additional decomposition of all these maps into on-off and off-on components, which would double the number of color feature maps is not possible. This is the case, since the decomposition of RG and BY map into four independent color maps is equivalent to an on-off/off-on decomposition. Furthermore, image pyramids for all four color maps are build in order to allow a separation between colored blobs of different sizes. The computed four independent color pyramids can be used for an attention-based task-driven search (e.g., search for red objects of a certain size). The concept of task-driven attention (so-called top-down attention) is described in detail in Sect. 4.4..

However, colors themselves are not a cue for the contrast-driven attention (so-called bottom-up attention). For example, a monotonous red image should not lead to contrast-driven attention. How such a contrast-driven (bottom-up) attention is computed will be described in Sect. 4.. A color-based contrast-driven attention should be guided to image positions showing color contrasts (e.g., a green blob on a red background). The color feature type required for such operations is termed double color opponency in literature. Said double color opponent maps are received by filtering all four RGBY color maps with a Difference of Gaussians kernel based on image pyramids. As a result, for each color map five double color opponent maps are received, also allowing a differentiation between red blobs on a green background and vice versa. The received color contrast maps can now be used to detect targets based on their color contrast (e.g., traffic signs of typically bright colors in a typically less colorful traffic environment). Additional to bottom-up searches, such color contrasts can be used for the top-down search for objects with high color contrasts.

In sum, the color feature space consist of four RGBY color pyramids (i.e., 20 color feature maps) and 20 double color opponent maps. Top-down search hence disposes of 40 color feature maps and bottom-up search of 20 color maps.

Discussion

In the following, the performance of the RGBY color space is assessed and compared qualitatively to RGB. For that a complex traffic scene in twilight is used (see Fig. 16a), in which the present signal board should be found based on color information. As it can be expected, the absolute R-channel of RGB shown in Fig. 16b is not sufficient for a successful color-based detection of the signal board. However, even when normalizing the RGB R-channel to the overall sum of all three color channels, the signal board can not be detected (see Fig. 16c). Reason is that the low light situation changes the color of the signal board despite the automatic white balance of the camera. When using the proposed non-linear RGBY colors a separation on the RGBY R-channel is possible, despite the challenging lighting conditions (see Fig. 16d). An attention-based search for such signal boards can hence rely on the highly discriminating R-channel, which boosts the performance of the attention system as compared to the usage of RGB colors. Extensive testing with HSV colors has also shown inferior performance compared to the proposed RGBY color space.

4.3. Real-World Challenges for Top-Down Attention Systems

In the following paragraph, challenges are described a TD attention system is faced with when used on real-world images.

High Feature Selectivity: In order to yield high hit rates in TD search an attention system needs high feature selectivity to have as much supporting and inhibiting feature maps as possible. For this the used features must be selected and parameterized appropriately. Even more important for high selectivity is the use of modulatory TD weights on *all* sub-feature maps and scales. Many TD attention approaches allow TD weighting only on a high integration level (e.g., no weighting on scale level [37]) or without using the full potential of features (e.g., no on-off/off-on feature separation [32]) which leads to a performance loss. The here presented system fulfills both aspects. Based on the extended selectivity of the attention sub-system, the specific challenges of the car domain can be handled, as dealing with the horizon edge present in most images.

Comparable TD and BU Saliency Maps: Typically the TD and BU saliency maps are combined to an overall saliency, on which the Focus of Attention (FoA) is calculated. The combination requires comparable TD and BU saliency maps, making a normalization necessary. Humans undergo the same challenge when elements popping out compete with task-relevant scene elements for attention. A prominent procedure in literature normalizes each feature map to its current maximum (see [32] that is based on [36]), which has some drawbacks the here presented approach avoids.

Comparability of Modalities: Similarly, the combination of different a priori incomparable modalities (e.g., decide on the relative importance of edges versus color) must be

(a)   (b)

(c)   (d)

Figure 16. (a) Input image of road scene in twilight (signal board marked in red), (b) Absolute R-channel of RGB-space, (c) Relative R-channel of RGB-space (i.e., R-channel normalized to the sum of RGB-channels, with thresholding), (d) R-channel of RGBY space (with thresholding).

achieved. The presented approach realizes this by the biological principle of homeostasis that is defined as the reversible adaptation of essential processes of a (biological) system to the environment (see e.g., [65]).

Support of Conjunctions of Weak Object Features in the TD Path: Another important robustness aspect is the support of conjunction of weak object features in the TD path of the attention sub-system. That is, an object having a number of mediocre feature activations but no feature map popping out should still yield a clear maximum when combined on the overall saliency.

Changing Lighting Conditions: In a real-world scene, changing lighting conditions heavily influence the features the saliency map is composed of and hence the performance of attention system suffers. As the calculated TD weights are based on the features of training images (see Sect. 4.4.), the TD weights are illumination-dependent as well. Put differently, the TD weights are optimal for the specific illumination and thereby to the contrast that is present in the training images. The usage of TD weights on test images with a differing illumination will lead to an inferior TD search performance. Instead of adapting the TD weights dependent on the illumination, a local exposure control is proposed in order to adjust the contrast of the training images as well as the test images before applying TD weight calculation and TD search. The following attention system description will elaborate on the means taken to solve the named five challenges.

4.4. Attention System Description

The organization of Sect. 4.4. is led by the consecutive processing steps of the current ADAS attention sub-system as depicted in Fig. 17. After a short description of the general purpose of the BU and TD pathways, their combination to the overall saliency is described. Following this overview, the used modalities (feature types) are specified followed by the entropy measure that is used for the camera exposure control. Next, the different steps of the feature postprocessing are described. The TD feature weighting, the homeostasis process to get the conspicuity maps (i.e., modalities) comparable, as well as the final BU/TD saliency normalization are the final processing steps in the attention architecture.

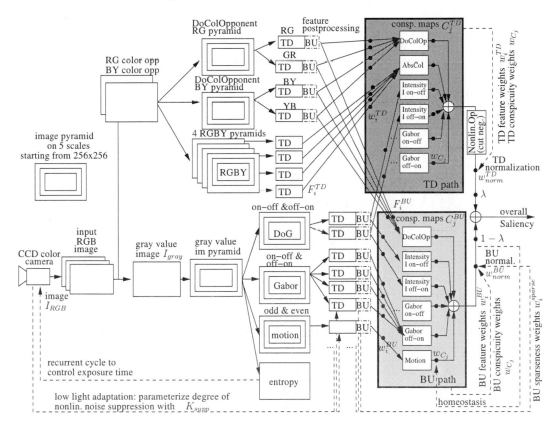

Figure 17. Visual attention sub-system (dashed lines correspond to TD links).

The attention system consists of a BU and a TD pathway. The TD pathway (red enclosed region in Fig. 17) allows an object- and task-dependent filtering of the input data. All image regions containing features that match the current system task well are supported (excitation), while the others are suppressed (inhibition) resulting in a sparse task-dependent scene representation. Opposed to that, the BU pathway (blue enclosed region in Fig. 17) supports an object- and task-unspecific filtering of input data supporting scene elements that differ from their surroundings. The BU pathway is important for a task-unspecific analysis of the scene supporting task-unrelated but salient scene elements.

The BU and TD saliency maps are linearly combined to an overall saliency map. This map is used to generate FoAs that represent the scene elements higher system layers work on. The combination is realized using parameter λ (on the right hand side in Fig. 17) that is set dependent on the system state emphasizing the BU and/or TD influence (see Equ. (43)). Due to this combination the system also detects scene elements that do not match the current TD system task. By ensuring a certain BU influence such scene elements are not suppressed, which would otherwise lead to the so-called inattentional blindness phenomenon (i.e., complete perceptual suppression of scene elements as described in [33]).

Turning to the processing details, the following modalities are calculated on the captured color images: RGBY colors (inspired by [1]), intensity by a Difference of Gaussian (DoG) kernel, oriented lines and edges by a Gabor kernel, motion by differential images (see Sect. 4.2. for details on the applied static feature maps) and entropy using the structure tensor.

In the following, a rough repeated description of the modalities is given, after which the entropy feature is specified that is used to set the camera exposure. The features motion and color are used differently for the BU and TD path. The BU path uses double color opponency from RGBY colors by applying a DoG on 5 scales on the RG and BY color opponent maps. The filter results are separated into their positive and negative parts (on-off/off-on separation, whose importance is emphasized in [1]) leading to 4 pyramids of double color opponent RG,GR,BY and YB-maps. The TD path uses the same color feature but additionally 4 pyramids of the absolute RGBY maps. Absolute RGBY colors do not support the BU pop-out character and are hence not used in the BU path. A DoG filter bank is applied on 5 scales separating on-off and off-on effects. Furthermore, a Gabor filter bank on 4 orientations (0, $\pi/4$, $\pi/2$, $3/4\pi$) and 5 scales is calculated separately for lines and edges (even and odd Gabor). The realized Gabor filter bank ensures disjoint decomposition of the input image. The detailed mathematical formulation of the used Gabor filter bank can be found in Sect. 4.2.2.. Motivated from DoG the concept of on-off/off-on separation is transferred to Gabor allowing e.g., the crisp separation of the sky edge or street markings from shadows on the street. Motion from differential images on 5 scales is used in the BU path alone. Since this simple motion concept cannot separate static objects from self-moving objects, it is not helpful in TD search. The entropy T is based on the absolute gradient strength of the structure tensor A on the image I_{gray}:

$$T \quad = \frac{det(A)}{trace(A)}. \tag{36}$$

The matrix A is calculated using derivatives of Gaussian filters G_u and G_v and a rectangular filter of size W:

$$A = \begin{bmatrix} \Sigma_W(G_u * I_{\text{gray}})^2 & \Sigma_W(G_u * I_{\text{gray}})(G_v * I_{\text{gray}}) \\ \Sigma_W(G_v * I_{\text{gray}})(G_u * I_{\text{gray}}) & \Sigma_W(G_v * I_{\text{gray}})^2 \end{bmatrix} \quad (37)$$

$$G_u(u,v) = -\frac{u}{2\pi\sigma^4}exp(-\frac{u^2+v^2}{2\sigma^2}),$$

$$G_v(u,v) = -\frac{v}{2\pi\sigma^4}exp(-\frac{u^2+v^2}{2\sigma^2}).$$

The entropy is used as a means to adapt the camera exposure and not as a feature.

The local exposure control works on the accumulated activation $T_{sum} = \Sigma_{RoI}T$ on an image region of interest (RoI) (e.g., coming from the appearance-based object tracker that is part of the ADAS, for details see Sect. 3.). Here inspiration came from the human local contrast normalization. The exposure time is recursively modified in search of a maximum on T_{sum}, which maximizes the contrast on the defined image regions. As described in Sect. 4.2., the system disposes of 136 independently weighable sub-feature maps.

Following the calculation of the raw features, a postprocessing step on all sub-feature maps is performed (see Fig. 18). The feature postprocessing consists of 5 steps. First,

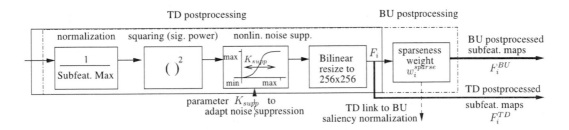

Figure 18. Postprocessing of feature maps in BU and TD path.

all sub-features are normalized to the maximal value that can be expected for the specific sub-feature map (not the current maximum on the map). For example, for DoG and Gabor this is done by determining the filter response for the ideal input pattern, i.e., the maximum possible filter response. The ideal input pattern is generated by setting all pixels to 1 whose matching pixel positions in the filter kernel are bigger than 0. Figure 19 shows the resulting ideal DoG and 0° even Gabor input patterns that are derived from the given filter kernels. This procedure ensures comparability between sub-features of one modality (e.g., all sub-feature maps of the motion modality).

Next, the signal power is calculated by squaring and a dynamic neuronal suppression using a sigmoid function, which is applied for noise suppression. A parameter K_{supp} shifts the sigmoid function horizontally, which influences the degree of noise suppression respectively the sparseness of the resulting sub-feature maps. After a bilinear resize to the resolution 256x256, which allows a the later feature combination, for the BU feature postprocessing a sparseness weight w_i^{sparse} is multiplied that ensures pop-out by boosting sub-feature

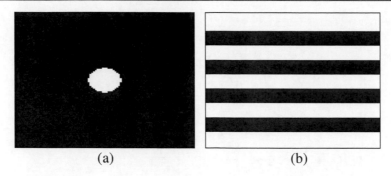

(a)   (b)

Figure 19. Input patterns that maximize the filter response. The maximum of this filter response is used for sub-feature normalization: (a) Ideal DoG input pattern, (b) Ideal 0° even Gabor input pattern.

maps with sparse activation:

$$w_i^{sparse} = \sqrt{\frac{2^s}{\sum\limits_{\forall u,v \; F_{i,k}(u,v) > \xi} F_{i,k}(u,v)}} \tag{38}$$

$$\text{for } s = [0,4] \text{ and } \xi = 0.9 \cdot Max(F_{i,k}).$$

The sparseness operator is not used in the TD path (see red enclosed region in Fig. 18) in order to prevent the suppression of weak object features.

Later in the TD path a weighting on all 136 sub-feature maps takes place to realize inhibition and excitation. The TD-related tuning on the feature level is motivated from the fact that neurobiological studies have shown that attentional influences are present very early in the human visual pathway (see [3]). Furthermore, neurophysical studies on monkeys have shown that attention-based modulation of neuronal activities lead to an increase in activity in case the bias matches the preferences of cell populations. But also a suppression of neuron populations can be encountered in case the attended features do not match the preferences of the cells (see [3]). These measurements motivate the usage of supporting (excitation) and suppressing (inhibition) feature TD weights as realized in the presented attention system.

As referenced earlier, the TD weights w_i^{TD} are calculated based on Equ. (2). The weight calculation scheme is inspired by [37] but was extended to match the scene complexity of the car domain. The average activation in the object region is related to the average activation in the surround on each feature map F_i^{TD} taken only the N_i pixels above the threshold $\phi = K_{conj} Max(F_i^{TD})$ with $K_{conj} = (0,1]$ into account. As opposed to the weighting scheme proposed by [37], in the here presented approach the threshold ϕ assures that numerous small values on a feature map do not even out rarely present big ones. The proposed threshold ϕ improves the TD search performance, since big values influence the TD search performance overproportionally. In the BU path only excitation ($w_i^{BU} \geq 0$) takes place, since without object or task knowledge in BU nothing can be inhibited. For a more detailed discussion of feature map weighting see [66, 1].

As visualized in Fig. 17, the $j = 1..M$ conspicuity maps C_j^{BU} and C_j^{TD} result from a weighted combination of N_j BU and TD sub-feature maps within a feature type j:

$$C_j^{BU} = \sum_{i=1}^{N_j} w_{i,j}^{BU} F_{i,j}^{BU} \tag{39}$$

$$C_j^{TD} = \sum_{i=1}^{N_j} w_{i,j}^{TD} F_{i,j}^{TD}. \tag{40}$$

The already introduced sub-feature normalization procedure ensures intra-feature compara-bility, but for the overall combination, comparability between modalities (i.e., conspicuity maps) is required as well. The normalization problem of the conspicuity maps is solved by dynamically adapting the conspicuity weights w_{C_j} for weighting the BU and TD con-spicuity maps C_j^{BU} and C_j^{TD}. This concept mimics the homeostasis process in biological systems (see e.g., [65]), which can be understood as the property of a biological system to regulate its internal processes in order to broaden the range of environmental conditions in which the system is able to survive. More specifically, the $\tilde{w}_{C_j}(t)$ are set to equalize the activation on all $j = 1..M$ BU conspicuity maps, taking only the N_j pixel over the threshold $\xi = 0.9 \cdot Max(C_j^{BU})$ into account:

$$\tilde{w}_{C_j}(t) \quad = \frac{1}{\frac{1}{N_j} \sum_{\forall u,v \text{ with } C_j^{BU}(u,v) > \xi} C_j^{BU}(u,v)} \tag{41}$$

$$\text{with} \quad \xi - 0.9 \cdot Max(C_j^{BU}).$$

Exponential smoothing is used to fuse old conspicuity weights $w_{C_j}(t-1)$ with the new optimized ones $\tilde{w}_{C_j}(t)$:

$$w_{C_j}(t) \quad = \alpha \tilde{w}_{C_j}(t) + (1-\alpha) w_{C_j}(t-1) \quad \text{for} \quad j = 1..M. \tag{42}$$

The parameter α sets the velocity of the adaptation and could be adapted online depen-dent on the gist (i.e., basic environmental situation) via a TD link. In case of fast changes in the environment, α could be set high for a brief interval, e.g., while passing a tunnel or low in case the car stops. Additionally, thresholds for all M conspicuity maps are used based on a sigma interval of recorded scene statistics to avoid complete adaptation to extreme environmental situations.

$$S^{total} = \lambda S^{TD} + (1-\lambda) S^{BU} \tag{43}$$

Before combining the BU and TD saliency maps using the parameter λ (see Equ. (43) and Fig. 17) a final normalization step takes place. Like the sub-feature and conspicuity maps, the saliency maps are normalized to the maximum expected value. This maximum value is determined by stepping backwards through the attention sub-system taking into account all weights (w_i^{sparse}, w_i^{BU}, w_i^{TD}) and the internal disjointness/conjointness of the features to determine the highest value ($v_{max,j}^{BU}$ and $v_{max,j}^{TD}$) a single pixel can achieve in each BU and TD conspicuity map j. A feature is defined as internally disjoint (conjoint), when the input image is decomposed without (with) redundancy in the sub-feature space. In other words the recombination of disjoint (conjoint) sub-feature maps of adjacent scales or orientations is equal to (bigger than) the decomposed input image. Since DoG and Gabor are designed to be internally disjoint between scales and orientations (see Sect. 4.2.) the maximum pixel value on a conspicuity map j is equal to the maximum of the product of all sub-feature and/or sparseness weights of the sub-features it is composed of (w_i^{sparse} and w_i^{BU} for BU as well as w_i^{TD} for TD). Motion is conjoint between scales, therefore the product of all sub-feature motion weights w_i^{BU} and their corresponding w_i^{sparse} are summed up to get the maximally expected value on the motion conspicuity map. The contribution of the color feature to the saliency normalization weight is similar but more complex.

Since appart from DoG and Gabor there is disjointness between conspicuity maps the maximum possible pixel values for all BU and TD conspicuity maps, calculated as described above, are multiplied with the corresponding w_{C_j} and added to achieve the normalization weights w_{norm}^{TD} and w_{norm}^{BU} for the TD and BU attention (please also refer to Fig. 17 for the position the normalization weights are applied):

$$w_{norm}^{BU} = \frac{1}{\sum_{j=1}^{M} k_j w_{C_j} v_{max,j}^{BU}} \tag{44}$$

$$w_{norm}^{TD} = \frac{1}{\sum_{j=1}^{M} k_j w_{C_j} v_{max,j}^{TD}}. \tag{45}$$

With:
$$k_j = \begin{cases} 0.5 & \text{for} \quad j \in \{DoG, Gabor\} \\ 1 & \text{for} \quad j \notin \{DoG, Gabor\}. \end{cases}$$

Using this approach, w_{norm}^{TD} will adapt when the TD weight set changes.

It is important to note that DoG and Gabor features are conjoint, meaning that they represent the same signal characteristics. Put differently the conspicuity maps for DoG and Gabor are not independent. As discussed in Sect. 4.2. using both DoG and Gabor is still helpful, since the signal decomposition is different for both filter types. The conjointness is taken into account in the attention normalization procedure in Equ. (44) and (45) in the form of the factor k_j that decreases the integral influence of DoG and Gabor on the overall attention.

4.5. Functional Comparison to Other Top-Down Attention Models

Taken the abundance of computational attention models (see [44] for a review), the two related approaches of [32] and [1] were selected for a detailed structural comparison, since these impacted the presented work most. Then, it is summarized what makes the introduced approach particularly appropriate for the real-world car domain.

The system of **Navalpakkam and Itti** [32] is based on the BU attention model Neuromorphic Vision Toolkit (NVT) [36] but adds TD to the system. Each feature map is normalized to its current maximum, resulting in a loss of information about the absolute level of activity and a boosting of noise in case the activation is low. Taken such a normalization procedure and the object dependence of the TD weights, the BU and TD saliency maps are not comparable, since the relative influence of the TD map varies when the TD weight set is changed. Additionally, the BU and TD saliency maps are not weighted separately for combination. As features a speed-optimized RGBY (leading to an inferior separability performance), a DoG intensity feature and Gabor filter on 4 orientations (both without on-off/off-on or line/edge separation) are used on 6 scales starting at a resolution of 640x480. The system uses TD weights on all sub-feature maps resulting in 42 weights that allow reasonable selectivity. A DoG-based normalization operator (see [36]) is applied for pop-out support and to diminish the noise resulting from the used feature normalization. However, the absolute map activation and therefore comparability is lost.

The system of **Frintrop** [1] integrates BU and TD attention and is real-time capable (see [67]). It was evaluated mainly on indoor scenes. The system normalizes the features to their current maximum, resulting in the same problems as described above. The BU and TD saliency maps are weighted separately for combination. Following the argumentation above the used normalization makes the combination weight (corresponding to *lambda* in the here presented attention system) dependent on the used TD weight set and thereby object-dependent. As features, the system uses double color opponency based on an efficient RGBY color space implementation, a DoG intensity feature (with on-off/off-on separation), and a Gabor with 4 orientations starting from 300x300 resolution. A total of 13 TD weights are used on feature (integrated over all scales) and conspicuity maps. For pop-out support a uniqueness operator is used.

Most important differences comparing the systems: In the presented system high selectivity is obtained by decomposing the DoG (on-off/off-on separation) and Gabor (on-off/off-on separation, lines and edges) features without increasing the calculation time. Furthermore, the usage of TD weights on all sub-feature maps and scales results in 136 independent tunable feature weights that increase the selectivity. The resulting scale variance of the TD weights is not a crucial issue in the car domain. The RGBY is used as color and double color opponency. In contrast to [32, 1], in the here presented system motion is used to support scene dynamics. All sub-feature maps and the BU respectively TD saliency maps are normalized without loosing information or boosting noise and by that preventing false-positive detections. Comparability of modalities is assured via homeostasis. The attention sub-system works on 5 scales starting at a resolution of 256x256. Experiments have shown that in the car domain bigger image sizes do not improve the attention system performance.

The presented system supports conjunction of weak features since the sparseness operator is not used in the TD path. Illumination invariance is reached by image-region-specific exposure control that is coupled tightly to the system.

4.6.   Application notes: Attention-based Recognition of Traffic Signs

Currently available traffic sign recognition systems typically focus on circular signs in restricted application areas, like e.g. highways. Additionally, said traffic sign applications are only used as comfort functions, e.g. to warn the driver about the current speed limit. However, taking the next step towards crash prevention in a complex system a number of traffic signs classes has to be recognized simultaneously. From our point of view, this has to be done by a single integrated approach, instead of an individual approach for each traffic sign class. Otherwise, the amount of required processing power is not available in the medium term. In addition, the system should be able to cover scenes of high complexity in order to cope with inner-city scenarios.

(a)   (b)

(c)   (d)

Figure 20. Examples for traffic sign conditions and scene complexities: (a) blurred due to camera movement, (b) various textures in the surrounding, (c) similar colors in the backround, (d) partly covered by other objects.

The first approaches for traffic sign detection date back to the 1980s (see [68] for an overview of the early approaches). The large magnitude of publications covering that topic can be explained by the high degree of variations of traffic signs between different countries. This work focuses on German traffic signs, however the generic nature of the attention system would allow an international application of the system. Recently, also the first commercial systems for the recognition of speed signs are available. Nevertheless, they are restricted to circular speed signs and also targeted at highways/country roads as application area. Many of the publications focus on the recognition of a single or a small number of classes of traffic signs. Still, some authors aim at recognizing all or numerous sign classes, like [69, 70, 71]. The work of Fang et. al. [69] uses two neural nets to recognize all speed sign categories, one for color and one for edges. However, the neural nets are only trained with signs of a single size and therefore, can only recognize one size for each traffic sign. Therefore, the approach [69] is not optimal in the sense that the recognition of signs must be possible for all sizes and hence distances to a traffic sign.

The general procedure for the majority of algorithms is similar and can be divided in two parts. First, the algorithms try to extract all regions with possible traffic sign candidates

(Region of Interest (RoI)), termed as detection phase. Second, the previous detected regions are classified or recognized, filtering out the false positive detections, referred to as classification phase. Additionally, a recognized sign can be temporally integrated to increase the recognition performance even further. But this can be done with every recognition approach and therefore, is not treated here. Because of limitations in space only the central aspects of the different approaches are raised.

4.6.1.   Related Work - Detection Phase

The detection phase can be divided in two types of approaches: on the one hand color based algorithms and on the other hand shape based approaches. Starting with the former, the image is segmented by typical traffic sign colors, which can be done by color relations in the RGB color space [72, 73, 74, 75] and also sub-spaces of RGB as shown by [76] can be used. Even more prominent is a thresholding in the HSV color space as used by [77, 78, 79, 80, 81] in order to get more independent to lighting conditions. Also some exotic color spaces as the CIECAM97 are used [82]. Besides the simple thresholding a number of more complex region growing approaches can be found, as e.g., the Color Structure Code (CSC) based on a hierarchical region growing with a hexagonal topology as used by [83]. Also possible is a segmentation by fuzzy sets as introduced by [84].

The second type, the shape-based approaches use, e.g., a Sobel operator [70], a Canny edge detector [85], or similar approches running on a grayscale image. Afterwards, the resulting edge image is analyzed and decomposed to find regions of interest, with candidates of road signs. To this end, [70] propose a new method for the detection phase by searching for vertical symmetry axes, which should enable the detection of all types of traffic signs. Nevertheless, their example images show only highway scenes with a rather low scene complexity, leaving in doubt if the approach will also show good performance on inner-city scenarios with a lot of structure.

However, a large part of publications proposes a combination of the former two, starting with a color segmentation and afterwards some kind of shape extraction. The work of Paclik et al. [79] proposes a shape-based template matching after the color segmentation in the HSV-colorspace. Garcia et al. [86] use a Prewitt-operator to extract edges of the red color plane. Afterwards a maximum search for each of the image axes is done to find RoIs. Another approach by Oh et al. [87] starts by deriving color segments followed by the computation of a number of symmetry properties to get candidate regions for traffic signs. Zhu et. al. [71] introduce the concept of the Color-Shape Pair (CSP), were a certain color segmentation is followed by a specific shape extraction depending on the type of traffic sign. To this end, the approach should be able to detect all types of traffic signs. Nevertheless, it is not stated how the color segmentation or shape extraction is done. Additionally, the evaluation is only done with emulated images and also no meaningful evaluation data (e.g., false positive and false negative rates) is provided.The work of Tsai et. al. [88] apply a RBF-network for the color segmentation and afterwards some kind of edge filtering is applied.

Most approaches are marked by the fact that their detection stage is targeted at mainly one type of traffic sign class and can not easily be extended to additional traffic sign classes.

4.6.2. Related Work - Classification Phase

After the initial detection phase, several regions of interest are available. These RoIs contain traffic signs, but also regions with only similar appearance (false positive detections). Therefore, the task of the classification phase is the verification of the RoIs and thereby the identification of true positive traffic signs.

Most of the publications apply well-known approaches for classification with also common assets and drawbacks. One of these is template matching ([72, 77, 87, 89]), were a normalized cross correlation of a traffic sign template from the database with the RoI patch is applied. Additionally, the RoI patch should be previously normalized to get the same size for RoI and template. Nevertheless, the result of a normalized cross correlation is strongly dependent on the similarity of the template and the RoI patch, making the approach vulnerable to normally imperfect traffic sign patches. Another method is the Hough-transformation ([85, 90]) applicable to all kind of geometric shapes as, e.g., lines, circles and so on. The method can also handle partial occlusions, but is restricted to a single type of shape at a time. Also commonly used for classification are neural networks ([69, 73, 75, 80, 81, 88]). Neural networks can cope with large variances, however the input data has to be rescaled to a certain common size, which results in difficulties in case of traffic signs with varying diameters. Also for every sign class a different network has to be trained. Furthermore, a Support Vector Machine can be used for the classification as done by [71], which is similar to a neural network. Other approaches develop special classification methods, as e.g., the comparison of a vector (containing specific extracted features) with a template from the database as [82]. Some approaches not even apply an additional classification stage, but use a combination of color and shape as described in the detection stage (e.g. [86, 84]) for the recognition of traffic signs. Nevertheless, to our knowledge there is no generic approach for the detection and classification of traffic signs, being able to handle complex inner-city scenes and also varying diameters of traffic signs.

In the following, a rough overview of our approach for traffic sign recognition is given (see Fig. 22). Thereafter, all processing steps and their theoretical background are described in more detail.

The overall system can be divided into two main parts. The first one is the biologically motivated attention system (see Sect. 4.) acting as detection stage. The attention system searches for traffic sign classes based on a number of templates (3-4 templates are sufficient) for each class. The templates are used to derive an object-specific weight set that is computed online. Afterwards, each detected region is post-processed by an array of weak features acting as classification stage. The result is a probability value for each RoI and traffic sign class. Since, the attention system was already explained in full detail, the following section will only highlight the most important steps.

4.6.3. Detection Stage - Attention System

As general detection stage the 400x300 RGB input image (recorded by our test vehicle, see [66]) is analyzed by calculating the attention map S^{total} (see Equ. (43)).

The top-down (TD) attention can be tuned task-dependently to search for specific traffic sign classes by calculating a TD weight set w_i^{TD} based on Equation (2), where $\phi = K_{conj}Max(F_i)$ with $K_{conj} = (0, 1]$.

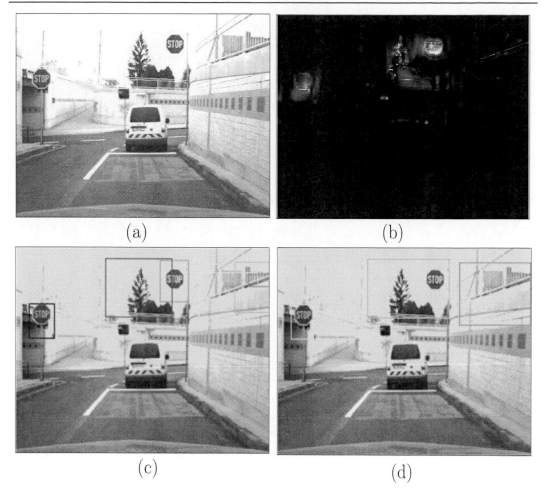

Figure 21. Detection stage: (a) Input image of attention system, (b) Attention map for the TD search, (c) RoIs for all sign classes, (d) Fused RoIs for classification stage.

The bottom-up (BU) weights w_i^{BU} are set object-unspecifically in order to detect in the general case unexpected potentially dangerous scene elements. The parameter $\lambda \in [0, 1]$ (see Equation (43)) determines the relative importance of TD and BU search and is set to one for the current task of traffic sign detection. Therefore, only the mechanism of top-down attention is used for the detection of regions with traffic signs. For more details regarding the used attention system, see Section 4..

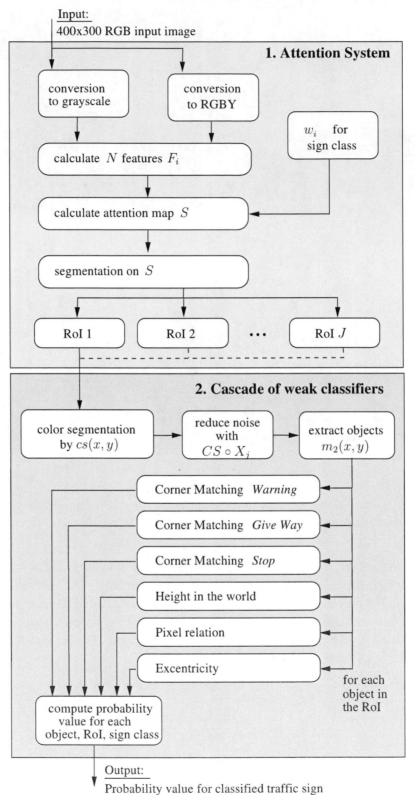

Figure 22. System structure for traffic sign recognition.

Each of the traffic sign classes (Stop-, Give Way-, Warning-, Prohibitive-signs, etc.) can be actively searched by using the TD attention. After the computation of the TD attention map, we detect the maximum on it and get the focus of attention (FoA). In the following, the segmented FoA is treated as region of interest (RoI) for the classification stage. Nevertheless, the different sign classes have different numbers of occurrences per image and also a visually diverse clearness. To this end, a different number of RoIs have to be extracted for a class on each image, varying from three for *Stop*-signs up to 5 for *Give Way*-signs (three for circular-, five for triangular warning signs). The size of the RoIs can vary from 15x15 pixels to 80x80 pixels, which corresponds to the minimum and maximum size of a traffic sign. The fusion of the resulting RoIs for different sign classes is realized by an overlap criterion of 30% on the smaller RoI, providing a reduced computation time by computing each image region only once. For further details on the online implementation of the attention system please refer to [24].

4.6.4. Classification Stage - Cascade of Weak Classifiers

The second part of the algorithm handles the extraction of relevant information from each of the RoIs. Each RoI is handled independently, while the procedure for all of the RoIs is the same. For the sake of simplicity, we switch sometimes between the matrix notation (e.g., A) and the function notation (respectively $a(x,y)$), nevertheless the content of both is the same.

The result for each of the weak classifiers is a probability value, providing the correspondence of an object within a RoI to a certain sign class (the extraction of objects from a RoI is discussed later). At the end, all results for one object and class are multiplied, providing the final result for a certain traffic sign.

Since our detection stage uses a combination of color and shape features, it appeared sufficient to apply a simple color thresholding (see Equation (46)) to extract relevant structures, similar to other approaches as described in 4.6.1.. To become more independent from ligthing conditions we use the RGBY color space (see Sect. 4.2.3.). In this respect, to our knowledge the usage of the RGBY colorspace for the classification of traffic signs is novel. The intervals of the color thresholds were extracted from the set of training images and therefore, show the variation within the data set. See Figure 24b for the result of the color segmentation.

$$cs(x,y) = 1 \begin{cases} 0.035 \leq roi_r(x,y) \leq 0.481 \\ G_{min} \leq roi_g(x,y) \leq G_{max} \\ B_{min} \leq roi_b(x,y) \leq B_{max} \\ Y_{min} \leq roi_y(x,y) \leq Y_{max} \end{cases}$$

$$cs(x,y) = 0 \text{ otherwise} \tag{46}$$

After the color segmentation, a morphological (see [64]) opening operation $CS \circ X_j$ with a number of structuring elements j is applied. The structuring elements are chosen to support the geometrical shapes of the traffic signs, while removing noise (see Fig. 24c for the result and Fig. 23 for the structuring elements). The resulting image patch NR after the noise reduction is given in Equation (47).

$$\begin{bmatrix} 1 & 1 & 1 & 1 & 1 \end{bmatrix} \quad \begin{bmatrix} 0 & 0 & 1 \\ 0 & 1 & 0 \\ 1 & 0 & 0 \end{bmatrix} \quad \begin{bmatrix} 1 \\ 1 \\ 1 \\ 1 \\ 1 \end{bmatrix} \quad \begin{bmatrix} 1 & 0 & 0 \\ 0 & 1 & 0 \\ 0 & 0 & 1 \end{bmatrix}$$

Figure 23. The X_j structure elements.

$$NR = \sum_{j=1}^{4} CS \circ X_j \tag{47}$$

Finally, a mask is generated by evaluation of the local neighbourhood (see [64]) for each pixel. To this end, k_i operators (given by Equation (48) to (53)) are applied in two stages on the result of the noise reduction stage NR. The computation of the first stage (with result $m_1(x,y)$) is started at the upper left and continued to the right in a row-wise manner. While, the computation of the second part (with overall result $m_2(x,y)$) is started at the upper right part and continued to the left, also in a row-wise manner. The resulting mask is depicted in Fig. 24d.

$$m_1(x,y) = \begin{cases} 1 : k_1(x,y) = 1 \vee k_2(x,y) = 1 \vee \\ \quad nr(x,y) = 1 \\ 0 : otherwise \end{cases} \tag{48}$$

$$\begin{aligned} k_1(x,y) = 0.25 \cdot [&nr(x-1,y-1) + nr(x-1,y) + \\ &nr(x-1,y+1) + nr(x,y-1)] \cdot (1 - nr(x,y)) \end{aligned} \tag{49}$$

$$\begin{aligned} k_2(x,y) = 0.25 \cdot [&nr(x-1,y-1) + nr(x-1,y) + \\ &nr(x+1,y) + nr(x,y-1)] \cdot (1 - nr(x,y)) \end{aligned} \tag{50}$$

$$m_2(x,y) = \begin{cases} 1 : k_3(x,y) = 1 \vee k_4(x,y) = 1 \vee \\ \quad m_1(x,y) = 1 \\ 0 : otherwise \end{cases} \tag{51}$$

$$\begin{aligned} k_3(x,y) = 0.25 \cdot [&m_1(x-1,y-1) + m_1(x-1,y) + \\ &m_1(x-1,y+1) + m_1(x,y-1)] \cdot (1 - m_1(x,y)) \end{aligned} \tag{52}$$

$$\begin{aligned} k_4(x,y) = 0.25 \cdot [&m_1(x-1,y-1) + m_1(x-1,y) + \\ &m_1(x+1,y) + m_1(x,y-1)] \cdot (1 - m_1(x,y)) \end{aligned} \tag{53}$$

The procedure described so far is generic, and therefore work with all kinds of sign shapes (octagonal, rectangular, triangular, circular).

In the following, the weak classifiers (also called features) will be described. Due to space limitations, the contribution focuses on the pixel relation feature in order to describe the overall concept, whereas similar processing steps for the other features will be left out.

To extract all relevant objects from the RoI, the Neumann neighborhood is applied on M_2 defining all independent objects. The order of the objects is defined by the results of

Figure 24. Classification stage: (a) Input RoI of classification system, (b) Result of the color segmentation, (c) After opening operation, (d) Masks for each object within the RoI.

the corner matching feature. Hence, starting with the object having the highest result of the corner matching, followed by the second highest and so on. Therefore, the mask of each object is multiplied with the initial RoI providing only the relevant pixels.

The pixel relation is defined by the ratio of red to white pixels. Therefore, the amount of pixels for each of the classes has to be determined. This has already been done for the class of red pixels with the initial color segmentation. An additional color segmentation (similar to the initial one) for white pixels is applied to extract all white pixels of the RoI. Afterwards, the mask $m_2(x, y)$ separates the independent objects, facilitating the counting of red and white pixels to allow the use for the computation of the pixel relation. As ground truth data the red and white area sizes of the signs have been estimated from the specifications of German road traffic regulations (see Equation (54) for *Give Way* and Equation (55) for *Stop*).

$$\left.\frac{p_{red}}{p_{white}}\right|_{GW,ideal} = \frac{A_{red}}{A_{white}} = 0,98. \tag{54}$$

$$\frac{p_{red}}{p_{white}}\bigg|_{\text{STOP,ideal}} = 5,04. \tag{55}$$

Due to a number of noise sources (e.g., slant, blurred, light conditions) the pixel relation is marked by a certain variation. To this end, the pixel relation is transformed to a kind of fuzzy set (see Figure 25 for *Give Way* signs) providing the membership function of the pixel relation to a certain traffic sign class. The membership function was acquired from the image test set and provides in our case the probability value P_{pix} for a certain sign class.

$x_{p_{red}/p_{white}}$ yP_{pix}^{GW} 11 0,9 0,80.8 0,10.1 0 0.2 0.40.4 0.6 0.80.8 1 1.21.2 1.4 1.61.6 1.8 22 2.2 2.42.4 2.6

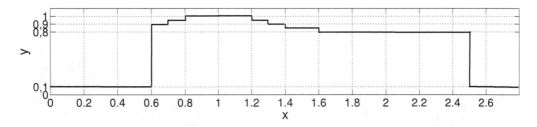

Figure 25. Fuzzy membership function of the pixel relation for the *Give Way* sign class.

The next feature is the corner matching, which is similar for all sign classes, but differs in the number and type of corner templates that are used (see Fig. 26 for used corners of different sign classes).

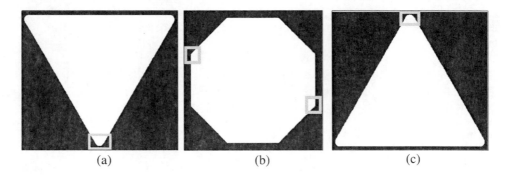

Figure 26. Used corners for matching: (a) *Give Way*, (b) *Stop*, (c) *Warning*.

Therefore, it will be sufficient to elaborate on the application of the corner matching on *Give Way* signs only. The corner matching is a template matching (see [64]) with an ideal template of certain characteristic corners for a traffic sign class. As an example, the template of the lower corner from a *Give Way* sign is given in Fig. 27. Every template W_l will be cross-correlated with each mask $m_2(s,t)$ from an RoI by use of Equation (56) (N and O define the size of $m_2(s,t)$).

$$cr_l(x,y) = \sum_s \sum_t m_2(s,t)w_l(x+s,y+t)$$

$$\text{for } x = 0,1,2,...,N-1,$$
$$y = 0,1,2,...,O-1$$

(56)

The result $cr_l(x,y)$ contains the cross correlation values for a complete RoI and therefore, the highest result determines the position of the object. Additionally, for each object the highest correlation result is transformed by a fuzzy set (each corner w_l has its own fuzzy set) to a probability value (similar to the pixel relation). Based on that, each detected object is marked by a certain probability P_{w_l} that the characteristic corner w_l is present. If there is more than one corner for a certain sign class (e.g. *Stop* sign), not only the single probabilities P_{w_l} will be computed but also a combined probability P_{rs}, which evaluates the spatial relation of the single corners to each other. This is also transformed by a fuzzy set, which takes into account that specific corner have to be positioned at specific locations in the image than the other one.

2	1	1	1	1	1	2
-1	4	2	2	2	4	-1
-2	-1	4	4	4	-1	-2
-4	-2	-1	6	-1	-2	-4
-6	-4	-2	-1	-2	-4	-6

Figure 27. Template W_1 for *Give Way* sign.

The next feature is the eccentricity, which defines the relation between length to width of an object. In order to compute the eccentricity, the mask of each object is used to determine the smallest and biggest row and column belonging to the object. Given this information the eccentricity of an object can be easily computed. Afterwards, the eccentricity will also be transformed by a fuzzy set to a probability P_{exc}, describing the presence of a certain traffic sign corresponding to the chosen fuzzy set. The ground truth for most of the traffic signs concerning the eccentricity is about one, nevertheless we use independent fuzzy sets for the different sign classes since their noise sensitivity differs.

The final weak classifier is the height in the world. Due to the stereo camera system in our test vehicle we are able to estimate the world position of all pixels. For further details about the camera and matrix transformations please refer to Sect. 6.. Hence, for each object the median of height values of all object pixels is computed and again transformed by a fuzzy set to a probability value P_{height}.

Finally, the overall probability for each of the traffic sign classes has to be evaluated. Based on that, the Equation (57), (58), and (59) provide the overall probability for the supported traffic sign classes *Stop*, *Give Way* and *Warning*.

$$P_{GW} = P_{w_1} \cdot (1 - P_{w_4}) \cdot P_{pix}^{GW} \cdot P_{exc}^{GW} \cdot P_{height}$$

(57)

$$P_{STOP} = P_{w_2} \cdot P_{w_3} \cdot P_{pix}^{STOP} \cdot P_{exc}^{STOP} \cdot P_{height} \cdot P_{rs}^{STOP}$$

(58)

$$P_{WARN} = P_{w_4} \cdot (1 - P_{w_1}) \cdot P_{pix}^{WARN} \cdot P_{exc}^{WARN} \cdot P_{height}$$

(59)

The attention system as a whole as well as the described traffic sign recognition is evaluated in Sect. 8.1.1..

5. Scene Classification

Currently available Driver Assistance Systems (DAS) focus on restricted application areas, like, e.g., highways. Information about the current scene context is not included. Said applications make a number of assumptions based on the designated context, which results in a predefined set of rules and parameters. Normally, these simplifications restrict the usability of these systems to one application area only. Different from that, the here presented ADAS is able to tune its modules dependent on the current context and environment, thereby allowing its robust application on highways, country road, and inner-city. Therefore, knowledge about the scene type is valuable as a tuning channel of the Attentive Co-Pilot, allowing more dedicated and also diverse reactions in different surroundings.

In the following section, the fast and robust approach for the classification of the scene is presented. The algorithm is independent of potentially outdated map data as well as errors and inaccuracies of Global Positioning System data. Furthermore, it is independent of precoded context information in the map data, because it requires only an image of the scene. Based on the novel Hierarchical Principal Component Classification (HPCC), the algorithm reliably classifies the scene (over 97%) in various, complex scenarios (evaluated on 9000 images). As the evaluation in Sect. 8.1.2. will show, the presented approach is an important step towards a holistic understanding of the driving situation, as well as the basis for a wider operational range of the ADAS.

5.1. Related Work

The concept of visual scene classification has gained increasing interest in recent years. Numerous publications handle this topic in a general fashion, but only a few cover the driver assistance domain. The typical procedure of existing algorithms is as follows: A number of features from the image is extracted, which will either be processed at once or gradually depending on previous results. Afterwards, a classification is done. A possible classification approach compares extracted features with mean values derived during a training phase. Publications of visual scene classification, mostly use a number of selected categories, like, e.g., indoor/outdoor, landscape/city, and coast/landscape/forest/mountains. Typical low level features for the classification are color histograms (see [91, 92, 93]), texture orientation (see [93, 94, 95]) or a combination of these features.
Another approach is the usage of special features on the intermediate level, like grayscales, color spots, and SIFT descriptors as done by [96], using probabilistic Latent Semantic Analysis (pLSA) for the classification. A further intermediate level approach was proposed by [97], which segmented the image by its RGB, HSV and texture values, by assigning each pixel to one of six categories like, e.g., water, sand, sky. Afterwards, pixels of the same category are connected to regions, segmenting the overall picture. The regions and their spatial relation to each other are used for the classification. Oliva and Torralba (see [98, 99]) have shown a more promising approach for the classification of the scene based on the usage of the frequency domain. They introduced so called Discriminant Spectral Templates (DST),

Figure 28. Examples for the different scene categories and illumination conditions: (a) Highway, (b) Country road, (c) Inner city, (d) Country road.

which are generated from a large number of sample images. Therefore, the spectrum of an image is sampled by a number of frequency-selective filters and assigned to each of the classes (like, e.g., artificial/natural, open/closed, expanded/enclosed, see [100]) with a value between 0 and 1 corresponding to their respective membership. Hence, each class has a continuous scale describing the membership of the image to the class. The sampled frequency results for each of the features allows the generation of templates, which describe all relevant frequencies with their corresponding intensity for a certain class. However, the proposed method by Oliva and Torralba is on the one hand continuous regarding the obtained classification results, which makes a crisp decision for a certain class difficult. On the other hand the approach is not discriminative enough in case of similar categories as present in the car domain.

Only few publications handle scene classification applicable for driver assistance systems. One of these is the work of [101], which uses features of the HSV-color space to identify the number of image pixels having the color of, e.g., bricks or grass. These features are evaluated by a set of fuzzy rules to classify the scene.

Nevertheless, most of the categories (in the general case) differ quite strongly regarding their visual features (e.g., landscape/city), in contrast to typical scenes in the traffic domain. A typical scene for an ADAS will always contain street in front of the car. The upper middle part often shows sky. Objects can always occlude the view on the scene and there are no unique objects for different categories, which would simplify the task. Additionally, the classification has to deal with changes in lighting conditions and also great variety within a scene category, e.g. a country road through a forest compared to a country road surrounded by grassland (see Fig. 28 for some exemplary categories).

5.2.   System Description - Scene Classification

In the following, a rough overview of our approach for scene classification is given (see Fig. 29). Thereafter, all processing steps and their theoretical background are described in more detail.

The overall system can be divided in three main parts. The first one is the preprocessing, where adaptations of the image take place to reduce the amount of data, as well as to reduce the influence of changes in lighting conditions (see [98]). In the last step of the preprocessing, the image is divided in 16 equally sized square sub-parts, which will be processed independently in the following feature extraction part. In the second part a feature extraction is done for obtaining the relevant information of the image. As already mentioned, our system uses the frequency domain to get a compact representation of the data. To this end, for each of the 16 sub-parts the Discret Fourier Transform (DFT) is used to compute a spectrum. Afterwards, each spectrum is sampled (i.e., weighted) with a number of Gaussian filters, which is inspired by [102], that used oriented Gabor filters for the sampling of the spectrum. The sampled data is normalized with the computed mean and variance values from the training phase, to provide comparability between the different scales of the sub-parts. To further reduce the amount of data, while keeping the relevant information, the principal component analysis (PCA) is applied. Finally, in the third part the classification takes place, which is independent of the previous steps, due to the fact that different methods could be chosen. Therefore, two versions of the newly developed HPCC classifier have been evaluated.

5.2.1.   Preprocessing

The input of the system is a 400x300 RGB image, which in the first step will be converted to a grayscale image. Afterwards, the influence of changes in lighting conditions is reduced. To this end, the image is rescaled using a logarithmic curve to change the distribution of the intensity values. This is motivated by early processes in the human vision pathway. The intensity values are rescaled to cover the complete dynamic range (see Fig. 30b). The next step is a high-pass filtering to reduce low spatial frequencies, attenuating large differences in contrast as well as side effects of the DFT. For that reason, the image is filtered with a filter whose frequency response is given in Equation (60) (see [103]).

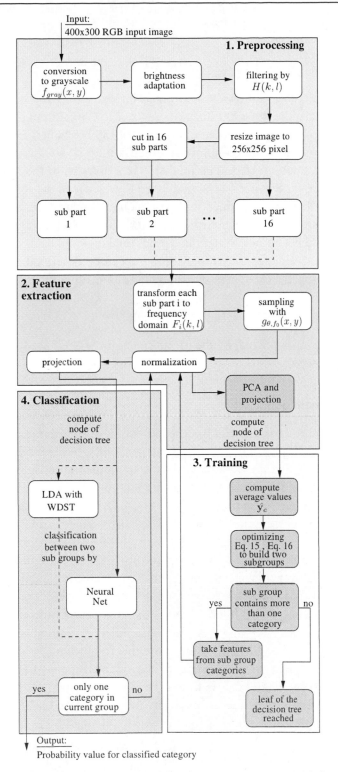

Figure 29. System structure for scene classification (gray system modules are only used in the training phase)

$$H(k,l) = \begin{cases} 1 & \text{for } k = 0 \cap l = 0 \\ 1 - \left(1 - 0.9e^{-\frac{k^2+l^2}{156.25}}\right) & \text{otherwise} \end{cases} \tag{60}$$

The filtering leads to a uniformly distributed intensity over the complete image (see Fig. 30c). Afterwards, the 400x300 image is resized to 256x256 pixel, which leads to a compression of the vertical axis and an elongation of the horizontal axis in the frequency domain. Since the resize is carried out during the training as well as execution phase the classification result is not effected. The final step is a division of the image in 16 equally sized square sub-parts of the size 64x64 pixel (see Fig. 30d). In the following, each of the sub-parts is independently transformed to the frequency domain. The division in sub-parts is done in order to draw conclusions from characteristic amplitude values at certain image regions, which would not be possible if the overall image would be directly transformed to the frequency domain. Hence, each of the sub-parts can be described as a complex spatial frequency function separated in magnitude and phase (see Equation (61)).

$$F_i(k,l) = |F_i(k,l)|e^{\phi(k,l)} \tag{61}$$

In the following, only the magnitude of the spectrum will be used and the phase information will be neglected.

5.2.2. Feature Extraction

The second part of the algorithm handles the extraction of relevant information from each of the 16 spectra. Each spectrum is handled independently, while the procedure for all the spectra is the same. When aiming at a real-time implementation a spectrum with 64x64 values is a description of the image with a too high dimensionality and therefore unsuitable for a direct classification. Additionally, the knowledge of single magnitude values at a certain frequency and phase is not of interest, because changes of object positions in the image will also cause small changes at the energy level of the spectrum. Therefore, the energy distribution of certain areas of the spectrum will be evaluated, instead of single magnitude values. Another point is the general applicability of the approach, if single magnitude values at a certain position and phase would be used, a possible overfit to the training data might occur, which interferes with the goal of reaching a good generalization of the classification. Therefore, the spectrum is sampled by a number of Gaussian filters, which are scaled, rotated and shifted to get different resolutions for different frequencies and can be interpreted as a weighted mean of the sampled areas. Each of the 16 spectra is filtered with an array of 100 Gauss filters (see Fig. 31b), which have been adapted to the spectrum providing a high resolution at low frequencies and a low resolution at high frequencies. The applied filter kernel (see Fig. 31a) is defined by Equation (62)(see [104] for details).

$$g_{\theta,f_0}(x,y) = Ae^{-(a(x-x_0)^2 + 2b(x-x_0)(y-y_0) + c(y-y_0)^2)} \tag{62}$$

For the rotation of the filter kernel by the angle θ the following parameters a, b and c have to be adapted (see Equation (63), (64), and (65)).

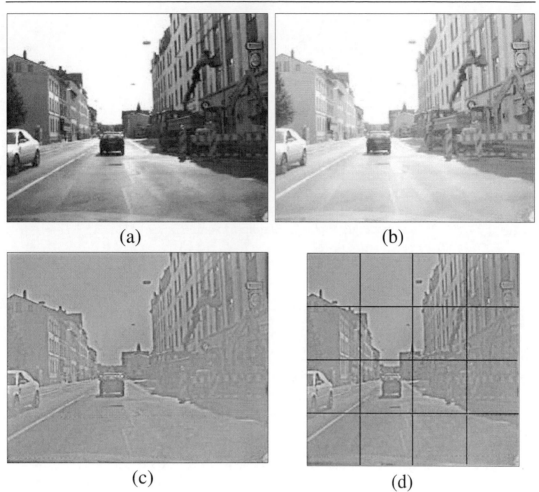

(a)   (b)

(c)   (d)

Figure 30. Different steps of the preprocessing stage: (a) Grayscale Image, (b) Image after adaptation of intensity, (c) Image after suppression of low frequencies, (d) Rescaled image with sub-parts

$$a = \frac{\cos^2 \theta}{2\sigma_x^2} + \frac{\sin^2 \theta}{2\sigma_y^2} \tag{63}$$

$$b = -\frac{\sin 2\theta}{4\sigma_x^2} + \frac{\sin 2\theta}{4\sigma_y^2} \tag{64}$$

$$c = \frac{\sin^2 \theta}{2\sigma_x^2} + \frac{\cos^2 \theta}{2\sigma_y^2} \tag{65}$$

Finally, the width and height of a filter kernel can be adapted by σ_x and σ_y and where chosen in a way that the -3dB border frequencies of the filters touch each other. The shifting of the filter kernel's center is carried out by the adaptation of x_0 and y_0, defined by the spatial frequency f_0, as well as the angle θ (see Equation (66) and (67)).

$$x_0 = f_0 \frac{N}{2} \cos \theta \tag{66}$$

$$y_0 = f_0 \frac{M}{2} \sin \theta \tag{67}$$

For each of the sub-parts i the result of the sampling is a vector $\tilde{y}_i$ ($i = 1 \ldots 16$) with 100x1 dimensions. The overall result are 16 vectors having 100 values each, making in total a number of 1600 attributes per image.

Before a further reduction of the data can be done, each sub-part i should be normalized to generate a similar range of values for each vector element h of $\tilde{y}_i(h)$. For the normalization, the mean and standard deviation vectors have to be estimated for each of the sub-parts from the training data. The database for the training holds N images, which results in 16 matrices $\tilde{Y}_i$ for each of the sub-parts i with an overall dimension of $100 \times N$. A row j of matrix $\tilde{Y}_i$ for sub-part i contains the data $\tilde{y}_i$, which represent the samples from image j. Hence, the mean estimator (see [105] for details on this concept) for each vector element h from the sampling vector $\tilde{y}_i$ can be described by Equation (68).

$$\bar{y}_i(h) = E(\mu_i(h)) = \frac{1}{N} \sum_{n=1}^{N} y_i^n(h) \tag{68}$$

The standard deviation (see [105]) is derived by Equation (69) were n denotes the image.

$$s_i(h) = \sqrt{E(\sigma_i^2(h))} = \sqrt{\frac{1}{N-1} \sum_{n=1}^{N} y_i^n(h) - \bar{y}_i(h)} \tag{69}$$

The normalization of a sub-part i and element h of the feature vector $\tilde{y}_i(h)$ is carried out based on Equation (70).

$$y_i(h) = \frac{\tilde{y}_i(h) - \bar{y}_i(h)}{s_i(h)} \tag{70}$$

The normalization of the overall training data $\tilde{Y}_i$ (all elements h of sub-part i) is defined by Equation (71).

$$\mathbf{Y}_i = \frac{\tilde{\mathbf{Y}}_i - \mathbf{I}^{N \times 1} \cdot \bar{\mathbf{y}}_i^T}{\mathbf{I}^{N \times 1} \cdot \mathbf{s}_i^T} \tag{71}$$

Where $\mathbf{I}^{N \times P}$ is the unit matrix of dimension $N \times P$, $\bar{\mathbf{y}}_i$ the mean vector and $\mathbf{s}_i$ the variance vector of sub-part i.

As already mentioned, a further reduction of the extracted features is carried out based on the results of a PCA (during the training phase). In the following, the PCA (see [106]) will be computed for each matrix $\mathbf{Y}_i$ (containing data of N training images of sub-part i), which can be seen as a coordinate transformation, where the first new coordinate axis aligns along the maximum variance of the data, the second axis along the second largest variance and so on. To this end, the result of the PCA is the transformation matrix $\mathbf{T_i}$, where each column contains the coefficients for a single principal component and the columns are in descending order of their importance. To reduce the size of each $y_i(h)$ only the first v principal components will be used for the projection. Therefore, a shortened transformation matrix $\hat{\mathbf{T}}_\mathbf{i}$, containing only the first v principal components, is constructed.

The final step of the feature extraction is the projection of the matrices $\mathbf{Y}_i$ to their new coordinate system by Equation (72).

$$\hat{\mathbf{Y}}_i = \mathbf{Y}_i \cdot \hat{\mathbf{T}}_\mathbf{i} \tag{72}$$

Similarly, the transformation is carried out for a single feature vector $\mathbf{y}_i$ by Equation (73), which is the input for the following classification step.

$$\hat{\mathbf{y}}_i = \mathbf{y}_i \cdot \hat{\mathbf{T}}_\mathbf{i}. \tag{73}$$

5.2.3. Training and Classification

Due to limitations in space, only the HPCC will be explained in detail, while the underlying methods are not described here, but can be found in the literature. Details on classification approaches as the Linear Discriminant Analysis (LDA) with Windowed Discriminant Spectral Template (WDST) can be found in [100] and for details on neural networks please refer to [107].

Typically, a classification algorithm tries to distinguish between all possible categories in one step, by simply extracting the principal components from all categories. A different approach was developed for the Hierarchical Principal Component Classification (HPCC) of the here described system. More specifically, a decision tree is build, always separating between two groups and each group contains a number of categories (at least one). At the first view, this is not a novelty if the classification is based on the same data or the same principal components. But this changes if during each classification step only the principal components from the current two groups are used. At first, the average values $\hat{\mathbf{y}}_c$ of the feature vectors in principal component space for each category are computed. On the basis of these average values the categories will be divided in two groups $A, B \subseteq C$ (with A, B satisfying $A \cap B = \emptyset$ and $A \cup B = C$) optimizing the criterion of Equation (74).

$$\min_{A,B \subseteq C} \left(\sum_{i,j \in A, i \neq j} |\hat{\mathbf{y}}_i - \hat{\mathbf{y}}_j|_2 + \sum_{i,j \in B, i \neq j} |\hat{\mathbf{y}}_i - \hat{\mathbf{y}}_j|_2 \right) \tag{74}$$

Whereas $|\mathbf{x} - \mathbf{y}|_2$ describes the Euclidean Distance between vector $\mathbf{x}$ and $\mathbf{y}$ (see [106]). At the same time, the Euclidean Distance between the average values of group A and B should

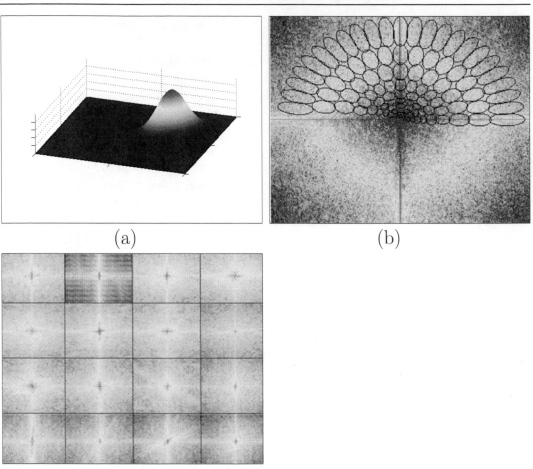

(a)   (b)

(c)

Figure 31. (a) Two dimensional Gauss function, (b) Spectrum and filter array with -3dB level lines , (c) Image after transformation to frequency domain

reach a maximum (for a mathematical description, see Equation (75)).

$$\max_{A,B \subseteq C} \left| \frac{1}{|A|} \sum_{i \in A} \hat{\mathbf{y}}_i - \frac{1}{|B|} \sum_{j \in B} \hat{\mathbf{y}}_j \right|_2 \tag{75}$$

The separation in groups A and B is the initial step at the first node of the decision tree. If for example group A contains more than one category the procedure above is repeated. The normalization is now done with the mean and standard deviation of the categories, which are part of group A and combined in matrix $\mathbf{Y}_A$. Again, the principal components are computed and the matrices projected to the principal component sub space of group A with $\hat{\mathbf{Y}}_{cA} = \hat{\mathbf{T}}_A \cdot \mathbf{Y}_c$. Also the average values $\hat{\mathbf{y}}_{cA}$ of the categories are calculated and the previous criteria (Equation (74), Equation (75)) optimized to sub-divide the group A into AA and AB. This method is applied for group B as well as for all sub-groups containing more than one category. The total number of categories is initially defined by the training data. The advantage of the method is the specific calculation of the principal components at each node of the decision tree. Only at the first node the overall training data is used to form two groups, which are maximally heterogeneous to each other, but at the same time maximally homogeneous for the members of the group (concerning the average values $\hat{y}_c$ of the categories). The classification at each node can either be carried out with LDA and WDST (see [100]) or a neural net (see [107]).

Hence, at each node a specific classification task is trained. The overall system with the classification step is depicted in Figure 29. In a nutshell, the training and subsequent classification is carried out in the following way: As first step, a preprocessing on the complete training data is performed, afterwards each image with its sub-parts is transformed independently and their spectra sampled. In the second step, the decision tree is learned. Thereby the matrices for the transformation to principal component space as well as mean and standard deviation vectors for each node are stored. The last step is the classification of an image, therefore, the features of the image are extracted and stored in the sampling vector $\tilde{y}_i$. At each node, the sampling vector is normalized with the corresponding mean and standard deviation vectors and afterwards projected to the principal component space. The result is classified by one of the named methods and assigned to one of the sub-groups. This procedure is repeated until a leaf of the tree is reached, which results in the classification of the image to the category of the leaf. In another variant of the HPCC a decision tree for each of the sub-parts of an image is generated. Thereby, 16 decision trees are build for each of the sub-parts and finally a majority voting is carried out for the 16 results. The approach of a single classification tree for the overall image will be called HPCC 1 and the approach with 16 single classifications will be called HPCC 2.

For an abundant evaluation of the scene classification system refer to Sect. 8.1.2..

6.   Depth Features

Accurate depth information is of vital importance for a driver assistance system. Typical commercial applications for assisting the driver use Radar or Lidar data. Such sensors deliver accurate but sparse depth information of the scene. So far, only few commercial driver assistance systems use vision, despite the fact that the information density is comparatively high. During the projection of the 3D world to the 2D image chip, one dimension - the depth information - is lost. Recovering the depth cannot be done with 100% certainty, i.e. 2D images are ambiguous in terms of depth. For solving this challenge several depth cues are fused. After a biological motivation, the implemented depth cues are described.

6.1.   Biological Motivation

Following [17] several stereo-related cues and at least nine monocular depth cues exist that allow the human to reliably perceive the depth in the environment. In the following, some of these monocular cues are listed and described shortly:

- Depth from object knowledge (known object size in the world as reference for the measured object size on the camera plane)

- Depth from ground plane assumption (assuming a flat world, the vertical image position is proportional to the object depth)

- Depth from blur (optimizing the edge sharpness by changing the focal length of the camera)

- Depth from Time to Contact (infer the time that remains until collision from the growth of perceived object size)

- Depth from relative size (several objects of the same type in different distances)

- Depth from shading (positioning of shades relative to objects)

- Depth from texture gradient (depth-dependent image frequencies on homogenous textured surfaces)

- Depth from aerial/atmospheric perspective (blue bias on objects that are far away)

The following subsections describe four monocular and binocular (stereoscopic) depth cues the presented ADAS is based on in order to perform its various vision tasks.

6.2. Depth from Stereo Disparity

The perception of stereoscopic depth is based on the interpretation of the differences between the projected images of both eyes (so-called parallax). An isolated point in the 3D world is projected to slightly different positions on the retina of both eyes, since these have a horizontal distance, the so-called basic distance. The horizontal shift between the images is called lateral disparity, see [53]. In addition to the lateral disparity, other flavors of disparity exist (see [53]) that can also cause an impression of depth - still the lateral disparity seems to be the most important disparity-related depth cue and is therefore also in the focus of the following reflections. For detecting lateral disparity (for simplification called disparity in the following) the detection of correspondences between the left and right eye is necessary. Here, ambiguities are possible, due to differences in illumination and partial occlusion between both images. Especially, local regions of low texture can lead to the well-known aperture problem, which is also a challenge for the optical flow computation (refer to [108]). Furthermore, differences and changes in the internal optical parameters of both eyes exist that influence the projections and hence the detected lateral disparity. Still, the human vision system can cope with these challenges by continuous adaptation mechanisms. How these challenges are resolved by the human vision system is largely unknown. Designing a technical stereo system that closely mimics the processing steps in the brain is therefore not possible up to now. However, the existing engineered approaches show sound results, but also have their limitations.

Figure 32 depicts the individual processing steps, which are needed for computing dense 3D world coordinates from stereo based on an engineering-driven approach.

After capturing pairs of images, the camera lens distortion is corrected for both cameras independently. The undistortion step is essential in order to make the mapping of the 3D world to the 2D image plane comparable for both cameras, which is a prerequisite when computing the stereo disparity in the following step. Based on the captured stereo images, the undistorted vertical and horizontal pixels v and u are computed on the initial (distorted) vertical and horizontal pixels v_d and u_d:

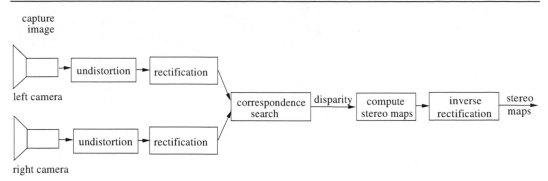

Figure 32. Processing steps for computing dense 3D world coordinates from stereo.

$$u \quad = (1 + k_1\beta^2 + k_2\beta^4)u_d + 2k_3u_dv_d + k_4(\beta^2 + 2u_d^2) \tag{76}$$

$$v \quad = (1 + k_1\beta^2 + k_2\beta^4)v_d + k_3(\beta^2 + 2u_dv_d) + 2k_4u_dv_d \tag{77}$$

$$\text{with } \beta = \sqrt{u_d^2 + v_d^2}.$$

The undistortion is based on a lens distortion model (described in [109]) that uses radial (k_1 and k_2) and tangential distortion coefficients (k_3 and k_4). For both cameras, these coefficients are determined offline using captured images of a checkerboard pattern based on the camera calibration toolbox [110] that is available in the internet.

Furthermore, the cameras are oriented differently in the world (i.e., the camera angles θ_X, θ_Y, and θ_Z are different for both cameras). In order to allow an efficient search for correspondences between the two camera images, these angles need to be compensated (i.e., the optical axes of both cameras need to be parallel). In theory, this could be done physically by adapting the camera position. However, this is not possible with the needed accuracy. The usual approach is to virtually adapt the camera angles by shifting and remapping the image pixels of both cameras, which is called rectification. Typically, a linear rectification is realized, which means both camera images are rescaled, rotated and shifted in horizontal and vertical direction in order to compensate the differences in the camera angles. The rectification is done using the commercial "Small Vision System" software [111].

For the rectification process the camera angles of both cameras are required. These can be computed based on the previously introduced Equations (3) and (4) that describe the 3D world to 2D image mapping.

Equation (3) and (4) use the 3 camera angles θ_X, θ_Y, and θ_Z, the 3 translational camera offsets t_1, t_2, t_3 (see Fig. 33b), the horizontal and vertical principal point u_0 and v_0 as well as the horizontal and vertical focal lengths f_u and f_v (focal lengths that are normalized to the horizontal and vertical pixel size respectively, see Fig. 33a). In sum, 12 unknown variables exist (the elements of the rotation matrix Equ. (78) as well as the position of the camera in the world $t_1, t_2,$ and t_3).

$$R \quad = R_X R_Y R_Z = \begin{bmatrix} r_{11} & r_{12} & r_{13} \\ r_{21} & r_{22} & r_{23} \\ r_{31} & r_{32} & r_{33} \end{bmatrix} \tag{78}$$

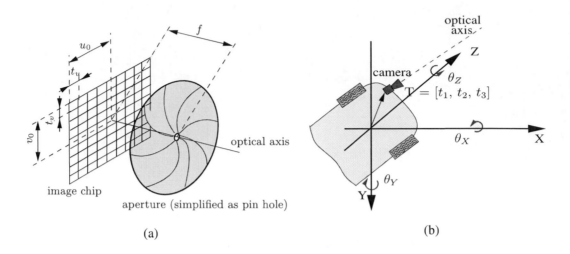

(a)   (b)

Figure 33. (a) Visualization of internal camera parameters, (b) Coordinate system and external camera parameters.

For determining these 12 variables the calibration scene shown in Fig. 34 is used, for which the 3D world position of the marked points was measured manually with a laser device and stored.

(a)   (b)

Figure 34. Calibration scene with measured 3D world calibration points: (a) Left image (calibration points marked), (b) Right image.

Based on internal interdependencies (orthogonality equations of the rotation matrix, see Equ. (79)) and the correspondences between the stored 3D world position and the measured image position for 3 points, all 12 parameters and hence the camera angles θ_X, θ_Y, and θ_Z

can be determined.

$$
\begin{aligned}
r_{11}^2 + r_{12}^2 + r_{13}^2 - 1 &= 0 \\
r_{21}^2 + r_{22}^2 + r_{23}^2 - 1 &= 0 \\
r_{31}^2 + r_{32}^2 + r_{33}^2 - 1 &= 0 \\
r_{11}r_{21} + r_{12}r_{22} + r_{13}r_{23} &= 0 \\
r_{11}r_{31} + r_{12}r_{32} + r_{13}r_{33} &= 0 \\
r_{21}r_{31} + r_{22}r_{32} + r_{23}r_{33} &= 0
\end{aligned}
\tag{79}
$$

After repeating the described procedure for the second camera, the image rectification can be done. After the rectification, an efficient search for correspondences between the left and right image can be realized. More specifically, for each pixel and its neighborhood in one of the camera images the best match in the other camera image is determined using a correspondence search with a probabilistic matching algorithm (refer to [108]). Since both images are undistorted and rectified the correspondence search between the images can be restricted to horizontal shifts, which makes the procedure very efficient. The result of the correspondence search is a dense disparity map $D(u,v)$, which contains a measured horizontal shift for all image positions.

Based on the disparity image the 3D world position for all image pixels can be computed using:

$$
Z_{\text{stereo}}(u,v) \quad -\frac{f_u B}{D(u,v)} + t_3
\tag{80}
$$

$$
Y_{\text{stereo}}(u,v) \quad = \frac{Z(v - v_0)}{f_v} + t_2
\tag{81}
$$

$$
X_{\text{stereo}}(u,v) \quad = \frac{Z(u - u_0)}{f_u} + t_1.
\tag{82}
$$

With: B ... basic distance between the left and right cameras principal point

f_u, f_v ... normalized focal length [in pixels]

$D(u,v)$ ... disparity

u_0, v_0 ... principal point

t_1, t_2, t_3 ... translational camera offset.

The equations are derived by transforming Equ. (3) and (4), setting all camera angles to zero, since the disparity computation was done on rectified images.

In the last step, the stereo maps are unrectified (i.e., the prior rectification is neutralized) to make them comparable to the input image on which all other processing steps are running. This is realized by remapping the pixel values of the rectified stereo maps based on Equ. (3) and (4), which results in unrectified stereo maps.

Figure 35 depicts a typical example for the resulting unrectified stereo maps in an inner-city scenario.

RGB input image   X position in m

Y position in m   Z position in m

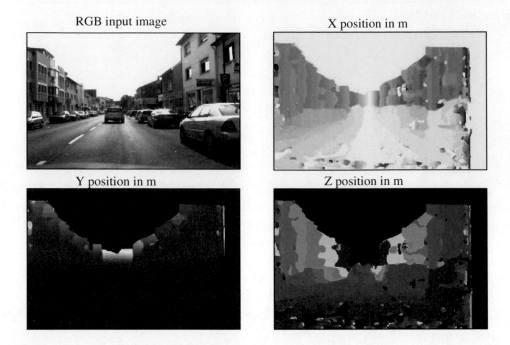

Figure 35. Dense 3D world positions for all image pixels based on stereo from a probabilistic matching approach [108].

Conceptional Extensions

Analyzing the Equ. (80) to (82) and Fig. 35, it can be seen that the stereo maps are dense (i.e., for all image pixels a 3D world position is computed). However, at image positions near to the car the computed values are not sufficiently accurate. When using a threshold on the stereo confidence map that was calculated during the disparity computation, these pixels can be identified. Furthermore, the thereby identified pixels can be corrected using an inter-modality depth cue fusion with the depth cues described in the following (see [26] for details on that approach).

6.3. Depth from Object Knowledge

Depth from object knowledge calculates the distance of an object Z_{obj} based on approximate knowledge about the area the object covers on the image plane (width W_{pixel} H_{pixel}), the width and height of the object in the world drawn from experience (W_{world} and H_{world}) as well as the intrinsic parameters of the sensor ($f_u = f/t_u$ and $f_v = f/t_v$, with the focal length f and the horizontal and vertical pixel size t_u and t_v):

$$Z_{obj,W} \approx \frac{W_{world} f_u}{W_{im}} \quad \text{and} \quad Z_{obj,H} \approx \frac{H_{world} f_v}{H_{im}}. \tag{83}$$

Equation (83) can be derived by applying and transforming the 3D to 2D pinhole camera Equations (3) and (4) (see [49] for the detailed derivation).

6.4. Depth from Bird's Eye View

For computing the distance of objects that are positioned on the drivable path the bird's eye view is used. The bird's eye view is a metric representation of the scene as viewed from above (see Fig. 36). The cue is able to detect and estimate the distance of objects present on the ego-vehicle's and neighboring lane (as opposed to the perspective image). Working on this representation for estimating object distances has the advantage that the cumbersome non-linear projection from 3D world coordinates to the 2D image plane (see Equ. (3) and (4)) is compensated. As such, world position coordinates can directly be assigned to a detected object without further processing. Furthermore, by this transformation, the detection of lanes and objects can be realized easier than working on the projected camera image, since expectations regarding typical metric lane widths can be integrated easily into the algorithm.

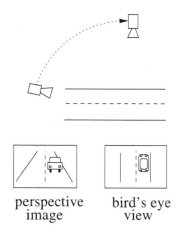

Figure 36. Visualization of the bird's eye view.

The bird's eye view is calculated on the undistorted pixels v and u based on Equ. (3) and (4) by inverse perspective mapping of the 3D world points X, Y, and Z (see Fig. 33b for a visualization of the used coordinate system) to the 2D (u,v) image plane. The equations describe how to map a 3D position of the world to the 2D image plane (refer to [112]). More specifically, only the image pixels (u,v) that are required to get the metric bird's eye view (i.e., the XZ-plane) dense, are mapped. The approach also leads to low computational demands. The usage of inverse perspective mapping makes the inversion of Equ. (3) and (4) obsolete, when computing the bird's eye view.

As can be seen in Equ. (3) and (4) the 3D world position coordinates X, Y, and Z of all image pixels (u,v) are required. By using a monocular system, one dimension (the depth Z) is lost. A solution to this dilemma is the so-called flat plane assumption. Here, for all pixels in the image, the height Y is set to 0. Based on this, only objects in the image with $Y = 0$ (especially, the street the system aims to detect) are mapped correctly to the bird's eye view, while all the other regions are stretched to infinity in the bird's eye view (for example the car in Fig. 37d).

Now, a vertical grow algorithm with dynamic thresholds searches for discontinuities in the bird's eye view and assigns a distance value to them (see Fig. 37d).

In the rectified image (i.e., the image is virtually remapped to be equivalent to an image with all 3 camera angles zero, see Sect. 6.2. for details on the image rectification) the following direct relation between the vertical pixel value v and the depth Z_{birds} exists:

$$Z_{birds} = \frac{f_v \, t_2}{(v - v_0)} \tag{84}$$

With:

t_2 ... camera height above the ground

v_0 ... the vertical principal point

v ... vertical pixel position with significant contrast change

f_v ... Normalized focal length.

In case the flat plane assumption is not fulfilled (i.e., the street surface is not flat) the bird's eye view is inaccurate, which decreases the quality of all algorithms that run on the bird's eye view (e.g., depth estimation or temporal road integration, see [20]). An approach that allows a stable bird's eye view even in case of non-flat street surfaces and pitching of the vehicle is described in [49].

6.5. Depth from Radar

Depth from Radar (Radio Detecting and Ranging) is obtained from a commercial standard vehicle equipment sensor (76-77 GHz, Long Range Radar), which delivers sparse point-wise measurements of low longitudinal but higher lateral uncertainty (for an example see Fig. 37b). Radar sensors evaluate the reflections (echoes) of bundled micro wave beams (typically between 400 MHz and 80 GHz) for detecting, localizing, tracking, and classifying objects. More specifically, the time of flight t_{tof} is used to determine the object distance Z_{radar}:

$$Z_{radar} = \frac{c_0 \cdot t_{tof}}{2}. \tag{85}$$

With: c_0 ... velocity of propagation (speed of light)

$$\approx 300000 \, \frac{km}{s}$$

t_{tof} ... time of flight (to the object and back).

For measuring the time of flight, the individual beam packages must be marked and recognized, which can be done by modulation and demodulation of the signal amplitude, frequency or phase. The object velocity v_{dop} is determined based on the Doppler shift Δf:

$$v_{dop} = \frac{c_0 \cdot \Delta f}{2 f_0}. \tag{86}$$

With: c_0 ... velocity of propagation (speed of light)

$$\approx 300000 \, \frac{km}{s}$$

Δf ... measured Doppler frequency shift

f_0 ... carrier frequency.

Using Radar sensors, the object distance and velocity can hence be measured with independent approaches. Different from visual sensors, Radar is very robust against changing weather conditions, which makes it an important cue that increases the system robustness.

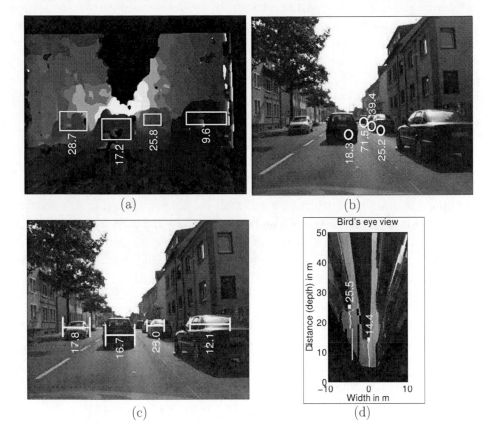

Figure 37. Used depth cues: Depth from (a) Stereo disparity, (b) Radar, (c) Object knowledge, (d) Bird's eye view.

7. Road Detection Sub-System

The importance of driver assistance systems for further decreasing the number of traffic accidents is a widely acknowledged fact. The growing complexity of tasks, which these Advanced Driver Assistance Systems have to handle leads to complex systems that use information fusion from many sensory devices and incorporate processing results of multiple other modules. One important field of interest for said systems are applications like, e.g., the "Honda Intelligent Driver Support System" [4] supporting the driver to stay in the lane and to maintain a safe distance from the car in front. Other systems focus on collision avoidance based on autonomous steering and braking (see, e.g., [113]) as well as path-planning even in unstructured environments (see, e.g., [114]). All these applications need a robust detection of the drivable road area. The more safety-relevant applications become, the more the required quality of the detected drivable road area must be improved. As "drivable road area" we define the space in front, which the car can move on safely in a physical sense, but without taking symbolic information into account (e.g., one-way-street, traffic signs).

First vision-based approaches for detecting the drivable road area on unmarked streets were introduced in recent years. Although most of these visual-feature-based approaches show sound results in scenarios of limited complexity, they seem to lack the necessary system-inherent flexibility to run in complex environments under changing lighting conditions. To cope with such environments, in Sect. 7.1. we introduce an architecture for robust unmarked road detection. The system relies on four novel approaches that permit the autonomous adaptation of important system parameters to the environment. As the presented results show, the approach allows for robust road detection on unmarked inner-city streets without manual tuning of internal parameters. This is different from most approaches in literature that rely on strong rigid road models and offline set parameters. In order to further stabilize the gathered results, in Sect. 7.2. a novel, generic approach for improving unmarked road detection systems by temporal integration is proposed. Since the dedicated analysis of the remaining road detection errors after the temporal integration has shown that in challenging situations the curbstone can be surpassed by the detected road segment, we extended the system and added the here presented system as final postprocessing step (see Sect. 7.3.). More specifically, all road segments surpassing the detected curbstones were corrected (clipped).

7.1.   Adaptive Multi-Cue Fusion for Detecting Unmarked Roads in Inner-City

In this section, a robust system approach for detecting the drivable area on unmarked roads is presented. Based on four novel techniques, which extend known unmarked road detection approaches, the proposed system reliably detects the road in complex scenarios by autonomously adapting its internal parameters. As evaluation on inner-city sequences shows, the presented techniques are an important step toward more generic and robust driving-path detection for unmarked roads. Unlike other approaches, no scene-dependent manual adaptation of system parameters is required. The input images used for the evaluation, corresponding ground truth data, and a result sequence are accessible on the internet [115].

7.1.1.   Related Work

Initial approaches for lane detection on marked roads date back to the 1990s (see [112] for an overview of the early approaches). These to date commercially available systems are restricted to marked roads with a predictable course, based on a clothoid lane model that is also used for road construction of motor-ways. In recent years, the field of research for road detection has shifted to unmarked country roads and inner-city streets. To this end, current prototype systems evaluate and fuse different visual features. In the following, the structure of such visual-feature-based systems is analyzed. It is shown that despite the large number of existing road detection systems some important techniques for increasing the road detection robustness are not considered so far.

Image Training Regions: Current approaches for road detection often use street training regions in front of the car in order to parameterize the probability distributions that describe the road feature characteristics (e.g., [116, 117], see also Fig. 41). Only very few approaches partially incorporate information of non-road image regions to improve road detection (e.g., [54, 118]). However, to our knowledge no approach uses the full potential of non-road information, e.g., for the autonomous adaptation of internal system parameters and the dynamic online assessment of the cue quality, as it is done in our system.

Features: Typical visual features for road detection in state-of-the-art systems are: texture (edge density) on the intensity [119, 54, 120], stereo disparity [121, 117], HSI color [54, 116, 117, 122], or depth from Lidar / Radar [123, 124]. Many system approaches use the feature edge density (structure) on the intensity map. However, edge density on further feature maps is so far not considered. To our knowledge no approach uses the edge density on color maps for road detection. During the evaluation of our system, we experienced the edge density computed on color maps as a robust cue for detecting the road.

Feature Granularity: Numerous system approaches rely on probabilistic methods for classifying street and non-street pixels (e.g., [54, 55, 125, 118, 126]). Such iconic (i.e., pixel-based) approaches do not include information of the neighborhood of a pixel, but handle all pixels independently. Nevertheless, discontinuities in the feature maps often contain important information that allow improved scene decomposition (e.g., curbstones that separate the road from the sidewalk). Other approaches stress the importance of region-based information and use region growing or vertical filling (e.g., [116, 127, 128]). Such approaches are often sensitive to changing lighting conditions causing large gradients in the feature maps (e.g., shadows on the road). Both, the iconic and the region-based system approaches have important advantages that partially compensate their drawbacks. However, to our knowledge no system approach for road detection uses both approaches to the same extend.

Road Modeling: Many of the recent feature-based systems use road models of varying complexity that support the feature-based road detection (e.g., [54, 55, 56] use clothoids, [121] distinguishes between left, right, and straight street course, [129] uses second order polynomials). For country roads and highways such approaches seem to yield sound results. Nevertheless, as further discussed in Sect. 7.1.2., we claim that said rigid street models are not flexible enough to robustly run on inner-city streets that often show abrupt changes in their course as well as occlusions of significant parts of the drivable road area. However, some kind of road model seems to be necessary in order to improve robustness of the road detection. This dilemma can be resolved by relying on a generic and flexible road model that makes only simple assumptions about the course of the road. One of the few system approaches that follows this idea is presented in [122]. The authors point out that the road area typically covers between 30 to 85% of the image. The feature thresholds are adapted in order to reach this ratio. Unfortunately, the proposed approach is restricted in its flexibility, since the ratio is set offline without constantly adapting it to match the current characteristics of the scene.

To sum up, existing state-of-the-art road detection systems are marked by a limited flexibility, which restricts their application to country roads and highways. In order to allow reliable road detection in more complex inner-city scenarios, we propose four novel techniques to enhance robustness and system-inherent flexibility by enabling adaptation to the environment. To our knowledge a combination of these techniques have not been used for road detection before.

In detail, these techniques are:

- Using street *and* non-street training regions (see Fig. 41) that both adapt the feature probability distributions,

- Using edge density (structure) feature, computed on the HSI hue and saturation maps,

- Combining iconic *and* region-based feature processing,

- Fusing feature-based road detection with a dynamic and generic road model.

In the following section, details about our road detection system embedding these four techniques are given. The presented system approach is not restricted to inner-city streets, but was tested on country roads and highways as well.

7.1.2. System Description

In the following, the realized system architecture for unmarked road detection is described (see Fig. 38). It relies on our four novel techniques that enhance the system-inherent flexibility. After giving a rough overview on the individual processing steps, all system modules are described in detail.

Our system takes RGB input images, stereo disparity (from two parallel cameras), and Radar data as input. Knowledge about previously detected objects in the scene can be used as optional input. The system detects the road based on six robust features that are evaluated and fused in a probabilistic way. For this step, street and non-street training regions are defined in the input image. In parallel, the system detects present lane markings with a biologically motivated filter approach. The lane markings are fused with the detected road segments. In the final step, a binary road map is computed relying on a road model that adapts itself to the environment.

Next, the system is described in more detail. In the first step, different features are calculated on the 400x300 pixel RGB input images. The features we use are saturation and hue of the HSI color space (see, e.g., [64]). Furthermore, we apply the structure tensor in Equ. (87) (with W being a 9x9 region around the current pixel) to compute the edge density E_j (see Equ. (88)) on the hue, saturation, and intensity of the HSI color space:

$$A_j(u,v) \quad = \begin{bmatrix} \Sigma_W (G_u * F_j)^2 & \Sigma_W (G_u * F_j)(G_v * F_j) \\ \Sigma_W (G_v * F_j)(G_u * F_j) & \Sigma_W (G_v * F_j)^2 \end{bmatrix} \tag{87}$$

with $j \in \{\text{hue, saturation, intensity}\}$ and

$$G_u(u,v) \quad = -\frac{u}{2\pi\sigma^4} exp(-\frac{u^2+v^2}{2\sigma^2})$$

$$G_v(u,v) \quad = -\frac{v}{2\pi\sigma^4} exp(-\frac{u^2+v^2}{2\sigma^2})$$

$$E_j(u,v) \quad = \frac{det(A_j(u,v))}{trace(A_j(u,v))}. \tag{88}$$

Typically, the edge density computed on these feature channels is different for the road and the rest of the scene, which makes it a reliable feature.

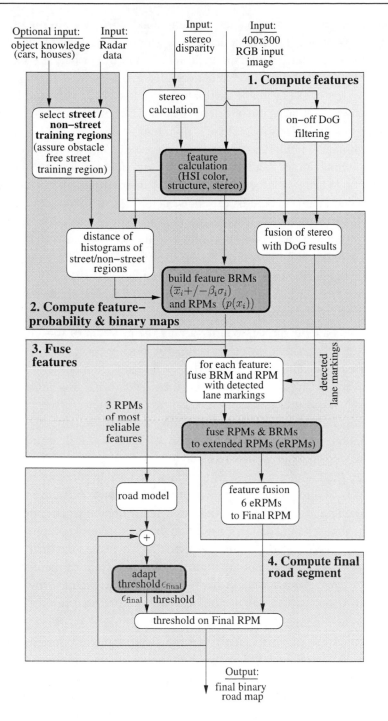

Figure 38. System overview: Adaptive road detection system (red modules contain novel techniques).

Furthermore, vision-based stereo data is used as feature. For computing stereo vision, the camera images are rectified in order to facilitate the correspondence search between the two camera images (i.e., the images are remapped, virtually aligning the two camera coordinate systems with the world coordinate system). The thereby necessary intrinsic (i.e., internal camera properties, like the focal length and the principal point) and extrinsic (i.e., external camera properties, like camera angles and offsets) camera parameters were determined using the freely available calibration toolbox [110]. The toolbox was applied on a calibration scene similar to the one described in [130] (see also Sect. 6.2. for details on the computation of stereo disparity). There is no dynamic change of the camera pitch angle, since on the one hand the input images are pitch-corrected using a correlation-based method similar to [131]. On the other hand, we assume a flat road, which is present in most inner-city environments. When using the system in an urban environment, the course of the road and hence the camera angles could be estimated using a surface model (e.g., a hyperplane, please refer to [20] for details). The image rectification assures that the camera angles (including the static pitch angle) will not influence the stereo results. The correspondence search yields a disparity map. Based on the disparity map three dense maps containing the 3D-world positions for all image pixels can be obtained (see Fig. 35). The stereo data is remapped using the measured camera angles in order to have the stereo maps and the image comparable in terms of the pixel position of objects.

The stereo maps are postprocessed for solving the problem of missing disparity values near to the car (see Fig. 39b). More specifically, during the computation of the stereo disparity no correspondence search is possible at image regions near to the car, since this would come at the cost of high computation time. We solve this problem by searching line-wise for high horizontal gradients in the bird's eye view of the camera image (for information on this representation see [112]) taking only the area directly in front of the car (e.g., first 10 meters) into account (see example in Fig. 39a). It is assured that no objects are present in the said area based on Radar and low vertical gradients in the bird's eye view. The area between the found gradients, which mark the road borders, is assumed to be road. The image regions in bird's eye view representation are mapped to the perspective image with a pin hole camera model, which includes the determined intrinsic and extrinsic camera parameters (e.g., static camera angles). Based on the perspectively mapped road regions the three stereo maps are corrected assuming a perfectly flat plane (see the resulting corrected depth map in Fig. 39c). Since only the region directly in front of the car is corrected, the error induced by a non-flat road plane can be considered as small. However, to eliminate this error the estimated camera angles coming from the optional surface model could also be included into the pin hole camera model.

Tests have shown that huge shadows on the road result in poor stereo quality, since the correspondence search gets difficult on dark, noisy image regions. This supports using more cues that are to some extend more invariant to shadows as done in the presented system (e.g., HSI color space). Altogether, our system relies on six different cues for road detection (see Tab. 3 for an overview).

In the second step, binary road maps (BRM) and road probability maps (RPM) for the six feature maps are computed. The BRMs are binary maps that hold "1" for pixels belonging to the detected street and zero for the rest. The six BRMs are calculated with a region-growing algorithm, by which region-related feature properties are incorporated. Opposed to that, the six RPMs contain continuous probability values that assess the "road-likeness" of the feature values for all pixels independently. Both map types rely on the same

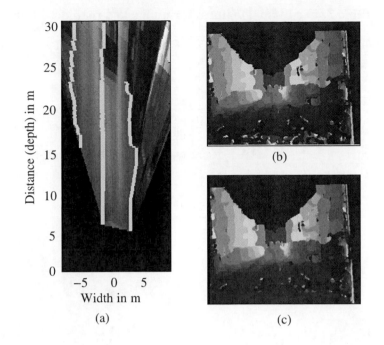

Figure 39. (a) Gradient-based road search on the bird's eye view on the image depicted in Fig. 41, (b) Missing disparity values near to the camera vehicle induce false and missing depth values, (c) Corrected depth map

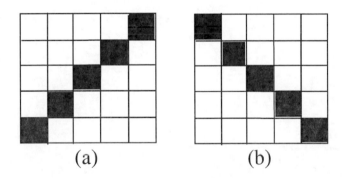

Figure 40. Structuring element for region growing for (a) left image half, (b) right image half.

normal distribution, see Equ. (99) and (100). The parameters of the normal distribution are calculated using a street and at least 2 non-street training regions (see Fig. 41). Please note that the training region needs to be set beyond the regions of corrected height values (see Fig. 39c). The training regions are adapted dynamically depending on the scene. For example, it is assured that no obstacle is within the training region by incorporating Radar data. Furthermore, the size of the street training region is set proportionally to the velocity of the ego vehicle, to exploit the fact that typically no near obstacles exist during fast driving, e.g., on highways. The street and non-street training regions are chosen by considering the

Table 3. Used visual features for unmarked road detection

MODALITY	Cue #	VISUAL ROAD DETECTION FEATURE
Color	1	Hue
	2	Saturation
Structure	3	Edge density on Hue
	4	Edge density on Saturation
	5	Edge density on Intensity
Stereo	6	Height of objects in scene

Figure 41. Visualization of street and non-street training regions.

height map of the scene derived from the stereo disparity map (see Fig. 35) and existing knowledge about objects in the scene. In the following, the computation of the BRMs and RPMs is described in more detail. For computing the BRMs a region-growing algorithm, which connects continuous regions in the feature maps is applied (i.e., the neighborhood of a pixel is evaluated). The latter approach is done, in order to get crisp borders between the road and the sidewalks that often have road-like features. The region growing uses two different structuring elements for the left and right half of the image (see Fig. 40), which is motivated from the typical course of roads in a perspective image. The region-growing algorithm recursively sets all pixels that are adjacent to the currently known street segment in BRM_i to "1", when the corresponding pixels in the feature map i are within the confidence interval (see Equ. (89) and Equ. (90)).

$$\bar{x}_i - \beta_i \sigma_i < \quad x_i < \bar{x}_i + \beta_i \sigma_i \quad \forall i = 1..5 \tag{89}$$
$$\text{with } \beta_i \quad = 4 d_i(H_{s_i}, H_{n_i}) \; \forall i = 1..6$$

$$\bar{x}_6 - \varepsilon_Y(v) < \quad x_6 < \bar{x}_6 + \varepsilon_Y(v) \tag{90}$$
$$\text{with } \varepsilon_Y(v) \quad = \beta_6(\sigma_6 - \sigma_q(v_{\text{train}})) + \sigma_q(v) \tag{91}$$

$$d_i(H_{s_i}, H_{n_i}) \quad = \sqrt{1 - \gamma_i(H_{s_i}, H_{n_i})} \; \forall i = 1..6 \tag{92}$$

$$\gamma_i(H_{s_i}, H_{n_i}) \quad = \sum_{\forall x} \sqrt{H_{s_i}(x) H_{n_i}(x)} \; \forall i = 1..6 \tag{93}$$

The region-growing algorithm starts from the road-training region. The normal-distribution-based confidence interval in Equ. (89) uses the feature thresholds $\bar{x}_i$ +/ $\beta_i \sigma_i$, which are independently calculated for all five visual features. Here, the parameter $\bar{x}_i$ is the mean and σ_i the standard deviation of the normal distribution calculated on the street training region. The parameter β_i is introduced in order to adapt the confidence interval to the current scene properties. Different from $\bar{x}_i$ and σ_i, which are calculated on the street training region alone, the threshold parameter β_i changes dynamically depending on the characteristics of the street *and* non-street training regions. More specifically, the parameter β_i, which influences the feature thresholds, is calculated from d_i (see Equ. (92)). The parameter d_i is the distance between the two histograms H_{s_i} and H_{n_i} of the street and non-street training regions for the i=1..6 features. The measure d_i is based on the Bhattacharya coefficient $\gamma_i(H_{s_i}, H_{n_i})$ (see Equ. (93)), which assesses the similarity of two histograms. Based on β_i the confidence interval is adapted (see Equ. (89)). The larger the difference between the street versus the non-street areas on a feature map is, the bigger the confidence interval becomes.

Different from the five visual cues (hue, saturation, and the three edge density maps), the normal distribution of the stereo height Y also depends on the measured distance to the car. This is empirically plausible, since Y is a function of the stereo disparity $D(u,v)$ and the relative influence of the quantization error of $D(u,v)$ (measured in pixels) grows the smaller $D(u,v)$ and hence the bigger the distance of a road segment is to the car. Hence, the part σ_q of the standard deviation of the stereo height cue that is induced by the quantization error of $D(u,v)$ increases with growing distance to the car. In order to mathematically assess the error propagation of the quantization error of disparity $D(u,v)$ to the stereo height Y their functional relation is required. The stereo height $x_6 = Y$ can be computed using Equ. (94) (with B as the horizontal distance between the stereo cameras, h the camera height, v the vertical pixel position and v_0 the vertical principal point of the camera).

$$x_6 \quad = Y = \frac{B \cdot (v - v_0)}{D(u,v)} - h \tag{94}$$

$$D_{\mathrm{surf}}(v) \quad = \frac{B \cdot (v - v_0)}{h} \tag{95}$$

$$\sigma_D \quad = \frac{\Delta g}{\sqrt{12}} = \frac{1}{\sqrt{12}} \tag{96}$$

$$\sigma_q(v) \quad \approx \sigma_D \left| \frac{dY}{dD} \right|_{D(u,v)=D_{\mathrm{surf}}(v)} \tag{97}$$

$$\approx \sigma_D \left| -\frac{B \cdot (v - v_0)}{[D_{\mathrm{surf}}(v)]^2} \right|$$

$$\sigma_q(v) \quad \approx \frac{1}{\sqrt{12}} \left| \frac{h^2}{B \cdot (v - v_0)} \right| \tag{98}$$

Equation (96) defines the standard deviation σ_D of the disparity (measured in pixels), which is induced by the quantization error (the step size Δg is set to 1 pixel). For computing the propagated standard deviation σ_q (required in Equ. (91)), we use Equ. (97) (refer to [64]), which describes how the standard deviation of a random variable (here the disparity $D(u,v)$) is propagated through a function (here $Y(D)$). We are interested in the disparity on road surface D_{surf} alone (see Equ. (95), gathered after reforming Equ. (94) with Y=0). Hence, D_{surf} defines the position at which Equ. (97) is linearized. Here, the vertical pixel position v is a parameter of the distribution. For the quantization-error-induced standard deviation of the height cue Y, we finally find Equ. (98). The hyperbolic form of Equ. (98) confirms the made empirical assumptions. Based on that, the confidence interval ε_Y for the stereo height Y (see Equ. (90)) includes the standard deviation $\sigma_q(v)$ that is adapted depending on the current vertical image position v of the current pixel in focus (see Equ. (91)). Besides adding $\sigma_q(v)$ in Equ. (91), the standard deviation σ_6, computed on the training region on the Y map, needs to be corrected by $\sigma_q(v_{\mathrm{train}})$ present at the vertical image position v_{train} of the training region. As result, we now have six BRMs for six features.

Additionally to the region-based processing for calculating the BRMs, a pixel-based (iconic) processing for computing the RPMs is done (i.e., each pixel is handled independently from its surround). All pixel values x_i receive a probability value $p(x_i)$, which results in six independent Road Probability Maps (RPMs) for the six features:

$$p(x_i) \quad = e^{-\frac{(x_i - \bar{x}_i)^2}{2\sigma_i^2}} \quad \forall i = 1..5 \tag{99}$$

$$p(x_6) \quad = e^{-\frac{x_6^2}{2[\sigma_6 - \sigma_q(v_{train}) + \sigma_q(v)]^2}} . \tag{100}$$

The probability distribution for the stereo-based height cue Y (see Equ. (100)) assumes the mean height zero $\bar{x}_6 = 0$ and adapts $\sigma_q(v)$ during the computation of RPM_6 and BRM_6 dependent on the vertical pixel position v. The approach assumes a normal distribution of the six features in the street training region and beyond. As described for x_6 a position-dependent variance was introduced. The assumed normal distribution was verified with statistical tests of goodness of fit for all features independently.

In the third step, the computed BRMs and RPMs are fused with the detected lane markings. More specifically, the RPMs for all features are set to a high probability for the detected lane markings. The lane-marking detection is done with the biologically motivated Difference of Gaussian (DoG) kernel (see Fig. 42a), which takes the receptive fields of neurons in the retina as a role model. The DoG filter kernel is adapted to be selective to bright structures on a dark background, the so-called on-off contrasts without reacting to dark structures on a brighter background. Figure 42c shows the filter response on the inner-city frame shown in Fig. 42b. All image regions with on-off contrasts, that have a height within the confidence interval Equ. (90), and that are below the horizon are detected as being lane markings (see Fig. 42d). The separation between on-off and off-on contrasts reduces the number of false positive road marking detections. For example, in [57] the prefiltered road image still contains the lane marking unspecific off-on contrasts (e.g., traffic signs in front of a bright sky). Such off-on contrasts are filtered out in our approach to improve the road detection performance.

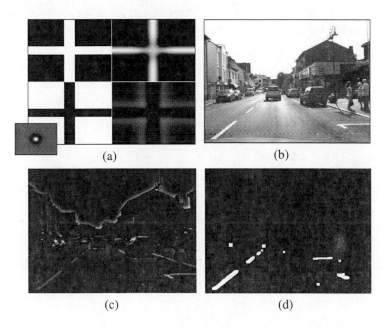

(a)   (b)

(c)   (d)

Figure 42. (a) On-off Difference of Gaussian (DoG) filtering on two test images with on-off and off-on contrast (left) as well as the respective filter responses (right), (b) Inner-city test frame, (c) On-off DoG filter response for bright contrasts on a dark background (with lane markings popping out), (d) Detected lane markings (after fusion of DoG and object height from stereo).

The six iconic RPMs and their respective BRMs are combined by multiplication, which leads to six extended RPMs (eRPM):

$$eRPM_i \quad = RPM_i BRM_i \ \forall i = 1..6. \tag{101}$$

Based on this, the advantage of probability-based computation is preserved. At the same time, discontinuities in the feature maps can be detected. As a result, the advantages of both approaches are combined.

Next, all eRPMs are fused resulting in the final RPM (fRPM) using the geometric mean:

$$\text{fRPM} \quad = \left(\prod_{i=1}^{6} \text{eRPM}_i \right)^{1/6}. \tag{102}$$

In the forth and final step, the Final Road Map is determined by applying a threshold $\varepsilon_{\text{final}}$ to the fRPM:

$$\text{Final Road Map}(u,v) \quad = \left\{ \begin{array}{ll} 1 & \forall\ \text{fRPM}(u,v) > \varepsilon_{\text{final}} \\ 0 & \text{else} \end{array} \right. . \tag{103}$$

The threshold $\varepsilon_{\text{final}}$ is set dynamically based on the correlation results of the three currently most reliable features maps, in order to get a prediction of the current relative size of the road versus the rest of the image. For these three features the currently best HSI color feature (hue or saturation), the best structure feature (structure on hue, saturation, or intensity), as well as stereo are selected. For the selection process the Bhattacharya coefficient $\gamma_i(H_{s_i}, H_{n_i})$ is evaluated (see Equ. (93)), by which the separability of street versus non-street histograms H_{s_i}, H_{n_i} can be assessed.

Hence, the computation of the Final Road Map relies on a simple road model (expected fraction of the road area in the current image, termed road-to-image-ratio). No assumptions are made regarding the current position of the road in the image. As extensive evaluation has shown, it is of crucial importance to adapt the said expected fraction dynamically to the current scene. This dynamic adaptation enables the system to run robustly in complex scenes, as in inner-city scenarios.

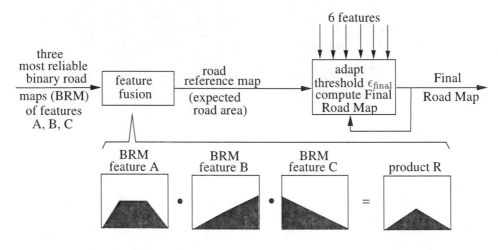

Figure 43. Control loop to adapt the final road detection threshold $\varepsilon_{\text{final}}$.

For adapting $\varepsilon_{\text{final}}$ the control loop depicted in Fig. 43 is used. The threshold $\varepsilon_{\text{final}}$ is adapted by a gradient method based on Equ. (108). In the following, the applied procedure is described in detail. It uses the BRMs of the three most reliable feature maps A, B, and

C that are combined to the road reference map (i.e., feature product R that represents the expected road area), depicted in Fig. 43. The four binary maps are summed up, which results in four scalar values $S_{\{A,B,C,R\}}$:

$$S_X \quad = \sum_{\forall(u,v)} \text{BRM}_X(u,v) \text{ with } X \in \{A,B,C,R\}. \tag{104}$$

The values $S_{\{A,B,C,R\}}$ represent the integral number of pixels detected as road for the three feature maps and the road reference map.

Then, the parameter κ is calculated:

$$\kappa \quad = \frac{\frac{S_R}{S_A} + \frac{S_R}{S_B} + \frac{S_R}{S_C}}{3}. \tag{105}$$

It represents the mean percentage with which the three most reliable feature maps correspond to the road reference map R. The larger κ is, the more the features match to each other, i.e., the more similar the three features maps are. The degree of similarity of these features gives a hint about what to expect from the remaining cues and can hence be used to adapt $\varepsilon_{\text{final}}$. The Final Road Map is computed (see Equ. (103), where $\varepsilon_{\text{final}}$ is set to a typical initial value for bootstrapping) and summed up yielding the scalar value S_{FRM}:

$$S_{\text{FRM}} \quad = \sum_{\forall(u,v)} \text{Final Road Map}(u,v). \tag{106}$$

Next, it is checked if the calculated scalar value S_{FRM} fulfills:

$$\frac{1}{\kappa} < \quad \frac{S_{\text{FRM}}}{S_R} < 1.2\frac{1}{\kappa}. \tag{107}$$

If the inequality is fulfilled, the Final Road Map is valid. If not, $\varepsilon_{\text{final}}$ is adapted incrementally based on the following Equation (with $\alpha^- < 1$ and $\alpha^+ > 1$), until the following inequality is fulfilled:

$$\varepsilon_{\text{final}}(t) \quad = \begin{cases} \alpha^- \varepsilon_{\text{final}}(t-1) & \text{when } \frac{S_{\text{FRM}}}{S_R} < \frac{1}{\kappa} \\ \\ \alpha^+ \varepsilon_{\text{final}}(t-1) & \text{when } \frac{S_{\text{FRM}}}{S_R} > 1.2\frac{1}{\kappa}. \end{cases} \tag{108}$$

Equation (108) is motivated from the well-known Resilient Backpropagation (RPROP) approach. The step sizes α^+ and α^- are adapted using the SuperSAB approach (see [132] for details). The processing stops after 100 iterations at the latest.

In the following section, our system approach is evaluated based on an inner-city scenario.

In the following section, a tracking procedure based on temporal integration is proposed, which steadies the gained road detection results, e.g., in case of difficult lighting conditions.

7.2. Temporal Integration for Feature-Based Road Detection Systems

Although existing state-of-the-art systems for unmarked road detection show promising results, the detected road segments often contain holes and show a detection performance that strongly varies in time depending on environmental conditions (see also previous Section 7.1.). The varying detection performance is due to the changing content of the training region in front of the car. Thereby, the system possibly adapts to local characteristics present in the current training region that might differ from the global road characteristics. Furthermore, local illumination changes that depend on the current view angle and lighting conditions influence the detection performance. See Fig. 44 for a visualization of both effects.

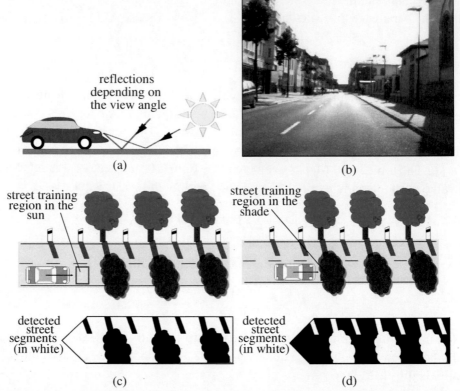

Figure 44. Causes for varying road detection performance: (a) Illumination change with dependence on the view angle, (b) Sample image showing typical illumination gradient, (c) Schematic example: Training region in the sun and resulting detected street segment (in white), (d) Schematic example: Training region in the shade and resulting detected street segment (in white).

In the following section a real-time capable approach for improving the road detection results for this type of state-of-the-art system is presented that adds a generic postprocessing step. Our proposed architecture removes the drawbacks of these systems using a temporal integration approach based on the bird's eye view. In order to test the proposed approach, the visual-feature-based road detection system described in Sect. 7.1. is used. Still, this road detection system can be exchanged with any other state-of-the-art system. Evaluation results computed on inner-city data show that this approach is an important enhancement for all visual-feature-based road detection systems. One of the used sequences and corresponding ground truth data is accessible on the internet for benchmark testing. The proposed approach is a crucial step toward robust road detection in complex scenarios that allows building high-level applications, as, e.g., active collision avoidance or trajectory planning, based on vision as the major cue.

7.2.1. Related Work

The concept of temporal integration is used in various applications in the field of computer vision for driver assistance. For example, [133] uses spatiotemporal integration to improve the classifier performance when detecting signal boards and cars. Other applications for improving the classifier performance rely on (temporal-integration-based) voting mechanisms, which are widely used in numerous domains (see [134] for an overview). Also the well-known Kalman filter approach [135] stabilizes its state estimate by temporal integration (fusion of measured and predicted data). In [136] temporal integration is used to determine the camera parameters, thereby stabilizing the input image of a marked lane detection system running online in a car.

Also for clothoid-model-based lane detection on highways and country roads (see, e.g., [56] and [54]) temporal integration was found to improve the detection performance. Still, the usage of such model-based approaches for road detection in complex inner-city scenes is heavily restricted, due to the unpredictable and abruptly changing course of the road and various occlusions of road parts. Figure 45a shows the complexity of a hand labeled ground truth road segment for an inner-city frame that can hardly be modeled using, e.g., a clothoid model. Therefore, also a model-based temporal integration is not possible and will not show the desired results in such complex scenarios.

Newer road detection approaches that rely on the statistical evaluation of different image features (see, e.g. [116] and [117]) can handle such scenarios but have the drawbacks discussed at the beginning of Sect. 7.2. (see page 140). Nevertheless, also for these systems temporal integration can and should be used for making the road segment detection more robust. To this end, the most direct approach would be to use the optical flow that reflects the magnitude and direction of the motion of image regions, as shown in Fig. 45b. Based on that, the current position of a street segment detected in the past can be determined and used for a fusion with the current road detection results. However, the optical flow has certain drawbacks. First, it's to date high computational costs make it scarcely applicable in domains with hard real-time constrains, as the car domain. Second, the optical flow cannot be calculated at the borders of an image and is error prone due to ambiguities resulting from the aperture problem, illumination change, and camera noise [137]. Instead of detecting the motion of all image regions based on the optical flow, the approach proposed here concentrates on the drivable street plane alone, relying on the bird's eye view (see Fig. 45c and Fig. 47).

7.2.2. System Description

In the following, a rough overview of our approach of bird's-eye-view-based temporal road integration is given (see Fig. 46). Thereafter, all processing steps and their theoretical background are described in more detail.

As input data our system uses 400x300 monocular gray value images and a binary map of the currently detected street segment. The images are used for calculating the bird's eye view, which is a representation of the scene as viewed from above (see Fig. 47a and

(a)   (b)   (c)

Figure 45. Exemplary inner-city frame: (a) Hand-labeled ground truth street segment, (b) Optical flow (colors code the direction of the motion), (c) Bird's eye view.

Fig. 45c). In the following step, the bird's eye view is used for detecting the motion of the static vehicle environment based on Normalized Cross Correlation (NCC). Based on these correlation results the current and past street segments are fused by temporal integration on the bird's eye view. The fused street segments are then mapped back to the perspective view corresponding to the input image.

The system takes optional input data that improves the quality and makes the temporal integration more robust. As such optional input data, stereo images as well as the longitudinal ego velocity and yaw rate of the CAN bus of our prototype vehicle are processed. The depth map that is calculated from stereo images (using the commercial "Small Vision System" [111], see Sect. 6.2.) is the basis for correcting the changes in the pitch and roll angle. An uncompensated change in the pitch and roll angles make the bird's eye view unstable in case the car brakes or the street profile is not flat. The CAN data is used for predicting the motion of the car based on a single track model. The predicted motion is used for determining the anchor for the correlation on the bird's eye view. The usage of CAN data makes the system faster. Still, without CAN data the detection quality is not reduced.

In the following, the processing steps (as depicted in Fig. 46) are described in more detail. First, the camera lens distortion is corrected. The undistorted vertical and horizontal pixels v and u are computed on the initial (distorted) vertical and horizontal pixels v_d and u_d based on Equation (76) and (77).

The undistortion is based on a lens distortion model (described in [109]) that uses radial (k_1 and k_2) and tangential distortion coefficients (k_3 and k_4). The undistortion step is essential in order to allow a correct mapping of the image pixels to the bird's eye view. It is important to note that for the bird's eye view as a metric representation, the undistortion step makes sure that the proportions in the bird's eye view match the world.

Then the bird's eye view is calculated on the undistorted pixels v and u based on Equ. (3) and (3) by inverse perspective mapping of the 3D world points X, Y, and Z to the 2D (u,v) image plane (see Fig. 47b for the notation in our coordinate system). The equations

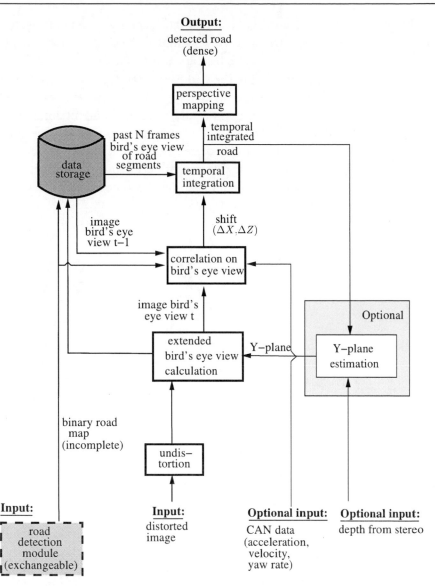

Figure 46. System structure: Temporal road segment integration (the dashed module can be exchanged with the road detection algorithm preferred by the user, optional module highlighted in red).

describe how to map a 3D position of the world to the 2D image plane (refer to [112]). More specifically, only the image pixels (u,v) that are needed to get a dense metric bird's eye view plane are mapped into the XZ-plane. The usage of inverse perspective mapping makes the inversion of Equ. (3) and (4) for calculating the bird's eye view obsolete.

As can be seen in Equ. (3) and (4) the 3D world position coordinates X, Y, and Z of all image pixels (u,v) are needed for computing the bird's eye view. However, by using a monocular system, one dimension (the depth Z) is lost. A solution to this dilemma is the so-called flat plane assumption. Here, for all pixels in the image, the height Y is set to 0.

Based on this, only objects in the image with $Y = 0$ (especially, the street we are interested in) are mapped correctly to the bird's eye view, while all the other regions are stretched to infinity in the bird's eye view (for example the cars in Fig. 45c).

In case this assumption is not fulfilled (i.e., the street surface is not flat) the bird's eye view is inaccurate, which leads to decreasing quality of the temporal integration. To allow a stable bird's eye view even in case of non-flat street surfaces and pitching of the vehicle, stereo data from our stereo camera setup is used. In order to enhance the robustness of the correction, only pixels that belong to the currently detected street segment are used for surface estimation. More specifically, the differences between the coordinate axes and the street surface in terms of the pitch $\Delta\theta_X$ and roll angle $\Delta\theta_Z$, as well as the height of the camera over the ground Δt_2 are computed:

$$Y \quad = Y_0 + aZ + bX \tag{109}$$
$$\Delta\theta_Z \quad = atan(b) \tag{110}$$
$$\Delta\theta_X \quad = atan(a) \tag{111}$$
$$\Delta t_2 \quad = Y_0. \tag{112}$$

This is done based on the 3D position for all image pixels derived from the stereo disparity (see Fig. 35 for 3D data of a sample image). The flat plane assumption $Y = 0$ is then replaced by $Y = f(X,Z)$ leading to an extended bird's eye view. In our implementation a first order model for the street surface (linear hyperplane) is used as shown in Equ. (109) (see [138] for more details). Results have shown that higher order models lead to inferior performance. The reason for this is the restraint number of 3D measurement points at the borders of the image, since only reliable pixels belonging to the detected street are used for the surface estimation. Since the estimated surface is noisy (stereo data is calculated

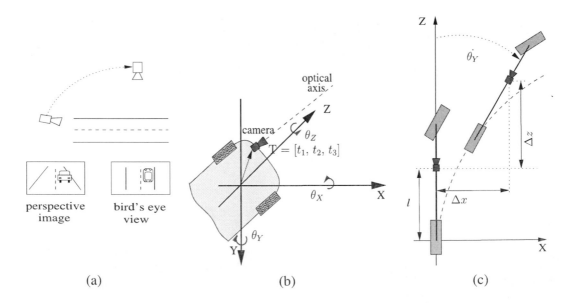

(a)   (b)   (c)

Figure 47. (a) Visualization of the bird's eye view, (b) Coordinate system and position of the camera (car is heading in Z-direction), (c) Single track vehicle model.

based on error prone correlation between the left and right image), a linear Kalman filter is used on the parameters Y_0, a, and b that raise the performance considerably. A possible improvement would be to use a model of the vehicle kinetics (containing damper and spring characteristics, realistic distribution of the vehicle mass) for the Kalman prediction (as proposed in [139]) instead of the linear prediction model used here.

By NCC-based correlation between the current and the stored previous bird's eye view the vehicle motion (ΔX, ΔZ) since the previous time step is detected. A single track vehicle model, as depicted in Fig. 47c, predicts the starting point $x_t = x_{t-1} + \Delta x$ and $z_t = z_{t-1} + \Delta z$ of the NCC correlation patch of time step t-1 in the current bird's eye view map. The values Δx and Δz are calculated based on the sample time T, the distance of the camera from the rear wheel l, as well as the yaw rate $\dot{\theta}_Y$, and lateral velocity $\dot{Z}$ from the CAN bus (see single track model Equ. (113) and (114)):

$$\Delta x = \frac{\dot{Z}}{\dot{\theta}_Y}(1 - cos(\dot{\theta}_Y T)) + sin(\dot{\theta}_Y T)l \tag{113}$$

$$\Delta z = \frac{\dot{Z}}{\dot{\theta}_Y} sin(\dot{\theta}_Y T) + cos(\dot{\theta}_Y T)l - l. \tag{114}$$

The derived longitudinal and lateral motions as well as rotational change (i.e., yaw angle) between the current and the previous bird's eye view are stored along with the incremental motion between the previous $N = 40$ frames (equivalent to 4 seconds of processing by our prototype vehicles' vision system).

The NCC correlation patch on the bird's eye view is selected to contain enough structure (using the entropy-based measure described in Sect. 4.4.), which improves the accuracy of the NCC. Furthermore, it is assured that the patch belongs to the detected street and that it is not too far away from the ego vehicle, since the resolution of the bird's eye view decreases with growing distance to the vehicle.

The bird's eye view maps of the detected street segments of the previous $N = 40$ frames are calculated and stored. The stored incremental motion during the past 4 seconds is integrated and used to shift all stored bird's eye view street segments correspondingly. Then the shifted previous 40 bird's eye view street segments are weighted (weights α_t) and summed up by:

$$S_{\text{integ}} = \sum_{t=1}^{N} \alpha_t S_t \text{ with } \sum_{t=1}^{N} \alpha_t = N. \tag{115}$$

Thereafter, the sum of the street segments $S_{\text{integ}}(X,Z)$ is related to the maximum possible number of overlaid street segments $S_{\text{max}}(X,Z)$, which results in an Integrated Road Probability Map (IRPM):

$$IRPM = \frac{S_{\text{integ}}(X,Z)}{S_{\text{max}}(X,Z)}. \tag{116}$$

Please note that $S_{\text{max}}(X,Z)$ changes depending on the position in the bird's eye view map. The following final threshold operation determines the final temporal integrated street segment S_{final} in the bird's eye view representation:

$$S_{\text{final}} = \begin{cases} 1 & \forall\, IRPM(X,Z) \geq \beta \\ 0 & \forall\, IRPM(X,Z) < \beta \end{cases}. \tag{117}$$

The weight α_1 in Equation (115) is set high to ensure that the pixels in the current detected street segment are with a high probability also present in the final temporal integrated street segment. The other weights α_t could be set dynamically dependent on a quality measure of the bird's-eye-view-based NCC or the road detection system as well as the capturing time t. The threshold β in Equ. (117) is currently set to 0.7. This means that a pixel is classified as street if at least 70% of the overlaid past street segments have voted for street.

Next, the final temporal integrated street segment S_{final} is mapped back to the image using Equ. (3) and (4). For this operation the resolution of the street segment in the bird's eye view representation needs to be high (which is done by upsampling the size by factor of 4) in order to allow a lossless perspective mapping of the street segment. The perspective mapping step produces equidistant, periodic spaces in the street segment directly in front of the car (see Fig. 48a). These spaces are filled using a morphological close operation with a small morphological structuring element to prevent adding too many false positive street pixels (see Fig. 48b). In other words, openings in the bird's eye street segment (that, e.g., correspond to objects on the street) are retained in the final perspectively mapped street segment. Such openings are explicitly checked for objects in the implemented ADAS (see Sect. 3.).

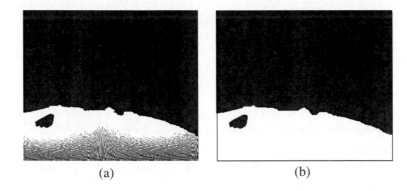

(a)   (b)

Figure 48. Final morphological fill operation for closing spaces in the street segment that are due to perspective mapping (justified openings are preserved): (a) Raw perspectively mapped street segment, (b) After morphological closing.

The following section shows that the proposed temporal integration procedure results in an enhanced street segmentation. The final detected street segment has fewer holes and is dynamically more stable than that of other approaches, which allows complex path-related applications.

7.3. Self-Adaptive Approach for Curbstone and Roadside Detection

As part of the human-like "Attentive Co-Pilot", a subsystem for the detection of curbstones and elevated roadsides was developed that relies on biological principles. This system will be described and evaluated in this section.

In general, a robust approach for the detection of curbstones and elevated roadsides would improve various other system percepts in an ADAS (e.g., in a more precise environmental map a pedestrian could be assigned to the sidewalk, the vision processing could be guided to suspicious objects near the detected roadside, a precise localization in a digital map would be possible). Furthermore various system tasks in inner-city become possible (improvement of autonomous parking maneuvers, improved collision avoidance in inner-city or more precise analysis of intersections).

As the following Sect. 7.3.1. will show, only few dedicated approaches for curbstone and elevated roadside detection exist that mainly suffer from different limitations. Most of them rely on a single sensor approach, disregarding the full potential of sensor fusion. As opposed to that, the approach described in Sect. 7.3.2. relies on the fusion of different sensor modalities using biologically inspired methods.

7.3.1. Related Work

Only few dedicated approaches for the detection of curbstones and elevated roadsides exist. Typically these approaches rely on a single sensor for the generation of 3D data. Based on this 3D data a height map of the environment can be generated and suspicious edges are detected and refined.

More specifically, in [140] a laser scanner is used to derive 3D data of the environment. The derived differences in height of neighboring scan points are thresholded, filtered and a line model is fitted. The laser scanner used in this application is marked by a relatively low frame rate, which restricts the maximum supported velocity. Furthermore, the range of robust detection of curbs is restricted due to the growing influence of noise with increasing distance to the ego vehicle.

Another more sophisticated approach is presented in [141]. For generating dense 3D data, a stereo camera setup is used. The authors propose the computation of a so-called Digital Elevation Map (DEM), which is a height map of the scene as viewed from above. On the DEM an edge detection, filtering and spline fitting is realized. Although the presented DEM is very noisy, the gathered results appear to be robust. As the presented results show, only curbs that are near to the vehicle can be detected. This is due to the growing influence of inaccuracies (e.g., the quantization error) with increasing distance to the ego vehicle (see [26] for a comprehensive treatment of this issue).

Other approaches fuse different sensor outputs in order to improve the detection robustness. For example, in [142] a laser sensor is combined with a monocular camera. The single-layer laser sensor is used to detect the position where the curbstone cuts the sensed layer. This point is used as starting point for the image processing. More specifically, a static edge detector is applied starting from the laser-sensed curbstone. Since, in some cases the appearance of curbstones only slightly differs from the road (i.e., virtually no edge is present in the captured image) this approach is marked by a restricted robustness. Another multi-sensor approach is described in [143]. Here stereo data and vision data is fused using probabilistic methods. The described approach realizes a late fusion of the road detection results of all present sensors. More specifically, curbstones are detected by specific edge filters and elevated roadsides by the stereo sensor. No early information fusion between the detection results takes places, limiting the achievable performance gain from sensor fusion.

Newly emerging multilayer laser scanners offer novel possibilities for the detection of curbstones and road boundaries, since such sensors combine high frame rates with a high accuracy 3D scan (see e.g., [144] for typical high precision applications of such sensors).

However, it is important to note the relatively high costs of this sensor type.

As opposed to that, stereo cameras are getting affordable and technologically sound (e.g., robust solutions for calibrating the cameras exist) and require a comparatively low amount of space in the vehicle. Still, as described above sufficient accuracy for curb detection can only be gained in the first few meters from the ego-vehicle. To solve this dilemma, our contribution proposes a specific fusion of 3D and vision data. Vision data is marked by its high information density. The vision-based detection of curbstones and lane borders is possible even at large distances. Still, curbstones and lane borders can have various appearances, which makes the design of a generic appearance-based model difficult. As described in the following, in the here proposed system stereo data is used to detect curbstones near the vehicle. At greater distances a complete switch to vision takes place. The detection result of the stereo cue is used to adapt a vision template of the present curbstone/elevated roadside, while relying on biologically inspired approaches for signal processing.

7.3.2.   System Description

The proposed overall system concept for the adaptive detection of curbstones and elevated roadsides is depicted in Fig. 49. After giving a rough overview of the major processing steps, all system modules are described in detail.

The proposed system consists of two major parts. First a stereo-based detection step, second a vision-based detection step that is initialized and modulated by the results of the first. The stereo-based curbstone detection relies on dense 3D data coming from a stereo camera setup. Based on that, a specific height map (the so-called Digital Elevation Map) is computed and temporally integrated in order to reduce noise. On this thereby extended Digital Elevation Map, a specific biologically motivated edge filtering is applied resulting in a robust curbstone detection up to a distance of 9 meters from the vehicle. Based on the stereo detection result a vision template of the roadside is generated and adapted. Using this template, the course of the roadside is detected via means of computer vision. The second detection step stops, when the statistical properties of the road and nonroad area (on both sides of the road) change abruptly. This change typically marks an erroneous vision-based curbstone detection far in the distance or an object that occludes the roadside.

In the following, all system modules are described in detail. The system uses pairs of color images of 300x400 pixels captured by a stereo camera setup mounted in the car as input information. After an image undistorsion and rectification step (see [109]) as well as a transformation into grayscale, a dense disparity $D(u, v)$ is computed using correspondence search with a probabilistic matching algorithm (see [108] for details). Based on the disparity image the 3D world position for all image pixels can be computed using the previously introduced Equation (80), (81), and (82).

Please refer to Fig. 35 for a visualization of the used dense stereo data and Fig. 47b for the here applied coordinate system.

In the following step, the stereo maps $Z_{\text{stereo}}(u, v)$, $Y_{\text{stereo}}(u, v)$, $X_{\text{stereo}}(u, v)$ are unrectified (i.e., the prior rectification before disparity computation is neutralized) to make them comparable to the input image in terms of pixel position. Now, the so-called Digital Elevation Map (DEM) is computed, which is a metric height map of the scene as viewed from above (see [145] for details). However, as dedicated testing has revealed, the plain

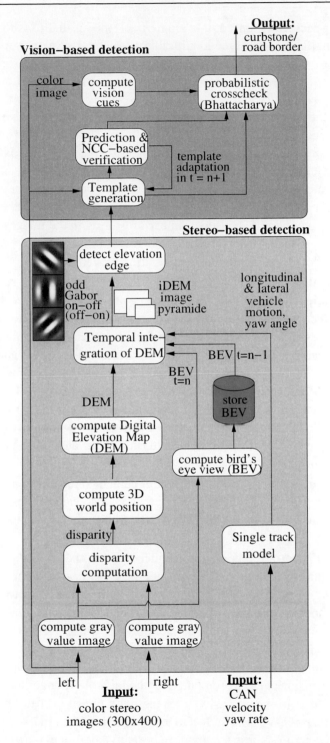

Figure 49. System architecture of the curbstone detection system.

DEM is too noisy for a direct elevation edge detection (see Fig. 50e). Therefore different from [145] and hence as a novel approach a temporal integration procedure is applied on the DEM. More specifically, based on a single track model that uses the vehicle velocity and yaw-rate from the CAN bus, the longitudinal and lateral vehicle motion as well as yaw angle is estimated. Furthermore, from the right camera image a bird's eye view representation (see [112] for background information) is computed for all input images. The birds eye view (BEV) is a metric representation of the scene as viewed from above that results from remapping the gray scale input image (see Fig. 47a and 50b). Using the BEV of the current and previous image the motion of the vehicle is computed using Normalized Cross Correlation (NCC). In order to reduce the computational costs of the NCC, the estimated motion of the vehicle from the single track model is used to define an anchor point for the correlation template in the current BEV. Based on this procedure, the vehicle motion of the previous 10 time frames is determined and stored. The DEMs of the previous 10 time frames are shifted accordingly and superimposed resulting in the integrated DEM (iDEM). As Fig. 50d shows the iDEM is marked by much less noise as the DEM in Fig. 50c (see [20] for technical details on the temporal integration procedure).

Finally, on the iDEM an elevation edge detection is realized. More specifically, odd Gabor filters of the orientations 45, 90 and 135 degree are applied on three scales for reducing the computational costs, while allowing the detection of different edge widths. For that, on the iDEM a three level Gaussian image pyramid is computed. The applied Gabor filters are biologically motivated image filters that were shown to exist in the vision pathway of the mamal brain (see [17] for the biological and [52] for a theoretical background on this filter type). For the right/left roadside odd Gabor filters with off-on/on-off contrast type selectivity are used (refer to Fig. 51 and 50e for an example and [146] for technical details on this specific decomposition technique for Gabor filters). By decomposing the Gabor filters, a simple and effective way for side-specific filtering of elevated edges on the right and left roadside becomes possible.

Dedicated evaluation has shown that (for our camera setup) from a distance of about 9 meters on a curb detection on stereo starts to get noisy and cannot run robustly. Therefore, stereo is used as cue for roadside detection for the first 9 meters distance from the vehicle only.

As stated by [17], also psychophysical evidence exists that marks stereo as the primary depth cue of the human for the first few meters only. After that other (monocular) vision features take over. In accordance to that, the processing is switched to vision-based edge detection. More specifically, the last stereo-based elevation edge measurement is used to adapt a vision template using the data of the left color image. After a prediction step (a segment-wise linear line model is applied) the template is used to verify and correct the real position of the roadside using NCC. In case of a low NCC value a probabilistic crosscheck is done. For that 5 vision cues are computed on the left color image: the hue and saturation channel of the HSI color space, as well as the edge density on the hue, saturation and intensity. All 5 features have been shown to be robust cues for unmarked road detection (see [26] for technical details on these features). In order to determine, if a vision-based detected roadside segment is valid, image patches left respectively right of the roadside segment (subsequently called "road patch" P_{road} and "nonroad patch" $P_{nonroad}$) are compared to their template counterparts T_{road} and $T_{nonroad}$. The named templates are derived from the valid roadside region that was previously determined using the DEM. The comparison between the road/nonroad patches and their templates is realized by applying the distance measure

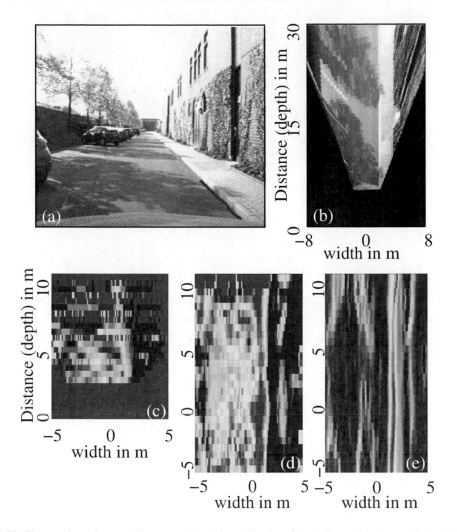

Figure 50. Exemplary inner-city scenario (visualization for right curbstone only): (a) Captured image with detected right curbstone (blue line: stereo-based, green line: vision-based), (b) Bird's eye view, (c) DEM, (d) Temporal integrated DEM, (e) Odd Gabor off-on filtered.

$\delta(P_k, T_k)$ with $k \in \{\text{road, nonroad}\}$ that is based on the Bhattacharya coefficient (a measure for determining the similarity between two histograms) calculated on the histograms $H_i^{P_k}$ and $H_i^{T_k}$ of the image patches of all $N = 5$ vision cues:

$$\delta(P_k, T_k) = \sum_{i=1}^{N} \sqrt{1 - \gamma(H_i^{P_k}, H_i^{T_k})} \tag{118}$$

$$\gamma(H_i^{P_k}, H_i^{T_k}) = \sum_{\forall u, v} \sqrt{H_i^{P_k}(u, v) H_i^{T_k}(u, v)}.$$

In case $\delta(P_k, T_k)$ is bigger than the maximum distance between all previously found (valid) DEM road/nonroad patches, the newly found roadside segment is invalid and the

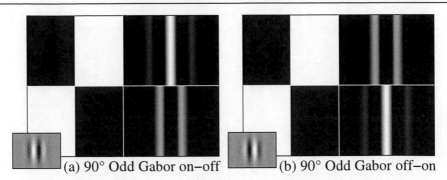

(a) 90° Odd Gabor on–off   (b) 90° Odd Gabor off–on

Figure 51. Application of 0 degree odd Gabor filter kernels on simplified road border images: (a) Kernel for on-off contrasts (left road border), (b) Kernel for off-on contrasts (right road border).

algorithm stops. A big distance $\delta(P_k, T_k)$ can result from a detection error (typically happening far in the distance) or from an object that occludes and interrupts the roadside. The thereby gathered information can be used in our biologically motivated ADAS to guide the attention. In case the roadside is interrupted in the vicinity of the camera-carrying ego-vehicle, the attention system could be set to analyze the specific image region more closely in order to rule out a potential danger coming from a so far unknown object on the road.

In the following, an abundant evaluation of the described algorithm will allow the assessment of its capabilities and robustness.

8. Evaluation Results

In Sect. 8.1. individual system modules are evaluated that play an important role for the presented cognitive ADAS architecture. In Sect. 8.2. the overall system properties will be assessed. In Sect. 8.2.1. the system ability of purely vision-driven autonomous braking on a stationary vehicle is tested in an exemplary highway construction site. Then in Sect. 8.2.2., based on a complex inner-city scenario it is shown how the system proactively plans and verifies expectations in order to allow a safe interaction with the environment (corresponding to the control instances 6. and 7. in Sect. 3. on page 69).

8.1. Evaluation of System Modules

In the following section, the attention sub-system, the depth features, classifier performance, and the road detection sub-system are evaluated.

8.1.1. Evaluation of Attention Sub-system

First, the system properties related to the challenges defined in Sect. 4.3. are evaluated. All results are calculated on five real world data sets (cars, reflection post, construction site, inner-city sequence, toys in an indoor scene) accessible in the internet (see [147]).

High Feature Selectivity

The gain of this approach was exemplarily shown in Sect. 4.2.2. based on the suppression of the horizon edge (see Fig. 14c for a visualization of the diminished influence of the horizon edge on the (TD modified) BU saliency on a real world example). For evaluation, the measures average FoA hit number ($\overline{Hit}$) and average detection rate ($\overline{DRate}$) were calculated. The named evaluation measures were introduced by [18]. While $\overline{DRate}$ is the ratio of the number of found task-relevant objects to the overall number of task-relevant objects, $\overline{Hit}$ states that the object was found on average with the $\overline{Hit}$'th generated FoA. Hence, the smaller $\overline{Hit}$ is, the earlier an object is detected (see [1] for more details on these measures). Table 4 qualitatively shows the significant performance gain of attentional sky suppression versus no horizon edge handling based on real world benchmark data.

Table 4. Benefit of attentional sky suppression on real world data

Search target	# test images	a) original BU $\overline{Hit}$ ($\overline{DRate}$)	b) attentional sky supp. $\overline{Hit}$ ($\overline{DRate}$)	c) sky masked $\overline{Hit}$ ($\overline{DRate}$)
Cars	54	3.06 (56.3%)	2.19 (71.4%)	2.47 (71.4%)

Comparable TD and BU Saliency Maps

The used feature normalization prevents noise on the saliency map and ensures the preservation of the absolute level of feature activation. Using a TD weight set that supports certain object-specific features, the normalization procedure hence ensures that the TD map will show high activation if and only if the searched object is really present. Figure 52f shows that the maximal attention value on the TD saliency map for cars rises when the car comes into view (see [147] for downloadable result sequence).

In order to evaluate the generic nature of the attention-based TD search, cars and reflection posts (useful for unmarked road detection as done, e.g., in [148]) were used as LTM search objects. The results are presented in Tab. 5, showing that incorporating TD information improves the search performance considerably. Please note that when changing the LTM search object, besides an exchange of the LTM image patches and an appropriate training of the object classifier no modification in the system structure is required. Again, for evaluation the measures average FoA hit number ($\overline{Hit}$) and average detection rate ($\overline{DRate}$) were calculated. The choice of training images has only small influence on the search performance as the comparable results for different sets of training images show (see Tab. 5).

The evaluation revealed the highest hit numbers and detection rates for pure TD search ($\lambda = 1$). However, the influence of task-unspecific saliency (i.e., $\lambda < 1$) has to be preserved to avoid inattentional blindness (see Sect. 4.1. and [33] for details on this concept).

The presented results support the generic nature of the TD tunable attention sub-system during object search. Moreover, the attention system can be perceived as a common tunable front-end for the various other system tasks, e.g., as lane marking detection (as described in Sect. 3.). Following this concept, the task-specific tunable attention system can be used for scene decomposition and analysis, as it is shown exemplarily on two typical German highway scenes in Fig. 53.

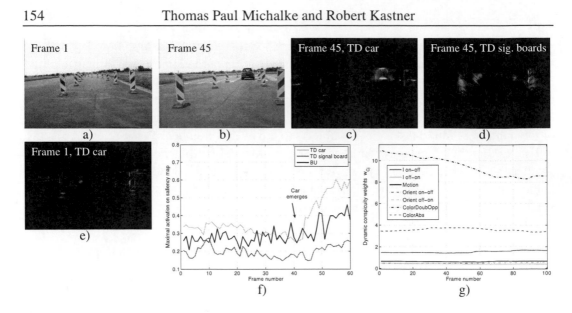

Figure 52. Evaluation of normalization: a),b) Input images c)TD saliency tuned to cars, d)TD saliency tuned to signal boards, e)TD saliency tuned to cars (noise, since no car is present), f)Maximal saliency activation level on BU, TD car and TD signal board map, g) Dynamically adapted conspicuity weights w_{C_j} (homeostasis) for the M=7 modalities.

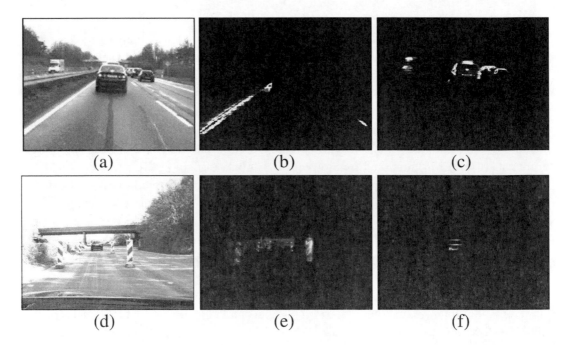

Figure 53. Attention-based scene decomposition: (a) Highway scene, (b) TD attention tuned to lane markings, (c) TD attention tuned to cars, (d) Construction site, (e) TD attention tuned to signal boards, (f) TD attention tuned to cars.

Comparability of Modalities

The used dynamic adaptation of w_{C_j} (for a theoretical background of the biological

Table 5. Search performance for BU- and TD-based LTM object search for cars and reflection posts for 2 different training sets

Target	# Test images (objects)	# Trai-ning im	$\overline{Hit}$ (DRate) pure BU ($\lambda = 0$)	pure TD ($\lambda = 1$)
Cars		54 (self test)		1.53 (100%)
Training set 1	54 (58)	3	3.06 (56.9%)	1.82 (96.6%)
Training set 2		3		1.74 (93.1%)
Reflect. posts		56 (self test)		1.85 (66.3%)
Training set 1	56 (113)	6	2.97 (33.6%)	2.25 (52.2%)
Training set 2		7		2.36 (52.2%)

concept of homeostasis, see Equation (42)) causes a twofold performance gain. First, the a priori incomparable modalities can be combined yielding a well balanced BU and TD saliency map. Secondly, the system adapts to the dynamics of the environment preventing varying modalities from influencing the system performance (e.g., in the red evening sun the R color channel will not be overrepresented in the saliency). Figure 52g) depicts the dynamically adapted w_{C_j}. Table 6 shows a noticeable gain in the signal to noise ration (SNR) on the overall saliency for 26 traffic relevant objects (e.g., traffic light, road signs, cars), comparing the dynamically adapted w_{C_j} vector with a locally optimized static w_{C_j} vector.

Table 6. Comparability of modalities via homeostasis

Traffic-relevant objects	#images (obj)	$\overline{SNR}_{obj}$ using static w_{C_j}	$\overline{SNR}_{obj}$ using dynamic w_{C_j}
Inner-city sequenc	20 (26)	2.56	2.86 (+11.7%)

Support of Conjunctions of Weak Object Features in the TD Path

The support of conjunctions of weak object features in the TD path is assured since w_i^{sparse} is used in BU only. Evaluation on 54 images with cars as TD search object shows that the average object signal to noise ratio ($\overline{SNR}_{obj}$) on the TD saliency map (defined as the mean activation in the object versus its surround) decreases by 9% when w_i^{sparse} is also used in the TD path. For evaluation, weak object feature maps are defined as having the current maximum outside the object region but still having object values of at least 60%

of the maximum within the object. For the used 54 traffic scene images on average 11% of all feature maps are weak. In case weak feature maps are used to optimally support the TD saliency in an excitatory way $\overline{\mathrm{SNR}}_{obj}$ on the TD saliency map increases by 25%. The results are aggregated in Tab. 7. Figure 54a shows that the number of excitatory TD weights w_i^{TD} decreases the bigger K_{conj} (see Equation (2)) is. An object-dependent trade-off exists since the TD saliency map gets sparser the bigger K_{conj} is.

Table 7. Improvement due to support of weak feature conjunctions

TD search target	# test image	$\overline{\mathrm{SNR}}_{obj}$ with w_i^{sparse}	$\overline{\mathrm{SNR}}_{obj}$ without w_i^{sparse}	$\overline{\mathrm{SNR}}_{obj}$ with optimal weak feat. excitation
Cars	54	6.72	7.32 (+9%)	8.41 (+25%)

Changing Lighting Conditions

The feature activation of an image region depends on the illumination. Hence the TD weight set is only optimal for the lighting conditions of the training images and the TD search performance decreases when illumination changes without an adaptation of the camera exposure. It is important to note that in a real world scene the optimal exposure in varying illumination is different for all objects (see Fig. 54b and c), making the exposure control dependent on the current task of the system.

Evaluation is conducted based on a complex indoor test setting showing a collection of toys. In the setup it was possible to control and measure the illumination. As it is shown, the realized exposure control leads to illumination invariance of the TD weight sets (see the reached FoA hit number for the system running the exposure control Tab. 8).

Table 8. Illumination invariance of TD weight sets using dedicated exposure control

Target	# Test im (obj)	Average hit number (and detection rate [%]), TD search $\lambda = 1$				
Toys in a complex in-door setup		Traning illu-mination 75 lx	without expos. control		with expos. control	
			150 lx	15 lx	150 lx	15 lx
	20 (20)	1.95 (100%)	2.74 (95%)	2.83 (30%)	1.80 (100%)	2.0 (100%)

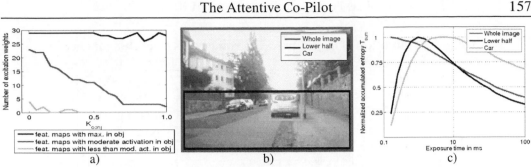

Figure 54. Evaluation of illumination influence: a)# of excitatory TD weights depending on K_{conj}, b)Image regions used for exposure optimization (whole image, lower half, car), c)Energy function: Accumulated entropy T_{sum} with object-dependent optima.

Attention-based Tracker Support

In the following, the performance gain of the described attention-based-tracker-support (see Fig. 3c) is given based on the scenario shown in Fig. 65. In the scenario, a bicycle is tracked over 100 frames. For evaluation the measures defined in the Equ. (119), (120), (121), as well as the center accuracy are used. The equations define different ground-truth-based measures that are used here to assess the position and size of a tracked area in the image that contains an object. The measures are motivated from [121] (with pixels being True Positive (TP), False Negative (FN), False Positive (FP)).

$$\text{Completeness} \quad = \frac{TP}{TP + FN} \tag{119}$$

$$\text{Correctness} \quad = \frac{TP}{TP + FP} \tag{120}$$

$$\text{Quality} \quad = \frac{TP}{TP + FP + FN} \tag{121}$$

On a descriptive level Completeness states, based on given ground truth data, how much of the real object region is covered by the tracked and hence relocalized region. Correctness states how much of the relocalized region actually belongs to the object to allow a better assessment of large regions that show a high Completeness. Quality combines both measures, since between Completeness and Correctness a trade-off is possible. Based on this, the Quality measure should be used for a comparison, since it weights the FP and FN pixels equally. For a more detailed analysis, the Completeness and Correctness state what exactly caused a difference in Quality. The center accuracy describes the mean absolute position error of the middle axis of the object region in pixels. The necessary ground truth data was produced by accurate manual annotation of the bicycle region. As Tab. 9 shows, the applied saliency-enhanced tracking is superior to a classical NCC-based approach. Furthermore, a spatial prior that depends on the Kalman object position uncertainty improves the tracking result.

Attention-based Traffic Sign Recognition

In the following, we evaluate the performance of our traffic sign recognition system with a total of 820 images, taken from two image sequences. The 820 images show 117

Table 9. Evaluation of object tracking robustness (bicycle sequence)

Evaluation measure	NCC-based tracking	Saliency-enhanced tracking without spatial prior	**Saliency-enhanced tracking with spatial prior**
Completeness	0.23	0.60	**0.73**
Correctness	0.31	0.23	**0.37**
Quality	0.16	0.20	**0.30**
Center accuracy	22.05	20.5	**4.6**

relevant traffic signs on 93 images. Therefore, a number of images contain two relevant traffic signs. Nevertheless, the approach and also the evaluation measure treats each traffic sign independently. Based on that, each of the traffic signs on an image has to be classified. No temporal integration (usage of sign information from previous images) of a traffic sign is done here to show the single image performance.

The images were manually labeled, providing the exact position and type of each traffic sign. The images show various inner-city scenes, with different scene complexities (see Fig. 20).

In order to evaluate our algorithm, we adopt the Equations (119), (120), and (121).

The measures have to be interpreted slightly different from the previous application. On a descriptive level the Completeness states, based on given ground truth data, how many of the traffic signs were actually detected. The Correctness states how many of the detected regions were actually relevant traffic signs. The Quality combines both measures. A traffic sign is counted as true positive detection if the corresponding traffic sign class as well as position (with a range of five pixel to the ground truth center) on the image is detected.

The three measures were calculated on the detected traffic signs over all images of the two inner-city sequences. The gathered results are depicted in Tab. 10.

Table 10. Results of the traffic sign recognition evaluation

Traffic signs	# number signs	Correct-ness	Comple-teness	Quality
Stop	64	100%	97%	97%
Give way	53	96.2%	98.1%	94.4%
Both	**117**	**98.3%**	**89.8%**	**88.5%**

An in-depth comparison with other approaches is difficult to realize. This is due to the fact that, there is no well-known benchmark database with image sequences, providing the same input images for all approaches. Some publications use images that always contain traffic signs, others use images of traffic signs with a certain size only, others use images

of highway scenes only and a few generate synthetic images. In general, the class of recognized traffic signs as well as their appearance varies in different countries. Additionally,
numerous publications do not state the reached classification rates. Due to the mentioned
difficulties, a direct comparison with other approaches was not carried out. Nevertheless, an
overall Quality of nearly 90% shows the reliability of our approach, especially when taking
into account that no temporal integration was used.

8.1.2. Evaluation of Scene Classification

In the following, we evaluate the performance of our scene classification by training and test
with a total of 10800 images, taken from several image sequences. The images were manually assigned to one of the categories highway, country road and inner city (see Fig. 28).
The images show various scenes, some containing cars, trucks, and pedestrians, others do
not contain traffic relevant objects. The scenes also show strong differences in the present
lighting conditions. The training was conducted with 600 images per category. Afterwards,
the evaluation was done by five independent runs with 1800 images each (also 600 images
per category). The results of the HPCC on the different test sets showed similar performance on the classification rate (variation of 2%). Table 11 shows the average results over
the five evaluation runs. In the following, the scene classification approach with a single
classification tree for the overall image is called HPCC 1 and the one with 16 single classifications is called HPCC 2.

Table 11. Average results of the scene classification on all test sets

Method	correct classification			total
	Highway	Country road	City	
HPCC 1 with LDA/WDST	98,37	94,03	96,17	96,19
HPCC 1 with Neural Net	98,60	97,77	97,30	97,89
HPCC 2 with LDA/WDST	98,73	84,70	92,80	92,11
HPCC 2 with Neural Net	98,63	96,60	94,93	96,72

To draw a comparison, a system only comprising of LDA with WDST was set-up.
Hence, the LDA/WDST system generates a template for each category without sub-parts. It
is comparable to the work of Oliva and Torralba [98] and showed a total result of nearly 68%
on a single evaluation run. Compared to our results, the HPCC 1 with a neural net reliably
classifies the scene with over 97% accuracy and also requires the fewest computation time.
Again, no temporal integration was conducted. This would improve the detection results
considerably, since the scene context typically is rather stable over time. The HPCC is able
to reliably provide the current scene context as an input for higher level ADAS applications.

The images being incorrectly classified (see Fig. 55 for two examples), show on the one
hand, largely covered areas, due to cars and trucks in front. On the other hand, they show
ambiguous scenes, which would also be difficult for a human to classify correctly, without
temporal integration. Figure 55a shows the driveway to a highway, which is not a typical
scene for highways but should be interpreted as belonging to this category. The Figure 55b

was captured during a stop at a traffic light on a country road, which underlines the smooth transition between the different categories.

Figure 55. Two example images resulting in a wrong scene classification: (a) Driveway to a highway as country road, (b) Country road as inner city

8.1.3. Evaluation of Depth Fusion

Figure 56 shows the EKF-based fusion of depth measurements for a car that drives in front of the prototype vehicle through an inner-city scenario (see Fig. 37b for a visualization of the scenario). For the EKF the sensor variances $\sigma_{radar} = 0.3$, $\sigma_{birds} = 2.8$, and $\sigma_{obj} = 2.7$ as well as the process variance $\sigma_{process} = 0.023$ for the prediction step are used. Note that the usage of two additional monocular depth cues of high variance fused with the low variance Radar cue ensures the availability of depth values even if the interesting objects are outside of the Radar beam.

8.1.4. Evaluation of Classifier Performance

For a proof of concept, the classifier (see Sect. 3.) was trained to distinguish cars from signal boards and clutter. A set of image segments generated by the presented vision system during online operation was used for training. It contains 11000 square image patches of size 64x64 pixels, and was divided into the classes "cars" (2952 patches), "signal boards" (2408 patches) and "clutter" (5803 patches) by visual inspection. Car segments contain complete back- und front-views of cars (at any position) which must be at least half as large as the patch in both dimensions. At equal false positive and true negative rates, for cars an error of 4.7% and for signal boards an error of 9.7% was obtained on equally large test sets. The performance of the trained classifier is shown in Fig. 57 in form of a receiver operator characteristic (ROC) curve that visualizes the trade-off between false positive (clutter recognized as object) and false negative (object recognized as clutter) detections when varying the classification thresholds. The ROC curve was generated using 5-fold cross validation. Furthermore, the quality of the classification is enhanced by the voting process described in Sect. 3..

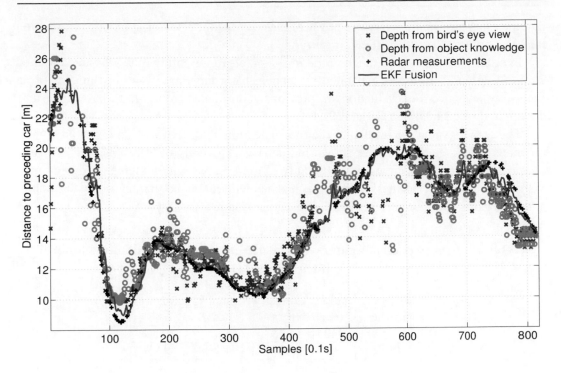

Figure 56. Depth from bird's eye view, object knowledge, Radar and fusion with EKF.

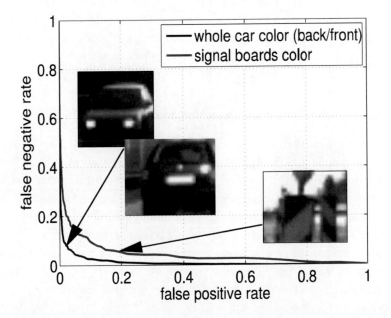

Figure 57. Receiver operator characteristic curve for cars (back and front views) and signal boards.

8.1.5. Evaluation of Unmarked Lane Detection

In the following the performance of the unmarked road detection system is evaluated. The sub-system is able to detect the "drivable road area", which is defined as the space in front that the car can move on safely in a physical sense, but without taking symbolic information into account (e.g., one-way-street, traffic signs).

In order to evaluate how much of the image pixels representing road area are classified correctly, ground truth was generated by manual hand labeling of 440 test images of an inner-city sequence. For evaluation, the previously introduced ground-truth-based measures are applied (see Equation (119), (120), (121).

The gather evaluation results for the road detection algorithm with and without temporal integration (see Sect. 3.) are shown in Tab. 12. A Quality of 89.9% is reached using temporal integration as opposed to a Quality of only 60.5% without temporal integration. While the highest Correctness of 98.1% is reached without temporal integration, this comes at the cost of a low Completeness and, consequently, a low Quality.

Table 12. Comparison of unmarked lane detection with and without temporal integration (TI)

Road detect. approaches	#test im.	Correct- ness	Complet- ness	Quality
Without TI	440	98.1%	61.5%	60.5%
With TI	440	**95.2%**	**94.1%**	**89.9%**

For further evaluation Fig. 58 shows the street detection results on a number of example frames of the inner-city sequence used for evaluation. Please refer to [20] and [26] for more evaluation results concerning the road detection and temporal integration system described. The input images and stereo data used for the evaluation as well as the ground truth data and results are accessible on the internet [149] for open benchmark testing.

8.1.6. Evaluation of the Curbstone Detection System

In Sect. 7.1. a robust unmarked road detection system for inner-city application was presented. Based on that Sect. 7.2. described a temporal integration system for unmarked road detection results. Since the specific analysis of the remaining road detection errors of said system has shown that in challenging situations the curbstone can be surpassed by the detected road segment, we extended the system and added the here presented system as final postprocessing step. More specifically, all road segments surpassing the detected curbstones were corrected (clipped). In order to evaluate the benefit of the here presented curbstone detection system, we used an inner-city sequence (210 images with hand-labeled groundtruth) and the same evaluation methods as before (see Equation (119), (120), and (121)). The evaluation was realized on road detection results with and without temporal integration.

In this context, the Completeness states, based on given ground truth data, how much of the present road was actually detected. The Correctness states how much of the detected road is actually road, in order to avoid classifying all pixels as road leading to a Completeness of 100%. The Quality combines both measures, since between the Completeness and Correctness a trade-off is possible. Based on this, the Quality measure should be used for

Results of standard approach
(Input street segment for us)

Temporal integration
approach

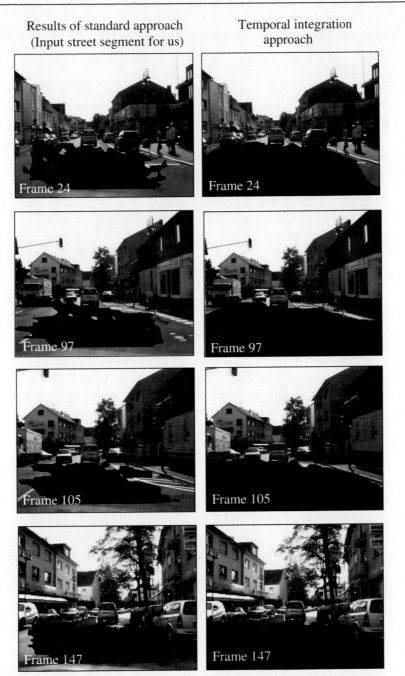

Figure 58. Road detection on example images of an inner-city sequence (left column: Without temporal integration, right column: With temporal integrated street segment).

a comparison, since it weights the FP and FN pixels equally. For a more detailed analysis, the Completeness and Correctness can be evaluated and thereby determining what exactly caused a difference in Quality.

As Tab. 13 shows using the curbstone detection results in a postprocessing step im-

Table 13. Evaluating the infuence of detected curbstones on unmarked road detection results with and without temporal integration

Road detection approaches	# test images	Correct-ness	Comple-teness	Quality
Road detection system [26] without temp. integ.	210	83.9%	77.1%	66.4%
Curb detection, without temp. integ.	210	**95.8%**	**76.7%**	**73.7%**
Road detection with temp. integ.[20]	210	80.2%	88.7%	72.3%
Curb detection, with temp. integ.	210	**94.9%**	**88.1%**	**83.8%**

proved the detection Quality from 66.4% to 73.7% (without applying temporal integration) respectively from 72.3% to 83.8% (with applying temporal integration). When analyzing Tab. 13 more closely, it can be perceived that postprocessing with curbstone detection results lowers the Completeness by a small extend. For both cases the Completeness is diminished: without temporal integration (from 77.1% to 76.7%) and with temporal integration (from 88.7% to 88.1%). More specifically, that means that some true-positively detected road segments were falsely corrected and hence clipped by applying the curbstone detection results. Still, the postprocessing step corrects more false-positive pixels than it falsely corrects true-positive ones. For both cases the Correctness grows: without temporal integration (from 83.9% to 95.8%) and with temporal integration (from 80.2% to 94.9%). Summing up, the Correctness is overproportionally improved leading to the measured significant increase in Quality. In order to facilitate the empirical assessment of the gathered results, in Fig. 59 some typical frames of the used inner-city sequence are depicted.

For our experiments we use a Honda Legend prototype car equipped with a mvBlueFox CCD color camera from Matrix Vision delivering images of an initial resolution of 800x600 pixels at 10Hz, which is hence the processing rate our road detection module has at least to reach. The image data as well as the vehicle state data from the CAN bus is transmitted via LAN to several Toshiba Tecra A7 (2 GHz Core Duo) running our RTBOS integration middleware [150] on top of Linux. As most of the system's submodules are already part of our ADAS running in real-time (e.g., stereo computation, bird's eye view, temporal integration architecture, single track model), we expect the remaining currently Matlab-implemented submodules to fulfill real-time requirements also.

8.2. Evaluation of Overall System Performance

In the following, the overall system performance will be assessed based on a construction site (see Sect. 8.2.1.) and an inner-city scenario (see Sect. 8.2.2.).

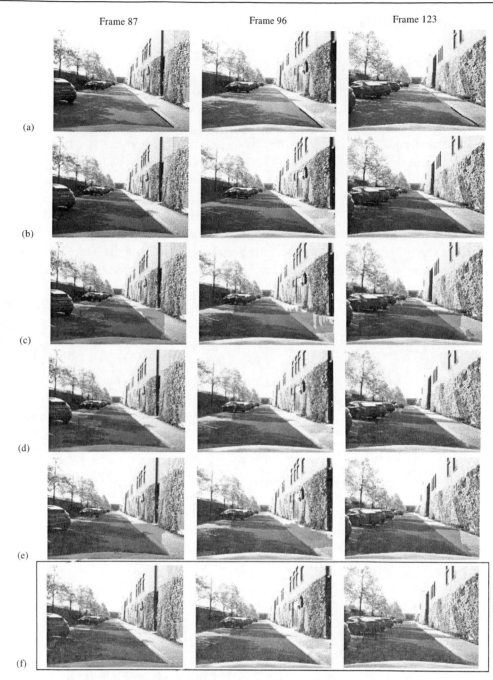

Figure 59. Typical frames of inner-city sequence: (a) Captured images with detected right curbstone (blue line: stereo-based, green line: vision-based), (b) Hand-labeled groundtruth road segments, (c) Detected road without temporal integration, (d) Incorporating curbstone detection result (without temporal integration), (e) Detected road with temporal integration, (f) Final detection result: Incorporating curbstone detection (with temporal integration)

8.2.1. Highway Performance

Scenario

In order to evaluate the proposed system in a challenging situation, the focus is on typical construction sites on highways. This situation is quite frequent and a traffic jam ending exactly within a construction site is a highly dangerous situation: due to the S-curve in many construction sites, the driver will notice a braking or stopping car quite late as the signal boards limit the field of view (see Fig. 60a). The ADAS implementation uses a 3-phase danger handling scheme depending on the distance and relative speed of a recognized obstacle. For example, when the vehicle drives around 40 km/h and a static obstacle is detected in front at less than 33 meters, in the first warning phase a visual and acoustic warning is issued and the brakes are prepared. If the dangerous situation is not resolved by the human driver, the second phase triggers the belt pretensioner and the brakes are engaged with a deceleration of 0.25 g followed by hard braking of 0.6 g in the third phase.

(a)   (b)

Figure 60. Scenario: (a) Schematic sketch of the construction site scenario. Stationary car is visible from 48 meters on. (b) Real scenario.

Technical Setup

For the experiments, a Honda Legend prototype car is used that is equipped with a mvBlueFox CCD color camera from Matrix Vision delivering images of 800×600 pixels at 10 Hz. The image data as well as the Radar and vehicle state data from the CAN bus can be recorded. The recorded data is used during offline evaluation. For online processing all data is transmitted via Ethernet to two laptops (2 GHz Core Duo) running the RTBOS (Real-Time Brain-like Operation System) integration middleware [150] on top of Linux. The individual RTBOS components are implemented in C using an optimized image processing library based on the Intel performance primitives (IPP) [151].

Test Data for Training and Evaluation

In order to gain sufficient training data and for evaluating the actual system performance, an exemplary construction site was set up on a private driving range where data was recorded and the actual online tests were performed.

Influence of Parameters on Detection Performance

All results described in the following are obtained by averaging over 10 recorded sequences in order to lessen statistical outliers. As performance metric, the detection distance is used as this is a good indicator for the efficiency of the saliency system in analyzing complex visual scenes under time constraints. As in each time step of the system running at 10 Hz, one FoA is analyzed in the "what" pathway and potentially added to the STM, [frames] (equivalent to $\frac{1}{10}$ second) are used as time unit.

In the first step, the object detection distance is evaluated depending on STM size N and the TD parameter λ (setting the amount of TD influence, see Equation (1)) while using a TD weight set trained on cars. Figure 61 shows the distance to the stationary car when the first

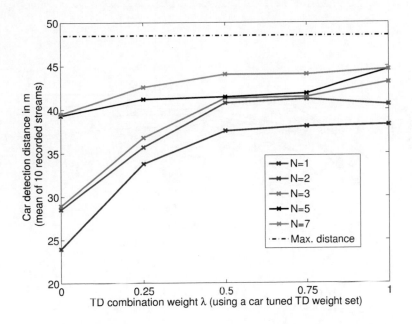

Figure 61. Stationary car detection distance depending on the TD attention parameter $\lambda=0$, 0.25, 0.5, 0.75, and 1 as well as the STM size N=1,2,3,5, and 7 when using ground truth for detecting a hit.

FoA hits the car, which is defined by hand-labeled ground truth on the recorded sequences. It can be seen that the larger the TD influence (search task: find cars) expressed by λ, the earlier the car is detected. Similarly, the more objects are stored in the STM (object number N), the earlier the car is detected as a large part of the visual scene is already contained as (unknown) objects in the STM and therefore inhibited in the saliency map. It can also be deduced that with growing N the influence of TD is reduced since the scene coverage increases.

Including the task of object recognition in the evaluation, Fig. 62 shows the distance to the stationary car when the first FoA hits the target and this RoI is recognized as car by the object classifier. Since the used classification threshold was set high to obtain a low false-positive error rate at the cost of a high false-negative error rate, the distance when the car is detected is smaller than in the evaluation with ground truth. Differing from Fig. 61, at large values of N (see Fig. 62 for N=7) the detection distance worsens again. The reason for this effect is that the system is not using object segmentation algorithms but performs segmentation directly on the saliency image which can lead to enlarged patches suppressing the surround of the found objects as well. In this way, the borders of the car might be suppressed by adjacent signal board patches leading to incomplete car FoAs that are not sufficient for correct classification by the used object classifier. The likelihood that this happens is growing with the growing size N of the STM. However with a growing N also the scene coverage improves. This trade-off leads to the measured results.

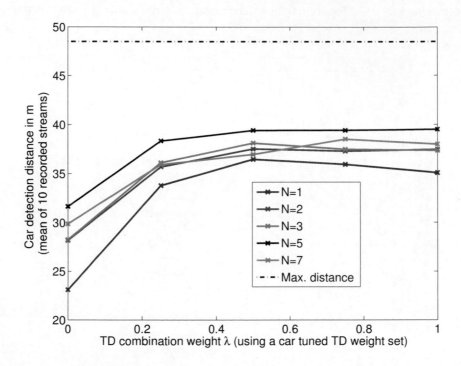

Figure 62. Stationary car detection distance depending on the TD attention parameter λ=0, 0.25, 0.5, 0.75, and 1 as well as the STM size N=1,2,3,5, and 7 when using the classifier for detecting a hit.

Based on Fig. 62 the best choice of λ for detecting cars would be 1, which equals pure TD search mode. However, such a parameterization is not appropriate because this leads to a reduced capability of detecting other objects that are only prominent in the BU saliency (see Fig. 63). Here, it can be seen that with growing λ the average detection distance of signal boards (the only other object class besides cars in the evaluation) drops. Stated differently, the system ignores all other objects while searching for cars in pure TD mode ($\lambda = 1$), which might lead to dangerous situations. The default value for λ was hence set to 0.5 for the online tests.

In the previous evaluations it was assumed that the scene contains more than N objects and used a fixed STM size which is equivalent to storing any object for N frames independent of, e.g., whether it is was correctly recognized. Now an object-specific Time To Live (TTL) is introduced, defining for how many frames an object is stored in the STM before it

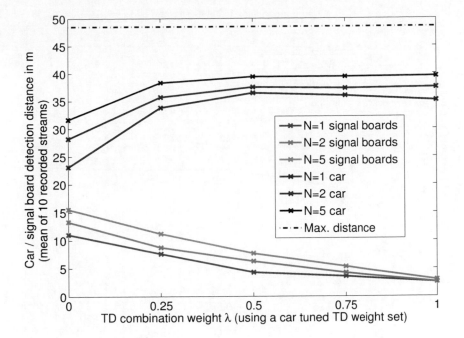

Figure 63. Detection distance depending on the TD attention parameter λ=0, 0.25, 0.5, 0.75, and 1. Average detection distance of signal boards and the stationary car using the object classifier for an STM size of N=1,2, and 5.

is removed. In this way, unknown objects can be tracked for only a short time before a new recognition attempt is carried out if the image region is still salient. Figure 64 shows how the choice of the TTL influences the system performance.

For an object-unspecific TTL of 5 frames the curve is identical to Fig. 63 for N=5. For the object-specific case, the following parameters were chosen $TTL_{sigboard} = 6$ frames for signal boards, $TTL_{cars} = 20$ frames, and $TTL_{unknown} = 3$ frames, leading for the construction site sequences on average to N=5 objects in the STM. Note that the low value of $TTL_{unknown}$ and the high value of TTL_{cars} both support to set the object recognition threshold high, i.e., it is very likely to get an unknown object, which is a false negative car but rather unlikely to get a car that is a false positive.

A clear gain in detection performance can be seen when using object-dependent TTL values, which is due to the fact that FoAs, which hit the car very early are often too small for a reliable classification. These unknown scene parts are suppressed only for 3 frames before the classifier gets a second chance to detect the car. This object-specific TTL parameterization was used during the online tests described below.

Aggregated Evaluation of the Autonomous Braking Behaviour

In the last sub-section, the warning generation was evaluated in detail on 10 recorded construction site sequences used also for evaluation in the previous subsection. In all sequences, the ADAS was able to recognize and track the car from a distance between 42 and 32 meters, while the car was fully visible at a distance of about 48 meters.

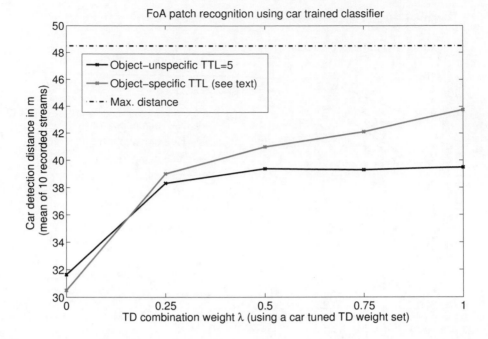

Figure 64. Stationary car detection distance depending on the TD attention parameter λ=0, 0.25, 0.5, 0.75, and 1 while using object-unspecific and object-specific TTL values.

During documented online system tests in the setting depicted in Fig. 60 with the prototype vehicle driving 40 km/h the system detected in 57 of 60 cases the stationary car in time and issued the 3 warning phases as expected including autonomous braking. In the remaining cases, either the object recognition detected a signal board as car and the braking was performed too early or the FoA generation did not deliver a good car RoI position so that the fusion of the car RoI with Radar data failed and no warning/braking was performed at all. Note that the presented vision-based proof-of-concept system completely relies on vision and does not make use of an additional Radar-based emergency braking that would be needed in real traffic as backup for situations in which the presented vision system fails.

8.2.2. Inner-city Performance

In order to qualitatively evaluate the control aspects presented in Sect. 3., results in form of 4 sample frames of a test sequence are presented that show a complex real-world scenario (see Fig. 65). The test sequence is accessible in the internet (see [147]). After a description of the visualized internal system percepts based on Fig. 65a, a detailed description of the gathered results is given. In the top row in Fig. 65a (from left to right) the object-unspecific bottom-up saliency, the top-down attention tuned to the tracked bicycle, and their combination (here with $\lambda = 1$ and a sharp spatial prior for the attention-based tracking support) is shown. In the bottom row left in Fig. 65a the input image including a visualization of the detected road area is shown. In the bottom row in the middle, the input image including the predicted vehicle trajectory (the longer the green region, the faster the camera vehicles moves), the detected dynamic object including its predicted trajectory (the red region codes a negative relative velocity: the longer the red region, the faster the dynamic object moves), and the area covered by the radar sensor (in magenta) is visualized. The bottom right image shows an environmental representation that visualizes the task-relevant dynamic object. An aura around the object codes the position uncertainty of the detected object.

In the scenario, while exploring the scene (with $\lambda=0$, no spatial prior set, and the STM holding up to 5 objects) the camera ego-vehicle detects a dynamic, i.e., moving, object based on the procedure described in Sect. 3. (see Fig. 65a). The object is tracked (in one "what" pathway, the parameter λ is set to 1 allowing an attention-based tracking support, a spatial prior is set that depends on the object position uncertainty, as described in Sect. 3.). The ego-vehicle overtakes the bicycle,giving a blind spot warning. Based on the presented internal 3D representation the bicycle position is predicted linearly even while it is outside the field of view of the camera (see Fig. 65b, the growing position uncertainty is visualized by the growing object aura in the bird's eye view representation). Without any dynamic object in the field of view, λ is set to 0 again, the spatial prior is reset, and the object decay rate is reset to allow the tracking of up to 5 objects. All these adaptations support an object-independent scene exploration. Now, the ego-camera vehicle stops to turn right. The ADAS "remembers" the bicycle and gives a blind spot warning. The ego-vehicle waits for the bicycle to reappear. In order to allow a fast redetection, the top-down attention is tuned to the bicycle, setting a spatial prior with low sharpness. This allows its instantaneous redetection (see Fig. 65c). The object position is updated lowering the position uncertainty. The system tracks the object relying on the attention-based-tracker-support (see Fig. 65d). Summing up, the system at runtime builds up and verifies expectations of the environment, thereby autonomously tuning internal parameters and processes that improve and accelerate the system reaction.

The processing described above relates to one "what" pathway (see Fig. 1), which concentrates on the detection, tracking, and prediction of one dynamic and hence potentially dangerous object. As visualized in Fig. 1, multiple "what" pathways run in parallel. For example, further "what" pathways handle the detection of cars, signal boards, and other traffic-relevant objects using the previously described LTM search (see Sect. 3.) that relies on object-specifically tuned saliency maps. The control of these pathways is realized by the functional mapping described in Sect. 3.. For each of these "what" pathways the object-specific LTM search can be interrupted by a STM search in case an object was lost during tracking (see Sect. 3.). The complete result video is accessible in the internet at [152].

For further qualitative system evaluation, Fig. 66 depicts internal system variables for three sequential frames of another inner-city sequence with cars as LTM search object. As described in Sect. 3., for each new image the attention is calculated and a new FoA is generated via maximum search and segmentation on the saliency map. The detected road area (and thereby also the present lane markings) are mapped out of the saliency map, which decreases the false positive rate of generated FoAs, i.e., less non-car FoAs are generated. In the first frame, the car in front is detected and stored in the representation based on a car-like hole in the detected street segment that modulates the attention (see highlighted region in the saliency map of frame 194 in Fig. 66). Please note that the cars 2 and 3 are not stored in the internal representation, since their position is beyond the represented road environment.

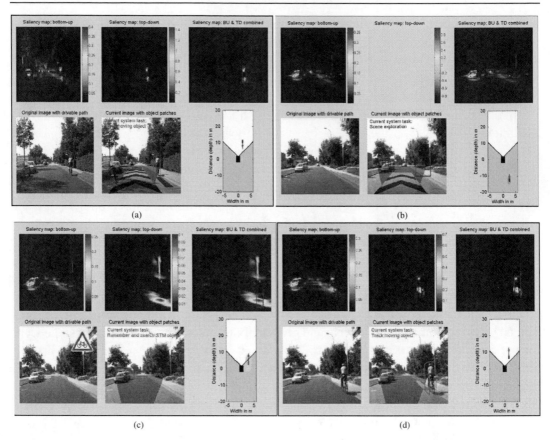

Figure 65. Visualization of system states for bicycle sequence: (a) After its detection the bicycle is tracked, ego-vehicle is closing in, (b) Blind prediction of bicycle, (c) Ego-car searching actively for the bicycle, waiting to turn right, (d) Bicycle redetected successfully, ego-vehicle turns right.

9.   Summary

In modern vehicles, numerous driver assistance functionalities exist that support the driver in typical traffic situations. In general, all these functionalities bring own sensors, processing devices, and actuators. No information fusion takes places between the functionalities, due to among other things unsolved questions in system design that come along with high system complexity. Thereby, the potential to improve the robustness of so far independent system modules as well as the potential to develop higher level functionalities is ignored. Furthermore, the number of driver assistance functionalities is growing constantly in today's vehicles. In the near future, this will lead to problems regarding the limited number of interaction channels to inform the driver of dangerous events (so-called human machine interface (HMI)). Already today, in specific traffic scenarios a contradicting HMI access of different driver assistance functionalities can occur. For solving these challenges, a large-scale driver assistance system is required that integrates and fuses various functionalities (leading to so-called advanced driver assistance systems (ADAS)). Despite the apparent ne-

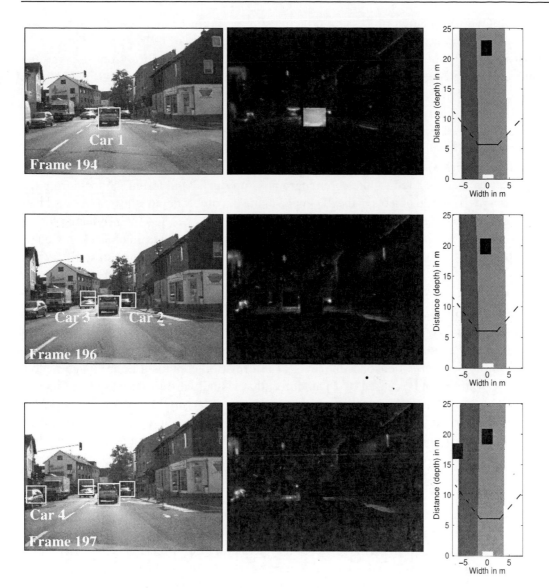

Figure 66. System evaluation on example images of an inner-city sequence. Left column: visualization of found FoAs, middle: calculated saliency map S^{total} (previously found objects are suppressed by inhibition of return), Right column: Visualization of internal representation (dashed line marks the border of the vision field).

cessity of such systems, only a few of these approaches exist in literature. Said systems typically rely on rigid system structures and safely run in clearly defined scenarios only. While it may be argued that the quality of such engineered systems in terms of isolated aspects, e.g., object detection or tracking, is often sound, the solutions lack the necessary flexibility.

Instead of following classical engineering-based approaches, in the contribution at hand, an ADAS is developed that solves the challenges of complex system design by mimicking known information processing principles in the human brain. On the micro-level the realized system copies the signal processing characteristics of neurons in order to reach robust image filtering. On the macro-level the system gets inspiration from the way the human brain organizes higher level signal flows in order to reach a generic system structure (e.g., a task-dependent tunable attention system).

More specifically, on the micro-level various static and dynamic visual features are introduced that are biologically inspired. Inspiration is drawn from known processing principles of the vision pathway in the human brain (i.e., the signal processing characteristics of neurons in the brain). Features for the detection of specific intensity changes, oriented lines and edges as well as a retina-like color space are introduced and tested. Since during the projection of 3D world objects to the 2D image plane the object depth is lost, a distance feature becomes necessary. Four biologically motivated depth cues and their dynamic fusion are described. The realized depth sources are stereo disparity, depth from object knowledge, depth from the bird's eye view and Radar-based depth. Thereby, in sum 130 static feature maps are accessible, by which the proposed ADAS can sense the world. Together with six dynamic feature maps, the ADAS disposes of an overall number of 136 feature maps.

The 136 biologically inspired feature maps are combined in the attention system that is used as common front-end of all vision processes of the presented ADAS. The key aspect and output of the attention system is the saliency map, whose amplitude (i.e., its activation in neurobiological terms) encodes the level of information contained in an image region. A high activation can be caused by 1) an object that visually differs strongly from its surrounding environment (sensory-driven or bottom-up attention) or 2) by an image region that matches the current searched object properties (goal-driven or top-down attention). Both the bottom-up (BU) and top-down (TD) attention use a weighted combination of the features. Five novelties increase the adaptivity of the attention system to the scene and thereby assure a high robustness, which allows for building applications for outdoor scenarios of the dynamic vehicle domain.

The importance of context information for improving the performance of driver assistance functionalities is a widely acknowledged fact in the community. Therefore the ADAS contains a real-time unmarked road detection system that relies on vision as the major cue. As evaluation showed, the so detected road segments match ground truth data well in most situations. However, in case of shadows on the road the detected road segments contain holes and get unstable in time. As a further novelty, for solving these challenges a generic tracking approach for unmarked road detection systems is applied that is based on temporal integration (i.e., integration of road detection results over time). The temporal integration approach was successfully tested on the implemented system described before, but would be suitable to improve any comparable state-of-the-art unmarked road detection system.

In the central part of the contribution, the realized visual features, the attention subsystem, and the unmarked road detection sub-system including the temporal integration approach are combined to a generic, biologically motivated Advanced Driver Assistance System. The attention sub-system, which weights and combines all visual features, allows a task-dependent scene decomposition that enables the system to react in real-time to challenging situations. In the developed ADAS, the attention sub-system is used as front-end for the detection of a stationary vehicle in a highway construction site. In case a quickly approaching vehicle is detected by the system, a danger handling scheme is initiated that in the final phase allows the system to brake autonomously. Different from commercially available systems and approaches in literature, the object detection is based on vision as the main cue.

Based on an abundant system evaluation, system properties could be demonstrated that were measured in psychophysical studies on humans as well. Similar to humans, it could be shown that a number of 5 to 7 stored and tracked objects in the short term memory results in the best overall system performance when searching for a dangerous object under time constraints. Furthermore, it could be shown that the reaction time to unexpected traffic-relevant objects grows with an increasing focus on a specific object class (a phenomenon that is called inattentional blindness in psychophysical studies with humans). Based on these results, it can be stated that the realized ADAS closely models important human information processing principles allowing the usage of the system as attentional co-pilot for human drivers.

10. Future Directions

The performance assessment of the human vision system has revealed capabilities that exceed all known computational vision systems having a comparable image resolution. For example, [153] provides the following Equation for computing the maximum distance D_v, a human is able to visually classify an object in good weather conditions:

$$D_v = \frac{a}{\tan\left(\frac{\pi}{S\,10800}\right)}. \tag{122}$$

With:

a   =   object size in m

S   =   factor of acuteness of vision - usually 1.0.

A vehicle of width $a = 2.5m$ with an acuteness factor $S = 1.0$ can hence be classified from approximately 2500 meters on.

As stated in Sect. 8.2.1. the here proposed ADAS is able to classify cars from about 42 meters on. Among other things (like, e.g., differences in image resolution), the large difference in performance between the human and a technical vision system might be due to the fact that the human integrates information about the scene context and gathered experience. In the discussed example, context information about the road (e.g., the object is positioned on the road), which restricts the potential type of object and object class-related experience (e.g., a car is a fast moving object on the road) is crucial. First approaches to include context into the ADAS are realized in the contribution at hand, in order to improve the object detection. More specifically, the detected road is searched for car-like openings and used to modulate the attention and object segmentation (see Sect. 3.). However, more context information (e.g., scene type: inner-city, urban road, highway) needs to be included, in order to further improve the system performance. In [154] a robust, real-time capable system extension for said basic scene classification is described, which will be incorporated in the "Attentive Co-Pilot" in the near future.

The contribution at hand concentrates mainly on saliency-based attention and building of a generic system that allows the dynamic modulation of modules and links between modules at run-time. The further development of the ADAS focuses on ways to control the designed cognitive system based on reinforcement learning on high system level. After the successful test of the low complexity control approach, in the next step, learning of the functional mapping between the measured input feature space and the output control parameter space will be in the focus. More specifically, it is planned to replay stored sequences of critical traffic situations from a data base. As learn-signal dangerous objects will be manually labeled in these sequences. The system task is to detect the objects early enough. In case the system react too late, the scenario is replayed by the learning algorithm while changing the functional mapping between input and output data of the behavior control module. Also measuring and mimicking the reactions of an experienced driver is envisioned in the future. The introduced system contains first approaches towards such an efficient cognitive control concept. The central assumption, as proposed in this contribution, is that a robust (and as envisioned also learning) system requires a generic system structure with a high number of degrees of freedom for controlling the system reaction and measuring the system state. Therefore, if required, it is planned to further increase the input feature space as well as output control parameter space of the behavior control module in order to increase the number of possible system behaviors and prove the scalability of the approach.

References

[1] S. Frintrop, *Vocus: A visual attention system for object detection and goal-directed search*, Ph.D. thesis, University of Bonn (2006).

[2] H. I. Christensen, H.-H. Nagel (Eds.), *Cognitive Vision Systems: Sampling the Spectrum of Approaches, LNCS,* Springer-Verlag, 2006.

[3] S. Treue, Visual attention: the where, what, how and why of saliency., in: *Current Opinion in Neurobiology*, Vol. 13, 2003.

[4] M. Ikegaya, N. Asanuma, S. Ishida, S. Kondo, Development of a lane following assistance system, in: *Int. Symp. on Advanced Vehicle Control*, Nagoya, 1998.

[5] K. Kodaka, M. Otabe, Y. Urai, H. Koike, Rear-end collision velocity reduction system, in: *Proc. 2003 SAE World Congress*, Detroit, 2003.

[6] K. Kodaka, J. Gayko, Intelligent systems for active and passive safety - Collision Mitigation Brake System, in: Proc. of the ATA_EL conference 2004, Parma, 2004.

[7] WWW, DARPA Urban Challenge, http://www.darpa.mil/grandchallenge/ (2007).

[8] WWW, European Commission Information Society Intelligent Car Initiative, http://ec.europa.eu/informationsociety/activities/intelligentcar/ (2007).

[9] N. Ouerhani, *Visual attention: From bio-inspired modeling to real-time implementation,* Ph.D. thesis, Université de Neuchâtel, Institute de Microtechnique (2003).

[10] R. Kastner, T. Michalke, T. Burbach, J. Fritsch, C. Goerick, Attention-based traffic sign recognition with an array of weak classifiers, in: *IEEE Intelligent Vehicles Symposium,* San Diego, 2010.

[11] E. Dickmanns, Three-stage visual perception for vertebrate-type dynamic machine vision, in: *Engineering of Intelligent Systems (EIS)*, Madeira, 2004.

[12] G. Färber, Biological aspects in technical sensor systems, in: *Proc. Advanced Microsystems for Automotive Applications*, Berlin, 2005, pp. 3–22.

[13] C. Stiller, G. Färber, S. Kammel, Cooperative Cognitive Automobiles, in: *IEEE Intelligent Vehicles Symposium*, 2007, pp. 215–220.

[14] S. Matzka, Y. Petillot, A. Wallace, *Proactive sensor-resource allocation using optical sensors,* in: VDI-Berichte 2038, 2008, pp. 159–167.

[15] WWW, European Project PReVENT, http://www.prevent-ip.org/ (2006).

[16] A. Torralba, Contextual priming for object detection, in: *International Journal of Computer Vision*, Vol. 53, 2003.

[17] S. Palmer, *Vision Science: Photons to Phenomenology*, MIT Press, 1999.

[18] S. Frintrop, *VOCUS: A visual attention system for object detection and goal-directed search,* Ph.D. thesis, University of Bonn Germany (2006).

[19] H. Wersing, E. Körner, Learning optimized features for hierarchical models of invariant object recognition, *Neural Computation* **15** (2) (2003) 1559–1588.

[20] T. Michalke, R. Kastner, J. Fritsch, C. Goerick, A generic temporal integration approach for enhancing feature-based road-detection systems, in: *IEEE Intelligent Transportation Systems Conference*, Beijing, 2008.

[21] R. Klein, Inhibition of return, *Trends in Cognitive Science* **4** (4) (2000) 138–145.

[22] M. Landy, L. Maloney, E. Johnsten, M. Young, *Measurement and modeling of depth cue combinations: in defense of weak fusion* (1995).

[23] S. Palmer, *Vision Science: Photons to Phenomenology,* MIT Press, 1999.

[24] J. Fritsch, T. Michalke, A. Gepperth, S. Bone, F. Waibel, M. Kleinehagenbrock, J. Gayko, C. Goerick, Towards a human-like vision system for driver assistance, in: *IEEE Intelligent Vehicles Symposium*, Eindhoven, 2008.

[25] J. Eggert, C. Zhang, E. Körner, Template matching for large transformations, in: *ICANN* (2), 2007, pp. 169–179.

[26] T. Michalke, R. Kastner, M. Herbert, J. Fritsch, C. Goerick, Adaptive multi-cue fusion for robust detection of unmarked inner-city streets, in: *IEEE Intelligent Vehicles Symposium*, Xian, 2009.

[27] M. Corbetta, G. Shulman, Control of goal-directed and stimulus-driven attention in the brain, *Nature Reviews Neuroscience* **3** (2002) 201–215.

[28] H. Egeth, S. Yantis, Visual attention: control, representation, and time course, *Annual Review of Psychology* **48** (1997) 269–297.

[29] J. Wolfe, T. Horowitz, What attributes guide the deployment of visual attention and how do they do it?, *Nat. Reviews Neuroscience* **5** (6) (2004) 495–501.

[30] C. Koch, S. Ullman, Shifts in selective visual attention: towards the underlying neural circuitry, *Human Neurobiology* **4** (4) (1985) 219–227.

[31] J. Tsotsos, S. Culhane, W. Wai, Y. Lai, N. Davis, F. Nuflo, Modeling visual attention via selective tuning, *Artificial Intelligence* **78** (1-2) (1995) 507–545.

[32] V. Navalpakkam, L. Itti, Modeling the influence of task on attention, *Vision Research* **45** (2) (2005) 205–231.

[33] D. Simons, C. Chabris, Gorillas in our midst: Sustained inattentional blindness for dynamic events, *British Journal of Developmental Psychology* **13** (1995) 113–142.

[34] S. Most, R. Astur, Feature-based attentional set as a cause of traffic accidents, *Visual Cognition* **15** (2) (2007) 125–132.

[35] H. Shinoda, M. Hayhoe, A. Shrivastava, What controls attention in natural environments, *Vision Research* (**41**) (2001) 3535 – 3546.

[36] L. Itti, C. Koch, E. Niebur, A model of saliency-based visual attention for rapid scene analysis, *IEEE Trans. Pattern Anal. Mach. Intell.* **20** (11) (1998) 1254–1259.

[37] S. Frintrop, G. Backer, E. Rome, Goal-directed search with a top-down modulated computational attention system, in: *DAGM-Symposium,* 2005, pp. 117–124.

[38] N. Hawes, J. Wyatt, *Towards context-sensitive visual attention, in: Proceedings of the Second Int. Cognitive Vision Workshop,* Graz, Austria, 2006.

[39] C. Goerick, H. Wersing, I. Mikhailova, M. Dunn, Peripersonal space and object recognition for humanoids, in: *Proc. Int. Conf. on Humanoid Robots,* 2005.

[40] V. Navalpakkam, L. Itti, An integrated model of top-down and bottom-up attention for optimal object detection, in: *Proc. IEEE Conference on Computer Vision and Pattern Recognition (CVPR),* 2006, pp. 2049–2056.

[41] J. Tsotsos, Y. Liu, J. Martinez-Trujillo, M. Pomplun, E. Simine, K. Zhou, *Attending to visual motion, CVIU* **100** (1-2) (2004) 3–40.

[42] G. Backer, B. Mertsching, Integrating depth and motion into the attentional control of an active vision system, in: G. Baratoff, H. Neumann, (Eds.), *Dynamische Perzeption,* St. Augustin (Infix), 2000, pp. 69–74.

[43] L. Itti, G. Rees, J. Tsotsos (Eds.), *Neurobiology of Attention,* Elsevier, 2005.

[44] D. Heinke, G. Humphreys, Computational models of visual selective attention: a review, in: G. Houghton (Ed.), *Connectionist Models in Psychology,* Psychology Press, 2005, pp. 273–312.

[45] S. Frintrop, E. Rome, H. Christensen, Computational visual attention systems and their cognitive foundation: a survey, *ACM Transactions on Applied Percerption (TAP).*

[46] J. Findlay, I. Gilchrist, *Active Vision: The psychology of looking and seeing,* Oxford University Press, 2003.

[47] A. Treisman, The perception of features and objects, in: A. Baddeley, L. Weiskrantz (Eds.), *Attention: Selection, awareness, and control, Clarendon Press,* Oxford, 1993, pp. 5–35.

[48] Z. Aziz, B. Mertsching, Visual search in static and dynamic scenes using fine-grain top-down visual attention, in: *Lecture Notes in Computer Science,* Vol. 5008, 2008, pp. 3–12.

[49] T. Michalke, *Task-dependent scene interpretation in driver assistance*, Ph.D. thesis, Darmstadt University of Technology (2010).

[50] N. Flores-Herr, *Das hemmende Umfeld von Ganglienzellen in der Netzhaut des Auges,* Ph.D. thesis, Frankfurt am Main, Johann Wolfgang Goethe-Universität (2001).

[51] W. von Seelen, Zur Informationsverarbeitung im visuellen System der Wirbeltiere, in: *Kybernetik,* Vol. 7, 1970, pp. 43–60.

[52] R. Trapp, *Stereoskopische Korrespondenzbestimmung mit impliziter Detektion von Okklusionen,* Ph.D. thesis, University of Paderborn Germany (1998).

[53] H. Mallot, Computational vision: *Information processing in perception and visual behavior,* MIT Press Robotica, 2002.

[54] U. Franke, H. Loose, C. Knoeppel, *Lane recognition on country roads, Intelligent Vehicles Symposium,* 2007 IEEE (13-15 June 2007) 99–104.

[55] O. Ramstroem, H. Christensen, *A method for following unmarked roads, in: IEEE Intelligent Vehicles Symposium,* 2005, pp. 650–655.

[56] E. Dickmanns, B. Mysliwetz, Recursive 3-d road and relative ego-state recognition, *IEEE Trans. Pattern Anal. Mach. Intell.* **14** (2) (1992) 199–213.

[57] T. Luo-Wai, Lane detection using directional random walks, in: *IEEE Intelligent Vehicles Symposium,* Eindhoven, 2008.

[58] D. Hubel, T. Wiesel, Receptive fields, binocular interaction and functional architecture in the cat's visual cortex, *Journal of Physiology* **160** (1962) 106–154.

[59] S. Marcelja, Mathematical description of the response of simple cortical cells, *J. Optical Society of America* **70** (11) (1980) 1297–1300.

[60] J. Jones, A. Stepnoski, L. Palmer, The two-dimensional spectral structure of simple receptive fields in the cats striate cortex, *Journal of Neurophysiology* **58** (6) (1987) 1233–1258.

[61] D. Gabor, Theory of communication, *J. IEE* **93** (1946) 429–457.

[62] A. Treisman, S. Gormican, Feature analysis in early vision: Evidence from search asymmetries, *Psychological Review* **95** (1988) 15–48.

[63] D. Forsyth, J. Ponce, *Computer Vision: A Modern Approach*, Prentice Hall, Berkeley, 2003.

[64] B. Jaehne, *Digital Image Processing*, Springer, Berlin, 2005.

[65] R. Hardy, Homeostasis, Arnold, 1983.

[66] T. Michalke, A. Gepperth, M. Schneider, J. Fritsch, C. Goerick, Towards a human-like vision system for resource-constrained intelligent cars, in: *Int. Conf. on Computer Vision Systems*, Bielefeld, 2007.

[67] S. Frintrop, M. Klodt, E. Rome, A real-time visual attention system using integral images, in: *Int. Conf. on Computer Vision Systems*, Bielefeld, 2007.

[68] P. Paclik, Road Sign Recogniton Survey, http://euler.fd.cvut.cz/research/rs2/files/skoda-rs-survey.html (1999).

[69] C. Fang, S. Chen, C. Fuh, Road-Sign Detection and Tracking, *IEEE Transactions on Vehicular Technology* **52** (5).

[70] C. Nunn, A. Kummert, S. Müller-Schneiders, A two stage Detection Module for Traffic Signs, in: *Proc. IEEE Internat. Conf. on Vehicular Electronics and Safety (ICVES)*, 2008, pp. 248–252.

[71] S. Zhu, L. Liu, X. Lu, Color-Geometric Model for Traffic Sign Recognition, in: *Proc. IMACS Multiconference on Computational Engineering in Systems Applications*, 2006, pp. 2028–2032.

[72] V. Andrey, K. H. Jo, Automatic detection and recognition of traffic signs using geometric structure analysis, in: *Proc. Internat. Joint Conference SICE-ICASE*, 2006, pp. 1451–1456.

[73] A. d. l. Escalera, L. E. Moreno, M. A. Salichs, J. M. Armingol, Road Traffic Sign Detection and Classification, *IEEE Transactions on Industrial Electronics* **44** (6) (1997) 848–859.

[74] H.-M. Yang, C.-L. Liu, K.-H. Liu, S.-M. Huang, Traffic Sign Recognition in Disturbing Environments, in: ISMIS 2003, *LNAI* **2871**, Springer Verlag, 2003, pp. 252–261.

[75] S. Kantawong, Road Traffic Signs Detection and Classification for Blind Man Navigation System, in: *Proc. Internat. Conf. on Control, Automation and Systems (ICCAS)*, 2007, pp. 847–852.

[76] M. Zadeh, T. Kasvand, C. Suen, Localization and Recognition of Traffic Signs for Automated Vehicle Control Systems, in: Conf. on Intelligent Transportation Systems, part of *SPIE's Intelligent System and Automated Manufacturing*, 1997, pp. 272–282.

[77] B. Cyganek, Road Signs Recognition by the Scale-Space Template Matching in the Log-Polar Domain, in: IbPRIA 2007, Part I, *LNCS* **4477**, Springer Verlag, 2007, pp. 330–337.

[78] N. Kehtarnavaz, N. C. Griswold, D. S. Kang, Stop-Sign Recognition based on Color and Shape Processing, *Machine Vision and Applications* **6** (1993) 206–208.

[79] P. Paclk, J. Novovicov, P. Pudil, P. Somol, Road Sign Classification Using Laplace Kernel Classifier, *Pattern Recognition Letters* **21** (2000) 1165–1173.

[80] S.-D. Zhu, Y. Zhang, X.-F. Lu, Detection for Triangle Traffic Sign Based on Neural Network, in: ISNN 2006, *LNCS* **3973**, Springer Verlag, 2006, pp. 40–45.

[81] Y. Wang, J. Dang, Z. Zhu, Traffic Signs Detection and Recognition by Improved RBFNN, in: *Proc. Internat. Conf. on Computational Intelligence and Security*, 2007, pp. 433–437.

[82] X. Gao, L. Podladchikova, D. Shaposhnikov, Application of Vision Models to Traffic Sign Recognition, in: *ICANN/ICONIP* 2003, *LNCS* **2714**, Springer Verlag, 2003, pp. 1100–1105.

[83] L. Priese, J. Klieber, R. Lakmann, V. Rehrmann, R. Schian, New Results on Traffic Sign Recognition, in: *Proc. IEEE Intelligent Vehicles Symposium*, 1994, pp. 249–254.

[84] H. Fleyeh, Traffic Sign Recognition by Fuzzy Sets, in: *Proc. IEEE Intelligent Vehicles Symposium*, 2008, pp. 422–427.

[85] M. A. Garca-Garrido, M. A. Sotelo, E. Martn-Gorostiza, Fast Road Sign Detection Using Hough Transform for Assisted Driving of Road Vehicles, in: EUROCAST 2005, *LNCS* **3643**, Springer Verlag, 2005, pp. 543–548.

[86] M. A. Garcia, M. A. Sotelo, E. M. Gorostiza, Traffic Sign Detection in Static Images using Matlab, in: *Proc. IEEE Conf. on Emerging Technologies and Factory Automation (ETFA)*, Vol. 2, 2003, pp. 212–215.

[87] J.-T. Oh, H.-W. Kwak, Y.-H. Sohn, W.-H. Kim, Segmentation and Recognition of Traffic Signs Using Shape Information, in: ISVC 2005, *LNCS* **3804**, Springer Verlag, 2005, pp. 519–526.

[88] L.-W. Tsai, Y.-J. Tseng, J.-W. Hsieh, K.-C. Fan, J.-J. Li, Road Sign Detection Using Eigen Color, in: ACCV 2007, Part I, *LNCS* **4843**, Springer Verlag, 2007, Ch. 169-179.

[89] A. d. l. Escalera, J. M. Armingol, J. M. Pastor, F. J. Rodriguez, Visual Sign Information Extraction and Identification by Deformable Models for Intelligent Vehicles, *IEEE Transactions on Intelligent Transportation Systems* **5** (2) (2004) 57–68.

[90] J. Turan, M. Fifik, L. Ovsenik, Transform Based System for TrafficSign Recognition, in: *Proc. 15th Internat. Conf. on Systems, Signals and Image Processing (IWSSIP)*, 2008, pp. 441–444.

[91] N. Serrano, A. Savakis, J. Luo, A computationally efficient approach to indoor/outdoor scene classification, Proc. of the Int. Conference on Pattern Recognition 04 (2002) 146–149.

[92] M. Szummer, R. W. Picard, Indoor-outdoor image classification, in: *IEEE International Workshop on Content-based Access of Image and Video Databases, in conjunction with ICCV'98,* 1998, pp. 42–51.

[93] A. Vailaya, A. Jain, H. J. Zhang, On image classification: City vs. landscape, in: *IEEE Workshop on Content - Based Access of Image and Video Libraries,* 1998, pp. 3–9.

[94] M. "Gorkani, R. W. Picard, "texture orientation for sorting photos "at a glance"", "ICPR-A" "94" ("1994") "459–464".

[95] K. Hotta, *Computer Vision Systems*, Vol. 5008/2008 of Lecture Notes in Computer Science, Springer, Berlin, Heidelberg, 2008, Ch. Scene Classification Based on Multi-resolution Orientation Histogram of Gabor Features, pp. 291–301.

[96] A. Bosch, A. Zisserman, X. Munoz, Scene classification via plsa, *Proceedings of the European Conference on Computer Vision.*

[97] D. Gökalp, S. Aksoy, Scene classification using bag-of-regions representations, in: *Proc. of the IEEE Conference on Computer Vision and Pattern Recognition,* 2007. CVPR '07, Vol. 1, 2007, pp. 1–8.

[98] A. Oliva, A. Torralba, A. Guerin-Dugu, J. Herault, Global semantic classification of scenes using power spectrum templates (1999).

[99] A. Oliva, Gist of the scene, in: L. Itti, G. Rees, J. K. Tsotsos (Eds.), *The Encyclopedia of Neurobiology of Attention*, Elsevier, San Diego, CA, 2005, pp. 251–256.

[100] A. Oliva, A. Torralba, Modeling the shape of the scene: A holistic representation of the spatial envelope, *International Journal of Computer Vision* **42** (3) (2001) 145–175.

[101] M. Wilson, Interclass fuzzy rule generation for road scene recognition from colour images, *Proc. of the 9th Int. Conference on Computer Analysis of Images and Patterns* **2124** (2001) 692–699.

[102] A. Oliva, P. Schyns, Coarse blobs or fine edges? evidence that information diagnosticity changes the perception of complex visual stimuli, *Cognitive Psychology* **34** (1997) 72–107.

[103] F. Wahl, *Digitale Bildsignalverarbeitung*, 2nd Edition, Springer, Berlin, Heidelberg, 1989.

[104] M. Lighthill, *An introduction to fourier analysis and generalized functions,* 1st Edition, Cambridge University Press, Cambridge, MA, USA, 1958.

[105] L. Fahrmeir, R. Künstler, I. Pigeot, G. Tutz, Statistik - *Der Weg zur Datenanalyse*, 6th Edition, Springer, Heidelberg, Berlin, 2007.

[106] K. Backhaus, W. Plinke, B. Erichson, R. Weiber, *Multivariate Analysemethoden,* 11th Edition, Springer, Berlin, Heidelberg, 2006.

[107] S. Russell, P. Norvig, *Artificial Intelligence: A Modern Approach*, 2nd Edition, Prentice Hall, Upper Saddle River, 2002.

[108] V. Willert, J. Eggert, J. Adamy, E. Koerner, Non-gaussian velocity distributions integrated over space, time and scales, IEEE Transactions on Systems, *Man and Cybernetics B* **36** (3) (2006) 482–493.

[109] J. Heikkila, O. Silven, *A four-step camera calibration procedure with implicit image correction* (1997).

[110] J. Bouguet, Camera Calibration Toolbox for Matlab, http://www.vision.caltech.edu/bouguetj (2007).

[111] K. Konolige, Small Vision System: *Hardware and implementation, in: Eighth International Symposium on Robotics Research*, 1997.

[112] A. Broggi, Robust real-time lane and road detection in critical shadow conditions, in: *Proc. Int. Symp. on Computer Vision*, IEEE, Parma, 1995.

[113] M. Schorn, U. Stahlin, A. Khanafer, R. Isermann, Nonlinear trajectory following control for automatic steering of a collision avoiding vehicle, in: *IEEE International Conference on Multisensor Fusion and Integration for Intelligent Systems*, 2006.

[114] T. Dang, S. Kammel, C. Duchow, B. Hummel, C. Stiller, Path planning for autonomous driving based on stereoscopic and monoscopic vision cues, in: *IEEE Proceedings of the 2006 American Control Conference*, 2006, pp. 191–196.

[115] BenchmarkData, http://www.rtr.tu-darmstadt.de/~tmichalk/IV2009_RoadDetectionSystem/ (2009).

[116] C. Rotaru, T. Graf, J. Zhang, Extracting road features from color images using a cognitive approach, in: *IEEE Intelligent Vehicles Symposium*, 2004.

[117] N. Soquet, D. Aubert, N. Hautiere, Road segmentation supervised by an extended vdisparity algorithm for autonomous navigation, in: *IEEE Intelligent Vehicles Symposium,* 2007.

[118] N. Apostoloff, A. Zelinsky, Robust vision based lane tracking using multiple cues and particle filtering, in: *IEEE Intelligent Vehicles Symposium,* 2003.

[119] T. Hong, T. Chang, C. Rasmussen, M. Shneier, Road detection and tracking for autonomous mobile robots, in: *Proceedings of SPIE Aerosense Conference,* 2002.

[120] Y. Sha, G. Zhang, Y. Yang, A road detection algorithm by boosting using feature combination, in: *IEEE Intelligent Vehicles Symposium,* Istanbul, 2007.

[121] P. Lombardi, M. Zanin, S. Messelodi, Unified stereovision for ground, road and obstacle detection, in: *IEEE Intelligent Vehicles Symposium,* 2005.

[122] X. Lin, S. Chen, Color image segmentation using modified HSI system for road following, in: *IEEE International Conference on Robotics and Automation,* 1991.

[123] C. Rasmussen, Combining laser range, color and texture cues for autonomous road following, in: *IEEE International Conference on Robotics and Automation,* Washington DC, 2002.

[124] H. Dahlkamp, A. Kaehler, D. Stavens, S. Thrun, G. Bradski, Self-supervised monocular road detection in desert terrain, in: *Proceedings of Robotics: Science and Systems,* Philadelphia, USA, 2006.

[125] R. Aufrere, V. Marion, J. Laneurit, C. Lewandowski, J. Morillon, R. Chapuis, Road sides recognition in non-structured environment by vision, in: *IEEE Intelligent Vehicles Symposium,* Parma, 2004.

[126] P. Smuda, R. Schweiger, H. Neumann, W. Ritter, Multiple cue data fusion with particle filters for road course detection in vision systems, in: *IEEE Intelligent Vehicles Symposium,* Tokyo, 2006.

[127] M. Chern, S. Cheng, Finding road boundaries from the unstructured rural road scene, in: *16th IPPR Conference on Computer Vision, Graphics and Image Processing,* 2003.

[128] D. Mateus, G. Avina, M. Devy, Robot visual navigation in semi-structured outdoor environments, in: *IEEE International Conference on Robotics and Automation,* Barcelona, 2005.

[129] M. Sotelo, F. Rodriguez, L. Magdalena, VIRTUOUS: Vision-based road transportation for unmanned operation on urban-like scenarios, in: *IEEE Transactions on Intelligent Transportation Systems,* Vol. 5, 2004.

[130] T. Marita, F. Oniga, S. Nedevschi, T. Graf, R. Schmidt, Camera calibration method for far range stereovision sensors used in vehicles, in: *IEEE Intelligent Vehicles Symposium,* 2007, pp. 356–363.

[131] A. Broggi, P. Grisleri, A software video stabilization system for automotive oriented applications, in: *Procs. IEEE Vehicular Technology Conference,* Stockholm, Sweden, 2005.

[132] J. Adamy, Fuzzy-Logik, Neuronale Netze und Evolutionäre Algorithmen, Shaker Verlag Achen, 2007.

[133] A. Gepperth, B. Mersch, C. Goerick, J. Fritsch, Color object recognition in real-world scenes, in: J. de Sa (Ed.), J. Marques de Sa et al. (Eds.): Artificial Neural Networks, *17th International Conference ICANN,* Part II, Lecture Notes in computer science, Springer Verlag Berlin Heidelberg New York, 2007, pp. 583–592.

[134] E. Bauer, R. Kohavi, An empirical comparison of voting classification algorithms: Bagging, boosting, and variants, *Machine Learning* **36** (1-2) (1999) 105–139.

[135] R. Kalman, A new approach to linear filtering and prediction problems, *Transactions of the ASME–Journal of Basic Engineering* **82** (Series D) (1960) 35–45.

[136] M. Nieto, L. Salgado, F. Jaureguizar, J. Cabrera, Stabilization of inverse perspective mapping images based on robust vanishing point estimation, in: *IEEE Intelligent Vehicles Symposium*, 2007.

[137] V. Willert, M. Toussaint, J. Eggert, E. Körner, Uncertainty optimization for robust dynamic optical flow estimation, in: *Proceedings of the 2007 International Conference on Machine Learning and Applications (ICMLA), IEEE,* 2007.

[138] X. Li, X. Yao, Y. Murphey, R. Karlsen, G. Gerhart, A real-time vehicle detection and tracking system in outdoor traffic scenes, in: *Proceedings of the 17th International Conference on Pattern Recognition*, 2004.

[139] M. Cech, W. Niem, S. Abraham, C. Stiller, Dynamic ego-pose estimation for driver assistance in urban environments, in: *IEEE Intelligent Vehicles Symposium*, 2004, pp. 43–48.

[140] R. Wang, B. Gu, T. Yu, L. Gou, Study on curb detection method based on 3d range image by laserradar, in: *IEEE Intelligent Vehicles Symposium*, Las Vegas, 2005.

[141] F. Oniga, S. Nedevschi, M. Meinecke, Curb detection based on a multi-frame persistence map for urban driving, in: *IEEE Conference on Intelligent Transportation Systems*, Beijing, 2008.

[142] R. Aufrere, C. Mertz, C. Thorpe, Multiple sensor fusion for detecting location of curbs, walls, and barriers, in: *IEEE Intelligent Vehicles Symposium*, 2003.

[143] R. Danescu, S. Nedevschi, M. Meinecke, T. To, A stereovision-based probabilistic lane tracker for difficult road scenarios, in: *IEEE Intelligent Vehicles Symposium*, Eindhoven, 2008.

[144] B. Roessler, K. Fuerstenberg, U. Lages, Laserscanner for multiple applications in passenger cars and trucks, in: Proceedings of AMAA 2006, *10th International Conference on Advanced Microsystems for Automotive Applications,* Berlin, 2006.

[145] F. Oniga, S. Nedevschi, M. Meinecke, T. To, Road surface and obstacle dectection based on elevation maps from dense stereo, in: *IEEE Conference on Intelligent Transportation Systems*, Seattle, 2007.

[146] T. Michalke, J. Fritsch, C. Goerick, Enhancing robustness of a saliency-based attention system for driver assistance, in: *The 6th International Conference on Computer Vision Systems (ICVS)*, Santorini, Greece, 2008. Lecture Notes in Computer Science, Springer, No. 5008, 2008, pp. 43–55.

[147] BenchmarkData, `http://www.rtr.tu-darmstadt.de/~tmichalk/ICVS2008_BenchmarkData/` (2008).

[148] M. von Trzebiatowski, A. Gern, U. Franke, U.-P. Kaeppeler, P. Levi, Detecting reflection posts - lane recognition on country roads, in: *IEEE Intelligent Vehicles Symposium*, 2004.

[149] BenchmarkData, `http://www.rtr.tu-darmstadt.de/~tmichalk/ITSC_TempIntegration/` (2008).

[150] A. Ceravola, F. Joublin, M. Dunn, J. Eggert, C. Goerick, Integrated research and development environment for real-time distributed embodied intelligent systems, in: *Proc. Int. Conf. on Robots and Intelligent Systems*, 2006, pp. 1631–1637.

[151] Intel, Integrated Performance Primitives, `http://www.intel.com/cd/software/products/asmo-na/eng/perflib/ipp/302910.htm` (2006).

[152] BenchmarkData, `http://www.rtr.tu-darmstadt.de/~tmichalk/IV2009_ADASControl/` (2009).

[153] K. Manz, D. Kooš, K. Klinger, S. Schellinger, Entwicklung von Kriterien zur Bewertung der Fahrzeugbeleuchtung im Hinblick auf ein NCAP für aktive Fahrzeugsicherheit, Universität Karlsruhe, Lichttechnisches Institut, 2007.

[154] R. Kastner, F. Schneider, T. Michalke, J. Fritsch, C. Goerick, Image-based classification of driving scenes by Hierarchical Principal Component Classification (HPCC), in: *IEEE Intelligent Vehicles Symposium*, Xian, 2009.

In: Computer Vision
Editor: Sota R. Yoshida

ISBN 978-1-61209-399-4
© 2011 Nova Science Publishers, Inc.

Chapter 4

TRAFFIC MONITORING; A PRACTICAL IMPLEMENTATION OF A REAL-TIME OPEN AIR COMPUTER VISION SYSTEM

Tomás Rodríguez
Tecnologías Avanzadas Inspiralia (ITAV).
PERA Innovation Network. Madrid, Spain

Abstract

Open air is a challenging environment where few computer vision applications succeed. The reasons behind these difficulties must be found in the uncontrolled nature of open air applications. Computer vision is a passive technology. Typically a camera mounted on a mast observes the scene while using "clever" algorithms to interpret the images. However, doing this interpretation is no easy task since almost any type of moving or static object may appear in scene. Also, there are many circumstances which are not under direct control of the system: illumination changes caused by passing clouds, movements of the sun or day / night transitions; presence of shadows and moving artificial lights; camera artifacts resulting from blooming or smearing; overreaction of camera compensation devices; occlusions; vibrations of the camera; weather elements, such as: rain, snow or fog; etc.

All these circumstances combined turns computer vision in open scenarios into a formidable task. Only those applications working under very constrained conditions and with very concrete objectives will have any opportunity to succeed. In this chapter we present a computer vision based traffic monitoring system able to detect individual vehicles in real-time. Our fully integrated system first obtains the main traffic variables of the vehicles: counting, speed and category; and then computes a complete set of statistical variables. The objective is to investigate alternative solutions to some of the difficulties impeding existing traffic systems achieve balanced accuracy in every condition; most notably: day and night transitions, moving shadows, heavy vehicles, occlusions, slow traffic and congestions.

1. Introduction

The use of Intelligent Transport Systems (ITS) is progressively becoming more important for the efficient management of road traffic infrastructures. These systems comprise a great number of technical aids and management strategies from different domains. In this chapter we focus our attention on a set of advanced sensing technologies categorized under the term Intelligent Vehicle Highway Systems (IVHS). The aim is to describe an adaptive, real-time, computer vision based, traffic monitoring system designed to detect and track vehicles in road traffic scenarios.

Our system is able to robustly detect individual vehicles, measure their speed and identify their category. Based on thee microscopic variables, the system computes a complete set of statistical parameters; such as: average speed, traffic intensity or flux, vehicle headway, occupancy, traffic density, etc. Traffic authorities typically use these data in public information services, traffic management, alert detection and infrastructure planning.

Computer vision presents significant advantages over other more traditional vehicle measurement technologies (i.e. current loops). Computer vision systems are more flexible, less invasive, more precise, more robust, are easier to maintain, produce richer information, do not affect the integrity of the road and offer, as an added bonus, the possibility to transmit images for human supervision.

Computer vision applied to traffic has been investigated since the late 80's, but there is still intense research work going on. The bibliography dealing with this subject is huge. There are lots of good scientific publications [1, 2, 3] and a few very systematic reports on massive testing experiences [4, 5, 6]. It is also possible to find a certain number of commercial systems [7, 8].

Unfortunately, despite its undeniable interest, computer vision is not massively used in traffic monitoring applications, since existing systems still suffer from poor reliability, high cost and unbalanced accuracy. The reason is computer vision systems are much affected by weather and illumination conditions. Their accuracy is seriously limited under changing weather and it is not uncommon to find blocked systems when conditions are adverse. In addition, not every system is able to work unattended 24x7; i.e. many systems cannot operate at night or in the periods between day and night. On the other hand, most systems are unable to cope with slow traffic or congestions and show important difficulties to correctly detect heavy vehicles. Occlusions and shadows are also important problems, causing lots of errors.

The system we present [9, 10] is autonomous, works unattended for long periods of time and adapts automatically to the changing environmental conditions. Several innovations, designed to deal with the above circumstances, are proposed: an integrated calibration and image rectification step, differentiated methods for day and night operation, an adaptive segmentation algorithm with automatic illumination compensation [11], a multistage shadow detection method [12] and special considerations for heavy vehicle identification and treatment of slow traffic. A specific methodology, developed to benchmark the accuracy of the different methods proposed, is presented at the end of the chapter.

2.   The Traffic Scenario

2.1.   Physical Environment

Traffic monitoring environments are generally complex [13, 2, 14, 15]. The scene is dominated by the road, which is usually gray, plane and texture less, except for the road lines, which are of a bright color. The road is assumed to be static and free of obstacles. The area under surveillance is typically between 10 and 20 meters long and may cover 1 to 3 lanes per camera.

Certainly our main interest is in the road and in the vehicles running along the road. However, in the images there appear other elements standing outside the road area, which might affect the detection of the vehicles: trees, traffic signals, lamp posts, bridges, etc. Those elements may be static or moving and might also project static or moving shadows on to the surveillance area.

The traffic scenario is influenced by the weather elements: rain, snow, fog; but also by changing illumination conditions resulting from the movement of the sun and by passing clouds. Weather elements may have different effects on the image. Rain causes speckle noise and reduces the perceived intensity in the image, but otherwise is not a big problem; if a step viewing angle is used for the camera. Snow increases the general intensity levels, while causing lots of reflections. Finally, fog reduces the contrast and visibility in the image to the point that might blind the system.

Variations in the illumination sources are also an important effect to be considered. The movement of the sun is the cause of a slow, systematic, variation in the intensity and the direction of the received illumination. This variation affects not only the intensity but also the chromaticity of the light reflected by the objects and determines the shape, size and direction of the shadows. Passing clouds also contribute to change the illumination levels in accordance with the movement of the cloud. Obviously, at night, there is no sun light. At night, traffic scenes may be dark or illuminated by artificial sources. In this last case illumination is diffuse, reasonably stable and comes from multiple sources located at fixed positions. While sun light shows a wide spectrum, artificial lighting is concentrated in a very narrow band. In the periods in between day and night a mixture of the above conditions is found.

Shadows are another important phenomena we need to take into account. Shadows may be cast by the vehicles or by the objects standing outside the surveillance area. Vehicles' shadows are always moving and joined to the vehicle. On the other hand, the objects located outside the surveillance area are usually static, but they can be moved by the wind, thus causing moving shadows. Under sun lighting each object cast a single shadow, but when artificial light is used multiple shadows per object are possible.

Next we need to consider the vehicles themselves. Vehicles are moving objects that can have any length between 3 and 15 meters and any color. Statistically, white cars dominate. Vehicles are composed of different parts, having different chromatic appearance: body, windows, tires, etc. Most vehicles present parts darker than the background and in many cases also brighter, due to illumination effects. Vehicles show very characteristic movements; they may change lanes, but enter and leave the image from the same direction and their speed can be considered uniform since, statistically, acceleration is little relevant in the surveillance area. Vehicles are solid objects; they never overlap, nor do they change positions in the lane. Most vehicles show cast shadows darker than the background, whose shape, size and orientation will depend on the illumination source and the atmospheric conditions. Vehicles' shadows can, in general, be differentiated from shadows cast by elements external to the surveillance area by their movement.

The final element we will consider in the physical scenario is the camera system. Most frequently, the camera is mounted on top of a pole at the side of the road, but can be also placed on a bridge or similar supporting structure crossing the road (see Fig. 1).

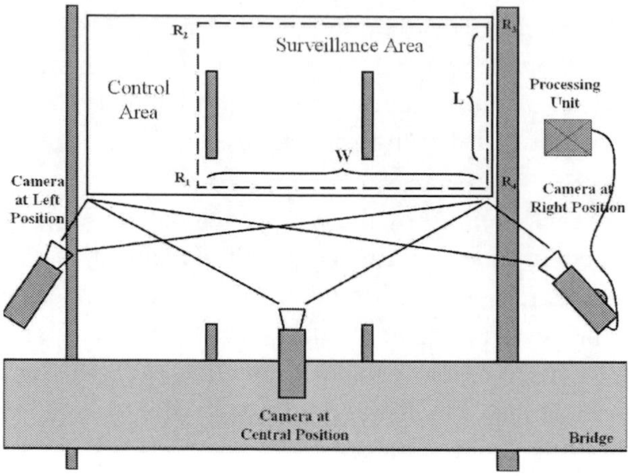

Figure 1. General layout of a traffic monitoring scenario showing typical camera configurations: *Left*, *Right* and *Central* camera positions. The diagram also presents the layout of the *Control Area* (filled) and *Surveillance Area* (dashed); as well as the four reference points $\tilde{R}_i$ used for calibration. W and L are respectively the width and length of the *Surveillance Area*, in meters.

Frequently, a compromise must be sought between several different factors, before an appropriate placement for the camera can be found. In that sense, the camera installation process must be flexible, so that it can be adapted to the varying external circumstances, but on the other hand, a minimum set of requirements must be defined so that an adequate performance of the system can be guaranteed (i.e. even if some authors claim their systems work in every possible situation, computer vision algorithms tend to offer best results under certain configurations only). The main factor to consider here are occlusions. Occlusions are produced when a vehicle intercepts the line of sight of another vehicle and constitute one of the most challenging problems in computer vision based traffic monitoring applications. In fact, avoiding occlusions must be one of the leading factors for deciding the placement of the camera.

Three parameters condition, to a great extent, the accuracy of the computer vision algorithms: the height of the camera, the position of the pole and the viewing angle. Practical considerations limit the height of the pole supporting the camera to between 12 and 15 meters. In consequence, the camera installation process is typically started by defining the length of the road and the number of lanes we desire to cover with the camera. Next we select the position of the pole according to the arrangement of the scenario. The cameras can be placed at a *central* position overlooking the road (on top of a bridge or similar structure), at the *left* side or at the *right* side of the road.

Once decided the camera position, we must aim the camera using the steepest possible angle that allow us to achieve the desired field of view. Steep angles are more convenient to avoid occlusions and also contribute to avoid blooming from the vehicles' headlights or from the sun. In fact one very sensible recommendation is to aim the camera so that the horizon is never included in the field of view.

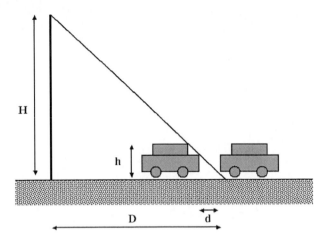

Figure 2. Diagram showing the viewing angle observed by the camera and the ability of the system to discern the separation between two vehicles.

As depicted in Figure 2, the ability of the system to tell the difference between two vehicles separated by a distance d is a function of the distance D from the camera to the vehicles, the height of the camera H and the height of the vehicle h; according to the following formula:

$$d = \frac{h * D}{H} \tag{1}$$

2.2. The Scenario as Observed by the Camera

In the previous section we presented the physical layout of a typical traffic scenario. However, when this scenario is projected on to the image plane of the camera it suffers a number of undesirable perspective deformations; therefore turning more complex subsequent image processing steps. Those effects can be described using the pin hole camera model [16] presented in Figure 3 and become apparent in the way the vehicles and their surrounding scenario are represented in the image:

- The shape of vehicles will be distorted. The distortion will acquire different aspects depending on the *intrinsic* and *extrinsic* parameters of the camera. If we assume vehicles can be approximated by regular parallelepipeds, the distortion will produce the following effects: the base and top of the vehicle will be deformed (i.e. they will no longer be rectangular); its height will appear projected to the left side (camera placed on the right side of the road), to the right side (camera placed on the left side of the road), or to the front / rear (camera in a front or back central position).

- The size of the vehicles will no longer remain constant in the image, but will depend on their position in the scenario (the more distant from the camera the smaller they will be represented in the image). In the same way, shape deformations will also depend on the distance to the camera.

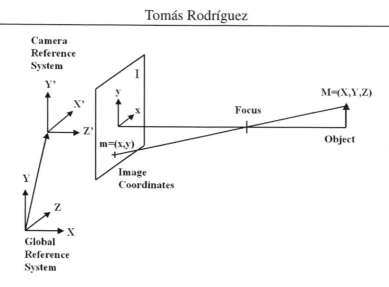

Figure 3. A representation of the Pinhole camera model [16], showing the layout of the different reference systems.

- The top / bottom borders of the vehicles will show different relative movements in the image sequence. Their deformation will depend on their height (i.e. If we take the plane of the road as our reference, top borders will be affected by the deformation in height, while bottom borders will not). As a consequence top borders will appear to move faster than their bottom counterpart. This is the reason why tracking methods tend to use the back-bottom border (the front-bottom border is always occluded in front views) to track the vehicle.

- Vehicles may certainly be occluded by other vehicles due to perspective projection. In practice, most occlusions are caused by large vehicles (i.e. trucks). While cars are usually of a moderate height and their shape is smooth, in the case of heavy vehicles, they tend to be very high and grow almost vertically over the road up to their maximum height; thus increasing the possibilities for occlusions.

- Occlusions can be longitudinal or lateral and they are almost impossible to avoid in certain circumstances. In free traffic conditions occlusions are not a big problem, since the distance between vehicles is sufficient to avoid most occlusions. However, under congested traffic, occlusions caused by large vehicles become more problematic. Occlusions are one of the most difficult problems to be found in computer vision traffic monitoring systems and minimizing occlusions must be one of the leading objectives of any method proposed.

- The shape of the *Surveillance Area*, as seen in the image, will be distorted according to perspective projection rules (i.e. a rectangular *Surveillance Area* will no longer remain rectangular in the image).

- In most traffic systems the length of the *Surveillance Area* is short enough so that the speed of vehicles can be assumed constant. However, due to perspective projection effects, the speed of the vehicle measured in the image is no longer constant; vehicles move faster in the front plane than they do in the horizon.

- Rectilinear paths in the scenario remain rectilinear in the image. However, vehicles' trajectories are no longer parallel and they cross at the vanishing point.

In addition to perspective deformations, the camera system induces other undesirable effects on the image representation:

- When the camera is moved, i.e. when it is moved by the wind or when the floor vibrates, the scene also moves.

- The image sensor suffers smearing or blooming problems when working close to its limits. Those problems typically happen when one of the elements of the sensor gets saturated due to reflections or direct sun light. The effect in the image is a saturated line of pixels or a white patch. The use of polarized filters greatly contributes to mitigate this effect.

- Automatic compensation devices (auto-iris, electronic shutter or AGC) are necessary in the cameras in order to adapt the image levels to the changing illumination conditions. However, compensation devices tend to overreact when faced with fast changes affecting a significant part of the image. The result is the level of continua in the image oscillates thus confusing the image processing algorithms. This circumstance systematically occurs when a large white vehicle suddenly enters into the scene.

- In spite of the protective measures implemented, it is difficult to avoid the accumulation of dirt, water or moisture on the camera lens.

3.   The Computer Vision Chain

The computer vision chain implementing the structure of the TRAFFIC system is presented in figure 4. The chain is composed of four main steps: Calibration, Segmentation, Detection and Tracking. Several auxiliary modules complete the chain. However, only the core modules will be described in this paper.

4.   Camera Calibration and Image Rectification

If we want to take physical measures of the objects in the scene from the camera images (i.e. to measure the vehicles' speed or category) it becomes necessary to calibrate the camera. In our simplified scenario, the Camera Calibration process is rather trivial and can be found in most introductory computer vision books [17]. However, we need to address two extraordinary circumstances: first, Camera Calibration must be achieved without stopping the traffic and second, we would like to compensate the perspective deformation effects discussed in section 2.2.. Both processes will be presented in the following sections. A more detailed description can be found in references [18, 19].

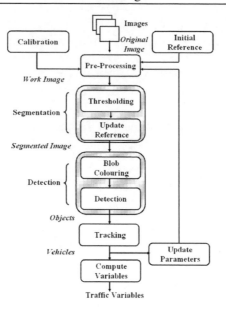

Figure 4. The computer vision chain of the TRAFFIC system. Notice how the system parameters are updated for every incoming image.

4.1. Camera Calibration

The computer vision algorithms need to know which is the image coordinate m that corresponds to a certain point M in the physical scenario (*World to Image* transformation) and conversely must also know which is the point in space M determined by an image pixel (*Image to World* transformation). Unfortunately, in a monocular view, this last is a one to many transformation, since the same image pixel m is in correspondence with all the points composing the line that joins M, the principal point of the camera and the image pixel m. For that reason, unless we impose additional constraints, it is not possible to find a single point in space that gives rise to the image pixel. In traffic monitoring applications, it is frequent to assume the interesting points observed by the camera lay on the road plane. We will see how this additional restriction allows us to calculate *Image to World* transformations for on the road pixels.

Given $\tilde{M}$, the coordinates of a *World* point in the three-dimensional space and $\tilde{m}$ its projection on to the image plane; both points are related by the projection matrix P according to the classical formula:

$$s\tilde{m} = P\tilde{M}; \tag{2}$$

where $\tilde{M} = \{X, Y, Z, 1\}$ and $\tilde{m} = \{x, y, 1\}$ are represented in homogeneous coordinates, and s is a scale factor.

One of the simplest methods to calculate the (*World to Image* transformation) is to start from the projection equation (2). In the general case, the projection matrix P has $3 \times 4 = 12$ elements, but only 11 degrees of freedom, since it is defined up to a scale factor. In our case we are interested only in points located in the plane of the road. For that reason, we define, for convenience, the Z axis perpendicular to the road plane and assume the coordinates of the scene points to be always $Z = 0$. Under such simplification, we may remove s from (2) and set, without loss of generality, $P_{34} = 1$. As a result, we obtain a system of two equations with 8 unkowns for every pair of corresponding points $[\tilde{M}, \tilde{m}]$:

$$x = \frac{P_{11}X + P_{12}Y + P_{14}}{P_{31}X + P_{32}Y + 1}$$

$$y = \frac{P_{21}X + P_{22}Y + P_{24}}{P_{31}X + P_{32}Y + 1} \tag{3}$$

Stacking a minimum of 4 such equations with their respective corresponding points $[\tilde{M}_u, \tilde{m}_v]$ and using traditional numerical methods (i.e. *Least Squares*), we can solve for the coefficients of the projection matrix P_{ij}. We must consider the selected points must be in the *general* position, i.e. not three of them aligned. It is also convenient to place the points covering the widest possible area on the road, so that numerical errors are minimized. Once the coefficients P_{ij} are known, equation (3) allows to obtain the pixel coordinates $\tilde{m}$ for every point $\tilde{M}$ on the road plane.

In order to compute the opposite (*Image to World*) transformation we need to solve for (X, Y) in (3), as a function of (x, y):

$$X = \frac{\begin{vmatrix} c & b \\ f & e \end{vmatrix}}{\begin{vmatrix} a & b \\ d & e \end{vmatrix}}; \quad Y = \frac{\begin{vmatrix} a & c \\ d & f \end{vmatrix}}{\begin{vmatrix} a & b \\ d & e \end{vmatrix}}; \quad with \quad \begin{array}{ll} a = P_{11} - P_{31}x; & d = P_{21} - P_{31}y; \\ b = P_{12} - P_{32}x; & e = P_{22} - P_{32}y; \\ c = x - P_{14}; & f = y - P_{24}; \end{array}$$

$$\tag{4}$$

Using (4), and provided the determinant in the denominator is not null, we are able to calculate the *world* coordinates of every image pixel. We must emphasize, once more, the above transformation is only valid for points placed on the plane of the road.

4.2. Image Rectification

In section 2.2. we described how Segmentation and Tracking algorithms [20, 21, 22] may experience important difficulties due to deformation effects induced by perspective projection rules. The most common difficulties are the following:

- Vehicle identification becomes more complex since the shape of the vehicle is deformed and its deformation changes with time. Also the size of the vehicle will depend on its position. These facts affect not only the initial detection of the vehicle, but also the matching of the successive instances of the vehicle in the respective images of the sequence.

- Tracking vehicles is more difficult since they no longer observe parallel trajectories and the vehicles' apparent speed will depend on its position in the image.

- Since the *Surveillance Area* is no longer regular, it becomes more difficult to isolate vehicles from their surrounding scenario; i.e. from objects located outside the road.

- Most traffic systems sub sample the input images in order to reduce redundant information and speed-up computation. However the reduction in the size of the vehicles due to perspective greatly affects the required resolution of the *Work Image*. One usual problem is resolution is far too high for vehicles in the front part of the image, while vehicles close to the horizon are only represented by a few pixels.

Not all these effects are treated adequately in existing computer vision systems [23, 24]. Some approaches cope with perspective deformations by designing more complex Segmentation and Tracking algorithms, others simply ignore them, or provide empirical solutions suitable only for very specific circumstances. In any case, perspective effects, if not taken into account, result in more computing overhead, decreased robustness and less accurate measurements. In our case, we compensate some of the above difficulties by means of the innovative *Image Rectification* method proposed below.

Perspective deformations cannot be avoided completely. However, they can be mitigated, to a great extent, if a bird's eye view over the road (camera pointing vertically to the plane of the road) can be selected. Placing the camera in this position is, in general, not possible. However, it is feasible to construct a virtual bird's eye view from a lateral view by applying *Image Rectification* techniques. On the other hand, the *Image Rectification* process has its limitations since it is only possible to transform correctly those points in the scene laying on a single plane (in our case the road plane). Conversely, points outside the road plane will remain distorted.

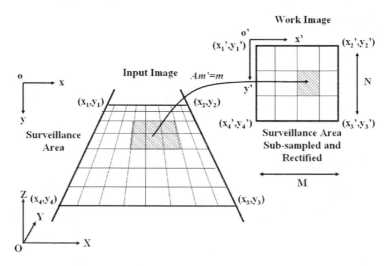

Figure 5. Example showing how a rectangle located inside the *Surveillance Area* of the *Input Image* is transformed to the reference frame of the *Work Image*, using the rectification method implicit in (6). Notice how the boundaries of the *Surveillance Area* are set in correspondence with the limits of the *Work Image*. M and N are respectively the horizontal and vertical resolution of the *Work Image*.

According to basic Epipolar Geometry theory [17], a certain relation can be found between two perspective views. In particular both views can be real camera views, or as it will be our case, one of them will be virtual. Given the coordinates of a *World* point in each of the two views, say $\{m \in I \mid m = (x, y, 1)\}$ and $\{m' \in I' \mid m' = (x', y', 1)\}$ in homogeneous coordinates, it can be verified [25] that in the general case the next relation becomes true:

$$m^T F m' = 0 \quad , \tag{5}$$

where F is the *Fundamental Matrix*. The 3×3 matrix F is of rank 2 and is defined up to a scale factor. In our case we are only interested in points lying on the road plane. Hence an additional constraint applies, which represents what is usually named a *collineation* [25]; thus determining the following relation between points in correspondence in the two views:

$$m = A m' \tag{6}$$

where m is a point in the real image and m' is the point in correspondence in the *Virtual Image* we desire to create. The 3×3 matrix A represents the *collineation* and is also defined up to a scale factor. In that way, it will be sufficient to take four pairs of corresponding points $\{m_i, m'_i\}$ in general position (i.e. no three of them aligned) to obtain a system of 8 equations with 8 unknowns that will allow us to calculate the 8 independent coefficients in $A_{i,j}$.

Now, if we take the four points m_i to be the vertexes of the *Surveillance Area* in the *Input Image* and m'_i the vertexes defining the limits of the *Virtual Image*, we can use *Least Squares* to calculate the coefficients $A_{i,j}$ that will allow us to perform the desired image transformation (see fig. 5). Once the $A_{i,j}$ coefficients are known, we may construct [1] the *Virtual Image* by assigning to every point $m'_i \in I'$ the pixel value of its corresponding point $m_i \in I$ using (6). We denote this *Virtual Image* as the *Work Image*. Once the *Work Image* becomes available, the *Input Image* can be discarded and all subsequent processing steps will be performed over the *Work Image*.

The method proposed will have the effect of obtaining the *Work Image* as a rectified and sub-sampled version of the *Input Image*. The trick will be to select the appropriate shape and dimensions of the *Surveillance Area* and *Work Image* so that the transformation produces exactly the effect we are expecting (i.e. a top view, with $z = 0$). For that purpose, the *Surveillance Area* must be rectangular and will enclose strictly that part of the road we desire to monitor (thus avoiding the inclusion of parts of the scenario outside the road). On the other hand, the *Work Image* must match exactly the image resolution we desire to obtain in the final result.

4.3. The Calibration Tool

We integrated the Calibration and Image Rectification steps described above in a single process; aided by a Calibration Tool. The aim was to provide a simplified non invasive installation procedure and achieve real time performance in the proposed image transformations.

The Calibration Tool (Fig. 6) provides graphical aids to define the required measurement areas and the metrical references on the images and also computes the transformation matrices.

---

[1]The inverse transform is preferred since that way every pixel in I' gets its correspondence in the *Input Image*.

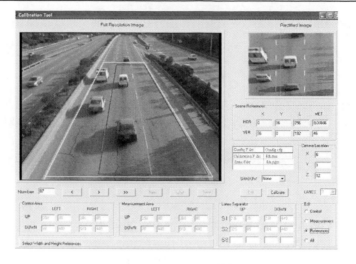

Figure 6. Screenshot of the Calibration Tool. The *Control* and *Surveillance* Areas are defined over the full resolution *Input Image* (720x576 pixels); while the metrical references are taken on the rectified *Work Image* (256x192 pixels). Notice how the *Work Image*, computed from the *Input Image* after sub-sampling and geometry correction, encodes only that part of the *Input Image* enclosed inside the *Control Area*.

The method is started by defining two rectangular areas in the scenario: the *Control Area* and the *Surveillance Area*. Both areas must be rectangular in *World* coordinates. We first select the vertexes of the *Control Area* using a graphical pointer over the *Input Image*. The *Control Area* must be selected so that it covers strictly that part of the road that must be supervised; i.e. we avoid including in the *Control Area* parts of the scene outside the road. The vertexes will be selected using existing references in the scenario (i.e. the traffic lanes), or more appropriate by placing four traffic cones on the road as physical points of reference.

Next, we define the vertexes of one or more *Surveillance Areas* using the same procedure. The *Surveillance Area* has been defined as a subset of the *Control Area*, which comprises strictly that part of the road (typically one or more traffic lanes) that will be *rectified* and processed by the computer vision algorithms; i.e. while the complete *Control Area* is calibrated, only the objects inside the *Surveillance Area* are processed. Following this approach we can change the area under supervision remotely without re-calibrating the camera; we just need to select another *Surveillance Area*.

Finally, the system requires to determine the relative distance (in meter) between two widely spaced points in the longitudinal and transversal directions of the road. The most common approach would be to measure the distance between the vertical and horizontal cones used for reference. This method is highly accurate and little invasive for the traffic. On the other hand we could use existing references (i.e. known distances between road markings, known size of passing vehicles, etc) to achieve similar results. This last method is very convenient since we are able to calibrate the camera remotely; however, it will be less precise. Distance measurements are taken using a pair of graphical sliders over the *Work Image*, after the rectification process has been correctly achieved.

Once defined the *Control* and *Surveillance* areas, as well as the metrical references, the Calibration Tool computes the transformation matrices. In our case we have three reference frames corresponding to the: *World, Input Image* and *Work Image* respectively. Where the *Work Image* has been introduced as a rectified and scaled projective transformation from the *Input Image* with the aim to arrange the content of the images in a way that is more appropriate for the needs of computer vision algorithms. In consequence, we will need to provide matrices for the most common transformations between any two reference frames. As described in section 4., our method will only require four *Reference Points* and two distance measurements in the *World* coordinate system to obtain all required relations. The result will be a set of structures that will allow the computation of the required transformations in real-time.

The four *Reference Points* $\tilde{R}_i$ are set in correspondence with the four vertexes delimiting the *Surveillance Area* (see Fig. 1). The system will use $\tilde{R}_i$ to compute the Projection matrix P using the procedure defined in section 4.1.. We will use the $Z = 0$ assumption; hence the coordinates of the $\tilde{M}_i$ points in (2) will be set to: $\{(0,0), (W,0), (0,L), (W,L)\}$; where W and L are respectively the width and length of the *Control Area*, measured in meters. Obviously the $\tilde{m}_i$ points will be the pixel coordinates of the corresponding reference points on the *Input Image*.

Next, the system will use the image pixels $\tilde{m}_i$ corresponding to the reference points $\tilde{R}_i$ to compute the Fundamental matrix F using the procedure defined in section 4.2.. The points $\tilde{m}'_i$ in (6) will be selected in correspondence with the vertexes of the *Work Image*: $\{(0,0), (M,0), (0,N), (M,N)\}$; where M and N are the desired horizontal and vertical resolutions of the *Work Image* respectively.

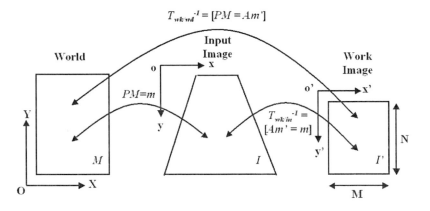

Figure 7. In the figure we show transformations between different reference systems. Only the transformations $T_{wk,wd}$, $T_{wk,in}$ and the respective inverses are, in practice, codified into the array of pointers structure.

Once P and F are known, we are able to transform between the respective coordinate systems. In practice (Figure 7), only the following transformations will be required: *Work to Input Image Transformation* ($T_{wk/in}$), *Work to World Transformation* ($T_{wk/wd}$) and its inverses.

One of our basic constraints was to be able to perform the transformations in real time. Even if traffic images are typically not very large, computing the transformations on-the-run would introduce unacceptable levels of overhead. For that reason, each transformation above is computed off-line and its results encoded into a two-dimensional array of pointers. This computation is done only once at start-up and, in general, need not be repeated, unless the camera is moved.

If we examine the transformation $T_{wk/in}$, we notice the pointers acts as a look-up table so that when one pixel $\{x', y'\}$ is indexed into the $T_{wk/in}$ structure, or *Work Image* for short, the pointer will return the intensity value of the corresponding pixel in the *Input Image*. This is an elegant way to perform the image transformation, while adding very little overhead. Similar structures are created for other transformations; i.e. Indexing the point $\{x', y'\}$ into the $T_{wk/wd}$ structure will provide the three-dimensional coordinates of the point in the world: $\{X, Y, 0\}$.

At run-time the above transformation structures are already pre-computed. Then for each *Input Image*, the corresponding *Work Image* will be obtained. The *Work Image* may remain as a two-dimensional array of pointers or physically copied into an image structure. At that point the *Input Image* can be discarded altogether since the *Work Image* already contains all the information that is required to perform the computer vision tasks.

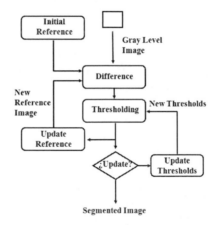

Figure 8. Structure of the *Segmentation* step. Notice how *Segmentation* operates on a single gray level image to produce the *Segmentation Masks*.

5. Segmentation

Our interpretation of the Segmentation step is a bit different from the approaches found in some of the references [26, 13, 27]. In our case, the objective of the Segmentation step is limited to extracting the moving objects of the scene and performing a preliminary classification. I.e. Segmentation does not attempt to identify shadows or vehicles since we consider at this stage we cannot identify the objects unambiguously and we understand the final decision must be delayed to later stages when the complete set of historical information become available.

Once the *Work image* has been created we segment the image by extracting the moving objects using an adaptation of well-known *Background Suppression* [28, 29, 30] techniques.

In our case *Background Suppression* is complemented with a statistical knowledge-based adaptive background estimation and an innovative method for the automatic computation of the Segmentation parameters. Due to the different environmental conditions, two algorithms are used for best operation under day and night. Both segmentation methods perform reasonably well in the transition periods; as described in the following section. A more detailed description of the Segmentation step can be found in [11].

5.1. Day Operation

The first segmentation stage computes the *image of differences D_t*:

$$D_t(x, y) = I_t(x, y) - B_{t-1}(x, y); \quad -255 < D_t(x, y) < 255 \tag{7}$$

Where I_t and B_t are the input and background images at time t. Our segmentation approach defines three categories: BCKGND, BRIGHT (potentially a pixel that belongs to a vehicle) and DARK (potentially a pixel that belongs to a moving shadow or a vehicle); according to the following classification:

$$U_t(x, y) = \begin{cases} BRIGHT & if & D_t(x, y) > T_b \\ DARK & if & D_t(x, y) < T_d \\ BCKGND & Otherwise \end{cases} \tag{8}$$

T_b and T_d are the thresholds for BRIGHT and DARK labels respectively. Both thresholds are calculated automatically using the procedure described in section 5.4.. Once the individual pixels have been labeled, contiguous pixels with the same label are grouped together using a 4-connected blob-coloring algorithm. The result from the one pass grouping algorithm is a list of objects masks complete with their most relevant descriptors: geometric center, mass center, enclosing rectangle, size in pixels, etc.

In contrast with [13], where early classification decisions may result in imperfect shadow removal and poor identification of dark vehicles, in (8) the objective is to preserve the compactness of the object masks and prevent the undesired removal of the dark part of the vehicles. This three label approach makes possible delaying the decision to remove the shadows until the tracking stage; where the relative temporal movement of vehicles and shadows can be better analyzed. This approach, combined with the automatic adaptation of the thresholds, allows for a simpler, faster and more robust segmentation (see Fig. 9).

The description above is meant for monochrome images. When dealing with color images, we use an HSV color space. In this case the *image of differences* (DH and DV) is calculated for the H and V channels independently and the segmentation criteria is modified as follows:

$$U_t(x, y) = \begin{cases} BRIGHT & if & DV_t(x, y) & > & TV_b & or \\ & if & DV_t(x, y) & < & TV_b & \wedge \\ & & |DH_t(x, y)| & > & TH & \\ DARK & if & DV_t(x, y) & < & TV_d & \wedge \\ & & |DH_t(x, y)| & \leq & TH & \\ BKGND & Otherwise \end{cases} \tag{9}$$

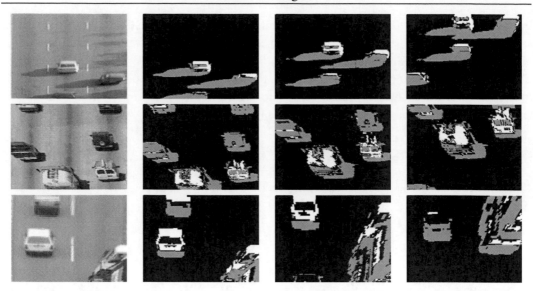

Figure 9. Segmentation results from input images taken at various resolutions in different ambient conditions: (first row) long shadows at the M30 highway-ring in Madrid, (second row) dense traffic in a US highway, (third row) heavy vehicle in a German highway.

Where TV_b, TV_d and TH are the corresponding thresholds for V BRIGHT, V DARK and H as described in section 5.3.. The principle behind the classification criteria in (9) says that an image patch clearer than the background is always classified as a vehicle, while a dark patch must also show a significant deviation (in any direction) in H to be considered as such. The reason for that is based on the experimental fact that shadows are always darker than the background and show little deviation in H. However, it must be noticed that a DARK label does not preclude shadow classification; it just defines a DARK pixel as unclassified foreground. During the tracking stage a DARK pixel can still be classified either as vehicle or shadow at convenience. The HSV approach provides better discrimination between background, moving shadows and vehicles, but at the cost of extra computing power.

5.2. Night Operation

During night operation we observe the vehicles from behind and take advantage of the strong transition occurring between the front of the vehicle and the headlights and also at the vehicle's rear lights. Both features will delimit the shape of the vehicle.

In a first instance the vertical and horizontal gradients in the *image of differences* will be calculated respectively:

$$GV_t(x, y) = D_t(x, y + \gamma) - D_t(x, y)) \tag{10}$$
$$GH_t(x, y) = D_t(x + \delta, y + \gamma) - D_t(x, y + \gamma)) \tag{11}$$

Then, only the gradients corresponding to moving features will be retained, using the classification criteria below:

$$U_t(x,y) = \begin{cases} DARK & if & GV_t(x,y) & < & Ta \\ BRIGHT & if & GV_t(x,y) & > & |GH_t(x,y)| \quad \wedge \\ & & GV_t(x,y) & > & Tb \\ BRIGHT & if & GV_t(x,y) & \geq & 0 \qquad\qquad \wedge \\ & & GV_t(x,y) & \leq & |GH_t(x,y)| \quad \wedge \\ & & |GH_t(x,y)| & > & Tc \\ BKGND & Otherwise \end{cases} \qquad (12)$$

Where Ta, Tb and Tc are the vertical negative, vertical positive and horizontal gradients respectively. It must be noticed that the vertical negative gradient, denoting the transition between the front of the vehicle and the headlights, will be given preference in the classification.

In this case the DARK label represents a vertical negative transition rather than a dark image pixel. A vehicle will be identified in the tracking stage when it is detected a DARK patch followed by a BRIGHT patch within a predefined distance. In that way the vehicles can be identified robustly while the multiple shadows caused by artificial illumination are ignored since shadows cannot, in general, produce the required vertical negative transition (see Fig. 10). The best results have been obtained empirically by setting δ and γ to 2 pixels. Only monochrome information is used during night operation.

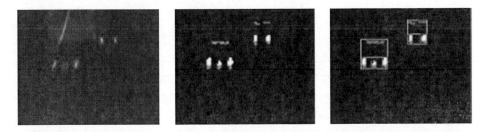

Figure 10. An example of night operation. (left) original image, (center) segmented image (right) detection masks. A white patch represents a BRIGHT label, while a gray patch is assigned a DARK label. It must be noticed how under night conditions headlights and shadows do not survive the *Segmentation* step.

5.3. Background Model Estimation

Acquiring and updating the background model is one of the most critical steps. In our case, as shown in Figure 11, the initial background is acquired by calculating the median of each pixel in the image over a temporal window. During the starting phase, two *Background Images* are taken separated by a specified time slice and its variance compared with a threshold. If the variance is below the threshold, system operation starts. Otherwise background initialization is restarted.

Once the initial background is acquired, it is necessary to continuously adapt it to the varying illumination changes. Illumination changes can be classified into "fast" and "slow" changes. This concept is somehow misleading depending on the frame rate the system is

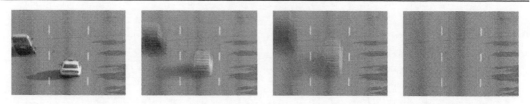

Figure 11. Construction of the background model; obtained after processing 256 gray level images.

able to achieve. At 25 frames/second, most illumination changes due to atmospheric effects are considered "slow" and are compensated in our approach using two methods: adaptation of the background levels and modification of the thresholds, see section 5.4..

For the adaptation of the *Background Image* we use a derivation of the Kalman filtering approach [31, 32], named *Exponential Forgetting*. Methods based on Kalman filtering assume the best information about the state of a system is obtained by means of an estimation which explicitly takes noise into account when measuring the parameters of the system. According to this approach, the estimation at time t is represented by:

$$\widehat{x}(t_i) = \widetilde{x}(t_i) + K(t_i) \cdot [z(t_i) - H(t_i) \cdot \widetilde{x}(t_i)] \tag{13}$$

where the prediction factor is defined by:

$$\widetilde{x}(t_i) = A(t_i) \cdot \widehat{x}(t_{i-1}) \tag{14}$$

In the above equations, $A(t_i)$ is the system matrix, $H(t_i)$ is named the measurement matrix, $z(t_i)$ is the input vector, while $K(t_i)$ is the gain matrix of the Kalman filter. The operation of the method can be summarized in the following steps: first, we take the prediction of the state of the system computed in a previous step; next we compare the prediction with the measured value of the parameter; finally we obtain a new estimation by computing the $K(t_i)$ weighted difference between the prediction and the measured value. The Kalman filter is recursive, so that every new estimation of the value of the parameter automatically accumulates the information acquired in previous steps. Hence, we avoid the need to store historic values individually.

Next, we will use basic Kalman filtering theory to implement our method for the adaptation of the *Background Image*. We name $s(x, y, t_i)$ to the intensity value of a pixel at a given time instant t_i. The estimated value of the pixel in the *Background Image* at this same time instant is represented by the vector $\widehat{s}(x, y, t_i)$ and the variation of the estimation is defined by $\dot{\widehat{s}}(x, y, t_i)$. According to equation 13, the new state of the system can be computed as follows:

$$\begin{bmatrix} \widehat{s}(x, y, t_i) \\ \dot{\widehat{s}}(x, y, t_i) \end{bmatrix} = \begin{bmatrix} \widetilde{s}(x, y, t_i) \\ \dot{\widetilde{s}}(x, y, t_i) \end{bmatrix} +$$

$$K(x, y, t_i) \cdot \left(s(x, y, t_i) - H(x, y, t_i) \cdot \begin{bmatrix} \widetilde{s}(x, y, t_i) \\ \dot{\widetilde{s}}(x, y, t_i) \end{bmatrix} \right) \tag{15}$$

where the prediction is:

$$\begin{bmatrix} \widetilde{s}(x,y,t_i) \\ \widetilde{\dot{s}}(x,y,t_i) \end{bmatrix} = A \cdot \begin{bmatrix} \widehat{s}(x,y,t_{i-1}) \\ \widehat{\dot{s}}(x,y,t_{i-1}) \end{bmatrix} \tag{16}$$

Without loss of generality we can simplify our model by considering the matrices A and H are constant:

$$A = \begin{bmatrix} 1 & a_{1,2} \\ 0 & a_{2,2} \end{bmatrix} \qquad\qquad H = \begin{bmatrix} 1 & 0 \end{bmatrix} \tag{17}$$

where $a_{1,2} = a_{2,2} = constant$ and matrix H takes this form because we are dealing with black and white images only. Finally, the gain matrix transforms into:

$$K(x,y,t_i) = \begin{bmatrix} k_1(x,y,t_i) \\ k_2(x,y,t_i) \end{bmatrix} \tag{18}$$

where $k_1(x,y,t_i) = k_2(x,y,t_i) = \alpha$. Now, if we expand the first element in equation (15), we notice:

$$\widehat{s}(x,y,t_i) = \alpha \cdot s(x,y,t_i) + (1-\alpha) \cdot \widehat{s}(x,y,t_{i-1}) + cte \cdot (1-\alpha) \cdot \widehat{\dot{s}}(x,y,t_{i-1}) \tag{19}$$

Finally, if we assume the variation $\widehat{\dot{s}}(x,y,t_{i-1})$ in the estimation of the *Background Image* between two consecutive time instants is small (which is about right) we arrive at the well-known *Exponential Forgetting* expression:

$$B(x,y,t_i) = \alpha \cdot I(x,y,t_i) + (1-\alpha) \cdot B(x,y,t_{i-1}) \tag{20}$$

where $I(x,y,t_i)$ is the intensity value of the pixel at present time, $B(x,y,t_i)$ is the newly estimated value of the *Background Image* for the present time, $B(x,y,t_{i-1})$ is the corresponding value of the *Background Image* computed in the previous time instant and α is known as the *learning* parameter. Equation 20 is more frequently found in the literature [31, 32] in the following form:

$$B_t(x,y) = \alpha \cdot B_{t-1}(x,y) + (1-\alpha) \cdot I_t(x,y); \quad \alpha < 1 \tag{21}$$

In consequence, given the current image I_t and the background in the previous time instant B_{t-1}, we can obtain the current background estimation for each pixel. In this case α is the time constant and represent the rate of adaptation of the background to the new image levels. Background updating will be affected by passing objects (particularly by slow moving objects). For that reason, the value of α will be lower, and hence the rate of adaptation higher, for pixels that belong to the background than the corresponding value for pixels belonging to a moving object or shadow.

This approach can be implemented by simply using a segmentation labeling criteria: i.e. pixels labeled BCKGND gets a lower value, or the most robust approach in [32] that uses feedback from the tracker. In the latter case the idea is that pixels that belong to recognized moving objects must be adapted more slowly, while pixels belonging to the background or static objects must be adapted much faster. In that way, in the case of traffic congestion, the background gets adapted very fast as soon as the congestion dissolves.

The coefficient α will be re-calculated periodically as a function of the period and the frame rate. The criteria used is to select the α coefficient that will allow us to achieve the desired rate of adaptation of the *Background Image* in a given time interval (assuming the input image remains constant). Since equation (21) is recursive, we need an estimation for the *Background Image* at the starting point. In our case we set the initial values of the *Background Image* to $B_0(x, y) = I(x, y)/2$. Next, if we apply equation (21) backwards until we reach the time instant m, we obtain the following expression::

$$B_m(x, y) = I(x, y)(1 - \alpha^m) \tag{22}$$

The rate of adaptation of the *Background Image* we desire to achieve is defined as:

$$Frac = \frac{|B_m(x, y) - B_0(x, y)|}{B_0(x, y)} = 1 - \alpha^m \tag{23}$$

From this relation we can obtain α:

$$\alpha = (1 - \frac{|B_m(x, y) - B_0(x, y)|}{B_0(x, y)})^{1/m} \tag{24}$$

Parameter m (the number of frames required to achieve the adaptation $Frac$ with a given α) can be obtained directly from the measured frame rate of the system V_p (normally 25 img / sec) and the recalculation time t_r as: $m = V_p \cdot t_r$. Our experiments demonstrated an adaptation of 10% with a recalculation interval of 30 seconds provides a good compromise between fast adaptation and robustness against ghost objects.

5.4. Automatic Parameter Adjustment

Parameters Tb and Td in Eq. (8) must be adapted automatically in order to cope with two types of illumination changes: long-lasting slow changes (i.e due to atmospheric effects) and fast changes of a short-duration (i.e. caused by the camera compensation devices). For this purpose, we propose to analyze two different versions of the histogram of the *image of differences* (Eq. 7): the *instant histogram* (calculated on a single image) and a window *time-averaged histogram*. The range of the histograms will be: -255 to 255.

The *time-averaged histogram* can be modeled as unimodal and Gaussian (Fig. 12), while, on the contrary, in the *instant histogram* a significant amount of noise and possibly a multi-modal distribution is to be expected. The basic idea is, that provided the background is reasonably updated, if the *time-averaged histogram* is analyzed over a sufficiently long period of time, the great majority of pixels differences will belong to the static part of the image and must be found in a small region around the peak. The objective would be to segment this population from the rest. However, global illumination changes in the current image may introduce a level of continua in the histogram before the mechanisms for slow adaptation can compensate it. As a result, the distribution representing the background differences will get displaced in the present image. This effect is masqueraded in the *time-averaged histogram* (since it has zero mean) and hence it must be compensated by locating the peak of the *instant histogram* and providing the necessary corrections.

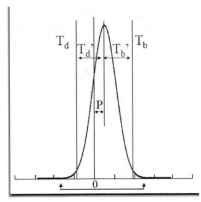

Figure 12. The figure shows how the *ideal* probability distribution representing the static background is displaced in the current image by an amount P, due to a global illumination change, caused for example by the actuation of the camera auto-iris. This effect cannot be detected on the *time-averaged histogram* since the averaging blurs the history of the histogram. However, parameters T_b and T_d, which represent the adaptation to slow illumination changes, are calculated from the *time-averaged histogram* with the aim to avoid the noisy influences that can be found in the *instant histogram*.

In that sense, the width of the *time-averaged histogram* will provide us an estimation of the required long term noise tolerance, while the position of the peak of the *instant histogram* represents the level of continua or displacement of the current image difference levels with respect to the optimal background estimation. The criteria will be to select first the relative thresholds Tb' and Td' as 2,5 standard deviations (σ) in both directions of the *time-averaged histogram* and then calculate the absolute thresholds Tb and Td at time t as follows:

$$T_b = P_t + T_b' \; ; \; T_d = P_t + T_d' \tag{25}$$

Where P_t signals the position of the peak of the *instant histogram*. Since the peak may move abruptly from one image to the other (even if the general shape of the histogram may remain), its position must be calculated for each incoming image. In order to avoid confusing the peak of the histogram with other prominent maxima, P_t is tracked from image to image in a window of the *instant histogram* range, centered at its previous position P_{t-1}. Once the absolute thresholds have been calculated, it will be necessary to update the *time-averaged histogram*. For that purpose, the level of continua is removed from the *instant histogram* and the result is time averaged with contributions from the pervious images. Since Tb' and Td' coefficients are meant to compensate slow changes, their evaluation is done only every 200 images.

When using the HSV color space (Eq. 9), the same technique for the calculation of the histogram is applied to the V channel (TVb and TVd), while the H channel uses a fixed threshold (TH). This is justified since image chromaticity is less affected by illumination changes. On the other hand, in the night algorithm (Eq. 12) we expect ambient illumination would be more stable. For that reason, Ta, Tb and Tc are set relative to a single base threshold computed from the dispersion of the histogram.

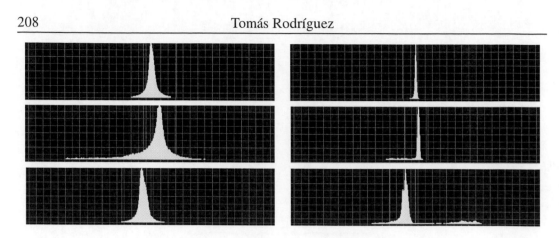

Figure 13. Examples of real *Histograms*. Top *Accumulated Histogram*. Middle and down two examples of *Instantaneous Histograms* for the same image sequences. Notice how the instantaneous histogram is more noisy and distorts the real width of the histogram but allows us to detect the displacement of the peak (level of continua).

The above method is fast, since it requires only two thresholds for the whole image, it uses both temporal and spatial information and, since we are using the histogram of differences and relative thresholds, it does not depend on the illumination levels. The algorithm correctly handles fast illumination changes and raises automatically the threshold levels in the presence of noisy images or poor background estimation.

5.5. Gamma Correction

Most frequently camera sensors are linear devices so that the electrical output in the sensor is proportional to the number of incident photons. On the contrary, human vision is inherently nonlinear and can be approximated by a 0.45 gamma function. For that reason, most cameras are bundled with an electronic image corrector providing gamma output similar to that in Figure 14. This compensation is very useful to visualize the images but produces the undesirable effect of modifying artificially the top level gray levels.

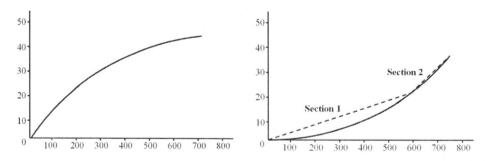

Figure 14. (Left) Typical output of a camera sensor with gamma 0.45. (Right) Correction function used to compensate the nonlinearity of the sensor, approximated by two linear sections.

The immediate consequence is similar increases in the incident intensity are transformed differently in the image, depending on the underlying gray level. Some important errors, such as segmentation faults in the border of traffic lines in presence of sudden intensity changes, can be traced back to inappropriate gamma correction.

The usual way to compensate the nonlinearity of the camera output is to apply an inverse function to the gray levels of every pixel in the image. However, this approach is very expensive computationally. For that reason, we opted to keep the gray levels but modify instead the segmentation thresholds. This solution is much faster, but it is still computationally intensive. In consequence we decided to approximate the inverse gamma function by two linear trams; as shown in Figure 14.

5.6. Other Segmentation Approaches Found in the Literature

5.6.1. Methods Using Temporal Differences

Temporal Differences is a classic method based on detecting object's movements by observing differences between consecutive images. For this method to work, the background scenario must be static or slow moving, as compared to foreground objects. The method identifies as a moving object any relevant discrepancy in the intensity between two time separated images. For that purpose we compare the value of each pixel in the current image with the same pixel in one or more of the previous images. This comparison can be done in many different ways but the most common approach simply computes the difference between the intensity levels of two consecutive frames and then threshold the result using any of the methods available in the literature.

$$D_t(u, v) = I_t(u, v) - I_{t-i}(u, v) \qquad (26)$$

Where D_t is the *image of differences* we desire to compute and i signals the position of the image in the temporal sequence (i.e. image comparison need not necessarily be done between two consecutive images).

The main advantage of this method is we do not need to compute a *Background Image*. This is an important factor to consider since acquiring and maintaining the *Background Image* is one of the main sources of difficulties for *Background Subtraction* methods. Furthermore, since the time between two frames is very short, this method is also free from the undesirable influence of most (but not all) ambient light variations. However, in spite of its undeniable advantages, the method also has important drawbacks; as described below.

In Figure 15 we show the result of applying the *Temporal Differences* algorithm to a simplified traffic scenario. Similarly to the *Background Subtraction* method, the system can only detect the vehicle if it is substantially different from the background in previous images. In this case when we differentiate two consecutive images we get front and rear borders separated by a valley region for each segmented vehicle. If the vehicle is clearer than the background the front border is made of negative differences, while the rear border is positive. In the case of a vehicle darker than the background results are just the opposite.

As observed in the picture, even in this "idealized" case, the resulting object masks are very difficult to discern. Every vehicle is associated at least two segmented regions. Furthermore, the size and separation of these regions is not constant, since they will depend on the speed of the vehicle; which normally is unknown. Also, the masks are not coincident with the real position of the vehicle. For that reason identifying the real size and position

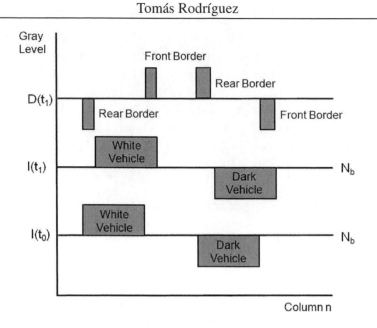

Figure 15. In the figure we show the intensity profile of the n column in image (I') at two different time instants (t_0 and t_1). We also show, at the top of the drawing, the resulting difference Image (D). In the input picture there are two "ideal" vehicles of uniform color: one white vehicle, closely followed by a vehicle of a dark color. N_b is the reference gray level of the background at this point.

of the vehicle becomes more complex. Finally, occlusions become a critical problem since the method favors overlapping of masks from different vehicles.

On the other hand, it is obvious this "idealized" case is very rare in practice. A real vehicle is heterogeneous and frequently it is composed of many different parts of different colors, which turns vehicle identification into a very challenging process. Some authors [33, 34] have tried to address this problem by computing, for each input image, two difference images: one between the current and previous image and a second one between the current and following images. Next, they use a border descriptor to extract the contour of the regions comprising the vehicles and computes the intersection of both resulting images. This method offers more accurate identification of the contour of the vehicle in the image. However, the large number or imperfections appearing in these contours pose new problems, which are, again, very difficult to solve. In practice the *Temporal Differences* method presents so many drawbacks it is hardly used alone. In most references [35, 34] this method is used as a complement or improvement of other more robust alternative solutions.

5.6.2. Background Mixture Models

A more sophisticated method to model the background [36] is based on the assumption that the value of each pixel in the image can be represented by a single population, affected by random noise, following a normal distribution (Gaussian). This method is a good approach if the value of the pixels are the result of observing light reflected by a single surface. In practice, in traffic scenes, the same pixel can be affected by light coming from multiple surfaces. For that reason, a single Gaussian does not represent accurately the information acquired from the scene.

With the aim to address this problem, in [37] it is proposed to use a mixture of three Gaussians, modeling respectively: the background, the vehicles and the shadows cast by the vehicles. Results can be improved further if we use multiple Gaussians to model the process; as described in [38]. Each Gaussian tries to handle the information coming from a single surface observed by the pixel in the course of time. Later, a heuristic criteria is used to determine which of these Gaussians or populations correspond to the background. A similar approach can be found in [39], while in [40] the author claims using a mixture of Cauchy distributions, instead of Gaussians, is a better representation of the different populations composing the scene.

According to the original "Background Mixture Model" method, described in [38], the recent history of each pixel $\{X_1, \ldots, X_t\}$ can be modeled with a mixture of K Gaussians. To that end, we represent the probability of observing the current value of the pixel by means of the following formula:

$$P(X_t) = \sum_{k=1}^{K} w_{k,t} \cdot \eta(X_t, \mu_{k,t}, \Sigma_{k,t}) \tag{27}$$

where $w_{i,t}$ is the *weight* assigned to each of the Gaussians of the mixture at time t and η is the probability density function. The distribution η is defined for each Gaussian as a function of the value of the pixel X_t, the average value $\mu_{i,t}$ of the distribution and its covariance matrix $\Sigma_{i,t}$, according to the following relation:

$$\eta(X_t, \mu, \Sigma) = \frac{1}{(2\pi)^{\frac{n}{2}} |\Sigma|^{\frac{1}{2}}} e^{-\frac{1}{2}(X_t - \mu_{k,t})^T \cdot \Sigma^{-1} \cdot (X_t - \mu_{k,t})} \tag{28}$$

With the aim to reduce the computational needs, it is usual to limit K to a maximum of between 3 and 5 Gaussians and we admit the simplification to consider the covariance matrix takes the form: $\Sigma_{k,t} = \sigma_k^2 \mathbf{I}$.

In that way, the distribution of the recent history of the observed values of each pixel in the image at a given time instant will be characterized by the mixture of Gaussians described above. When a new image is analyzed, the new value of the pixel can probably be found already in one of the components of the mixture. If the match is found, the new value is used to update the model of the corresponding component of the mixture. On the contrary, if it is not possible to find a match, the component distribution with lowest confidence level is removed from the mixture and a new component is created containing a single element. The new distribution is created with the value of the pixel as average and it is started with high variance and low weight.

Once the appropriate distribution has been found / created, we need to update the different parameters controlling the mixture model. Firstly, we proceed to update the weights using the following formula:

$$w_{k,t} = (1 - \alpha) \cdot w_{k,t-1} + \alpha \cdot M_{k,t} \tag{29}$$

where $M_{k,t} = 1$ for the distribution matched with the current value of the pixel and $M_{k,t} = 0$ for the rest. The α coefficient is named the *learning rate* and determines the speed of adaptation of the model. Once the weights have been updated, we re-normalize them again.

On the other hand, we only update the parameters μ and σ corresponding to the current value of the pixel. μ and σ are not modified in the rest of distributions. We use the following formulas to compute the new parameters μ and σ:

$$\mu_{k,t} = (1 - \rho) \cdot \mu_{k,t-1} + \rho \cdot X_t \tag{30}$$

$$\sigma_{k,t}^2 = (1 - \rho) \cdot \sigma_{k,t-1}^2 + \rho \cdot (X_t - \mu_{k,t})^T \cdot (X_t - \mu_{k,t}) \tag{31}$$

$$\rho = \alpha \cdot \eta(X_t | \mu_{k,t}, \sigma_{k,t}) \tag{32}$$

At this point, all the parameters of the mixture have been updated with the information contributed by the new image. Now, it is time to decide which is the distribution that better represents the background. The criteria used is to select the candidates having lower variance and highest weight. For that purpose we first order the Gaussians as a function of w/σ, so that the most promising distributions appear high in the list. Next, we select as representative of the background the first B distributions complying with the following condition:

$$B = argmin_b \left(\Sigma_{k=1}^b w_k > T \right) \tag{33}$$

where T signals the size of the space we want to model. In that sense, if T is low, we basically obtain an unimodal representation, while if T is increased, the background will be represented by multiple populations. Finally, we segment the image by identifying a pixel as belonging to a vehicle when its value is far from $2, 5 \cdot \sigma$ in all B distributions.

Thanks to the automatic adaptation of its parameters, the method is robust against slow illumination changes and offers the possibility to represent the background using information from various populations. One of the merits of the method is the possibility to incorporate new information without destroying the previous model. In that way, when a new value, not previously considered in the model, appears in the image, the new value is incorporated into a new distribution. However, the old distributions are still preserved, with the same μ and σ^2, but with lower *weight* w, until a model becomes the least probable and then it is removed from the mixture. In consequence, if the background is affected by temporal alterations, the method offers the possibility to recover its previous state. This is useful, for example, to cope with camera vibrations, where the background oscillates periodically. The same effect can be observed with moving trees or rain. Another possibility is to model the behavior of shadows and stopped vehicles.

Unfortunately, the ideal situation described above is not always realized in practice. The method only works if information is preserved in the model long enough to be recovered at a later time. However, there are several reasons why this may fail. For example, illumination conditions may change significantly during the time of the background alteration so that when it is finished and the information is recovered, it no longer represents the real conditions of the scenario. Another example is when the phenomena altering the background lasts longer than the time required to preserve the model.

These circumstances are not rare in traffic scenarios and for that reason it is questionable if the mentioned advantages justify the significant increase of the computational needs implicit in the method. If we use a low K, say 3 to 5, as proposed, the probability that a large temporal alteration may ruin the model is very high. In the methods using adaptive thresholds this circumstance would be handled by increasing the tolerance level of the threshold. On the contrary, in the methods using a mixture of Gaussians one of the distributions is removed from the list, resulting in an incorrect segmentation of the pixel. An effect that might last long after the disturbance has ended.

On the other hand, if K is high, the computational needs become unmanageable for an embedded system. Also a high K introduce the problem of how to decide which distributions belong to the foreground and which to the background. The real problem is, a priori, there is no clear criteria saying how many distributions must belong to the background.

Another possible source of errors has been reported in [41]. If the first value considered for a pixel belongs to the foreground, the algorithm will take $log_{(1-\alpha)}(T)$ times until the real value of the background is incorporated and $log_{(1-\alpha)}(0,5)$ times until it becomes dominant. For example, if we assume the background can be observed at least 60% of the time and $\alpha = 0,002$, it will be necessary 255 and 346 images respectively. The problem is even more critical in situations of dense traffic, when the road is less visible.

To solve this problem it has been proposed in [41] to use two models to update the different parameters, depending on the situation of the system. First the author defines a temporal observation window with the aim to give more relevance to recent information and adapt better to environmental changes. Next, he uses a different model for the initialization and runtime phases. The approach implemented during the initialization step is as follows:

$$w_{k,t} = w_{k,t-1} + \frac{1}{t}(M_{k,t} - w_{k,t-1}) \tag{34}$$

$$\mu_{k,t} = \mu_{k,t-1} + \frac{M_{k,t}}{\Sigma_{i=1}^{t}(M_{k,i})}(X_t - \mu_{k,t-1}) \tag{35}$$

$$\Sigma_{k,t} = \Sigma_{k,t-1} + \frac{M_{k,t}}{\Sigma_{i-1}^{t}(M_{k,i})}((X_t - \mu_{k,t-1}) \cdot (X_t - \mu_{k,t-1})^T - \Sigma_{k,t-1}) \tag{36}$$

Later, when the system has acquired at least L samples he uses the alternative approach described below:

$$w_{k,t} = w_{k,t-1} + \frac{1}{L}(M_{k,t} - w_{k,t-1}) \tag{37}$$

$$\mu_{k,t} = \mu_{k,t-1} + \frac{1}{L}(\frac{M_{k,t} \cdot X_t}{w_{k,t}} - \mu_{k,t-1}) \tag{38}$$

$$\Sigma_{k,t} = \Sigma_{k,t-1} + \frac{1}{L}(\frac{M_{k,t} \cdot (X_t - \mu_{k,t-1}) \cdot (X_t - \mu_{k,t-1})^T}{w_{k,t}} - \Sigma_{k,t-1}) \tag{39}$$

Another drawback of the K-Gaussianas method is the fact that the algorithm only considers information at the pixel level; i.e. it does not take advantage of global information affecting the whole image. This is unfortunate since the analysis of global changes is critical in traffic scenarios. Some examples are the global changes induced by passing shadows or the frequent over reaction of camera compensation devices. These effects, if not correctly handled, may corrupt the background model and may result in the erroneous classification of foreground and background pixels.

In summary, the Background Mixture Model method offers the possibility to handle multiple populations with the aim to build a model of the scene that would allow us cope with important events affecting traffic systems; such as: shadows, stopped vehicles, camera oscillations, etc. However, in practice, the increased computational needs are not compensated with an equivalent improvement in the accuracy of the system, since, as we mentioned above, other less sophisticated methods are able to achieve similar performance under free traffic. Unfortunately, the use of various populations offer no advantage under dense traffic because congestions take too long for the background information to be preserved.

Finally, it is interesting to note that if we take $K = 1$ and assume all values have the same probability ($\rho = \alpha$), then equation (30) is transformed into the limiting case so that we again recover a relation equivalent to that found in (20):

$$\mu_{k,t} = (1 - \alpha) \cdot \mu_{k,t-1} + \alpha \cdot X_t \tag{40}$$

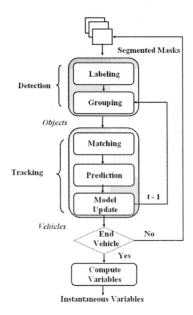

Figure 16. Structure of the Detection and Tracking process. Notice how the detection process uses feedback from previous (t-1) frame.

6.   Detection and Tracking

The mission of the Detection and Tracking step is to make an abstraction of the physical objects implicit in the Segmentation masks for every incoming image and then track those objects in the sequence until finally all vehicles and shadows present in the scene have been robustly identified. Ideally, the Detection stage works on information from a single image, while the tracking stage combines information from multiple previous images. In practice, the limits between the Detection and Tracking stages are blurred and information from the tracker is frequently used to lead searches in the Detection stage.

There is a wide variety of Detection and Tracking methods [15, 42, 43, 44, 45] in the literature. However, not many of them can be implemented in real time. Historically, research in traffic monitoring applications have been focused mainly on Segmentation but avoided specific developments for Detection and Tracking. This is unfortunate since general purpose trackers are overshooting in traffic environments, while on the other hand fail to take advantage of application specific information. In fact the vehicles' trajectories are rather simple; i.e. they are rectilinear and move at nearly constant speed, all in the same direction. However, these apparently simple trajectories are masqueraded by improper segmentation, the presence of shadows and other moving objects, occlusions, perspective effects, etc. In consequence standard trackers are poor performers in this application scenario.

```
objects_mask = compute_object_masks(input_image, background_image)
candidates_list = compute_candidates_list(objects_mask)
% Assign new instances of objects to objects list
do
{
  object = get_next_oldest_widest_object(objects_list)
  roi = compute_ROI(object)
  % Assign objects by checking if they overlap
  for_every (candidate in candidates_list)
  {
    if(check_overlapping_objects(roi, candidate) is true)
    {
      object = merge_objects(object, candidate)
    }
  }
}until(no more merges occur)

% Add objects entering the scene for the first time
objects_list = add_free_candidates(objects_list, candidates_list)

% Merge using safety distance
for_every (object1 in objects_list)
{
  roi = extend_object_with_safety_margin(object1)
  for_every (object2 in objects_list)
  {
    if(check_overlapping_objects(roi, object2) is true)
    {
      object1_merges_counter++
      if(object1_merges_counter > count_limit)
      {
        object1 = merge_objects(object1, object2)
      }
    }
  }
}
```

```
% Merge using predicted object category size
for_every (object1 in objects_list)
{
  if(object1_type is BRIGHT)
  {
    roi = extend_object_up_to_limits_of_category(object1)
    for_every (object2 in objects_list)
    {
      if(check_enclosed(roi, object2) is true)
      {
        object1_merges_counter++
        if(object1_merges_counter > count_limit)
        {
          object1 = merge_objects(object1, object2)
        }
      }
    }
  }
}

object_list = Compute_heavy_vehicles(objects_list)
object_list = Compute_shadows(objects_list)
% Compute traffic variables when object leves scene
for_every (object in objects_list)
{
  if(object_status is ended)
  {
    if(check_valid_object(object) is true)
    {
      traffic_variables = compute_traffic_variables(object)
    }
  }
}
```

Figure 17. Pseudo-code summarizing the Detection and Tracking processes. Main parameters: objects_masks = list of segmentation masks; candidates_list = list of candidate objects resulting from initial filtering of the objects masks; objects_list = the list of objects being computed (refined through subsequent image processing steps for the whole life of the detected objects); object = an element in the objects_list (i.e. a possible vehicle or shadow); traffic_variables = the computed traffic variables: counting, speed and category. See main text for details.

Our Detection and Tracking method performs in real time and is based on the vehicle model presented in section 2.1.. This model describes not only the intrinsic properties of the vehicles but more interestingly their behavior and their relations with other objects present in the scene; i.e. the shadows. The structure of the Detection and Tracking stages and a pseudo-code describing the process is shown in figures 16 and 17 respectively.

6.1. Object Detection

The three-label *object masks* resulting from the *Segmentation* step provide a pixel-wise description of the regions where the candidate vehicles or shadows are located. The masks are next transformed into an *objects list* structure in the *Labeling step*; where a one pass, four connected, blob coloring algorithm is used. The list may contain objects of three types: DARK, BRIGHT or SHADOW. Every object in the list is started with the following basic information: object type, geometric center, mass center, enclosing rectangle, size in pixels, etc. More properties are added to the list as the object progresses in the scene.

Because the *Segmentation* process is far from perfect, vehicles and shadows are typically represented in the *objects list* by multiple regions or objects. During the *Detection* stage, the objects composing a single vehicle or shadow are merged using the empirical knowledge implicit in the *vehicle* and *shadow models*. In our *Detection* approach vehicles' shapes will be approximated by rectangles (this is fair thanks to perspective correction) and the system will try to merge any compatible object of the same type using information such as: proximity, maximum allowed size and morphology. Again, we developed different Detection algorithms to handle day and night conditions.

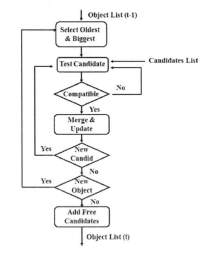

Figure 18. Object Detection Process. Compatible candidates are assigned to existing objects. Unpaired candidates are added as new objects.

While in *day* operation, the merging process (Fig. 18) is started with a list of candidate objects identified in the present image and the list of objects consolidated from previous images. The task is to take every object from the *objects list* and try to match it with any compatible object from the *candidates list*. With the aim to reduce the risk of incorrectly merging objects from different vehicles, we first select the oldest objects in the *objects list* and, from these, we choose the object showing the widest area. Then, the algorithm progressively tries to merge the selected object with objects of the same type in the *candidates list*, until no more compatible objects are found. The merged objects are automatically removed from the *candidates list* and the complete process is repeated with the next object

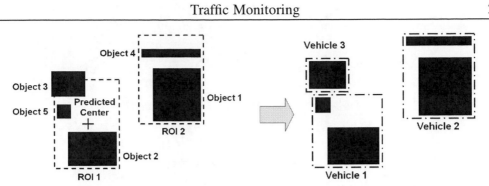

Figure 19. An example of the Merging Process. (a) Observe the candidate objects $1 - 5$ and the predicted center and ROI of the two objects currently being processed. (b) Notice how after the merging process, a new object 3 appears since the composed object exceeded the limits of the category.

in the *objects list* until all objects have been considered. Finally, all free objects in the *candidates list* are incorporated into the *objects list* as new objects.

During the merging process we construct a ROI (region of interest) for every object in the *objects list*. The ROI is placed at the position predicted for the object in the current image; as described in figure 19. The predicted position is computed from past observations of the same object. For BRIGHT objects the size of the ROI will be the *maximum allowed size* of the vehicle category or the maximum size observed for the selected object in previous images; whichever is bigger. The *maximum allowed size* of each vehicle category is obtained automatically at the calibration step by computing the size of the area projected on the *work image* by a parallelogram representative of the category. We select for merging that object in the *candidates list* overlapping more with the ROI. The merging will only take place if the size of the object resulting from the merging does not exceed the *maximum allowed size* of the category or the maximum observed size of the object. For DARK or SHADOW objects the process is similar; only the historical observed size of the object is not considered when computing the ROI in order or avoid undesirable growing of shadow areas.

At night the Detection process will be different since the objects masks are also different (see Fig. 20). If we remember from section 5.2., at night there are no shadows and the vehicles are represented by one or more DARK regions followed by one or more BRIGHT regions. The task will be to correctly group those regions. We first group every dark region with its corresponding BRIGHT region by placing a ROI aligned with the upper border of the DARK region. The width of the ROI will be coincident with the width of the DARK region and its length will be the *maximum allowed length* for the vehicle category. Any BRIGHT region overlapping with the ROI will be matched with the DARK region. When all DARK regions have been processed, the unmatched regions will be removed from the list; thus removing potentially dangerous features such as: shadows remains, reflections, etc.

Next all BRIGHT objects are converted into DARK objects and a new grouping process is started. First, we group all objects which are too close together by using a ROI with the

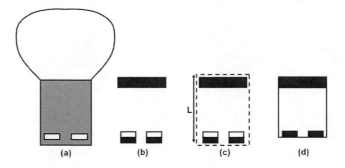

Figure 20. Example of a night detection process. (a) Ideal representation of a vehicle. (b) Segmentation masks. Notice a vehicle is composed of DARK and BRIGHT regions. (c) Detection ROI, where L is the *maximum allowed size* of the vehicle category. (d) Rectangle inscribing the resulting object. Notice how all BRIGHT objects have been transformed into DARK objects.

maximum allowed size of the category, extended a few pixels. Next we try to match the left and right lights of the vehicles. Typically this process is only required for large size vehicles, but we apply it to all objects for security. We use a ROI with the *maximum allowed length* of the category and a width computed from the detected width of the object, extended in the left and right directions up to the limits of the category. Any object overlapping with the ROI will be merged provided the composed object does not exceed the limits of the category. This approach allows us to capture any car light within the limits of the vehicle. Finally, the resulting candidate objects are subject to a matching process with the historical *objects list* similar to that described for day operation.

6.2. Object Tracking and Occlusion Reasoning

During the detection step we performed the matching between the candidate objects present in the current image and the objects detected in previous images. This process implicitly achieved a kind of merging of objects of the same type at the image level. However, the results are far from perfect and in practice, it is frequent to find vehicles are composed of one, two or all three types of objects: BRIGHT, DARK and SHADOW. In consequence, during the tracking stage, we will progressively merge all categories composing a single vehicle using the information compiled for the object since it first entered the scene. In our case, objects of different types are tracked independently and they are only merged at the end of the tracking process.

We first take advantage of one of the properties in the vehicle model saying a vehicle must observe a security margin with the preceding vehicle and also with other vehicles running in parallel. For that purpose we use a proximity criteria whereby two objects of the same type are merged when they are too close. We use a ROI centered at the object and extended in the amount of the defined vertical and horizontal security margins. We merge any overlapping object of the same type, but we also merge DARK objects with SHADOW objects. Again, the merging is only allowed if the merged object does not exceed the maximum allowed size of the category (all categories) or the maximum observed size (only for BRIGHT objects). To avoid incorrect merging due to temporal occlusions, we only merge the two objects when several successive merging attempts have taken place. A counter attached to the object is incremented with every merging attempt, but it is restored the first time the merging fails.

At this stage we should have a rather compact description of the objects in the list. However, to account for possible deficiencies in the Segmentation step (i.e. a vehicle appears broken into several parts), we implement one additional merging process for BRIGHT objects. In this case we allow the object to grow up to the limits of the category by capturing any BRIGHT object in its proximity; provided the usual size limits of the merged object are not exceeded. In this case we use a ROI extended in all four directions up to the maximum allowed width and length of the category. This is a risky process and can only be issued once the objects in the list have been compacted in the previous steps.

The above completes the merging approach, whereby we intend to identify one object with one vehicle or shadow. Now we will focus on the tracking process. Tracking vehicles is not a big deal. We just compute the average speed of the vehicle by line fitting the position detected in previous images, next we predict the position of the object in the current image assuming constant speed and finally match existing objects with new instances of the objects in the current image; following the procedure described in section 6.1.. Unfortunately, this apparent simple process gets masqueraded by the presence of shadows, occlusions and errors resulting from heavy vehicles.

Tracking BRIGHT objects is rather straightforward since a BRIGHT label provides an almost certain guaranty that the object belongs to a vehicle. However the case of DARK and SHADOW labels is more involved since an object may begin its history as DARK and then transform into SHADOW. Our approach is to count the number of times the object has been detected either as DARK or SHADOW and then decide which is the most appropriate label. For that purpose we use two counters: the first one (*detection counter*) counts the number of object detections regardless of its type; while the second one (*shadow counter*) counts the number of times this object has been identified as SHADOW.

Difficulties are increased due to occlusions. One of the sideways effect we were not able to solve in our perspective correction method is the height of vehicles is projected to the front and the side of vehicles. Thus, they appear larger than they are and we face the risk they might overlap. This problem is specially challenging in the case of heavy vehicles since, even if they usually observe larger security margins with the preceding vehicles, they are significantly higher and less aerodynamic. In fact it is not uncommon to find two overlapped vehicles or even vehicles which are mostly occluded, with the result any of them is miscounted. On the other hand occlusions are more severe close to the horizon.

Since occlusions imply some critical information is missing, our best opportunity to solve this problem with simple techniques suitable for real-time, is to compute their traffic variables while they are separate and allow for some tolerance for the case they again become apart after being occluded; i.e. a kind of ghost object tracking. This is reasonable since vehicles frequently show different relative speeds in the different lanes. Treatment of occlusions is done in our case by first, optimizing the aiming of the camera and second, implementing a tracking method tolerant to temporal faults.

The tracking algorithm is based on the state machine presented in figure 21. The first time a vehicle enters the scene, it is assigned the ENTERING state. Later, while it is being tracked, it gets the PASSING state and its *detection counter* is incremented for every new detection. On the contrary, the first time the detection fails, the object turns into a FAILED state but remains in the list in the form of a ghost object (this is only applicable to BRIGHT objects). A ghost object is subject to the usual matching and merging rules, but with every new fail its *failed object counter* is incremented. In the event a ghost object has succeeded the matching, its *failed object counter* is restored and returns to the PASSING state. Finally, an object gets the ENDED state when the *failed object counter* exceeds a threshold. Only at this point we consider the object is finished and we proceed to perform its final classification and evaluate its traffic variables.

BRIGHT and DARK objects who survive the merging at the end of the tracking process and offer a number of *object detections* above the threshold N_d will be identified as candidates for a physical vehicle. This candidate vehicle will only be validated if the object entered and left the scene from the appropriate points in the *control area* (i.e. top / bottom) and if the object is persistent. N_d is computed automatically as a function of the length of the *control area* (L) and the measured speed of the vehicle (V_V); so that the minimum allowed number of *object detections* guaranties the vehicle has covered at least half the length of the *control area*: $N_d = \frac{V_P \cdot L}{2 \cdot V_V}$. Where V_P is the processing speed of the system (typically 25 frames per second).

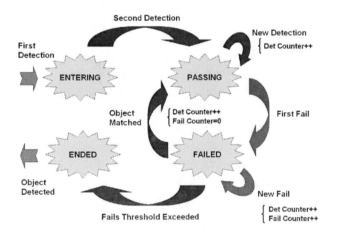

Figure 21. State Machine used in the tracking algorithm. Notice it provides certain protection against temporal occlusions.

On the other hand, surviving SHADOW objects must undertake one additional test. If the number of *shadow detections* is above the threshold N_d when the object leaves the scene (i.e. when it is not detected any more), the object will be classified as SHADOW. Otherwise, the total number of *object detections* will be checked against N_d and if the test is successful the object will be identified as an ordinary DARK object. Finished SHADOW objects will be simply discarded since it is certain its associated BRIGHT object already achieved the threshold N_d. This approach guaranties that given a sufficient number of detections, either the BRIGHT or SHADOW object is selected, but not both. The method also ensures DARK vehicles survive even if they might have been temporally classified as shadows and ensures certain protection against temporal occlusions.

6.3. Heavy Vehicle Identification

The effects resulting from heavy vehicles are frequently underestimated, since existing systems do not implement especial provisions to track them. Actually, heavy vehicles are responsible for many tracking errors and in particular occlusions effects; hence identifying the heavy vehicles is the first step to treat occlusions. Heavy vehicles are complex. They can be found in a wide variety of sizes, shapes and colors; from medium sized lorries to large trucks and buses. Furthermore, they can be decorated in vivid colors, thus confusing Segmentation algorithms.

We start the heavy vehicle identification process by determining the number of categories and the boundaries between them (in practice two categories are sufficient). The boundary in width is set to: $W_{light} + (W_{heavy} - W_{light})/2$; where W_i is the maximum apparent width of the respective categories, computed using the procedure described in section 6.1.. Similarly, the length limit is set to $1.25 \times L_{light}$. This is justified since we observe heavy vehicles are very similar in width, but can be of any length.

The first problem we must face is we do not know, a priory, if an object entering the scene for the first time belongs to a heavy vehicle or not. For that purpose we first check if the length of the object exceeds the boundary of the category and then change its category label accordingly. Discriminating heavy vehicles by length is more reliable since they are usually much longer than light vehicles. However, in some cases heavy vehicles are composed of multiple short objects. In that case we must also consider the width of the object. Width analysis is less reliable because the physical width of heavy and light vehicles is not much different. However, this difficulty gets alleviated thanks to the artificial width increase induced by the perspective correction method and the poor aerodynamics of heavy vehicles. Finally, two objects can be promoted to a single heavy object after an ordinary fusion process.

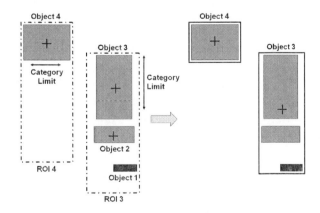

Figure 22. Heavy Vehicle Identification step. (a) See the ROI set for objects 3 and 4 and the category boundaries. See also how object 4 exceeds the width boundary, while object 3 exceeds the length boundary. (b) Results after the merging, assuming objects 3 and 4 had passed the confidence test.

Heavy vehicles are subject to the usual merging and tracking processes; only the category limits used are larger. Unfortunately, this approach does not work when the heavy vehicle is composed of multiple objects. In consequence, we apply a new merging process to certified heavy vehicles (see Fig. 22). In this case we use a ROI with a width equivalent to the maximum observed width for the object and the maximum allowed length of the heavy vehicle category. The ROI is aligned with the upper border of the object in order to avoid incorrectly merging with the preceding vehicles. As usual, we merge any overlapping object if the size of the resulting object does not violate the heavy vehicle category limits. This grouping process is risky since, if not careful, we may merge two physical vehicles. For that reason, we apply the merging only to heavy BRIGHT objects who have passed a confidence test; i.e. a *heavy vehicle counter* is incremented every time the size of the object exceeds the category boundary and the merging process is applied only after the counter exceeds a threshold. Also, we first select for merging the oldest and biggest objects in the list. The method can be extended to handle more than two categories, by setting additional category boundaries. However, the more categories you use, the less precise the results will be.

7. Shadow Removal

Vehicles typically exhibit one or more associated shadows in the image. Unfortunately, the process of discriminating vehicles' shadows from other vehicles present in their neighborhood is far from trivial. On the other hand, it is necessary to mention the added difficulty arising from shadows cast by objects other than the vehicles or multiple shadows resulting from artificial light sources at night.

A shadow is produced when an object intercepts the light path from the illumination source to the surface observed by the camera. The non-illuminated part of the obstructing object is called *self-shadow*, while shadows projected on to the background elements of the scene are referred as *cast-shadows*. Shadows are composed of: *umbra* and *penumbra*. In general we describe the *umbra* as that part of the shadow where the light source has been occluded almost completely, while in the *penumbra* is only partially occluded. The transition between both parts and between the *penumbra* and the illuminated part of the scene is typically smooth.

Most shadow removal methods [13, 27, 46]. present in the literature identify shadows based on its intrinsic properties (color, shape, or luminance levels). Several theoretical models have been proposed describing the differential chromatic characteristics of shadows. However, in practice, those models fail to represent the intricacy of shadows and tend to ignore its dynamical properties; thus wasting a significant amount of potentially useful information. As a consequence these methods are little robust since they frequently remove parts of the vehicles together with the shadows.

Our shadow removal method [12] is more involved, in the sense that shadows are treated as one more object within the computer vision chain. A type of object which shows certain differential intrinsic properties but also owns a rich history. The proposed approach is based on a complex *shadow model*. The *model* only considers the effects resulting from moving shadows. Conversely, static shadows are treated as part of the background. Compilation of information for shadow identification begins at the *Segmentation* step; as described in section 5.. As computation advances, more information is added to the *shadow model* from the *Detection* and *Tracking* stages. In that sense, in section 6., we learn how shadows are detected and tracked independently from the time they enter the scene until they finally disappear. We also noticed it is not possible to robustly remove the shadows until all available historical shadow information has been considered.

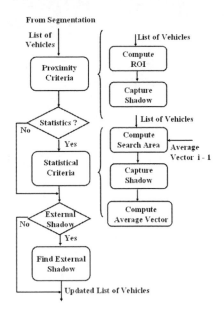

Figure 23. Decomposition of the shadow detection process. Notice how the two shadow detection methods are run in parallel and the results are compared for each input image.

Now, the critical missing part is the criteria used to decide when a DARK object should become a SHADOW object. For that purpose, we use three different processes: Detecting Shadows with the *Proximity Criteria*, Detecting Shadows with the *Directional Criteria* and Detecting Shadows from Outside the *Control Area*; as described in Fig. 23.

7.1. Detecting Shadows Using a Proximity Criteria

In this process we take advantage of one of the characteristics included in the *shadow model* saying shadows are in physical contact with the casting object. In that sense it is systematic to observe most vehicles present BRIGHT regions, but also DARK patches representing windows, tires, bumpers, etc. Our first step will be then to identify as SHADOW any DARK object that is close enough to a BRIGHT object.

For that purpose, we will use a region of interest (ROI) centered on the BRIGHT object. The size of the ROI will be selected from the maximum historical dimensions observed in the BRIGHT object up to this moment; extended with a security margin (typically 2 pixels in the vertical and horizontal directions). Any DARK object overlapping the ROI will become a candidate for a SHADOW object (see figure 24).

The above procedure will allow us to capture shadows that are in close contact with the BRIGHT object as well as any dark region enclosed inside. In the case a vehicle is composed only of DARK regions, this process does not apply since vehicle and shadow regions will typically form a single object. The capturing process is applied for every

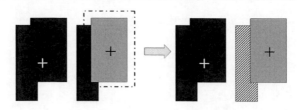

Figure 24. The figure presents the process of detecting the dark parts of a vehicle (before and after the shadows have been identified). It must be noticed how only BRIGHT objects can have associated shadows.

incoming image and every time a BRIGHT object and a DARK / SHADOW object are related, the *shadow counter* of the corresponding object is increased.

Based on the detected shadows, the *Proximity Criteria* allows us to compute statistically the *average shadow vector* linking the geometrical center of the BRIGHT object to the predicted mass center of the SHADOW object; as described in section 7.2..

The *average shadow vector* computed by the *Proximity Criteria* takes precedence at start-up, when directional information is not available, or as a second option when shadows are too small or when the average direction of the shadow calculated with the *Proximity* and *Directional* criteria are incongruent

7.2. Detecting Shadows Using a Directional Criteria

The hypothesis founding the *Proximity Criteria* are not always realized in practice. It is not uncommon to find situations where, due to poor segmentation, shadows are not in contact with the casting object or even appear broken. This circumstance is more usual at sun rise / set, when shadows are long and soft; but it is also frequent at any time under cloudy skies.

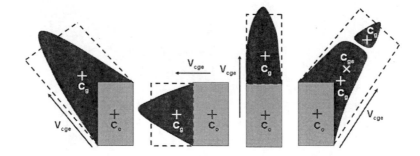

Figure 25. The figure shows several possible configurations involving shadows. (a) Long slanted shadow. (b) Short left shadow. (c) Long shadow in front. (d) Broken lateral shadow. For each object it is presented: its geometrical center C_o, the ROI, the mass center of the shadow C_g (white cross), the average mass center calculated for the period C_{ge} (inverted white cross) and the vector V_{cge} joining C_{ge} and C_o.

In order to solve this problem we propose to calculate the average magnitude and orientation of the cast shadows for each vehicle category using statistical methods. Once this parameter is known, we will identify as shadows those DARK objects whose relative position with respect to a BRIGHT object are in the correct direction and whose mass center is within the permitted range.

In this case we assume the simplification to consider all vehicles from a given category have associated shadows with similar orientation and magnitude at a given time instant. Again, this concept will be represented by the vector joining the center of the BRIGHT object and the mass center of the SHADOW object. We further assume this vector (*average shadow vector*) moves slowly and can be considered constant for extended periods of time (*learning time*). The *average shadow vector* can be computed by simply averaging the relative position of the mass center of the SHADOW with respect to the center of the BRIGHT object for each incoming vehicle, during the *learning time*. A reasonable *learning time* could be in the order of 30 seconds. One *average shadow vector* is calculated for each vehicle category in order to account for the different dimensions of the vehicles in the different categories.

The main purpose of the *average shadow vector* is to construct a ROI that will allow us to capture the shadows associated to each BRIGHT object. The ROI is started from the appropriate diagonal of the BRIGHT object; as can be observed in figure 25. Its width is set in accordance with the BRIGHT object's dimensions, and it has the same orientation and twice the length of the *average shadow vector*. Any DARK object whose mass center is within the ROI will be identified as a SHADOW object.

To ensure a smooth transition between periods, every new *average shadow vector* is only accepted if it fits inside the ROI of the vector calculated in the previous period. This approach implicitly performs a smooth tracking of the *average shadow vector*; as required by the shadow model. The algorithm is initialized using the *average shadow vector* computed with the *Proximity Criteria*.

The *Proximity and Directional Criteria* are complementary. The *Directional Criteria* is preferred during normal operation since it allows us to capture shadows detached from the casting object and broken shadows. It is also more robust in situations with long shadows overlapping the vehicles. However there are circumstances when the computation of the *average shadow vector* is not reliable. One such case is when shadows are too short to produce vectors of statistical significance; i.e. at midday, when the sun is high up in the sky. It is also possible that the algorithm loose track of the real *average shadow vector*.

To avoid those problems, both methods are run in parallel. Then, at every *learning time* the *average shadow vector* calculated with the *Proximity Criteria* is checked against the ROI of the *Directional Criteria*. If it does not fit within the ROI, shadows are temporally captured using the *Proximity Criteria* and the *Directional Criteria* is restarted.

7.3. Detecting Shadows from Outside the Control Area

The third shadow detection process attempts to remove shadows cast on the *control area* by vehicles running outside the *control area*. This is a systematic problem occurring when there exists parallel motorways or when the *control area* only covers part of the lanes present in the road under supervision.

External shadows can be discriminated attending to their movement properties. For example, static shadows are typically handled by the *background substraction* method; while oscillating shadows can be easily eliminated by the *tracker*. However, the case of shad-

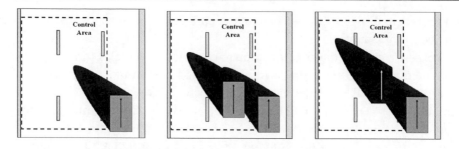

Figure 26. The figure presents several possible scenarios involving external shadows cast by vehicles running outside the *control area*. Scenarios (a) and (b) are easily handled by the proposed external shadow removal method. Scenario (c) is less frequent but presents a more difficult solution.

ows cast by vehicles running outside the *control area* requires specific measures since our present methods can not discriminate them from the DARK vehicles; i.e. the *Proximity* and *Directional Criteria* become useless because the casting object cannot be observed inside the *control area*.

To solve this problem we propose to label a DARK object as SHADOW whenever it touches the appropriate lateral border of the *control area*; as seen in figure 26. The appropriate border is determined by the orientation of the shadow. In general, we must check the border opposite to the direction of the *average shadow vector*. For example, if the *average shadow vector* points to the left we must check the right side limit. We also added two parameters that will allow us to deactivate the external shadow removal process when according to the configuration of the scene no external shadows are possible.

In figure 26 we present several possible scenarios involving external shadows. Scenarios (a) and (b) are easily solved with the method proposed. However in scenario (c) it is not possible to discriminate the vehicle from the overlapping shadow. We still have one more possibility to detect the vehicle if the shadow shows different relative speed with respect to the vehicle and both objects are overlapped only for a short period of time. On the other hand, if the tracker is not able to make them apart, this situation cannot be solved and a counting error will be produced. Fortunately, the induced error is not very relevant since dark-only vehicles are rare and the vehicle will be miscounted only when the above circumstances occur simultaneously. Some real examples involving shadows are presented in Fig. 27.

8.   System Implementation

We chose to implement our Traffic Monitoring system in a simple computer architecture with very limited resources, so that it can be ported to embedded platforms and allow space for further improvement. Currently, the system is running under Windows and is able to process over 40 frames per second in an old fashioned 800 Mhz microprocessor, with 256 Mb of RAM and low cost digital camera. The user interface of the application is presented in figures 28 and 29.

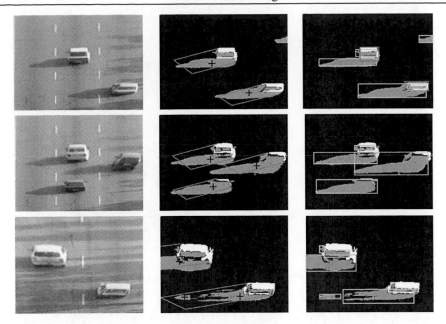

Figure 27. Three examples of the Shadow Removal process showing the original image (left), the *Directional* method (center) and the final classification of the shadow objects (right). In the first row we can see two vehicles with long shadows as well as an external shadow coming from a vehicle running on a parallel motorway. Notice also the abundant static shadows cast by trees from outside the *control area*. The *Directional* method correctly handles the long shadows since their mass center is easily captured by the ROI (second column). On the other hand, the dark patches inside the vehicle are successfully captured by the *Proximity* method. Finally the external shadow is also captured since it touches the right border of the *control area*. In the second row we can observe three vehicles running close together. It is apparent how the shadow removal algorithm correctly handles this difficult situation. Finally the third row presents an example of a broken shadow.

We also developed a specific methodology designed to benchmark the accuracy of the different computer vision methods. One of the difficulties we faced was, first to test the advantages of the different computer approaches during the research process and then to compare them with the results from other authors. Unfortunately, every author uses his own testing data (in many cases carefully selected to highlight the advantages of his method) and evaluation criteria. Our methodology is based on the use of a set of ground truth image sequences captured in various conditions. The vehicles in the sequences are first counted by a human operator and then compared with the results from the traffic system.

To improve this tedious and error prone process we have developed a specific tool which aids the human operator in the counting process. The operator is presented with an image sequence and every time a new vehicle appears in scene he presses the key appropriate for the lane and category. The tool automatically records the event in a file, together with its time stamp. Next we run our traffic monitoring system on the same sequence; thus producing an equivalent file. Finally, the Testing Tool is fed with both files and the results are automatically compared using a selectable integration period. In that way, once the

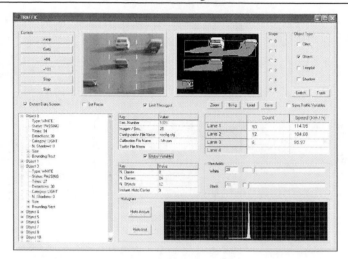

Figure 28. User Interface of the Traffic Monitoring system. Top left, navigation controls. Center, the *Work Image* and the *Segmented Image*. Top right, debugging controls. Left, object data viewer. Right, Traffic Variables. Bottom right, histograms and Segmentation controls.

ground truth file is available, we may run the comparison process with different algorithms, as many times as we desire, while the tool automatically computes the obtained error rates. The proposed testing method is objective, facilitates testing of individual components, saves a lot time and helps the researcher focus on the real thing; i.e. we only seek solution to problems which might affect the error rate.

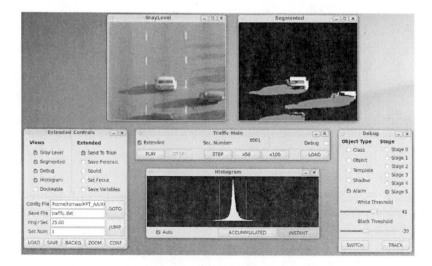

Figure 29. The User Interface of the Traffic Monitoring system running under Linux with extended functions and *dockable* synchronized windows.

Next, we describe the main traffic variables provided by the system; as well as the methods used to compute them.

8.1. Traffic Variables.

The traffic variables computed by the system can be classified into two groups: *Instantaneous* or *Basic* variables and *Statistical* variables. The *Basic* variables determine the microscopic properties of the individual objects detected in the images and comprise mainly: *Vehicle Counting*, *Instantaneous Speed* and *Vehicle Category*. In addition, each vehicle has an associated traffic lane.

Objects surviving in the *objects list* with the ENDED label are evaluated according to the criteria specified in section 6.2. If the result of the evaluation is successful we then compute the traffic lane associated to the trajectory of the vehicle. This calculation takes into account the last known position of the vehicle and the process is relatively simple since, due to geometry correction, most trajectories are parallel to the vertical edge of the image. At this point the *Vehicle Counter* for that specific traffic lane is increased by one.

Next, we determine the category of the vehicle by comparing the observed average size of the vehicle with the thresholds, in width and height, separating the different categories. Once more, calculations are simplified due to geometry correction since the apparent dimensions of vehicles are preserved no matter their position in the corrected image.

Finally, we compute the instantaneous speed of the vehicle in Km/h using the same procedure described in section 6.2. for the calculation of intermediate speeds. Here again the computing of the speed is free from perspective distortions thanks to geometry correction.

Once the *Basic* or *Instantaneous* variables have been determined, we proceed to compute the *Statistical Variables*. These variables are calculated by accumulating or averaging the data from the *Basic Variables* over a time interval: the *Integration Time*. The duration of the *Integration Time* is adjustable but typically range between 1 and 5 minutes. In the same way as we did with the *Instantaneous Variables*, the *Statistical Variables* will be presented classified by category and traffic lane.

The following *Statistical Variables* are computed by the system:

- *Average Speed*. It is computed as the average of the speed of the vehicles of a given category x, detected in a given traffic lane α, over the *integration period* t. It is presented in units of Km/h, using the formula below:

$$\overline{V}(t, x, \alpha) = \frac{\sum_i V_i(t, x, \alpha)}{N(t, x, \alpha)}, \tag{41}$$

  where $\overline{V}(t, x, \alpha)$ is the *Average Speed* in the interval; $V_i(t, x, \alpha)_i$ is the *Instantaneous Speed* for the i vehicle; and $N(t, x, \alpha)$ is the *Number of Vehicles* detected in the *Integration Period* t.

- *Traffic Intensity* or *Vehicle Flux*. Contains the number of vehicles of category x crossing the control area per hour in the given lane α. It is computed in units of $vehicles/hour$ with the following formula.

$$\varphi(t, x, \alpha) = \frac{N(t, x, \alpha)}{\Delta T}, \tag{42}$$

where $\varphi(t, x, \alpha)$ is the *Flux* computed in the *Integration Period* t; and ΔT is the time interval, measured in hours, used by the *Integration Period*.

- *Traffic Density*. The *Traffic Density* represents the number of vehicles of category x, detected in the given traffic lane α, per kilometer. It is certainly measured in $vehicles/Km$

$$\rho(t, x, \alpha) = \frac{\varphi(t, x, \alpha)}{\overline{V}(t, x, \alpha)}, \qquad (43)$$

where $\rho(t, x, \alpha)$ is the *Traffic Density* computed in the *Integration Period* t.

- *Vehicle Headway*. Computes the average time between two vehicles of category x running in lane α. It is computed in seconds.

$$L(t, x, \alpha) = \frac{1}{\varphi(t, x, \alpha)}, \qquad (44)$$

where $L(t, x, \alpha)$ is the *Vehicle Headway* computed in the *Integration Period* t and $\varphi(t, x, \alpha)$ is the *Flux* of vehicles.

- *Occupancy*. The *Occupancy* provides information about the average time a given traffic line α remains occupied by the vehicles.

$$O(t, \alpha) = \frac{\sum_i \Delta t_i}{\Delta T}, \qquad (45)$$

where $O(t, \alpha)$ is the lane *Occupancy* in the *Integration Period* t; and Δt_i is the time required by vehicle i to cross the control area. It is computed from its speed V_i and its length l_i: $\Delta t_i = \frac{l_i}{V_i}$.

The above variables are computed for each traffic lane and vehicle category independently. However, we also provide aggregated information comprising the same variables computed for all traffic lanes (i.e. the complete road) and vehicles' categories (i.e. all vehicles).

9. Results and Evaluation

Our evaluation process consisted of two different types of tests. In the first phase we compared our global results with the equivalent information compiled in different evaluation experiences; such as that performed by the FHWA [4, 5], the JPL [6] and the University of Utah [47]. We also considered the results reported by some commercial systems. All in all, seven different systems were examined: EVA, Traficon, Autoscope, CCATS, Iteris, Trafficam and Video-Trak. See summary in Table 1.

Doing a global analysis is no easy task due to the high number of testing experiences and the different aims and conditions prevailing in each test. Nevertheless, our main conclusion is the performance of the different systems is very much dependent on the environmental conditions. Current state of the art allows for an average counting error of 5% and

Table 1. Comparison of average global results from different systems. Sources: [1] FHWA-2002, Minnesota Guidestar [4]. [2] FHWA1439-7, Texas Transport Inst. [5]

	Our System	[1] EVA	[1] Traficon	[1] Autoscope	[2] Video Trak	[2] Iteris
Count	3.6 %	5 %	5-15 %	7-8 %	25 %	15 %
Speed	6 %	10 %	8-13 %	8 %	N/A	N/A

a 10% error in the measurement of the vehicles' speed. We compare favorably with these results since our global error rates are 3.59% and 6% respectively. These global results look reasonable, however, looking at the details we discover the dispersion is huge, with error values peaking over 15% in vehicle counting and 18% in speed. Again we obtain better marks since our peak rate is below 9%. Finally, we must highlight some of the systems analyzed do not operate at night or in slow traffic and present serious difficulties under adverse weather.

In the second testing phase we compared the results from our traffic system with the ground truth images using the Testing Tool described above. Tables 2 to 5 present the results achieved under day, night and transition periods, for various values of traffic flux and classified by vehicle category. The error rate was obtained by computing the average rate of the difference between the counting done by our system and the ground truth; as compared with the total number of vehicles in the ground truth.

If we observe the global results, we discover the average error rate is 3.59%. This error rate is much lower for light vehicles 2.94% than it is for heavy vehicles 6.49%. On the other hand we find the error rates are very similar during the day 3.29% and in the transition periods 3.61%; while it degrades during the night 5.45% due to the difficulties found to correctly identify the heavy vehicles at night.

Next, we analyze the results for different values of the flux: 800, 1800 and 2200 v/h; where 1800 v/h signals the accepted maximum capacity of a road. We obtain respectively: 3.69%, 3.71% and 3.67%. However, we must notice these results are biased by the low composition of heavy vehicles with high flux. We observe the error rate of light vehicles increase only slightly with increasing flux, while the same results for heavy vehicles degrades significantly due to the difficulties found to identify heavy vehicles under high density; when the vehicles are close together.

We also performed tests under different weather conditions. The system performed slightly better under cloudy skies 3.25%, followed by clear skies 3.49% and finally with moving clouds 3.63%. On the other hand, accuracy was little affected by rainy weather since the error rate was 3.89%. Unfortunately, we could not obtain sufficient testing data for snowy or foggy conditions. Finally, in table 6, we present the results with different shadows configurations. We discover shadows do do not affect significantly the accuracy of the system and hence it is demonstrated the correct operation of the shadow removal method.

Overall, the best results are systematically obtained during the day, for light vehicles and with flux values of 800 v/h: 2.80%. On the other hand, heavy vehicles at night achieve a worst rate of 9%. With respect to classification of heavy vehicles we obtained a success

Table 2. Results with values of flux below 800 Vehicles / Hour

	Vehicle	Composition	Light	Heavy	Total
Day	6.280	19%	2,45	4,70	2,68
Night	3.140	14 %	4,82	9,45	5,17
Transition	1.570	18%	2,87	5,90	3,32
Total	10.990		3,21	5,97	3,69

Table 3. Results with values of flux between 800 and 1800 Vehicles / Hour

	Vehicle	Composition	Light	Heavy	Total
Day	25.552	20%	2,80	6,55	3,55
Night	1.704	15 %	5,02	9,65	5,71
Transition	6.388	17%	3,10	7,25	3,81
Total	33.644		2,98	6,79	3,71

Table 4. Results with values of flux over 2200 Vehicles / Hour

	Vehicle	Composition	Light	Heavy	Total
Day	23.988	18%	2,92	6,93	3,54
Transition	3.998	16%	3,15	7,53	3,75
Total	27.986		2,95	7,01	3,67

Table 5. Cumulated results with any flux value

	Vehicle	Composition	Light	Heavy	Total
Day	55.820	19%	2,73	6,20	3,29
Night	4.844	14%	4,89	9,52	5,45
Transition	11.956	17%	3,06	6,97	3,61
Total	72.620		2,94	6,49	3,59

Table 6. Results as a function of the length of the shadows

	Vehicle	Composition	Light	Heavy	Total
Short Shadows	19.152	20%	2,76	5,96	3,40
Long Shadows	32.680	18%	2,80	6,65	3,49
No Shadows	6.764	19%	2,73	5,78	3,31
Total	58.596		2,78	6,12	3,41

rate of 93.51% and our measurements of speed demonstrated the system is able to achieve an error rate below 6%. These results are well within the limits placed by traffic authorities who usually require an error rate of between 3% and 5% in vehicle counting, 5% and 10% in speed measurement and 5% and 10% in classification.

10.   Conclusion

An innovative computer vision based traffic monitoring system has been presented. The proposed system computes in real-time the microscopic traffic variables: counting, speed and classification; and based upon them produces the set of macroscopic variables: flux, density, composition and mean headway. The methods proposed are founded on a thoroughly analysis of the application scenario and careful attention was paid to implementation issues, such as: simple, non-invasive installation and real-time performance.

The system is self-adaptive and is able to operate autonomously for long periods of time; i.e. no hidden parameters to be adjusted. It performs in all weather and automatically selects the appropriate algorithm for day, night and transition periods. The system is robust against fast and slow illumination changes and is able to cope with long broken shadows, and shadows from parallel roadways. Ordinary camera movements (i.e. wind vibrations) hardly affect its performance because the system is tolerant against temporal tracking errors and strict constraints are used to identify the vehicles. We also provide an adequate treatment of occlusions and heavy vehicles, and obtain reasonable results in dense traffic; i.e. the system reports maximum occupancy and zero flush in the presence of traffic jams.

Several innovative contributions can be highlighted in the paper: an exhaustive analysis of the operational environment; an efficient calibration and image rectification method; an original Segmentation approach, complemented with an innovative method for the automatic selection of the Segmentation parameters; a Detection and Tracking approach specifically designed for traffic environments; a robust shadow removal method; specific provisions for heavy vehicle detection and the treatment of occlusions; and finally, a systematic testing and benchmarking methodology.

According to the results presented in section 9., our traffic system outperforms existing systems in terms of accuracy and already comply with most requirements placed by traffic authorities. Furthermore, our error rates are more balanced in adverse conditions and we are able to operate in situations where other systems fail; i.e. with long broken shadows, under high density of heavy traffic, in night conditions, with slow traffic, etc. However, even if our results are very good in usual traffic conditions, improvements would be desirable in some specific areas. In particular, more attention must be given to the detection of heavy vehicles in night conditions and also the treatment of occlusions under dense traffic must be improved. The system would benefit from an increase in the accuracy of the measured speed and more testing will be required in snowy and foggy weather. We may also revisit the S channel in color Segmentation, with the aim to better discriminate the vehicles from their shadows. On the other hand, some of the basic methods proposed could be adapted easily to other application scenarios; such as: incident detection, detection of suicide vehicles, intersection control, tunnel supervision, security surveillance, automatic signal management, presence detection for automatic barriers, etc.

References

[1] M.-C. Huang and S.-H. Yen, "A real-time and color-based computer vision for traffic monitoring system," in *IEEE International Conference on Multimedia and Expo*, vol. 3, June 2004, pp. 2119–2122.

[2] D. Koller, J. Weber, and J. Malik, "Robust multiple car tracking with occlusion reasoning," in *European Conf. Computer Vision*, 1994, pp. 189–196.

[3] T.-H. Chen, Y.-F. Lin, and T.-Y. Chen, "Intelligent vehicle counting method based on blob analysis in traffic surveillance," in *Proceedings of the Second International Conference on Innovative Computing, Information and Control*, vol. 0, 2007, pp. 238–242.

[4] MNDOT and S. C. Group, "Evaluation of non-intrusive technologies for traffic detection, final report, september 2002," Federal Highway Administration, U.S. Department of Transportation, Tech. Rep., September 2002.

[5] D. Middleton and R. Parker, "Initial evaluation of selected detectors to replace inductive loops on freeways," Texas Transportation Institute, Tech. Rep. FHWA/TX1439-7, April 2003.

[6] "Sensor development final report, traffic surveillance and detection technology development," Jet Propulsion Laboratory, Pasadena, California, Tech. Rep. FHWA-RD-77-86, March 1997.

[7] P. G. Michalopoulos, "Vehicle detection through image processing: The autoscope system," vol. 40(1), pp. 21–29, 1991.

[8] D. Panda, "An integrated video sensor design for traffic management and control," in *IMACS IEEE CSCC 99 International Multi-conference*, Athens, Greece, July 1999, pp. 176–185.

[9] T. Rodríguez, "Diseño e implementación de un sistema de visión artificial para la medida de variables de tráfico," Ph.D. dissertation, May 2007.

[10] T. Rodríguez and N. García, "An adaptive, real-time, traffic monitoring system," *Machine Vision and Applications Journal. Springer Verlag*, vol. 21, no. 4, pp. 555–576, 2010.

[11] T. Rodríguez, "Adaptive real-time segmentation in traffic sequences," *Machine Graphics and Vision Journal*, vol. 13, no. 1, pp. 39–52, 2004.

[12] ——, "Shadow removal for robust vehicle detection," *Machine Vision and Applications Journal, Springer Verlag*, Accepted, to be published in 2007.

[13] R. Cucchiara, C. Grana, and A. Prati, "Detecting moving objects and their shadows: an evaluation with the pets2002 dataset." in *Proceedings of Third IEEE International Workshop on Performance Evaluation of Tracking and Surveillance. ECCV 2002.*, Copenhagen, Denmark, May 2002, pp. 18–25.

[14] G. Foresti, C. Micheloni, and L. Snidaro, "Advanced visual-based traffic monitoring systems for increasing safety in road transportation," *Advances in Transportation Studies*, vol. 1, pp. 22–47, 2003.

[15] Q. Zang and R. Klette, "Object classification and tracking in video surveillance." in *CAIP*, 2003, pp. 198–205.

[16] A. Lai and N. H. C. Yung, "Lane detection by orientation and length discrimination," *IEEE Trans. Systems Man, and Cybernetics*, vol. 30, no. 4, pp. 539–548, 2000.

[17] G. Xu and Z. Zhang, *Epipolar Geometry in Stereo, Motion and Object Recognition.* Chap 3: Kluwer Academic Pub, 1996.

[18] T. Rodríguez, "Practical camera calibration and image rectification in monocular road traffic applications," *Machine Graphics and Vision Journal*, vol. 15, no. 1, pp. 51–71, 2006.

[19] ——, "Camera calibration and image rectification in a traffic monitoring system," *Advances in Transportation Studies*, vol. B, no. 8, pp. 81–96, April 2006.

[20] D. Comaniciu, V. Ramesh, and P. Meer, "Real-time tracking of non-rigid objects using mean shift," in *Proc. CVPR, vol. 2*, 2000, pp. 142–149.

[21] J. Melo, A. Naftel, A. Bernardino, and J. Santos-Victor, "Viewpoint independent detection of vehicle trajectories and lane geometry from uncalibrated traffic surveillance cameras." in *ICIAR (2)*, 2004, pp. 454–462.

[22] J. Owens, A. Hunterb, and E. Fletcher, "A fast model-free morphology-based object tracking algorithm," in *13th British Machine Vision Conference BMVC 2002*, Cardiff, UK, September 2002, pp. 767–776.

[23] M. C. Huang and S. H. Yen, "A real-time and color-based computer vision for traffic monitoring system," in *IEEE International Conference on Multimedia and Expo*, vol. 3, June 2004, pp. 2119–2122.

[24] A. Iera, A. Modafferi, G. Musolino, and A. Vitetta, "An experimental station for real-time traffic monitoring on a urban road," in *IEEE 5th International Conference on Intelligent Transportation Systems*, 2002, pp. 697–70.

[25] O. Faugeras, *Three Dimensional Computer Vision, A Geometric Viewpoint.* MIT Press, November 1993.

[26] R. Cucchiara, M. Piccardi, and P. Mello., "Image analysis and rule-based reasoning for a traffic monitoring system," *IEEE Transactions on Intelligent Transportation Systems*, vol. 1, no. 2, pp. 119–130, June 2000.

[27] S. Nadimi and B. Bhanu, "Physical models for moving shadow and object detection in video," vol. 26, no. 8, pp. 1079–1087, August 2004.

[28] T. Bouwmans, F. El Baf, and B. Vachon, "Statistical background modeling for foreground detection: A survey," in *HPRCV09*, 2009, pp. IV: 181–199.

[29] L. Cheng and M. Gong, "Realtime background subtraction from dynamic scenes," 2009, pp. 2066–2073.

[30] W. Guerra and E. Garcia Reyes, "A novel approach to robust background subtraction," 2009, pp. 69–76.

[31] C. Ridder, O. Munkelt, and H. Kirchner, "Adaptive background estimation and foreground detection using kalman-filtering," in *Proc. ICRAM 95193-195*, UNESCO, 1995.

[32] R. Cucchiara, C. Grana, M. Piccardi, and A. Prati, "Statistical and knowledge based moving object detection in traffic scenes," in *Proc. of IEEE Int'l Conference on Intelligent Transportation Systems*, Oct 2000, pp. 27–32.

[33] D. Dailey and L. Li, "Video image processing to create a speed sensor," Univesity of Washington, Seattle, Final WSDOT Research Report TNW-99-01, March 1999.

[34] K. Toyama, J. Krumm, B. Brummitt, and B. Meyers, "Wallflower: Principles and practice of background maintenance," in *International Conference on Computer Vision*, Corfu, September 1999, pp. 255–261.

[35] A. Lipton, H. Fujiyoshi, and R. Patil, "Moving target classification and tracking from real-time video," in *Proc. of the 1998 DARPA Image Understanding Workshop (IUW'98)*, November 1998.

[36] C. Wren, A. Azarbayejani, T. Darrell, and A. Pentland, "Pfinder, real-time tracking of the human body," vol. 19-7, pp. 780–785, July 1997.

[37] N. Friedman and S. Russell, "Image segmentation in video sequences: A probabilistic approach," in *Proc. Thirteenth Conf. on Uncertainty in Artificial Intelligence (UAI 97)*, 1997, pp. 175–181.

[38] C. Stauffer and W. Grimson, "Adaptive background mixture models for real-time tracking," in *Proc. IEEE Computer*, no. II, 1999, pp. 246–252.

[39] T. Chiang and W. Lau, "Segmentation of vehicles in traffic video," Standford University, Tech. Rep. EE3292J, 2002.

[40] Y. Ming, J. Jiang, and J. Ming, "Background modeling and subtraction using a local linear-dependence-based cauchy statistical model," in *Proc. of the VIIth Digital Image Computing: Techniques and Applications.*, Sydney, 2003, pp. 469–478.

[41] P. K. T. Pong and R. Bowden, "An improved adaptive background mixture model for real-time tracking with shadow detection," in *2nd European Workshop on Advanced Video Based Surveillance Systems. AVBS01*, September 2001.

[42] Carlo. and T. Kanade, "Detection and tracking of point features," no. CMU-CS-91-132, April 1991.

[43] J. Tai, S. Tseng, C. Lin, and K. Song, "Real-time image tracking for automatic traffic monitoring and enforcement applications," vol. 22, no. 6, pp. 485–501, June 2004.

[44] A. Yilmaz, O. Javed, and M. Shah, "Object tracking: A survey," *ACM Journal of Computing Surveys*, vol. 38, no. 4, pp. 13.1–13.45, 2006.

[45] Y. Sheikh and M. Shah, "Bayesian modeling of dynamic scenes for object detection," *IEEE Transactions on Pattern Analysis and Machine Intelligence*, vol. 27, no. 11, pp. 1778–1792, November 2006.

[46] A. Yoneyama, C. Yeh, and C. Kuo, "Moving cast shadows elimination for robust vehicle extraction based on 2d joint / vehicle shadow models," in *IEEE Conference on Advanced Video and Signal Based Surveillance. AVSS03*, 2003, pp. 229–236.

[47] P. T. Martin, "Detector technology evaluation," University of Utah, Department of Civil and Environmental Engineering, Tech. Rep. CMU-CS-91-132, April 2003.

In: Computer Vision
Editor: Sota R. Yoshida

ISBN 978-1-61209-399-4

Chapter 5

ALGEBRAIC TOPOLOGY FOR COMPUTER VISION

Daniel Freedman[1,*] *and Chao Chen*[2,†]
[1]Hewlett-Packard Laboratories, Haifa, Israel
[2]Institute of Science and Technology Austria and
Vienna University of Technology, Austria

Abstract

Algebraic topology is generally considered one of the purest subfield of mathematics. However, over the last decade two interesting new lines of research have emerged, one focusing on algorithms for algebraic topology, and the other on applications of algebraic topology in engineering and science. Amongst the new areas in which the techniques have been applied are computer vision and image processing. In this paper, we survey the results of these endeavours. Because algebraic topology is an area of mathematics with which most computer vision practitioners have no experience, we review the machinery behind the theories of homology and persistent homology; our review emphasizes intuitive explanations. In terms of applications to computer vision, we focus on four illustrative problems: shape signatures, natural image statistics, image denoising, and segmentation. Our hope is that this review will stimulate interest on the part of computer vision researchers to both use and extend the tools of this new field.

1. Introduction

Algebraic topology, with roots dating to Poincaré at the beginning of the twentieth century, has traditionally been considered one of the purest subfield of mathematics, with very few connections to applications. The last decade, however, has witnessed an explosion of interest in computational aspects of algebraic topology, and with the development of this computational machinery, a concomitant interest in applications. In this paper, we review some of these developments, and show how methods of computational algebraic topology may be fruitfully applied to problems of computer vision and image processing. We hope

---

*E-mail address: daniel.freedman@hp.com
†E-mail address: chaochen79@gmail.com

that this review will stimulate interest on the part of computer vision researchers to both use and extend these tools.

As we have noted, the new interest in algebraic topological tools has been fueled by two parallel developments: the design of new algebraic topological algorithms, and the application of these algorithms to various scientific and engineering f elds. The new algorithms have focused almost exclusively on computations involving homology groups; without going into detail at this point (we defer a formal description of homology theory until Section 2.), we may note that homology groups are topological invariants which, roughly speaking, count the number of holes of various dimensions that a topological space has. The great advantage conferred by homology groups is that these groups are relatively straightforward to compute with, as opposed to other topological concepts such as homotopy groups, or worse, homeomorphism equivalence classes. In particular, the concept of *persistent homology* as introduced by Edelsbrunner *et al.* [1], has proven to be very useful. The new framework has been applied to a number of f elds, including molecular biology [2, 3], sensor networks [4], robotics [5], graphics [6], geometric modeling [7], as well as computer vision and image processing.

Why use topological tools in computer vision? One answer is that, generally speaking, topological invariants tend to be very robust. If the topological space is stretched and deformed continuously, without any tearing or gluing, then the topological invariants of the space will be preserved. This is, of course, by design: topology is essentially the study of invariants of spaces under this group of transformations – continuous bijections with continuous inverses, also known as homeomorphisms. This property might be quite useful in the design of shape signatures, where the goal is to find a compact description of a shape which does not change much (if it all) when the shape undergoes some types of deformation.

Unfortunately, traditional topological invariants suffer from some problems from the point of view of the applied scientist. On the one hand, such invariants are perhaps "too robust:" very different shapes, such as the hand and the circle in Figure 1, may be topologically equivalent, thus leading to poor shape signatures. On the other hand, topological invariants can be quite sensitive to noise; this phenomenon is illustrated in Figure 1, in which two spaces – a torus and a two-handled torus – appear very similar, but are in fact topologically different due to the presence of the tiny handle.

Some of the methods developed in the last decade in the field of applied and computational algebraic topology attempt to deal with these two situations. In the case of shape signatures, one remedy involves augmenting the base topological space with extra geometric information, thereby creating a new topological space. Standard topological invariants can then be computed for this augmented space, leading to more discriminating shape signatures. We will see an example of this type of augmentation in Section 3.1. For the case of the sensitivity of topological invariants to noise, the theory of persistent homology has been developed. This theory deals with "topological noise," by examining not only the topological features of a space, but also their "lifetime," or significance. Aspects of persistent homology will be used throughout the paper.

The f elds of applied and computational algebraic topology are quite new, with most of the key developments having taken place in the last decade. The applications of these ideas to computer vision and image processing are even newer, with most of the relevant work have appeared in the last f ve years. As a result, this paper is perhaps slightly different

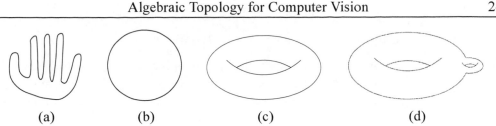

Figure 1. The problems with topological invariants. The hand-like shape in (a) and the circle in (b) are quite different shapes, but they possess the same topology. On the flip side, the ordinary torus in (c) is similar to the two-handled torus in (d), due to the fact that the second handle is very small (i.e. is "topological noise"). However, their topological descriptors will be different.

from a traditional survey or review of the literature. We focus on two goals: presenting the mathematical material – which can be quite daunting at f rst blush – in an accessible fashion, and reviewing some of the most interesting applications of this material to computer vision and image processing. The main goal of the paper is to stimulate interest in these new algebraic topological tools on the part of the computer vision community, so that the tools may be applied to new problems, and perhaps computationally and theoretically extended as well.

The remainder of the paper is organized as follows. In Section 2., we review the relevant material from algebraic topology, focusing in particular on homology theory and persistent homology. Although the material is presented in a way to make it as intuitive as possible, references to various standard texts and papers are given, to aid the reader interested in pursuing the topic further. Section 3. presents four interesting and illustrative applications of the topological techniques to computer vision and image processing. In Section 3.1., the problem of designing a shape signature is considered. Section 3.2. examines the problems of natural image statistics, and shows that the new topological techniques can contribute to a more accurate characterization of these statistics. Section 3.3. discusses the traditional problem of noise reduction, and simultaneously examines the problem of image segmentation. Persistent homology leads to a Mean Shift like algorithm, but one which has a rigorous way of merging segments. Finally, Section 4. concludes.

2. A Review of Persistent and Computational Homology

In this section, we provide the necessary background in algebraic topology, including a discussion of simplicial complexes, homology groups, and persistent homology. We will try to give an accessible introduction to the relevant notions, but given the space limitations our discussion will necessarily be somewhat brief. The interested reader is referred to [8, 9] for further details in general algebraic topology; [10, 11] for surveys of persistent homology; [12, 13] for surveys of computational topology; and [14] for an overview of topological data analysis.

2.1. Simplicial Complex

A *d-dimensional simplex* or *d-simplex*, σ, is the convex hull of $d + 1$ *affinely independent vertices*, which means for any of these vertices, v_i, the d vectors $v_j - v_i$, $j \neq i$, are linearly independent. In other words, given a set of $d + 1$ vertices such that no m-dimensional plane contains more than $m + 1$ of them, a simplex is the set of points each of which is a linear combination of these vertices, with all coeff cients nonnegative and summing to 1. A 0-simplex, 1-simplex, 2-simplex and 3-simplex are a vertex, edge, triangle and tetrahedron, respectively (Figure 2). The convex hull of a nonempty subset of vertices of σ is its *face*.

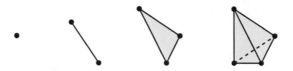

Figure 2. Simplices of dimension 0, 1, 2 and 3.

A *simplicial complex* K is a finite set of simplices that satisf es the following two conditions.

1. Any face of a simplex in K is also in K.

2. The intersection of any two simplices in K is either empty or is a face for both of them.

The *dimension* of a simplicial complex is the highest dimension of its simplices. If a subset $K_0 \subseteq K$ is a simplicial complex, it is a *subcomplex* of K.

Please see Figure 3 for an example simplicial complex. The triangulation of the solid cube provides 3-dimensional simplices. Therefore the simplicial complex is 3-dimensional.

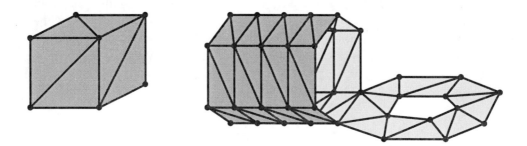

Figure 3. An example simplicial complex. It is the combination of the triangulation of a tube (open in both ends), an annulus and a solid cube. Note that the tube and the annulus share a common edge.

2.2. The Chain Group

In this paper, we only use simplicial homology of $\mathbb{Z}_2$ coeff cients, which is introduced in this section. For completeness, in Section 2.5., we briefly discuss simplicial homology of other coefficient rings.

Within a given simplicial complex K, a *d-chain* is a formal sum of d-simplices in K, namely

$$c = \sum_{\sigma \in K} a_\sigma \sigma, \quad a_\sigma \in \mathbb{Z}_2.$$

Note that since the field is $\mathbb{Z}_2$, the set of d-chains is in one-to-one correspondence with the set of subsets of d-simplices. A d-chain corresponds to a n_d-dimensional vector, whose entries are 0 or 1; the nonzero entries correspond to the included d-simplices. Here n_d is the number of d-simplices in K. For example, in Figure 4, the (formal sum of) red edges form a 1-chain and the (formal sum of) dark grey triangles form a 2-chain.

If we defne the addition of chains as the addition of these vectors, all the d-chains form the *group of d-chains*, $C_d(K)$. Note that addition is using $\mathbb{Z}_2$ (i.e. mod 2) arithmetic.

2.3.   The Cycle and Boundary Groups

The *boundary* of a d-simplex is the $(d-1)$-chain which is the formal sum of the $(d-1)$-simplices which are faces of the d-simplex. For example, the boundary of 1-simplex is the chain which is the formal sum of the two vertices which are its endpoints. The boundary of a d-chain c is then defned as the sum of the $(d-1)$-chains which are boundaries of each of the individual d-simplices appearing in the formal sum c. It is important to note that the sum over chains uses $\mathbb{Z}_2$ (i.e. mod 2) arithmetic, as described in Section 2.2.

This concept is best illustrated by way of example. In Figure 4, the green edges form the boundary of the 2-chain formed by the three dark grey triangles. Two out of seven 1-dimensional faces (edges) of the triangles do not appear in the boundary due to the mod 2 addition. Similarly, tetrahedra of the cube form a 3-chain whose boundary is the triangles of the box bounding the cube.

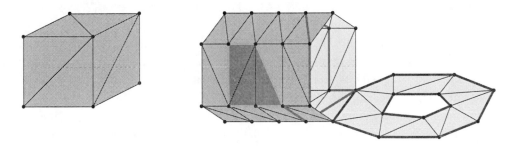

Figure 4. The green cycle is a boundary. The two blue cycles belong to a nontrivial class. The red cycle represents another nontrivial class.

The boundary operator $\partial_d : C_d(K) \rightarrow C_{d-1}(K)$ is a group homomorphism, which means that the boundary of the sum of any two d-chains is equal to the sum of their boundaries, formally,

$$\partial_d(c_1 + c_2) = \partial_d(c_1) + \partial_d(c_2), \quad \forall c_1, c_2 \in C_d(K).$$

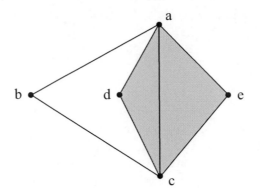

Figure 5. A simplicial complex K containing f ve 0-simplices, seven 1-simplices and two 2-simplices.

See Figure 5 for a simplicial complex whose boundary matrices are

$$\partial_1 = \begin{bmatrix} & ab & ac & ad & ae & bc & cd & ce \\ a & 1 & 1 & 1 & 1 & 0 & 0 & 0 \\ b & 1 & 0 & 0 & 0 & 1 & 0 & 0 \\ c & 0 & 1 & 0 & 0 & 1 & 1 & 1 \\ d & 0 & 0 & 1 & 0 & 0 & 1 & 0 \\ e & 0 & 0 & 0 & 1 & 0 & 0 & 1 \end{bmatrix} \quad \text{and} \quad \partial_2 = \begin{bmatrix} & acd & ace \\ ab & 0 & 0 \\ ac & 1 & 1 \\ ad & 1 & 0 \\ ae & 0 & 1 \\ bc & 0 & 0 \\ cd & 1 & 0 \\ ce & 0 & 1 \end{bmatrix}.$$

By convention, we def ne $\partial_0 \equiv 0$.

A *d-cycle* is a d-chain with zero boundary. The set of d-cycles forms a subgroup of the chain group, which is the kernel of the boundary operator, $\mathsf{Z}_d(K) = \ker(\partial_d)$. The set of d-boundaries are def ned as the image of the boundary operator, $\mathsf{B}_d(K) = \mathrm{img}(\partial_{d+1})$; this set is in fact a group. A d-cycle which is not a d-boundary, $z \in \mathsf{Z}_d(K) - \mathsf{B}_d(K)$, is a *nonbounding cycle*. In Figure 4, both the green and red chains are 1-cycles. (The red chain goes around the interior of the tube, but some parts are necessarily occluded in the rendering.) But only the red chain is nonbounding. It is not hard to see that a d-boundary is also a d-cycle. Therefore, $\mathsf{B}_d(K)$ is a subgroup of $\mathsf{Z}_d(K)$.

In our case, the coefficients belong to a field, namely $\mathbb{Z}_2$; when this is the case, the groups of chains, boundaries and cycles are all vector spaces.[1] Computing the boundary of a d-chain corresponds to multiplying the chain vector with a boundary matrix $[b_1, ..., b_{n_d}]$, whose column vectors are boundaries of d-simplices in K. By slightly abusing notation, we call the boundary matrix ∂_d.

2.4. The Homology Group

In algebraic topology, we want to capture all the nonbounding cycles, and more importantly, to classify them. We classify cycles into equivalence classes, each of which contains the set

---

[1]Note that this is not true when the homology is over a ring which is not a f eld, such as $\mathbb{Z}$.

of cycles whose difference is a boundary. A *homology class* is the set of cycles

$$\{z \mid z = z_0 + \partial_{d+1}c, \ c \in C_{d+1}(K)\},$$

for a fixed z_0. This set, denoted as $[z_0] = z_0 + B_d(K)$, is called a *coset*. Any cycle belonging to the class can be the *representative cycle*, z_0. When the representative cycle z_0 is a boundary, $[z_0] = 0 + B_d(K)$ is the boundary group itself.

The set of equivalence classes (one of which is the boundary group), under addition def ned by the addition of their representative cycles, forms a nice group structure. This group of equivalent classes is the quotient group $H_d(K) = Z_d(K)/B_d(K)$, and is called the *d-dimensional homology group*. The boundary group $0 + B_d(K)$ is the identity element of $H_d(K)$. Otherwise, when z_0 is a nonbounding cycle, $[z_0]$ is a *nontrivial homology class* represented by z_0. Cycles of the same homology class are said to be *homologous* to each other, formally, $z_1 \sim z_2$.

In Figure 4, the two blue cycles are homologous to each other, but not to the red and green cycles. The 1-dimensional homology group has four different members, represented by the green cycle (corresponding to the boundary group), the red cycle, one of the blue cycles, and the sum of a red cycle and a blue cycle, respectively.

In Figure 5, the simplicial complex has 1 nontrivial homology class, represented by four different nonbounding cycles, $(ab + ac + bc)$, $(ab + ad + bc + cd)$, $(ab + ae + bc + ce)$, and $(ab + ac + ad + ae + bc + cd + ce)$, whose corresponding vectors are $(1, 1, 0, 0, 1, 0, 0)^T$, $(1, 0, 1, 0, 1, 1, 0)^T$, $(1, 0, 0, 1, 1, 0, 1)^T$, and $(1, 1, 1, 1, 1, 1, 1)^T$ respectively.

All of the groups we have def ned thus far have the structure of vector spaces over the field $\mathbb{Z}_2$. We can therefore speak of the dimension of any of these groups, by which we mean the dimension of the corresponding vector space.[2] The dimension of the homology group is referred to as the *Betti number*,

$$\beta_d \qquad = \dim(H_d(K))$$
$$= \dim(Z_d(K)) - \dim(B_d(K)).$$

By linear algebra, the Betti number can be computed by computing the ranks of all boundary matrices.

$$\beta_d \ = (n_d - \mathrm{rank}(\partial_d)) - \mathrm{rank}(\partial_{d+1}).$$

As the dimension of the chain group is upper bounded by the cardinality of K, n, so are the dimensions of $B_d(K)$, $Z_d(K)$ and $H_d(K)$.

We note that the 0-dimensional homology group provides information about the number of connected components of a topological space. In particular, the 0th Betti number, β_0, is equal to the number of connected components. For dimensions d higher than zero, the Betti number yields information about the number of "independent d-dimensional holes" in that space. This last sentence is of course imprecise, and is meant only to convey intuition.

---

[2]The definitions which follow can be made without requiring the vector space property, but further mathematical apparatus is required.

2.5. Extensions of Homology Theory

Whereas the simplicial homology studies a topological space by studying its triangulation, for a general topological space, we could use *singular homology*. In singular homology, a simplex is def ned as a continuous mapping (not necessarily injective) from the standard simplex to the topological space. The definition is extended to chains, boundary operations and singular homology groups. It can be proven that the simplicial homology of a simplicial complex is isomorphic to the singular homology of its geometric realization (the underlying space). This implies, in particular, that the simplicial homology of a space does not depend on the particular simplicial complex chosen for the space. In the figures in this paper, we may sometimes ignore the simplicial complex and only show the continuous images of chains.

We restrict our discussion of simplicial homology to be over the $\mathbb{Z}_2$ field. In general, the coefficients may belong to arbitrary abelian groups. In such cases, the group structure of the homology can be more complicated. See [8] for more details.

2.6. Computation of Homology

Through a sequence of row and column operations, we can transform the boundary matrices. For example, in the simplicial complex of Figure 5, the boundary matrices can be rewritten as

$$
\partial_1' = \left[\begin{array}{c|ccccccc}
 & ab & ac & ad & ae & ab+ac+bc & ac+ae+ce & ac+ad+cd \\
\hline
a+b & 1 & 0 & 0 & 0 & 0 & 0 & 0 \\
a+c & 0 & 1 & 0 & 0 & 0 & 0 & 0 \\
a+d & 0 & 0 & 1 & 0 & 0 & 0 & 0 \\
a+e & 0 & 0 & 0 & 1 & 0 & 0 & 0 \\
a & 0 & 0 & 0 & 0 & 0 & 0 & 0
\end{array} \right] \quad \text{and}
$$

$$
\partial_2' = \left[\begin{array}{c|cc}
 & acd & ace \\
\hline
ac+ad+cd & 1 & 0 \\
ac+ae+ce & 0 & 1 \\
ab+ac+bc & 0 & 0 \\
ae & 0 & 0 \\
ad & 0 & 0 \\
ac & 0 & 0 \\
ab & 0 & 0
\end{array} \right].
$$

What is the purpose of such row and column operations? These operations effectively change the bases of the chain groups: 0- and 1-dimensional chain groups in the case of ∂_1, and 1- and 2-dimensional chain groups in the case of ∂_2. For the d-dimensional boundary matrix, the set of zero columns corresponds to a basis of the d-dimensional cycle group, i.e. $\{ab+ac+bc, ac+ae+ce, ac+ad+cd\}$. The set of nonzero rows corresponds to a basis of the $(d-1)$-dimensional boundary group. There is a one-to-one correspondence between this boundary basis and the set of d-chains corresponding to nonzero columns, specif ed by these nonzero diagonal entries in the new boundary matrix.[3] Each element of this $(d-1)$-

---

[3] The relationship may be more complicated if the homology is not over $\mathbb{Z}_2$ field.

dimensional boundary basis is the boundary of its corresponding d-chain. In our example, the chains $ac + ad + cd$ and $ac + ae + ce$ are the boundaries of the 2-chains acd and ace, respectively.

In general, combinations of such row and column operations are referred to as reductions. As can be seen from the example above, reductions enable the computation of Betti numbers by f nding the dimensions of the cycle and boundary groups. When the homology is over a field, as it is in our case, the reduction may be computed by Gaussian elimination.[4] If the homology is not over a field, a more complicated reduction using the so-called Smith Normal Form [15] must be used.

The idea of reducing the boundary matrices into canonical forms [8] has been extended to various reduction algorithms for different purposes [16, 10, 17]. Next, we will introduce one specif c reduction, namely, the persistent homology reduction.

2.7. Persistent Homology

We first give the intuition. Given a topological space $\mathbb{X}$ and a *filter function* $f : \mathbb{X} \to \mathbb{R}$, *persistent homology* studies changes in the topology of the sublevel sets, $\mathbb{X}^t = f^{-1}(-\infty, t]$. In Figure 6 the topological space is the 2-dimensional plane $\mathbb{R}^2$ and the filter function is the peaks function in MATLAB. Sublevel sets with different threshold t appear to have different topology (Figure 7).

As we increase the threshold t from $-\infty$ to $+\infty$, the sublevel set grows from the empty set to the entire topological space. During the growth, different homology classes may be born and then die. For example, in Figure 7(a), a new component is born. This component dies later (Figure 7(b)), when it merges into some component born earlier. In Figure 7(c), a new hole is born when a same component contacts itself. The newborn hole dies (Figure 7(d)) when it is sealed up.

The purpose of persistent homology is to characterize the f lter function in terms of the topological changes undergone by the sublevel sets of the function, as they proceed from the empty set to the entire domain. A key step in this process involves computing the birth and death times of these components (0-dimensional homology classes) and holes (1-dimensional classes), and more generally, higher dimensional homology classes. By birth, we mean a homology class comes into being; by death, we mean it either becomes trivial or becomes identical to some other class born earlier. The persistence, or lifetime of a class is the difference between its death and birth times. Those with longer lives tell us something about the global structure of the space $\mathbb{X}$, as described by the filter function.

Next, we introduce the formal definition of the persistent homology of a simplicial complex K f ltered by a scalar function, see for example [1, 18]. (In the example of Figure 7, we may imagine a triangulation of the relevant topological space, i.e. the plane.) A *filter function* $f : K \to \mathbb{R}$ assigns each simplex in K a real value, such that the function value of a simplex is no smaller than those of its faces. Without loss of generality, we assume that the filter function values of all simplices are different. Simplices of K are sorted in ascending order according to their filter function values,

$$(\sigma_1, \sigma_2, \cdots, \sigma_m), \quad f(\sigma_i) < f(\sigma_{i+1}), \quad \forall 1 \leq i \leq m - 1,$$

---

[4]More complex information than Betti numbers, such as representative cycles of the generators of the homology group, may also be computed by a variant of Gaussian elimination.

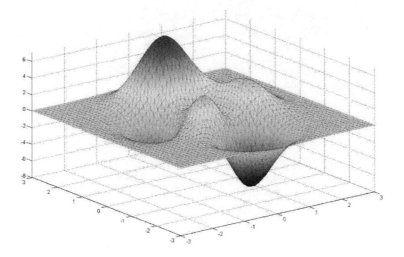

Figure 6. Illustrative example for persistent homology: the topological space is the 2D plane and the filter function is the `peaks` function in MATLAB.

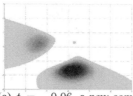
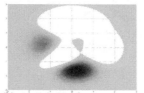

(a) $t = -0.06$, a new component is born (the patch in the center).

(b) $t = 0.41$, the new component dies. A new hole is born at almost the same time ($t = 0.3$).

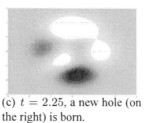
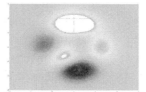

(c) $t = 2.25$, a new hole (on the right) is born.

(d) $t = 3.59$, the new hole dies.

Figure 7. Sublevel sets and their homologies. We draw the continuous sublevel sets whereas the persistence is computed through the simplicial complex.

namely, the *simplex-ordering* of K with regard to f. This is the order in which simplices enter the sublevel set $f^{-1}(-\infty, t]$ as t increases. Any sublevel set is a subcomplex, denoted as K_i, which exactly $\sigma_1, \cdots, \sigma_i$ as its simplices. The nested sequence of sublevel sets

$$\emptyset = K_0 \subset K_1 \subset \cdots \subset K_m = K$$

is called a *filtration*[5] of K. Let $f_i = f(\sigma_i)$ and $f_0 = -\infty$, $K_i = f^{-1}(-\infty, f_i]$.

---

[5]It is worth noting that in fact, the theory of persistent homology applies to *any* filtration, not only those which are derived from the sublevel set structure of a function.

For any $0 \leq i < j \leq m$, the inclusion mapping of K_i into K_j induces a group homomorphism of the corresponding homology groups,

$$F_d^{i,j} : \mathsf{H}_d(K_i) \to \mathsf{H}_d(K_j).$$

A homology class, h, is born at the time f_i if $h \in \mathsf{H}_d(K_i)$ but $h \notin \mathrm{img}(F_d^{i-1,i})$. Given h is born at f_i, h dies at time f_j if $F_d^{i,j-1}(h) \notin \mathrm{img}(F_d^{i-1,j-1})$ but $F_d^{i,j}(h) \in \mathrm{img}(F_d^{i-1,j})$. Any class in the coset $h + \mathrm{img}(F_d^{i-1,i})$ is born at f_i and dies at f_j.

The *persistence* of a homology class is defned as the difference between its death and birth times, which quantifes the signifcance of the feature. Not all the persistent homology classes die. Those which never die are *essential* classes, which correspond to nontrivial homology classes of K. An essential homology class has the $+\infty$ death time, and thus, an infnite persistence. For example, in the example of Figure 6, there are three 0-dimensional persistent classes. Only one of them has infnite persistence and the other two are relatively less signifcant and eventually die. The three 1-dimensional persistent classes also have different signifcances, measured by their persistences. In next section, we will discuss this in further detail.

An essential justification of the usefulness of persistence is its stability [19]. It has been proved that for a given topological space, the difference between the persistent homologies of two separate filter functions is upper bounded by the difference between the filter functions, as measured by the sup-norm. The distance between persistent homologies is defned as the distance between their persistence diagrams, which will be introduced in the next section. In a recent work [20], restrictions on the space and filter functions have been relaxed. Furthermore, the stability has been extended to two different topological spaces, e.g. a manifold and its fnite sampling.

The definition of persistent homology can be naturally extended to a general topological space with mild assumptions. The stability guarantees that the persistence of a general topological space filtered by a scalar function can be approximated by the persistence of its finite approximation (triangulation of the space and finite sampling of the filter function).

2.8. The Persistence Diagram and Barcodes

The persistent homology can be visualized and studied using a *persistence diagram*, in which each homology class corresponds to a point whose x and y coordinates are its birth and death times, respectively. Its persistence is equal to its vertical or horizontal distance from the diagonal. Important features correspond to points further away from the diagonal in the persistence diagram. Please see Figure 8(a) for the persistence diagram of the previous example. We plot 0-dimensional and 1-dimensional persistent classes with dots and crosses, respectively. From the diagram, we can see that there are two important persistent classes, corresponding to the component of the space itself, and the hole which is sealed up very late (when $t = 8.11$). For convenience, persistent classes with infinite death time (essential) are plotted on a horizontal line, whose y coordinate is infinity (the thickened line in the figure).

Formally, the persistence diagram includes all the points corresponding to persistent homology classes, as well as the diagonal line. It may be possible that several classes are born and die at the same time; thus, the points in the persistence diagram are assigned integer weights, according to their multiplicities. The persistence diagram has been proven to be stable to changes in the filter function [19]. This stability of persistence implies that the persistence diagram remains almost the same if we introduce noise into the filter function (Figure 8(c)).

Alternatively, we could plot the life intervals of persistent classes in the real line. For a persistent class, the birth and death time are the start and end points of the interval. We call this representation a *persistence barcode*. See Figure 8(b) for the persistence barcode representation of the persistent homology in the preceding example. 0-dimensional classes (resp. 1-dimensional) are drawn in solid (resp. dashed) lines with round (resp. square) marks on the start and end points. The essential 0-dimensional class has no death time.

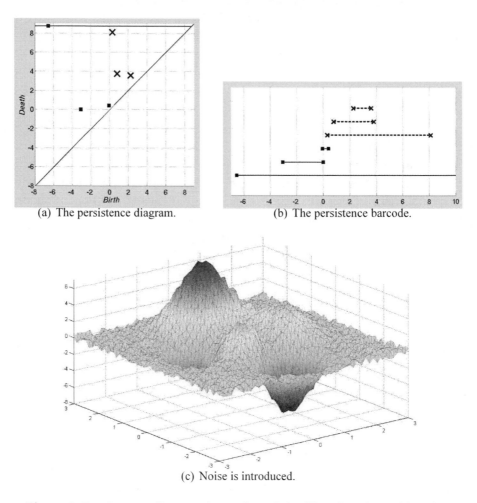

(a) The persistence diagram.

(b) The persistence barcode.

(c) Noise is introduced.

Figure 8. Persistence diagram, barcode and the filter function with noise.

2.9. Computing Persistence

Edelsbrunner *et al.* [1] devised an $O(n^3)$ algorithm to compute the persistent homology. Its inputs are a simplicial complex and a f lter function f, and its outputs are the birth and death times of all the persistent homology classes. The persistence algorithm for general spaces was developed in [17], which also explains the relationship of this algorithm to Gaussian elimination. A final version of this algorithm is contained in [21].

To explain the computation of persistence, we follow the exposition of [3, 10] which unif es boundary matrices of different dimensions into one overall *incidence matrix D*. Rows and columns of D correspond to simplices of K, indexed in the simplex-ordering. An entry of D is 1 if and only if its corresponding entry is 1 in the corresponding boundary matrix. The algorithm performs column reductions on D from left to right. Each new column is reduced by addition with the already reduced columns, until its lowest nonzero entry is as high as possible.

More specifically, during the reduction, record low (i) as the lowest nonzero entry of each column i. To reduce column i, we repeatedly find column j satisfying $j < i$ and $\text{low}(j) = \text{low}(i)$; we then add column j to column i, until column i becomes a zero column or we cannot f nd a qualified j anymore. If column i is reduced to a zero column, $\text{low}(i)$ does not exist. This is equivalent to reducing each boundary matrix into a canonical form, whose nonzero columns all have different lowest nonzero entries, and thus are linearly independent. It can be shown that while the order of reduction steps and the reduced matrix are not unique, the pairs – formed by grouping each column with its lowest nonzero entry – are unique.

The reduction of D can be written as a matrix multiplication,

$$R = DV, \tag{1}$$

where R is the *reduced matrix* and V is an upper triangular matrix. The reduced matrix R provides $\text{rank}(D)$ many pairs of simplices, $(\sigma_i, \sigma_j) : \text{low}(j) = i$. In such a pair, we say σ_j is paired on the right, σ_i is paired on the left. Each simplex appear in at most one pair, either on the left or on the right (cannot be both). For simplices that are not paired with any other simplex, we say they are paired with inf nity: (σ_k, ∞). Simplices paired on the right are *negative* simplices. Simplices paired on the left, with other simplices or with inf nity, are *positive* simplices.

A pair (σ_i, σ_j) corresponds to a persistent class, whose birth and death time are $f_i = f(\sigma_i)$ and $f_j = f(\sigma_j)$, respectively. That is, positive simplices give birth, while negative simplices cause death. A pair (σ_k, ∞) corresponds to an essential class, whose birth time is $f_k = f(\sigma_k)$.

The reduction is completely recorded in the matrix V. Columns of V corresponding to positive simplices form bases of cycle groups. Columns corresponding to positive simplices paired with $+\infty$ are cycles representing essential classes and form homology cycle bases.

3.   Applications to Computer Vision

In this section, we sketch out applications of the algebraic topological apparatus from the previous section to problems in computer vision and image processing. We focus on four illustrative applications: computation of shape signatures, the statistics of natural images, noise reduction, and image segmentation. In the case of the latter two, we treat them simultaneously, as the topological treatments of the two problems are closely related. For each of the problems of shape signatures and natural image statistics, we describe the technique of a single paper; in the case of noise reduction and image segmentation, we describe the results of a number of papers, as these latter problems have received somewhat more treatment in the still nascent literature.

3.1. Shape Signatures

A shape signature is a compact representation of the geometry of an object. Ideally, a signature should be the same for all of the objects within a particular class of objects. For example, if the class is the set of objects which are rigid motions (rotations plus translations) of a given smooth template curve in the plane, one might choose the curvature function as a signature. This is because the curvature function is equal for all objects in the set, and is different from the curvature function for an object from any other such set. However, the curvature function has problems: it amplif es noise, and it is not necessarily the case that two objects which have perceptually similar shapes will have similar curvature functions. A more relevant goal for computer vision, then, is to think in terms of broader classes of objects, and to find signatures which are similar within a class of interest, and as dissimilar as possible between classes, where similarity is measured by a particular distance function on signatures. For a survey of shape signatures, see [22, 23] and references therein.

In this section, we review the work of Collins *et al.* [24, 25] on shape signatures. The method presented in this work has the advantage that it is applicable to manifolds of any dimension; and with small modifications, to non-manifold spaces as well. Before delving into the details of this method, a natural question may arise: is the homology, on its own, sufficient to act as a shape signature? The answer is no, for two reasons. The first reason is that homology groups are sensitive to topological noise: as we have already seen in Figure 1, adding a small handle to a surface will completely change the homology of that surface. However, as we have noted, persistence is able to deal neatly with this problem. Thus, we may wonder whether persistent homology – with an appropriate filtration – is sufficient to act as a shape signature. The answer again is no, and this is the second reason homology (and persistent homology) is insuff cient: homology is too coarse a description of an object, as very different objects may have the same or similar homology groups. (This issue was also illustrated in Figure 1.) The key to the method of Collins *et al.* is to *augment* the underlying space to create a geometrically more informative space, and then to use the tools of persistence to compute signature of this space. We note in passing that [21] also used the notion of deriving a space, augmented with geometric data, for the purpose of f nding geometric descriptions of topological features.

We begin by describing the augmented space. Let $\mathbb{X}$ be the space of interest, which is a subset of $\mathbb{R}^n$. Def ne $T^0(\mathbb{X}) \subset \mathbb{X} \times \mathbb{S}^{n-1}$ as

$$T^0(\mathbb{X}) = \left\{ (x, \xi) \left| \lim_{t \to 0} \frac{d(x + t\xi, \mathbb{X})}{t} = 0 \right. \right\}$$

Then the *tangent complex* of $\mathbb{X}$, $T(\mathbb{X})$, is the closure of $T^0(\mathbb{X})$. In the case of a manifold, the tangent complex is similar to the tangent bundle of the manifold[6] – that is, each point is augmented with the set of unit tangent vectors to the manifold at that point. Thus, for

---

[6]Though not exactly the same, due to the use of unit vectors $\mathbb{S}^{n-1}$ in the definition of the tangent complex.

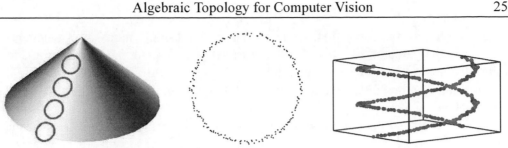

Figure 9. Two visualizations of the tangent complex. Left: the space is the blue cone, and the unit tangent vectors, which augment each point, are visualized as red circles. Middle and Right: the space is circle, here represented as a point cloud (middle); in this 1-dimensional case, the tangent complex can be represented explicitly (right). (Left figure taken from [24]. Copyright ©2005 World Scientific. Reprinted with permission. All rights reserved. Middle and right f gures taken from [25]. Copyright ©2004 Elsevier. Reprinted with permission. All rights reserved.)

example, in the case of a smooth surface living in $\mathbb{R}^3$, each point is augmented by a circle of tangent vectors, see Figure 9 (left). In the case of a smooth closed curve, each point is augmented by exactly two vectors (i.e., the two elements of $\mathbb{S}^0$), and the tangent complex can be visualized more explicitly, see Figure 9 (middle and right). The case of non-manifold behaviour is somewhat different. If a surface has a crease – e.g. imagine two planes meeting in a line – then at the crease, each point is augmented with not one, but two circles of tangent vectors.[7] See Figure 10 for an illustration.

Figure 10. The tangent complex for non-manifolds. Left: where the space is a 2-manifold, each point is augmented by a single circle of unit tangent vectors. Middle and right: where there is non-manifold behaviour, the space may be augmented by more than one circle of unit tangent vectors. (Figures taken from [24]. Copyright ©2005 World Scientific. Reprinted with permission. All rights reserved.)

In order to apply the tools of persistent homology, we will need a filter function for the space $T(\mathbb{X})$; ideally, the filter function should be geometric. Let us begin by focusing on the case when $\mathbb{X}$ is a curve, and consider the curvature $\kappa(x)$ at each point $x \in \mathbb{X}$. For any point in the tangent complex, $t = (x, \xi) \in T(\mathbb{X})$, we extend the curvature from the curve itself to the tangent complex in the natural way, $\kappa(t) = \kappa(x, \xi) \equiv \kappa(x)$. Then we may use the curvature as our f ltration function. In the case of curves, this has the effect of focusing

---

[7]In fact, the space $T^0(\mathbb{X})$ does not contain two circles of tangent vectors at a crease point; however, $T(\mathbb{X})$, which is the closure of $T^0(\mathbb{X})$, does.

on the flat parts of the curve first, while adding in increasingly more curvy segments as we increase the value of κ. This idea is illustrated in Figure 11 (middle column), for a family of ellipses. Note the way in which the ellipses with different eccentricities have different looking filtered tangent complexes; while the homology of the original ellipses are equivalent, the persistent homologies of these augmented spaces will be quite different, as desired. To extend the definition of this filtration to arbitrary manifolds – and indeed, arbitrary spaces – one may, for each $t = (x, \xi)$, define a circle of second order contact (akin to a classical osculating circle). The reciprocal of the radius of this circle gives an analogue to the curvature, which we may then use as a filter function. This quantity is essentially the sectional curvature at the point x in the direction ξ (though it is defined in [24, 25] to apply to non-manifold spaces as well). The interested reader is referred to [24, 25] for further details.

Finally, the shape signature for the space $\mathbb{X}$ is found by computing the persistent homology of the filtered tangent complex. This leads to a set of persistent barcodes, one set for each dimension. Recall, from Section 2.7., that the barcodes consist of intervals of the real line: the beginning of the interval is the birthtime and the end of the interval is the deathtime of the feature in question. These barcodes can be visualized by stacking the intervals, see Figure 11 (right column).

In order to compare two shapes, the barcode of a given dimension of the first shape is compared with the barcode of the same dimension of the second shape. The metric between barcodes is given by a matching algorithm: the cost of matching two intervals is given by the length of their symmetric difference, while the cost of unmatched intervals is simply their length. The distance between two barcodes is then given by the cost of the minimal matching; this distance, which can be computed by a bipartite graph matching algorithm, can be shown to be a metric, as desired.

We briefly mention some of the implementation details that are necessary for computing this signature when the shape of interest is given by a point cloud, which is a common case in practice. The tangent complex can be computed by using PCA on points in the neighbourhood of a given point (taken by the k nearest neighbours for a parameter k); if the space is not smooth, this information can be backed out of the eigenanalysis of the PCA, though this is more complicated. To compute the curvature at a given point, a circle of second order contact is fit to the data. To compute the persistence, a simplicial complex is first computed as the Cech complex, which is the *nerve* of the set of balls where each ball (of a fixed radius ε) is centered around a point in the tangent complex. That is, the complex is constructed as follows: where two balls intersect, an edge is placed; where three balls intersect, a triangle is placed; and so on. This complex can be shown to be homotopy equivalent to, and hence have the same homology as, the the union of balls [26]. Finally, the standard persistent homology algorithm (see Section 2.9.) can be applied to this simplicial complex. For further details, the reader is referred to [24, 25].

Results of applying the algorithm to the problem of computing shape signatures of a set of handwritten letters are shown in Figure 12. Quite obviously, there are mature technologies available for the optical character recognition (OCR) problem, and this technique does not outperform them; nonetheless, the results illustrate the power of the approach. In this example, there are eight letters, of which there are ten examples of each. In the experiment, each shape is assigned the barcodes described above, as well as extra barcodes derived from

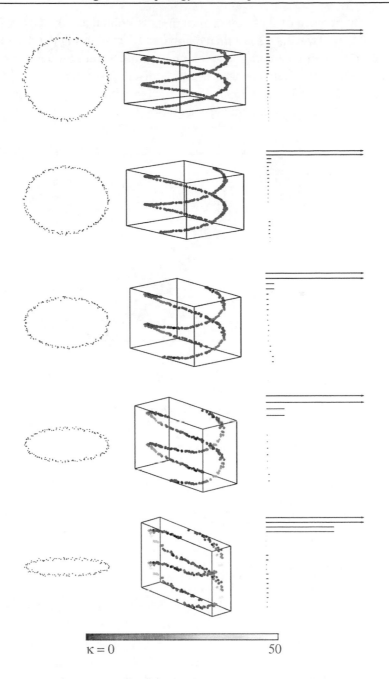

Figure 11. The persistence barcodes of shapes. Left: various ellipses, represented as point clouds. Middle: the filtered tangent complexes of these point shapes. The filter function is represented using colour, where the colour code is given at the bottom of the figure. Right: the corresponding barcodes (dimension 0), computing using persistent homology. (Figures taken from [25]. Copyright ©2004 Elsevier. Reprinted with permission. All rights reserved.)

other filtrations; the purpose of these other filtrations is to increase the power of discrimination between shapes. Two shapes are then compared by computing the distance between each pair their corresponding barcodes, and taking a weighted sum of these distances as the overall distance (see [25] for details). The resulting distance matrix for these 80 elements is shown in Figure 12: clearly, the shape signatures have the ability to capture the shape characteristics of the handwritten letters.

Figure 12. The distance matrix for the 80 letters (10 examples of each of 8 letters); dark represents a small value, and light represents a large value. (Figures taken from [25]. Copyright ©2004 Elsevier. Reprinted with permission. All rights reserved.)

We conclude this section by mentioning the very recent work on persistence-based shape signatures [27]. This work shows shapes can be endowed with certain quantities based on persistent homology, such that these quantities are stable when the shape undergoes a small change as measured by the Gromov-Hausdorff distance. Since the Gromov-Hausdorff distance is currently quite popular in the shape signature literature, this work may prove quite important.

3.2. Statistics of Natural Images

The problem of characterizing the statistics of natural images is a traditional topic in computer vision [28, 29, 30, 31, 32, 33]. The goal is to f nd the basic "rules" which describe images of natural scenes; these rules, once found, serve two purposes. The f rst purpose is an engineering one: the rules serve as a prior on images, which can be used in probabilistic or energy formulations of a variety of problems. For example, in the case of the so called Patch Transform [34], the goal is to reassemble the patches of an image in a jigsaw puzzle-like fashion while satisfying some user constraints. The natural image statistics provided by the Gaussian Mixture Model Field of Experts model [33] are used to ensure that the assembly process leads to a sensible image. In contrast to such an engineering view, the second purpose of the study of image statistics is a scientif c one. In this setting, the characterization of natural image statistics is interesting in its own right, and can lead to information about the way in which animals process visual data.

In this section, we review the work of Carlsson *et al.* [35], which uses a persistent homological approach to characterizing natural image statistics. The data used in this paper is the same as that of Lee *et al.* [32], which we briefy review.[8] A collection of more than $4,000$ images of natural scenes is used. From each image, $5,000$ 3×3 image patches are selected randomly, of which the top 20% with highest contrast in log-intensity are retained. These leads to a total collection of a bit more than 4 million patches.

More specifically, the process of choosing the top 20% of the image patches, per base image, works as follows. First, each 3×3 patch is represented as a 9-dimensional vector. Second, the elementwise-logarithm of each vector is taken. Third, for each vector, the mean of the vector is subtracted off of each element of the vector. Fourth, if the result of the prior computation is the vector v, then the so-called D-norm of v, i.e. $\sqrt{v^T D v}$, is computed; D is a particular 9×9 symmetric positive defnite matrix. Only the 20% of vectors with the highest D-norm are retained. Finally, each vector v is normalized by the D-norm, i.e. $v \leftarrow v / \sqrt{v^T D v}$.

Examining this process, we see that the in the first and second steps, the vectors live in $\mathbb{R}^9$. In the third step, after the mean has been subtracted off, the vectors live in an 8-dimensional subspace of $\mathbb{R}^9$. In the final step, after normalization, the transformed vectors live in $\mathbb{S}^7$, the 7-sphere.

In this setting, the goal is thus to characterize the statistics of the dense point cloud lying on $\mathbb{S}^7$. In order to do so, a filter function related to the density of the points is introduced. For each point x in the point cloud, let $\delta_k(x)$ be the distance from x to its kth nearest neighbour. Thus, $\delta_k(x)$ is inversely related to the density: the smaller is $\delta_k(x)$, the more densely represented is the area around a point. Setting the parameter k to have a small value results in a focus on the fine-scale structure of the data; whereas for k large, the coarse-scale structure of the point cloud becomes more apparent. For a fixed k, the function $\delta_k(x)$ is used as the filter function, with one caveat: the filtration ends when we have accumulated a fraction T of the points, where T is usually taken as 0.25. The reason for this latter restriction is that the high density points (i.e., the fraction T of points with the *smallest* values of $\delta_k(x)$) are said to form a "stable core," which best represent the image statistics. Finally, to speed up the computation, $5,000$ points at random are sampled from the data, and the persistence computation is performed on this subset. Many random samplings are taken to ensure consistency.

Given this filter function, what statistics are discovered? The first important discovery is that with a k value of 300 – that is, a large k value corresponding a relatively coarse scale – there is a single long-lived 1-dimensional homology class, see Figure 13 (top). To what does this circle on $\mathbb{S}^7$ correspond? An examination of the patches making up this circle indicates that they are patches with a light region on one side of the patch, and a dark region on the other: that is, they are edges. The circular structure turns out to be derived from the angle of the line separating the dark and the light regions; the angle can effectively take on all value from 0 to π. See Figure 13 (bottom) for an illustration.

The second important discovery uses a k value of 25, for a more fine scale analysis. At this scale, it is observed that there are 5 long-lived generators of the 1-dimensional homology group, see Figure 14 (top). There are several structures which can give rise to $\beta_1 = 5$ on the 7-sphere; on examination of the data, it turns out that the relevant structure is

---

[8]In fact, [32] uses both range and natural images; here, we focus only on the natural images, as these are what is used in [35].

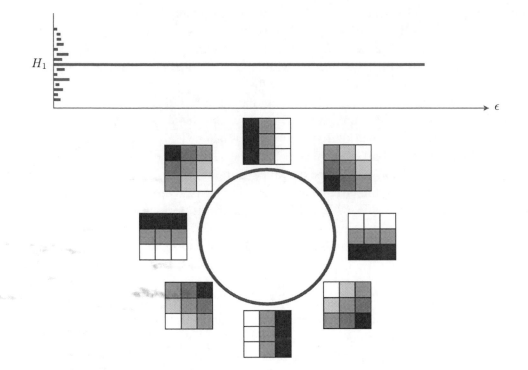

Figure 13. Coarse scale structure of the image statistics, corresponding to $k = 300$. Top: at this scale, the persistence barcode indicates that the data has one long-lived 1-dimensional homology class. Bottom: this single circle in $\mathbb{S}^7$ corresponds to edges, with the angle in the circle giving the angle of the edge. (Figures taken from [11]. Copyright ©2008 Robert Ghrist. Reprinted with permission. All rights reserved.)

a series of three interlocking circles, see Figure 14 (bottom). The first circle is the same as that already discovered at the coarse scale; the other two each intersect the original circle twice, but are disjoint from each other. It turns out that these two new circles represent patches which include three stripes, in which the stripes are not necessarily monotonic by grayscale, see Figure 15. Because they intersect the original circle, they include the edge patches described above (which are three stripe patterns, but where the stripes *are* monotonic by grayscale); but they also include non-edge patches, such as a patch consisting of two dark stripes sandwiching a light stripe. What is the difference between the two new circles? One circle represents horizontal stripes, and the other vertical stripes. Note that these horizontal and vertical stripes are *not* due to pixellization effects – if the images are all rotated by an angle of $\pi/4$, the true horizontal and vertical directions, represented as diagonals in this coordinate system, are still discovered [35].

Two more points deserve mention. First, more complex information can also be gleaned from the data, by looking at higher-order homology groups. For example, in looking at the 2-dimensional persistent homology, one finds a Klein Bottle structure. This structure has an explanation in terms of the underlying patches, but one which is somewhat involved to explain. The interested reader is referred to [35, 11] for a more in depth exposition. Second,

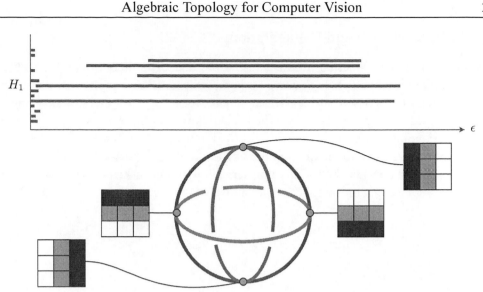

Figure 14. Fine scale structure of the image statistics, corresponding to $k = 25$. Top: at this scale, the persistence barcode indicates that the data has f ve long-lived 1-dimensional homology classes. Bottom: $\beta_1 = 5$ results from a series of three interlocking circles, in which the f rst circle is the coarse scale circle, while the other two each intersect the original circle twice, but are disjoint from each other. (Figures taken from [11]. Copyright ©2008 Robert Ghrist. Reprinted with permission. All rights reserved.)

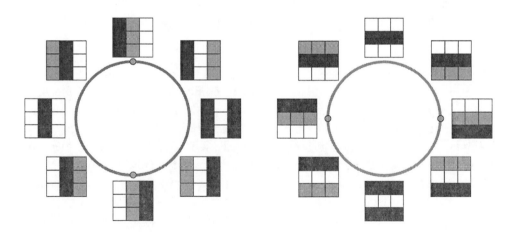

Figure 15. Analyzing the f ne scale structure. The two new circles represent patches which include three stripes, in which the stripes are not necessarily monotonic by grayscale. (Figures taken from [11]. Copyright ©2008 Robert Ghrist. Reprinted with permission. All rights reserved.)

this type of analysis has not been limited to natural image statistics; in a recent paper [36], Singh *et al.* have applied the same set of techniques to visual cortex data from experiments on primates. The latter should be of interest to the biological vision community.

3.3. Noise Reduction and Segmentation

The problem of noise reduction in images is an old one. The literature on this subject is vast, so no attempt will be made to survey it here; instead, let us simply note that classical approaches tend to be based on ideas from signal processing, estimation theory, and diffusion. In some instances, there are distinct features which one wishes to preserve in the image. For example, in terrain images, it is critical to preserve the large peaks, valleys, and passes, which correspond to maxima, minima, and saddles, respectively; see Figure 16. In ordinary images, it may also be useful to preserve "important" critical points, as this allows the image to retain a certain sharpness while noise is removed.

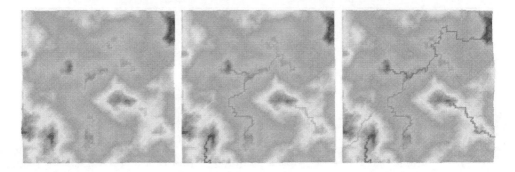

Figure 16. Simplification of a terrain image. Left: the original terrain image, in which heights range from blue (low) through cyan, green, yellow, and to red (high). Middle and right: simplifications of the terrain image which preserve large critical points. (Figures taken from [37]. Copyright ©2009 Dominique Attali. Reprinted with permission. All rights reserved.)

What is the connection between critical points and the homological tools that we have thus far discussed? The answer is that the critical points of a function and the persistent homology of that function are intimately related. In particular, the topology of the sublevel set of the function changes whenever there is a critical point; this can be seen in the example of Figure 7 and corresponding discussion in Section 2.7. As we know, the persistent homology itself is defned based on the changing homology of the sublevel sets. In fact, then, it turns out that the critical points of a function are in two-to-one correspondence with the points of the persistence diagram. That is, every birth time and every death time of a homological feature corresponds to a critical point of the relevant function. (Recall that each point in the persistence diagram consists of both a birth and death coordinate, which is why the correspondence is *two*-to-one.)

Note that this relationship between the homology of a space and the critical points of a function on that space dates to Morse and his eponymous Morse Theory [38, 39]. Classical Morse Theory assumes a smooth function, which in addition satisfies a mild genericity condition known as the Morse condition. The advantage of the persistent homology approach is that no smoothness is assumed for the function, so that a sensible defnition of critical points exists even when the underlying function is not smooth. That is, a homological critical value [19] of a function is a value at which the homology of the sublevel set of the function changes. This definition corresponds with the traditional critical point (at which the derivative vanishes) for smooth functions, but is more general. For example, it can be applied to a piecewise linear function, which is a standard case seen in applications.

Having established the relationship between critical points and points in the persistence diagram, we may now formulate the problem of feature-sensitive noise reduction as that of removing points with small persistence from the persistence diagram, while leaving other points in the persistence diagram alone. This has the effect of retaining important critical points, while discarding other, less significant ones. This problem has been addressed in the persistent homology literature, and goes under the title *persistence simplification*. The formal problem of persistence simplifcation, as described in [40, 37] is as follows:

Definition 1 *Given a topological space* $\mathbb{X}$ *and function* $f : \mathbb{X} \to \mathbb{R}$, *a function* $g : \mathbb{X} \to \mathbb{R}$ *is an ε-simplification of f if the two functions are close, $\|f - g\|_\infty \leq \varepsilon$, and the persistence diagram $D(g)$ contains only those points in the diagram $D(f)$ that are more than ε away from the diagonal.*

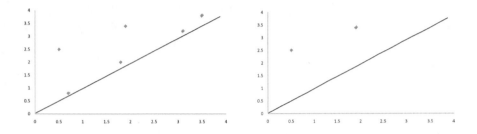

Figure 17. Persistence simplifcation. Left: the original persistence diagram for a given function f. Right: the persistence diagram for the ε-simplifcation g of the function f. Here $\varepsilon = 0.3$.

It should be clear that if such a g can be found, it will have solved the problem of feature-sensitive noise reduction, see Figure 17. Before examining algorithms for this general problem, however, we observe an interesting connection with the seemingly unrelated problem of segmentation. It will turn out that an important problem in segmentation admits a simpler version of persistence simplifcation, for which an algorithm has been developed. We will then return to a high-level discussion of results for the more general persistence simplifcation problem.

3.3.1. Segmentation

The connection between persistence simplifcation and segmentation comes about through the Mean Shift algorithm. In Mean Shift segmentation [41, 42, 43], each pixel in the image is assigned a feature vector – generally speaking, colour, texture, or some combination of the two, which is then often augmented by position. A non-parametric estimate of the probability density in this feature space – the Kernel Density Estimate (KDE) – is then constructed. Given this KDE, the image is segmented according to the *modes*, or local maxima, of the KDE. In particular, each local maximum of the KDE represents a segment of the image, and each pixel is assigned to the local maximum in whose basin of attraction the pixel lies.

Despite its success in many applications, the Mean Shift algorithm is known to generally yield an oversegmentation; that is, it produces too many segments. In some applications, this is tolerable; Mean Shift is sometimes used as preprocessing for a more sophisticated clustering algorithm, and is used simply to reduce the complexity of this second algorithm. On the other hand, it would be desirable if Mean Shift were able to yield a more precise segmentation on its own. Since Mean Shift tends to oversegment, the results might be corrected by forcing the algorithm to produce fewer clusters. Since each cluster corresponds to a local maximum of the KDE, the problem of mitigating oversegmentation is equivalent to the problem of filtering the KDE so as to preserve the most important local maxima, while eliminating smaller ones. In this sense, this problem is formally similar to a simpler version of the feature-sensitive noise reduction and persistence simplif cation outlined above. In particular, we are interested not in preserving all large critical points, but rather, only large local maxima.

Chazal *et al.* [44] present an elegant and practical method for attacking this problem. Before discussing their method, however, it is worth pointing out the contribution of Paris and Durand [45], who also attempt to tackle this problem. The basic idea of the paper is roughly in consonance with the approach of persistence simplification, and is the first work, to our knowledge, to try to tackle this problem in relation to segmentation. However, there are problems: the method is very "digital," in that it attempts to find basins of attraction and then to use a topological persistence oriented criterion for eliminating modes, by just using the digital grid, without a true simplicial complex (or other appropriate cell complex) underlying the analysis. The digitality proves to be a problem, both in theory and in practice. In theory, there is not much one can prove here; and in practice, some grid points are never classif ed as belonging to any basin of attraction, and a heuristic must be used.

The method of Chazal *et al.* [44], by contrast, is well-founded theoretically, and provides some nice practical properties as well. The set up is as follows. It is assumed that the topological space $\mathbb{X}$ is unknown and the function $f : \mathbb{X} \to \mathbb{R}$ is only specified on a finite subset $L \subset \mathbb{X}$. The specification of L itself is entirely coordinate-free; all that is needed is the set of pairwise distances between all points in L.[9] The goal is to compute the persistence of this sampled representation, and to simplify it, in the sense above: to eliminate local maxima whose persistence is smaller than a given threshold.

The first contribution is to show how the persistence diagram itself may be computed for the sampled representation. The *Rips Complex* of a f nite point set L and a positive real number δ is denoted $R_\delta(L)$ and is def ned as follows. A k-simplex σ with vertex set $v_0, \ldots, v_k \in L$ belongs to $R_\delta(L)$ if the distance between all pairs of vertices is less than or equal to δ: $d(v_i, v_j) \leq \delta$ for all i, j. It turns out that there is no value of δ for which the homology of the Rips Complex $R_\delta(L)$ matches that of $\mathbb{X}$, even for well-sampled spaces. Instead, the relationship between *a pair* of Rips Complexes, $R_\delta(L)$ and $R_{2\delta}(L)$, is suff cient to yield the persistent homology of the function $f : \mathbb{X} \to \mathbb{R}$. The details of this procedure are highly technical, relying on many algebraic concepts, such as persistence modules, which we do not def ne here. Instead we give a rough sketch, and the interested reader is referred to [44] for the full treatment.

Well-sampling means that the subset L is an ε-geodesic sample of $\mathbb{X}$, i.e. that any point

---

[9]Thus, $\mathbb{X}$ must also be a metric space; in practice, this is never a restriction, and most relevant spaces have even more structure, that is they are Riemannian manifolds.

in $\mathbb{X}$ has a geodesic distance of less than ε from some point in L, for ε less than $1/4$ of the *strong convexity radius of* $\mathbb{X}$ (which we do not define here). If $\mathbb{X}$ is well-sampled by L in the above sense, then Chazal *et al.* show that an approximation to the persistence diagram of $f : \mathbb{X} \rightarrow \mathbb{R}$ can be computed from the function values on L. Technically, let $L_\alpha = L \cap f^1(-\infty, \alpha]$ be the discrete analogue of the sublevel set; then the persistence diagram of f and the persistence diagram of the persistent homology module $\{R_\delta(L_\alpha) \hookrightarrow R_{2\delta}(L_\alpha)\}_{\alpha \in \mathbb{R}}$ have a bottleneck distance of at most a constant times δ, when δ is chosen to be greater than 2ε and less than $1/2$ the strong convexity radius of $\mathbb{X}$. This result relies on an earlier result [46] which showed that the relationship between the pair of Rips Complexes, $R_\delta(L)$ and $R_{2\delta}(L)$, is sufficient to provably approximate the homology of the domain $\mathbb{X}$.

Note that this result on its own is quite important, as it allows for the computation of persistence in high dimensional spaces, when an approach based on a simplicial complex would be too expensive (note that the size of the simplicial complex generally grows exponentially with the embedding dimension). In addition, though, the authors show how to use this scheme to simply deal with the oversegmentation problem from Mean Shift. First, a sampled version of Mean Shift is proposed: at any point, a steepest ascent vector is defined by looking at the highest (by function value) point in the neighbourhood of the point, where the neighbourhood is defined using 1 -skeleton of the the Rips Complex $R_{2\delta}(L)$. The point is then moved according to this steepest ascent vector, unless the point itself is the highest point in its own neighbourhood, in which case it is deemed a local maximum. The persistences of each such local maximum have already been computed using the algorithm sketched in the previous paragraph. In fact, the result of that algorithm is a diagram in which neighbouring maxima are linked. More formally, the diagram consists of pairs (v, e), where v is a local maximum and e is an edge of the 1-skeleton of the Rips Complex $R_{2\delta}(L)$ that links the connected component created by v in $R_{2\delta}(L)$ to the one created by some higher maximum u. If the lifespan of the connected component of v is shorter than some threshold, then the cluster of v is merged into that of u.

This algorithm, in addition to its provable properties (under appropriate sampling), can be shown to have a reasonable complexity. In particular, the complexity of the first part of the algorithm, the computation of persistence, is $O(n^3)$, where n is the number of points in L, whereas the second part is close to linear in n. Results of applying the algorithm are illustrated in Figure 18.

3.3.2.   General Persistence Simplification

As opposed to our treatment of the problems in the previous sections, in which we focused on one particular algorithm, we will, in this case, proceed to summarize the state of existing results in this field. This is mainly due to the fact that a somewhat larger literature has developed to tackle the problem of persistence simplification, though open problems certainly remain.

The first paper to introduce persistent homology [1] had already considered the problem of persistence simplification. In this paper, the setting is purely simplicial, and the filtration itself is given by an ordering of the simplices. An algorithm is given there for reordering of the simplices which simplifies the persistence. The main problem with this algorithm is that it reduces the persistence of *all* features; that is, all points in the persistence diagram

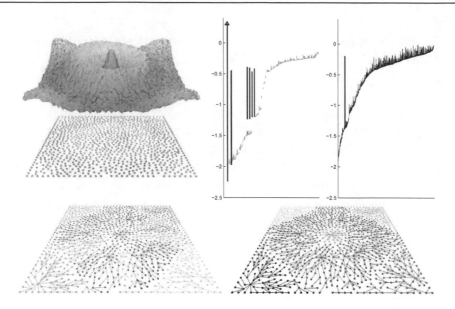

Figure 18. Segmentation. Top left: the function. Top right: the persistence barcode, illustrating the six large local maxima. Bottom left: the results of (discrete) Mean Shift. Bottom right: the results after merging clusters using persistence. (Figures taken from [44]. Copyright ©2009 Society for Industrial and Applied Mathematics. Reprinted with permission. All rights reserved.)

are moved closer to the diagonal, not just the smaller ones. This is not really desirable, as we wish to preserve the large features as precisely as possible, while removing the smaller ones.

Another series of papers tackle the problem of simplifcation of Morse-Smale complexes [47, 48, 49]. Briefy, the Morse-Smale complex bears a close relationship to the problem of Mean-Shift segmentation. The stable manifolds which are key ingredients in the construction of the Morse-Smale complex are essentially the same as the basins of attraction of the modes in Mean Shift; however, the Morse-Smale complex also uses the concept of unstable manifolds, which do not have a direct analogy in Mean Shift. (Unstable manifolds essentially allow points to run "down the hill" instead of up; this can be seen as performing mean shift on the negative KDE. The Morse-Smale complex then takes intersections of stable and unstable manifolds to build up a cell complex.) The main issue related to these results for simplifcation is that they are highly dependent on the low-dimension of the underlying topological space; the cases of dimension 2 and 3 are considered in the previously cited papers. In many cases, clustering occurs in spaces of somewhat higher dimension; for example, a common choice in image segmentation is $d = 5$, where each vector comprises 3 colour and 2 spatial dimensions.

The original paper to pose the problem of persistence simplifcation as in Defnition 1 was that of Edelsbrunner et al. [40]. In this paper, the problem was solved for piecewise linear 2-manifolds (surface meshes); the main problem with the approach is simply that it is very complicated, with many subcases considered. A more recent paper of Attali et al.

[37] also tackles the problem of simplif cation on surfaces and provides a simple algorithm, which is relatively simple to implement, and has a low complexity – linear in the number of simplices. Both of these papers are restricted to the low-dimensional setting.

Finally, we note that multiple simplification algorithms are introduced and discussed in [18].

4. Conclusions and Future Directions

In this survey, we have reviewed the new algorithms for computing with algebraic topology, in particular those of persistent homology; and the application of these algorithms to problems in computer vision and image processing. These techniques require some effort to master, but we believe that the effort is worth it: the techniques represent powerful new ways to attack interesting problems in vision. Furthermore, the methods have an inherent elegance which should be appealing to many vision researchers.

We believe that this is just the beginning of the application of the new topological ideas to image related problems. This paper ought merely to be an entryway for interested researchers into the exciting new developments in computational and applied algebraic topology. It is our hope that in five years, another survey will be required to cover the much larger number of developments that will have taken place over that time.

References

[1] H. Edelsbrunner, D. Letscher, and A. Zomorodian. Topological persistence and simplif cation. *Discrete and Computational Geometry*, **28**(4):511–533, 2002.

[2] H. Edelsbrunner. Biological applications of computational topology. *Handbook of Discrete and Computational Geometry*, pages 1395–1412, 2004.

[3] D. Cohen-Steiner, H. Edelsbrunner, and D. Morozov. Vines and vineyards by updating persistence in linear time. In *Proceedings of the Twenty-Second Annual Symposium on Computational Geometry*, pages 119–126, 2006.

[4] R. Ghrist and A. Muhammad. Coverage and hole-detection in sensor networks via homology. In *Proceedings of the 4th International Symposium on Information Processing in Sensor Networks*, 2005.

[5] V. de Silva, R. Ghrist, and A. Muhammad. Blind swarms for coverage in 2-D. In *Robotics: Science and Systems*, 2005.

[6] T.K. Dey, K. Li, J. Sun, and D. Cohen-Steiner. Computing geometry-aware handle and tunnel loops in 3D models. *ACM Transactions on Graphics (TOG)*, **27**(3):45:1–45:9, 2008.

[7] H. Edelsbrunner. Surface tiling with differential topology. In *Proceedings of the Third Eurographics Symposium on Geometry Processing*, pages 9–11, 2005.

[8] J. R. Munkres. *Elements of Algebraic Topology.* Addison-Wesley, Redwood City, California, 1984.

[9] A. Hatcher. *Algebraic Topology.* Cambridge University Press, 2002.

[10] H. Edelsbrunner and J. Harer. Persistent homology - a survey. In *Surveys on Discrete and Computational Geometry. Twenty Years Later. Contemporary Mathematics*, volume 453, pages 257–282. American Mathematical Society, 2008.

[11] R. Ghrist. Barcodes: The persistent topology of data. *Bulletin of the American Mathematical Society*, **45**(1):61–75, 2008.

[12] G. Vegter. Computational topology. *Handbook of Discrete and Computational Geometry*, pages 719–742, 2004.

[13] A. Zomorodian. *Computational topology*, volume 2 of *Algorithms and Theory of Computation Handbook*, chapter 3. Chapman & Hall/CRC, 2010.

[14] G. Carlsson. Topology and data. *Bulletin of the American Mathematical Society*, **46**(2):255–308, 2009.

[15] R. Kannan and A. Bachem. Polynomial algorithms for computing the Smith and Hermite normal forms of an integer matrix. *SIAM Journal on Computing*, **8**:499–507, 1979.

[16] T. Kaczyński, K.M. Mischaikow, and M. Mrozek. *Computational Homology*. Springer Verlag, 2004.

[17] Afra Zomorodian and Gunnar Carlsson. Computing persistent homology. *Discrete and Computational Geometry*, **33**(2):249–274, 2005.

[18] Afra Zomorodian. *Topology for Computing*. Cambridge Monographs on Applied and Computational Mathematics. Cambridge University Press, 2005.

[19] D. Cohen-Steiner, H. Edelsbrunner, and J. Harer. Stability of persistence diagrams. *Discrete and Computational Geometry*, **37**(1):103–120, 2007.

[20] F. Chazal, D. Cohen-Steiner, M. Glisse, L.J. Guibas, and S.Y. Oudot. Proximity of persistence modules and their diagrams. In *Proceedings of the 25th Annual Symposium on Computational Geometry*, pages 237–246, 2009.

[21] A. Zomorodian and G. Carlsson. Localized homology. *Computational Geometry*, **41**(3):126–148, 2008.

[22] D. Zhang and G. Lu. Review of shape representation and description techniques. *Pattern Recognition*, **37**(1):1–19, 2004.

[23] J.W.H. Tangelder and R.C. Veltkamp. A survey of content based 3D shape retrieval methods. *Multimedia Tools and Applications*, **39**(3):441–471, 2008.

[24] G. Carlsson, A. Zomorodian, A. Collins, and L. Guibas. Persistence barcodes for shapes. *International Journal of Shape Modeling*, **11**(2):149–187, 2005.

[25] A. Collins, A. Zomorodian, G. Carlsson, and L.J. Guibas. A barcode shape descriptor for curve point cloud data. *Computers & Graphics*, **28**(6):881–894, 2004.

[26] J. Leray. Sur la forme des espaces topologiques et sur les points f xes des représentations. *J. Math. Pures Appl., IX. Sér.*, **24**:95–167, 1945.

[27] F. Chazal, D. Cohen-Steiner, L.J. Guibas, F. Mémoli, and S.Y. Oudot. Gromov-Hausdorff stable signatures for shapes using persistence. In *Computer Graphics Forum*, volume 28, pages 1393–1403, 2009.

[28] D.J. Field. Relations between the statistics of natural images and the response properties of cortical cells. *Journal of the Optical Society of America A*, **4**(12):2379–2394, 1987.

[29] B. Olshausen and D. Field. Natural image statistics and eff cient coding. *Network: Computation in Neural Systems*, **7**(2):333–339, 1996.

[30] A. Van der Schaaf and JH Van Hateren. Modelling the power spectra of natural images: statistics and information. *Vision Research*, **36**(17):2759–2770, 1996.

[31] J. Huang and D. Mumford. Statistics of natural images and models. In *Proceedings of the IEEE Computer Society Conference on Computer Vision and Pattern Recognition*, volume 1, pages 541–547, 1999.

[32] A.B. Lee, K.S. Pedersen, and D. Mumford. The nonlinear statistics of high-contrast patches in natural images. *International Journal of Computer Vision*, **54**(1):83–103, 2003.

[33] Y. Weiss and WT Freeman. What makes a good model of natural images? In *IEEE Conference on Computer Vision and Pattern Recognition, 2007. CVPR'07*, pages 1–8, 2007.

[34] T.S. Cho, M. Butman, S. Avidan, and W.T. Freeman. The patch transform and its applications to image editing. In *IEEE Conference on Computer Vision and Pattern Recognition, 2008. CVPR 2008*, pages 1–8, 2008.

[35] G. Carlsson, T. Ishkhanov, V. De Silva, and A. Zomorodian. On the local behavior of spaces of natural images. *International Journal of Computer Vision*, **76**(1):1–12, 2008.

[36] G. Singh, F. Memoli, T. Ishkhanov, G. Sapiro, G. Carlsson, and D.L. Ringach. Topological analysis of population activity in visual cortex. *Journal of Vision*, **8**(8):1–18, 2008.

[37] D. Attali, M. Glisse, S. Hornus, F. Lazarus, and D. Morozov. Persistence-sensitive simplif cation of functions on surfaces in linear time. In *Proceedings of the TopoInVis Workshop*, 2009.

[38] J.W. Milnor. *Morse Theory*. Princeton University Press, 1963.

[39] Y. Matsumoto. *An Introduction to Morse Theory*. American Mathematical Society, 2002.

[40] H. Edelsbrunner, D. Morozov, and V. Pascucci. Persistence-sensitive simplification functions on 2-manifolds. In *Proceedings of the Twenty-Second Annual Symposium on Computational Geometry*, pages 127–134, 2006.

[41] K. Fukunaga and L. Hostetler. The estimation of the gradient of a density function, with applications in pattern recognition. *IEEE Transactions on Information Theory*, **21**(1):32–40, 1975.

[42] Y. Cheng. Mean shift, mode seeking, and clustering. *IEEE Transactions on Pattern Analysis and Machine Intelligence*, 17(8):790–799, 1995.

[43] D. Comaniciu and P. Meer. Mean shift: a robust approach toward feature space analysis. *IEEE Transactions on Pattern Analysis and Machine Intelligence*, pages 603–619, 2002.

[44] F. Chazal, L.J. Guibas, S.Y. Oudot, and P. Skraba. Analysis of scalar fields over point cloud data. In *Proceedings of the Nineteenth Annual ACM-SIAM Symposium on Discrete Algorithms*, pages 1021–1030. Society for Industrial and Applied Mathematics Philadelphia, PA, USA, 2009.

[45] S. Paris and F. Durand. A topological approach to hierarchical segmentation using mean shift. In *IEEE Conference on Computer Vision and Pattern Recognition, 2007. CVPR'07*, pages 1–8, 2007.

[46] F. Chazal and S.Y. Oudot. Towards persistence-based reconstruction in Euclidean spaces. In *Proceedings of the Twenty-Fourth Annual Symposium on Computational Geometry*, pages 232–241, 2008.

[47] H. Edelsbrunner, J. Harer, and A. Zomorodian. Hierarchical Morse–Smale complexes for piecewise linear 2-manifolds. *Discrete and Computational Geometry*, **30**(1):87–107, 2003.

[48] P.T. Bremer, B. Hamann, H. Edelsbrunner, and V. Pascucci. A topological hierarchy for functions on triangulated surfaces. *IEEE Transactions on Visualization and Computer Graphics*, **10**(4):385–396, 2004.

[49] A. Gyulassy, V. Natarajan, V. Pascucci, P.T. Bremer, and B. Hamann. Topology-based simplification for feature extraction from 3d scalar fields. In *Proceedings of the IEEE Conference on Visualization*, pages 535–542, 2005.

In: Computer Vision
Editor: Sota R. Yoshida

ISBN: 978-1-61209-399-4
© 2011 Nova Science Publishers, Inc.

Chapter 6

SPECTRAL IMAGING VERSUS NON-SPECTRAL IMAGING

Ismail Bogrekci

Mechanical Engineering Department, Faculty of Engineering,
Adnan Menderes University, Turkey

SUMMARY

Conventional approaches to Computer Vision harvested many opportunities for different disciplines and resulted in many applications and practices into our life. However, spectral imaging is promising many more looking into the future. Before we discuss what the difference between spectral and non-spectral imaging is, we shall define what the spectral and non-spectral imaging are at the beginning of this chapter. Later on, image acquisition tools and techniques will be discussed. Following on, the focus is intended to cover image processing techniques for spectral and non-spectral. Finally, the chapter is focused to discuss the advantages and disadvantages of spectral and non-spectral imaging.

INTRODUCTION

Spectral and non-spectral imaging should not be thought as competitors of each other. However, they both have pros and cons in terms of technology, application, and understanding. Since imaging technology is continuously developing, the future of imaging will show and surprise us with different approaches. From the beginning to end the light will interact with the material, this phenomenon will produce many different views, shows and images into the practical life.

Spectral and non-spectral imaging systems have wide varieties of applications using many varieties of platforms from space to human cell. These applications areas are Medicine, Space, Engineering, Agriculture, Security, Communication, Education, and etc. In this respect; the importance of imaging technologies is well understood. Without the imaging technology, the life would be blurry.

To give an example in Medicine, simply a surgeon or futures robot surgeons can not operate work without the imaging technology which is inevitable to use and operate a patient with minimal cut/disturbance.

THE CONCEPT

The concept of non-spectral and spectral imaging is essentially the same. Before the concept of spectral and non-spectral imaging is explained, the definitions for imaging are given for better understanding. Imaging is the creation of images from a physical scene using a camera or similar device. Imaging can be studied by dividing the area into two as analog and digital imaging. Currently, digital imaging is dominating the imaging world. A digital image may be created directly from a physical scene by a camera or similar devices. Alternatively, it may be obtained from another image in an analog medium, such as photographs, photographic film, or printed paper, by an image scanner or similar device.

There have been so called imaging practices in science without using a camera or similar device. Ultrasound images can be given as an example. Many technical images; such as those acquired with tomographic equipment, side-scan sonar, or radio telescopes are actually obtained by complex processing of non-image data. This digitalization of analog real-world data is known as digitizing, and involves sampling (discretization) and quantization.

Figure 1 illustrates the binary imaging representation of L shaped-item. Digital numbers (DNs) are given in Figure 1b and array voltage representation is shown in Figure 1c. An example of 4 by 4 pixel array detector is given here. It is assumed that minimum voltage level is 0 V while the maximum voltage level is 5 V. When L shaped black colored item is fixed to the white board, the image appears as seen in Figure 1a. The voltage levels of each detector are observed as in Figure 1c. Finally DN values of the image matrix would be as Figure 1b for 2 bit representation.

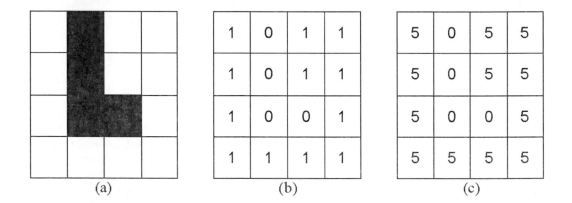

                (a)   (b)   (c)

Figure 1. Binary imaging representation of 4 by 4 pixel array a) image, b) DN values and c) voltages (volt).

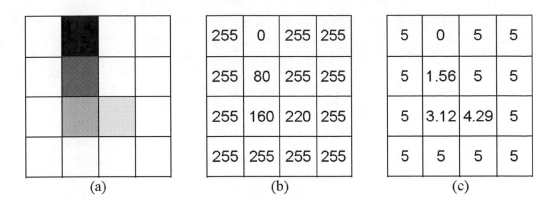

255	0	255	255
255	80	255	255
255	160	220	255
255	255	255	255

(a) (b)

5	0	5	5
5	1.56	5	5
5	3.12	4.29	5
5	5	5	5

(c)

Figure 2. Gray level imaging representation of 4 x 4 pixel array a) image, b) DN values and c) voltages (volt).

RED-DN

255	0	255	255
255	255	255	255
255	0	0	255
255	255	255	255

RED-VOLTAGE

5	0	5	5
5	5	5	5
5	0	0	5
5	5	5	5

GREEN-DN

255	0	255	255
255	0	255	255
255	255	0	255
255	255	255	255

GREEN-VOLTAGE

5	0	5	5
5	0	5	5
5	5	0	5
5	5	5	5

BLUE-DN

255	0	255	255
255	0	255	255
255	0	255	255
255	255	255	255

BLUE-VOLTAGE

5	0	5	5
5	0	5	5
5	0	5	5
5	5	5	5

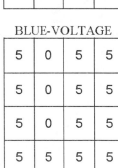

(a) (b) (c)

Figure 3. Color imaging representation of 4 x 4 pixel array a) image, b) DN values and c) voltages (volt).

Figure 2 illustrates the monochrome imaging representation of L shaped-item colored with black and different tones of grays for 8 bit imaging system. DNs are given in Figure 2b and array voltage representation is shown in Figure 2c. An example of 4 by 4 pixel array detector is given here. It is assumed that minimum voltage level is 0 V while the maximum voltage level is 5 V. When L shaped black and gray colored item is fixed to the white board, the image appears as seen in Figure 2a. The voltage levels of each sensor are observed as in Figure 2c. Finally DN values of the image matrix would be as Figure 2b for 8 bit representation.

Up to now non-spectral imaging is explained, in this approach, the light from the physical scene comes to the detector via optics with no spectral fragmentations. The detector sensitivity and digitalization of frame grabber/ AD converter are main factors in non-spectral imaging. The light intensity/ the amount of the reflection is the essential determinant factor in sensing. When we come to the color imaging, sort of fragmentations of the light into different wavelengths occurs.

Figure 3 illustrates the color imaging representation of L shaped-item colored with black, red, green and blue for 8 bit imaging system. DNs are given in Figure 3b for red, green and blue (RGB). The array voltage representations are shown in Figure 3c for RGB. An example of 4 by 4 pixel array detector is given here. It is assumed that minimum voltage level is 0 V while the maximum voltage level is 5 V. When L shaped black, red, green and blue colored item is fixed to the white board; the image appears as seen in Figure 3a. The voltage levels of each sensor are observed as in Figure 3c for RGB. Finally DN values of the image matrix would be as Figure 3b for 8 bit representation.

Airborne images of a farm in the Lake Okeechobee Drainage Basin in Florida, USA are shown in binary, gray level and color in figure 4. It is clear that color image has more information regarding the landscape than others. Features such as trees, vegetation, roads and ponds are more identifiable in color image than in gray and binary images.

Spectral imaging is the combination of imaging and spectroscopy that a complete spectrum is collected at every location of an image plane. This technique is studied and called as hyperspectral/multispectral imaging. Spectral imaging is not restricted to visible light, but works from ultraviolet to infrared. The spatial and spectral representation of multispectral imaging is shown in Figure 5.

Multispectral images are collected within several spectral bands. The resolution of bands is broader for multispectral imaging than that of hyperspectral imaging. The wavelength range of each common spectral band is described below depending upon the instrument used.

Blue; 450-515..520 nm, Green; 515..520-590..600 nm, Red; 600..630-680..690 nm, Near infrared; 750-900 nm, Mid-infrared; 1550-1750 nm, and Far-Mid-infrared; 2080-2350 nm.

For remote sensing applications, Blue is used for atmospheric and deep water imaging. Blue can reach within about 46 m deep in clear water. Green is used for imaging of vegetation and deep water structures. Green can reach up to 27 m in clear water. Red is used for imaging of man-made objects. Also it is used for soil, vegetation and water. Red light can reach up to 9.1 m deep in water. Near infrared is used for imaging of vegetation. Mid-infrared is used for imaging soil moisture content, vegetation and forest fires while Far-Mid-infrared is for imaging soil, moisture, geological features, silicates, clays, and fires.

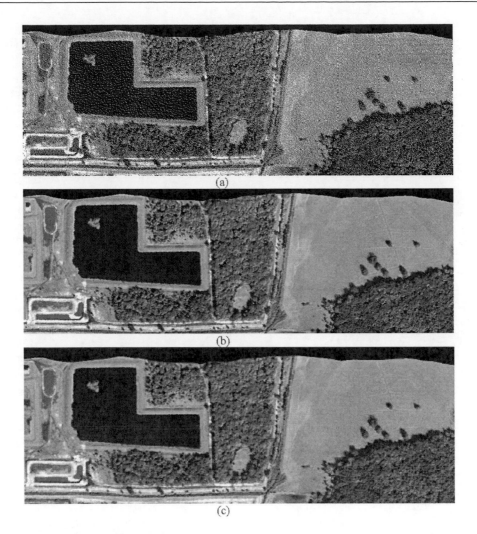

Figure 4. Airborne images of a farm in the Lake Okeechobee Drainage Basin in Florida, USA a) Binary, b) Gray level, and c) Color.

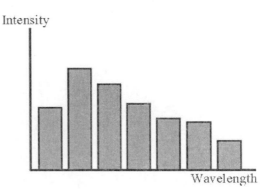

Figure 5. Multispectral imaging.

Hyperspectral imaging is collected with a resolution of less than 10 nm and the number of images is mostly more than that of multispectral imaging. Therefore, hyperspectral imaging contains more information than multispectral imaging.

Figure 6 shows the spatial and spectral representation of hyperspectral imaging. As seen many images are captured in hyperspectral imaging system than multispectral imaging. Therefore, hyperspectral images contain a lot more information than multispectral and non-spectral images.

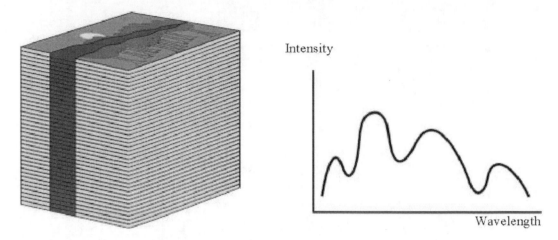

Figure 6. Hyperspectral imaging.

Multispectral and hyperspectral airborne images of a farm in the Lake Okeechobee Drainage Basin in Florida are illustrated in Figure 7. The images in Figure 7a takes less time to be captured when compared with the images in Figure 7b. Also image file sizes are smaller in Figure 7a than in Figure 7b. The imaging system for multispectral is cheaper than that for hyperspectral.

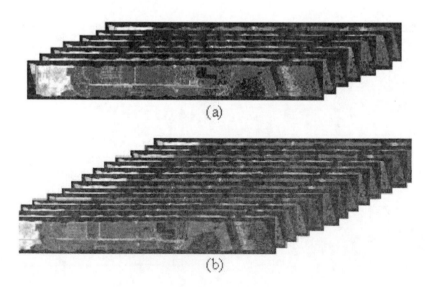

Figure 7. Airborne images of a farm in the Lake Okeechobee Drainage Basin in Florida, USA a) multispectral images and b) hyperspectral images.

IMAGING SYSTEMS

There are varieties of imaging systems for non-spectral and spectral imaging. They differ from each other on design approaches. However, the main difference between non-spectral and spectral sensing is that spectral sensing requires the acquisition of separated light with different wavelengths into the detector unit.

NON-SPECTRAL IMAGING

Non-spectral acquisition is the simplest way of imaging. A camera with black and white film used for photography is one of examples for the non-spectral imaging of analogue imaging system. For digital imaging systems, a black and white digital camera can be given as good example. In this sense, it can be explained that non-spectral imaging requires a light source, a scene/view/object, optics and detector (Figure 8). For a whole imaging system, off course, the electronic circuits, storage media and software are also needed. Direct or indirect light comes to the object. The light then is reflected, absorbed, and transmitted in order to explain simple. However, many other interactions happen between the material and the light which is out of aim of this chapter. Reflected light goes through the optics and shines on the detector. Depending upon the light intensity, potential differences occur in the detector cells. The voltages were digitized by an ADC circuit unit. The DNs are recorded by using different standards. Finally, the image is captured and stored in storage media.

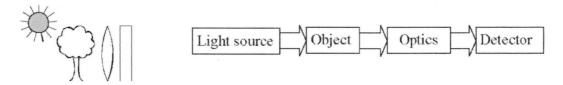

Figure 8. Non-spectral imaging.

For non-spectral imaging, there are few significant factors that affect the quality of the image. These can be explained as stated below:

1. CCD/CMOS detector pixel size,
2. f value (focal length) for focusing optics,
3. The distance between the object and the camera,
4. Light intensity,
5. Aperture size,
6. Shutter speed,
7. ADC digitization resolution (8, 16, 24 bit).

The parameters stated above are the main factors which defines the quality of images. Spatial resolution is one of the most important key factors. Figure 9 shows the effect of image resolution. The image in Figure 9a is a lot clearer than others in Figure 9. Also it has more information than others.

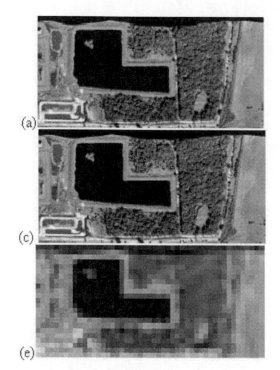

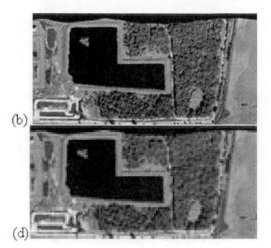

Figure 9. Imaging resolution.

SPECTRAL IMAGING

Spectral imaging can be described as obtaining images with spectral information. Multispectral and hyperspectral imaging are used. In spectral imaging, apart from light source, a scene/view/object, optics and detector, a wavelength selector is needed to use. Figure 10 illustrates the spectral imaging system.

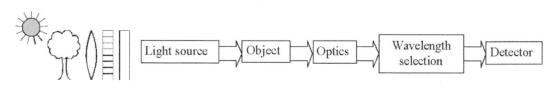

Figure 10. Spectral Imaging.

Depending upon the application area, the specifications of light source, optics, wavelength selectors, and detectors vary. Important part of the spectral imaging system is to have a wavelength selection unit. There are many ways to separate light photons to different wavelengths. Many of us observed that a piece of glass can separate the Sun light into different colors. From static to dynamic; from simple to advance; from cheap to expensive, different wavelength selectors have been invented and are on sale. Here, different wavelength selectors are mentioned below:

1. Band Filters,
2. Linear Variable Filters (LVFs),
3. Filter wheels,
4. Prisms,
5. Gratings,
6. Monochromators,
7. Liquid Crystal Tunable Filters,
8. Acousto-Optic Tunable Filters.

The light shines upon the object, depending upon the area of sensing, transmitted or reflected light goes through the optics and the light is separated into different wavelengths. Separated light waves are then shined on the detector. Finally, images are captured on a storage media.

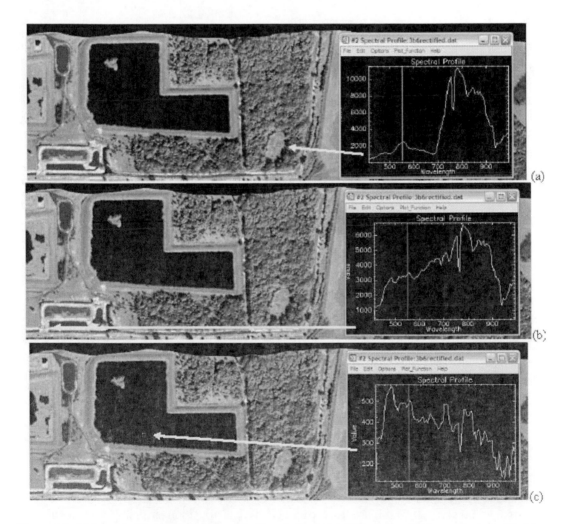

Figure 11. Airborne hyperspectral images of a farm in the Lake Okeechobee Drainage Basin in Florida, USA a) plant spectrum b) soil spectrum, and c) water Spectrum.

Airborne hyperspectral image of a farm in the Lake Okeechobee Drainage Basin in Florida is shown in Figure 11. A spectral signal of plants (Figure 11a) is extracted from Figure 11. It can be seen that signal at Figure 11a represents a fresh plant which has distinct wavelengths such as chlorophyll at/around 550 nm, red rising edge, and water peaks. Figure 11b shows the spectrum of soils while the water spectrum extraction from the image is illustrated in Figure 11c. Hyperspectral image in Figure 11 shows that water, plant and soil can easily be identified. A color imaging also can provide the same analyses but hyperspectral imaging can offer a lot more features to be identified / analyzed such as water stress in plants; illness of plants; deficiencies of nutrients in plants; soil (soil type: clay or sand etc.) and water properties (turbidity etc.).

IMAGE PROCESSING

The main aim of image processing is to enhance and analyze the images for obtaining real-world results. First attention is paid to image acquisition. The best image acquisition system should be able to mimic the real-world scene into digital medium. Real-time or static image processing systems can use hardware or software in order to process the signals. Image processing involves the enhancement, filtering, feature extraction before image analysis is conducted. The captured image is resized, filtered, enhanced and reformatted. These all cause some changes on DNs of image matrix. The regression or comparison of DNs with real world values such as length, temperature, and chemical concentration etc. are called as image analysis.

NON-SPECTRAL IMAGE PROCESSING

Non-spectral imaging mostly involves alteration, subtraction, addition, multiplication and division etc. of DNs at 2D matrix within or with other 1D/2D matrix or constant. In non-spectral imaging, some of image processing techniques can be stated below:

1. Resampling,
2. Resizing,
3. Filtering (low pass, high pass, band pass, edge filtering etc.)
4. Pattern recognition,
5. Blob analysis,
6. Contrast enhancement,
7. Geometric corrections/calibrations/enhancements.

Above mentioned techniques are some of the commonly used techniques. However, there are many more image processing techniques used for non-spectral image processing.

Images on the left of Figure 12 show the image acquisition errors. Image acquisition plane and angle introduces errors to the image. Therefore, results obtained from these erroneous images are far from the real values. Since the results are incorrect on the left images, geometric corrections are needed in order to obtain correct results. Figure 12 shows the geometric corrections done on two original images with/without grid on the left and geometrically corrected two images with/without grid on the right.

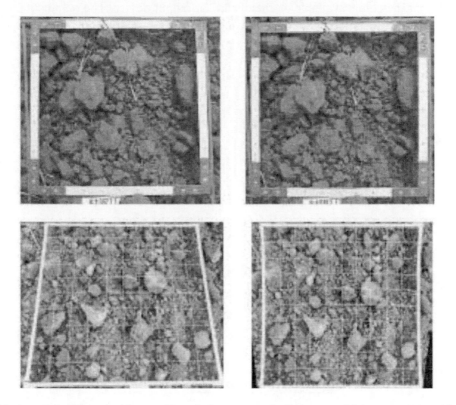

Figure 12. An original image without grid top left, a geometrically corrected image top right without grid, an original image with grid bottom left and a geometrically corrected image with grid bottom right.

a   b   c

Figure 13. Images (a) after geo-correction (b) after median filter (c) after frame removal.

Image of soil aggregates with grid and frame is illustrated in Figure 13a. A median filter is applied to the image in Figure 13a, and then image in Figure 13b is obtained. It is observed that the application of median filter to the image (Figure 13a) results in the removal of grid (Figure 13b). Later on, the image in Figure 13b is cropped to remove the frame.

The range of brightness values present on an image is referred to as contrast. Contrast enhancement is a process that makes the image features stand out more clearly by making optimal use of the colors available on the display or output device. The outputs represent the original images. Some information is lost during linear contrast stretching due to the nature of the operation. For example some lower grey values will be zero and some high grey values would be maximum. Figure 14 presents the linear stretching of the DN (Digital Number) values of each pixel in an image where; GLo: grey level of output GLi: grey level of input

c: cutoff

s: saturation

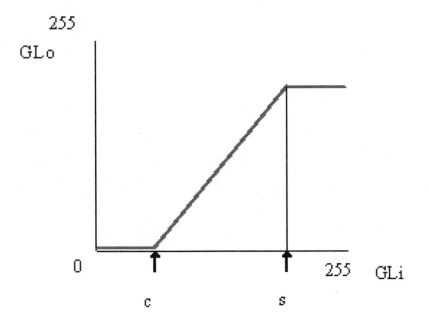

Figure 14. Linear stretching for contrast enhancement.

When the value of c increases, the output image gets darker and when the value of s increases output image becomes lighter. Figure 15 shows the effects of contrast enhancement on an image (left is input image and right is image with contrast enhancement). This technique has some advantages over binarising. Binarising is an image processing technique that can reduce the colour level of the image into two colours. To binarise an image, a threshold value is selected. When the value of the pixels in an image is greater than threshold, image becomes white and when the value of the pixels is smaller than threshold, image becomes black.

An edge may be regarded as a boundary between two dissimilar regions in an image. Many edge extraction techniques can be broken up into two distinct phases: Finding pixels in the image where edges are likely to occur by looking for discontinuities in gradients (Candidate points for edges in the image are usually referred to as edge points, edge pixels, or edgels). Linking these edge points in some way to produce descriptions of edges in terms of lines, curves etc. Figure 16 illustrates the edge detection of images.

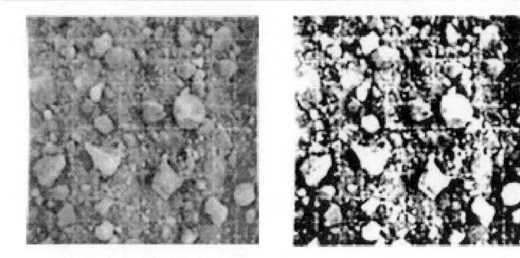

Figure 15. Representation of image contract enhancement.

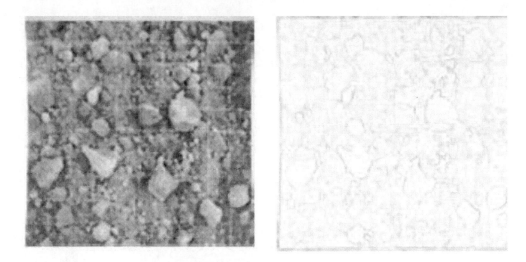

Figure 16. Representation of image edge detection.

Up to now, a few image processing techniques are mentioned and illustrated. However, there are many more image processing techniques for non-spectral imaging for different areas. It is not possible to mention and explain within the context and size of this chapter. It needs a book size to cover all.

SPECTRAL IMAGE PROCESSING

Spectral imaging involves alteration, subtraction, addition, multiplication and division etc. of DNs at 2D matrix within or with other 1D/2D matrix or constant with the computations involved in another dimension called z spectrum. In other words, in addition to the processing in non-spectral imaging, spectral information is computed. Some of image processing techniques for spectral imaging can be stated below:

1. Spectral Math,
2. Band ratios,
3. Classification (supervised, unsupervised, decision tree etc.),
4. Image sharpening (HSV, Brovey, Gram-Schmidt etc.),
5. Principle components,
6. MNF rotations,
7. Color transforms,
8. Stretches (decorrelation, photographic, saturation etc.),
9. NDVI or indexing,
10. Filterings (convolution and morphology, texture, adaptive and FFT etc.)

Above mentioned techniques are some of the commonly used techniques. However, there are many more image processing techniques used for spectral image processing. Some of the above mentioned images processing techniques are illustrated below.

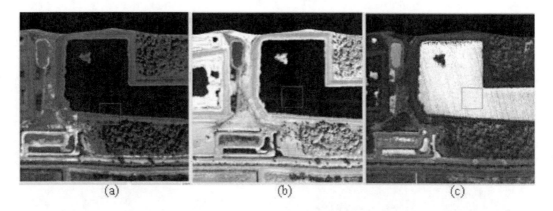

Figure 17. Band ratios application of 420 nm to 990 nm: (a) image at 420 nm (b) image at 990 nm and (c) the result image 420/990 nm.

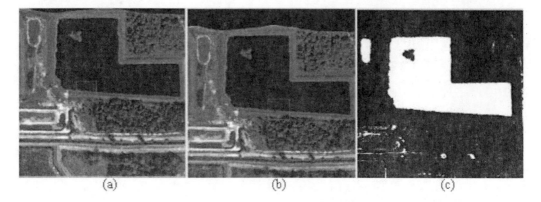

Figure 18. Spectral math application (a) image at 500 nm (b) image after Gram-Schmidt sharpening and (c) image after spectral math calculation (410+467)/550 nm.

COMPARISON OF NON-SPECTRAL AND SPECTRAL IMAGING

There are many parameters to compare non-spectral imaging with spectral imaging. Here are some of them discussed shortly. Table 1 describes the comparison parameters in summary.

Table 1. The comparison of non-spectral and spectral imaging

Criteria	Non spectral	Spectral	Comment
Type	2D/3D	3D/4D	
Information	Less	More	The amount of information in spectral images is vast.
The speed of image acquisition	Faster	Slower	
Light dispersion	Not needed	Compulsory	The light must be fragmented into different wavelengths/bands.
Handling	Very easy	Hard	
Algorithms	Simple	Complex	
Time for analyzing	Very quick	Very slow	
Complexity	Low	High	There are more components in spectral sensing systems.
Storage	Less	Much	
Price	Cheap	Expensive	

CONCLUSION

Spectral imaging and non-spectral imaging are part of our lives. They have different application areas from photography to Space. Humans will always use the imaging technologies in their life. Spectral sensing systems are becoming more available, cheap and user friendly. This virgin scientific area will give benefit the human beings; from brain studies to cells in Medicine; from maturity to quality in Agricultural Sciences; from fractures to defects in Engineering; etc.

The important thing is to know what to use when/where/how.

REFERENCES

[1] Russ John C. 2002. *The image processing handbook*. CRC Press LLC, USA, ISBN 0-8493-1142-X.

[2] Bogrekci Ismail. 2010. *Soil Tilth Sensing*. Lambert Academia Publishing, USA, ISBN 978-3-8383-8085-8.

[3] Gonzalez Rafael C., Richard E. Woods and Steven L. Eddins. 2009. *Digital Image processing using Matlab*. Gatesmark Publishing, USA, ISBN 978-0-9820-8540-0.

[4] Burke Michael. 2010. *Handbook of Machine Vision Engineering: Image Processing.* Chapman & Hall, USA, ISBN 978-0-4124-7930-4.

[5] McAndrew Alasdair. 2004. *Introduction to Digital Image Processing with Matlab.* Course Technology, USA, ISBN 978-0-5344-0011-8.

In: Computer Vision
Editor: Sota R. Yoshida

ISBN: 978-1-61209-399-4
© 2011 Nova Science Publishers, Inc.

Chapter 7

LEAST SQUARES FITTING OF QUADRATIC CURVES AND SURFACES

N. Chernov* and H. Ma[†]
University of Alabama at Birmingham
Birmingham, AL 35294, USA

Abstract

In computer vision one often fits ellipses and other conics to observed points on a plane or ellipsoids/quadrics to spacial point clouds. The most accurate and robust fit is obtained by minimizing geometric (orthogonal) distances, but this problem has no closed form solution and most known algorithms are prohibitively slow. We revisit this issue based on recent advances by S. J. Ahn, D. Eberly, and our own. Ahn has sorted out various approaches and identified the most efficient one. Eberly has developed a fast method of projecting points onto ellipses/ellipsoids (and gave a proof of its convergence). We extend Eberly's projection algorithm to other conics, as well as quadrics in space. We also demonstrate that Eberly's projection method combined with Ahn's most efficient approach (and using Taubin's algebraic fit for initialization) makes a highly efficient fitting scheme working well for all quadratic curves and surfaces.

Keywords: Least squares, orthogonal regression, fitting ellipses, conics, quadrics.

AMS Subject Classification: 62J.

1. Introduction

Fitting simple contours (primitives) to observed image data is one of the basic tasks in pattern recognition and computer vision. The most popular contours are lines, circles, and ellipses (recall that round objects appear as elliptic ovals on photos). In 3D space, one often fits planes, spheres, or more complex surfaces (such as ellipsoids) to point clouds. We review the most advanced fitting methods and extend them to all quadratic curves and surfaces.

---

*E-mail address: chernov@math.uab.edu
[†]E-mail address: hma@uab.edu

We begin with the 2D fitting problem. Let $(x_1, y_1), \ldots, (x_n, y_n)$ denote the observed points. Let $P(x, y; \Theta) = 0$ be the equation of the fitting contour, where Θ represents the vector of unknown parameters. For example, lines can be defined by equation

$$x \cos \theta + y \sin \theta + d = 0, \tag{1}$$

so $\Theta = (\theta, d)$. Circles can be described by

$$(x - a)^2 + (y - b)^2 - R^2 = 0, \tag{2}$$

so $\Theta = (a, b, R)$. Ellipses can be defined by

$$\frac{\breve{x}^2}{a^2} + \frac{\breve{y}^2}{b^2} - 1 = 0 \tag{3}$$

in the canonical coordinates $\breve{x}, \breve{y}$, which can be related to x, y by translation and rotation, i.e., $\breve{x} = (x - c_1) \cos \theta - (y - c_2) \sin \theta$ and $\breve{y} = (x - c_1) \sin \theta + (y - c_2) \cos \theta$; now $\Theta = (a, b, c_1, c_2, \theta)$, where (c_1, c_2) is the center, a, b are the semiaxes, and θ is the angle of tilt.

The classical least squares fit minimizes geometric distances from the observed points to the fitting curve:

$$\mathcal{F}(\Theta) = \sum_{i=1}^{n} d_i^2 = \sum_{i=1}^{n} (x_i - x_i')^2 + (y_i - y_i')^2 \quad \rightarrow \quad \min. \tag{4}$$

Here d_i denotes the geometric distance from the observed point (x_i, y_i) to the fitting contour, and (x_i', y_i') the (orthogonal) projection of (x_i, y_i) onto the contour.

The least squares fit (4) has many nice features. It is invariant under translations, rotations, and scaling, i.e., the fitting contour does not depend on the choice of the coordinate system. It provides the maximum likelihood estimate of Θ under standard statistical assumptions (where points are observed with an independent isotropic gaussian noise [9, 12, 15]). The minimization (4) is always regarded as the most desirable solution[1] of the fitting problem, albeit hard to compute in most cases.

Fig. 1 shows a sample of eight points (their coordinates are given in Table 1; they are borrowed from [19]) and the best fitting ellipse obtained by (4). We will explore this example at the end of Section 2.

When one fits lines (1), the problem (4) has a closed form solution, and its properties have been studied deeply [10, 15]. When one fits circles (2), the problem (4) has no closed form solution, but one has an explicit formula for the distances,

$$d_i = \sqrt{(x_i - a)^2 + (y_i - b)^2} - R, \tag{5}$$

hence one can easily compute the objective function (4), as well as its derivatives with respect to a, b, R. This makes the minimization of $\mathcal{F}$ rather straightforward – the standard

---

[1]In particular, (4) has been prescribed by a recently ratified standard for testing the data processing software for coordinate metrology [20].

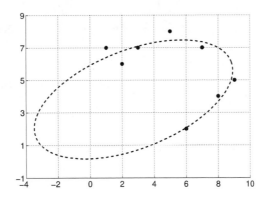

Figure 1. A sample of eight points and the best fitting ellipse.

Levenberg-Marquardt algorithm (the most popular and reputable scheme for solving least-squares problems [15, 19]) works well. Algebraic circle fits (say, the one by Taubin; see Appendix) provide good initial guesses.

When one fits ellipses, no simple explicit formulas are available for the distances d_i's or the projections (x_i', y_i'). Theoretically, the projection (x_i', y_i') can be found by solving a polynomial equation of degree four [28], but such a solution is complicated and inconvenient (it involves complex numbers), and even worse – it is numerically unstable [4]. Besides it is not clear how to differentiate d_i with respect to Θ. Since one cannot easily compute the objective function (4) or its derivatives, it appears that the Levenberg-Marquardt scheme is impractical (see [25] that mentioned such a point of view).

The first thorough investigation of the ellipse fitting problem was done in the middle 1990's by Gander, Golub, and Strebel [19]. They developed a roundabout way of minimizing $\mathcal{F}$ by using auxiliary parameters ω_i, $i = 1, \ldots, n$, describing the location of the projected points (x_i', y_i') on the ellipse; the latter, in the canonical coordinates (3) were expressed by $\breve{x}_i' = a \cos \omega_i$ and $\breve{y}_i' = b \sin \omega_i$. Thus the objective function becomes

$$\mathcal{F} = \sum_{i=1}^{n} (x_i - c_1 - a \cos \omega_i \cos \theta - b \sin \omega_i \sin \theta)^2$$
$$+ (y_i - c_2 + a \cos \omega_i \sin \theta - b \sin \omega_i \cos \theta)^2.$$

In [19], $\mathcal{F}$ was minimized with respect to $a, b, c_1, c_2, \theta, \omega_1, \ldots, \omega_n$ *simultaneously*. This procedure avoids the calculation of d_i's, but the minimization in the $(n + 5)$-dimensional parameter space is predictably cumbersome and slow. So the authors of [19] demonstrated that the minimization of geometric distances for ellipses was a prohibitively difficult task.

Recently Sturm and Gargallo [25] modified the above method in several ways. In particular, they used a projective matrix that allowed them to describe conics of all types (ellipses, hyperbolas, parabolas) with the same set of 5 parameters. Thus their method could freely switch between types during iterations. But they still work in an $(n+5)$-dimensional parameter space, in that sense their method is similar to that of [19].

In the late 1990s, in computer vision applications various alternative fitting schemes were developed, where so called algebraic distances were minimized; we review them in

Appendix. They produce ellipses that fit less accurately than those minimizing geometric distances (4). Some authors say that "the performance gap between algebraic fitting and geometric fitting is wide..." (see [7, p. 12]).

In the early 2000's another approach to the minimization of geometric distances (4) emerged, due to Ahn et. al. [4, 6, 7], that turned out to be very efficient. We describe it in a general form.

2. Fitting Implicit Curves and Surfaces

Least squares problems are commonly solved by the Gauss-Newton (GN) method or its Levenberg-Marquardt (LM) correction. If one minimizes a sum of squares $\mathcal{F}(\Theta) = \sum f_i^2$, then both GM and LM would use the values of f_i's and their first derivatives with respect to Θ, which we denote by $(f_i)_\Theta$.

Now suppose, as before, that we fit a curve defined by implicit equation $P(x, y; \Theta) = 0$ to observed points (x_i, y_i). Our goal is to minimize the sum of squares (4). The GN and LM methods can be applied here in two ways: we either treat $\mathcal{F}$ as a sum of n squares, $\mathcal{F} = \sum d_i^2$, or a sum of $2n$ squares, $\mathcal{F} = \sum g_i^2 + \sum h_i^2$, where $g_i = x_i - x_i'$ and $h_i = y_i - y_i'$. In the former case we will need d_i's and their derivatives $(d_i)_\Theta$. In the latter we need f_i's and g_i's, as well as their derivatives $(g_i)_\Theta$ and $(f_i)_\Theta$. The resulting algorithm is said to be *distance-based* if one uses d_i's, or *coordinate-based* if one uses g_i's and h_i's; see Ahn et al. [6, 7].

Obviously, it is enough to know the projections (x_i', y_i') in order to compute d_i's, g_i's, and h_i's. But their derivatives $(d_i)_\Theta, (g_i)_\Theta, (f_i)_\Theta$ present a more challenging problem. Sometimes finite differences are used to approximate these derivatives, which reduces the accuracy of the fit. But there are surprisingly simple formulas for these derivatives:

Proposition. *Let (x, y) be a given a point and (x', y') denote its projection onto the curve $P(x, y; \Theta) = 0$ (then x', y' depend on Θ). Denote $g = x - x'$, $h = y - y'$, and $d^2 = g^2 + h^2$. Then we have*

$$g_\Theta = \frac{P_\Theta P_x^2 - g P_y (P_x P_{y\Theta} - P_y P_{x\Theta})}{P_x (P_x^2 + P_y^2)}, \tag{6}$$

$$h_\Theta = \frac{P_\Theta P_y^2 + h P_x (P_x P_{y\Theta} - P_y P_{x\Theta})}{P_y (P_x^2 + P_y^2)}, \tag{7}$$

and

$$d_\Theta = \frac{P_\Theta}{\sqrt{P_x^2 + P_y^2}}, \tag{8}$$

where P_Θ, P_x, P_y denote the first order partial derivatives of P with respect to Θ, x, y, respectively, and $P_{x\Theta}$ and $P_{y\Theta}$ the corresponding second order partial derivatives; all the derivatives are taken at the projection point (x', y').

Proof. Since the vector $(x - x', y - y')$ is orthogonal to the curve,

$$g = x - x' = t P_x \quad \text{and} \quad h = y - y' = t P_y \tag{9}$$

for some scalar t. This immediately gives

$$d^2 = g^2 + h^2 = t^2(P_x^2 + P_y^2). \tag{10}$$

Next we use differentiation with respect to Θ. Differentiating the identity $P(x', y'; \Theta) = 0$ gives

$$P_\Theta = -P_x x'_\Theta - P_y y'_\Theta = (g g_\Theta + h h_\Theta)/t, \tag{11}$$

and differentiating the identity $d^2 = g^2 + h^2$ gives

$$d d_\Theta = g g_\Theta + h h_\Theta = t P_\Theta. \tag{12}$$

Now (8) follows from (12) and (10). Differentiation of (9) gives

$$g_\Theta = t_\Theta P_x + t P_{x\Theta}, \qquad h_\Theta = t_\Theta P_y + t P_{y\Theta}.$$

Eliminating t_Θ from these two equations yields

$$g_\Theta P_y - h_\Theta P_x = -t(P_x P_{y\Theta} - P_y P_{x\Theta}). \tag{13}$$

Solving (12) and (13) for g_Θ and h_Θ we obtain (6) and (7). $\qquad\square$

The formulas (6)–(8) were essentially obtained by Ahn et al. [6, 7]. Independently the formula (8) was derived in [3] (see eq. (24) there).

Practically, the calculation of the derivatives $d_\Theta, g_\Theta, h_\Theta$ by (6)–(8) is easy once the projection point (x', y') is located. The differentiation of $P(x, y; \Theta)$ with respect to Θ is usually straightforward; for example, one can easily find the derivatives of (3) with respect to a, b, c_1, c_2, θ.

Alternatively, one can try to change the parametrization scheme in order to simplify differentiation. For example, instead of (3) one can define an ellipse by equation

$$\sqrt{(x - p_1)^2 + (y - p_2)^2} + \sqrt{(x - q_1)^2 + (y - q_2)^2} - 2a = 0 \tag{14}$$

where (p_1, p_2) and (q_1, q_2) denote its foci and $2a$, as before, the major axis. These are sometimes called *Kepler's parameters* of an ellipse; they have certain advantages [11]. In particular, differentiation of (14) with respect to p_1, p_2, q_1, q_2, and a is quite straightforward.

We note that the coordinate-based scheme using g_i's and h_i's operates with $2n$ terms and involves the second order derivatives $P_{x\Theta}$ and $P_{y\Theta}$. The distance-based scheme operates only with n terms and does not involve the second order derivatives; cf. (8). As a result, the coordinate-based scheme seems to be less efficient, and we will only use the distance-based fit in what follows.

Remark. Since the distance d given must be differentiable, we have to treat it as a *signed* distance – it must be positive on one side of the curve and negative on the other, just as we had it in (5). For ellipses, one can make $d > 0$ for points outside the ellipse and $d < 0$ for points inside.

The above minimization scheme also works for surfaces in the 3D space, when they are defined by implicit equations $P(x, y, z; \Theta) = 0$. In that case the above formulas acquire an extra term corresponding to the z variable, otherwise they remain pretty much the same.

Table 1. A benchmark example with eight points [19].

x	1	2	5	7	9	3	6	8
y	7	6	8	7	5	7	2	4

Table 2. Comparison of two ellipse fitting methods.

	Failure rate	Avg. iter.	Cost per iter. (flops)
Implicit	11%	20	1640
GGS	26%	60	1710

Now the minimization problem (4) can be solved by the Gauss-Newton or Levenberg-Marquardt algorithm provided one can project any given point (x, y) onto a given curve/surface $P = 0$. We will discuss the projection subproblem later. The rate of converges of the GN and LM algorithms is nearly quadratic provided one has a good initial guess (which can be found, for example, by a non-iterative algebraic fit, such as the Taubin fit, see Appendix).

Ahn et al. have applied the above minimization scheme to quadratic curves (ellipses, hyperbolas, and parabolas) and some quadratic surfaces (spheres, ellipsoids, cones); see [4, 6, 7]. They compared it with several other minimization algorithms [5, 6, 7] and concluded that this one is the fastest and most robust. We have also tested it on quadratic curves and surfaces of various types and found that it has the following two advantages over other schemes: (i) it converges in fewer iterations, and (ii) it finds a smaller value of the objective function $\mathcal{F}$ more frequently than other methods do (i.e., the other methods tend to end up in a local minimum or diverge more often that this method does).

A benchmark example introduced in [19] and used later in [4] and other papers is a simple eight point set whose coordinates are shown in Table 1. The best fitting ellipse is known to have center $(2.6996, 3.8160)$, axes $a = 6.5187$ and $b = 3.0319$, and angle of tilt $\theta = 0.3596$; see Fig. 1. We have run two fitting algorithms – the implicit fit described here and the Gander-Golub-Strebel (GGS) method, which simultaneously optimizes $n + 5$ parameters, as mentioned earlier. Both methods were initialized by randomly generated ellipses (to get an initial ellipse, we just picked 5 points randomly in the square $0 \leq x, y \leq 10$ and used the ellipse interpolating those 5 points). After running these fitting methods from 10^5 random initial guesses, we found that the implicit fit failed to converged to the best ellipse in 11% of the cases, while the GGS method failed in 26% of the cases. In those cases where both algorithms converged, the implicit method took 20 iterations, on the average, while the GGS method took 60 iterations, on the average. The cost of one iteration was also higher for the GGS method. Table 2 summarizes the results.

We note that a high number of iterations here is not unusual. The authors of [19] used a modification of the best fitting circle to initialize their GGS procedure, and it took 71 iterations (!) to converge. A coordinate-based variant of the implicit fit used in [4] took 19 iterations to converge (it was also initialized with the best fitting circle). Our distance-based

Table 3. Comparison of two ellipse fitting methods.

	Initial ellipse		
	Best Circle	"Direct fit"	Taubin fit
Implicit (G)	16	17	17
Implicit (K)	14	16	16
GGS	50	54	54

implicit fit converged in 16 iterations.

In our experiment we used standard geometric parameters of the ellipse, i.e., c_1, c_2, a, b, θ. With Kepler's parameters (14), things get a little faster – the implicit method converged in 14 iterations. Table 3 gives the number of iterations taken by our fitting methods (the implicit method was implemented in geometric parameters (G) and in Kepler parameters (K)), initialized with the modified best fitting circle as in [19], the "direct ellipse fit" [18], and the Taubin fit (see Appendix).

3.   Projection onto Conics

The fitting scheme described above will work well only if one uses an efficient and reliable solution to the projection subproblem. The latter remains the time consuming part of the fitting process [6, 7].

In practice, various heuristic projection algorithms are employed [4, 5, 6, 7, 28] that are relatively fast, but their convergence is not guaranteed (and occasionally they do fail). On the other hand, certain theoretically reliable methods were proposed [2, 27], but most of them are overly complicated and too slow for practical use. For example, the projection of a point (u, v) onto an ellipse can be found as a root of a polynomial of degree four, but, as we said, this method is quite impractical and virtually never used.

A remarkable approach to projecting points onto ellipses was found by D. Eberly in 2004 [1, Section 14.13.1]. Not only it produces the desired projection faster than anything known previously (including heuristic schemes), but it comes with a mathematical proof of converging to the correct projection point in all cases, i.e., it is completely reliable. Below we describe Eberly's method for ellipses and then adapt it to other quadratic curves and surfaces. In each case we provide a theoretical proof of convergence. We consider such proofs as an important asset of the proposed methods.

Ellipses. It will be sufficient to project a point (u, v) onto an ellipse in its canonical coordinates:

$$\frac{x^2}{a^2} + \frac{y^2}{b^2} - 1 = 0. \tag{15}$$

Indeed, other ellipses can be translated and rotated to the canonical form (15), and then the projection point can be translated and rotated back to the original ellipse (the details are straightforward, we omit them).

Due to the obvious symmetry, it is enough to work in the first quadrant $u > 0, v > 0$; then the projection point (x, y) will also be in the first quadrant, i.e., $x > 0, y > 0$. (Other points can be reflected to the first quadrant about the axes, and then the projection point can be reflected back.) Also, we exclude the degenerate cases where $u = 0$ or $v = 0$; they are fairly simple and can be handled separately (see details in [1]).

Now the projection point (x, y) on the ellipse satisfies the orthogonality conditions (9), hence

$$u - x = tx/a^2 \quad \text{and} \quad v - y = ty/b^2 \tag{16}$$

for some real t (note that $t < 0$ for points inside the ellipse and $t > 0$ for points outside the ellipse). From (16) we find

$$x = \frac{a^2 u}{t + a^2} \quad \text{and} \quad y = \frac{b^2 v}{t + b^2} \tag{17}$$

Since $x, y > 0$, we have constraints $t > -a^2$ and $t > -b^2$. Assuming, as usual, that $a \geq b$ we get a single constraint $t > -b^2$. Substituting (17) into (15) we obtain a function

$$F(t) = \frac{a^2 u^2}{(t + a^2)^2} + \frac{b^2 v^2}{(t + b^2)^2} - 1, \tag{18}$$

whose root we need to find (because (x, y) must lie on the ellipse). Once we solve equation (18) for t, we can compute the projection point (x, y) by (17). Note that

$$\lim_{t \to -b^2+} F(t) = +\infty \quad \text{and} \quad \lim_{t \to \infty} F(t) = -1.$$

Taking the derivatives of F we see that

$$F'(t) = -\frac{2a^2 u^2}{(t + a^2)^3} - \frac{2b^2 v^2}{(t + b^2)^3} \tag{19}$$

and

$$F''(t) = \frac{6a^2 u^2}{(t + a^2)^4} + \frac{6b^2 v^2}{(t + b^2)^4}. \tag{20}$$

Thus on the interval $(-b^2, \infty)$ we have $F' < 0$ and $F'' > 0$, i.e., the function F is monotonically decreasing and concave; see Fig. 2. Thus standard Newton's method starting at any point t_0 where $F(t_0) > 0$ will converge to the unique root of F. Eberly suggests to start with $t_0 = bv - b^2$, because $F(t_0) > 0$ is guaranteed by (18). We found that it is more beneficial to start with

$$t_0 = \max\{au - a^2, bv - b^2\}. \tag{21}$$

Then Newton's method converges in 3-5 iterations in all practical cases and finds the root to within 7-8 significant digits. This is, on average, 2-3 times faster than solving equation of degree four or using general heuristics [4, 7]. The MATLAB code for this method is posted on our web page [29].

Hyperbolas. Now let us project a point (u, v) onto a hyperbola. Again, the latter can be defined in its canonical coordinates:

$$\frac{x^2}{a^2} - \frac{y^2}{b^2} - 1 = 0. \tag{22}$$

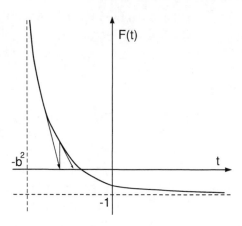

Figure 2. A typical graph of $F(t)$ for $t > -b^2$ and the progress of Newton's iterations toward the root.

Due to symmetry, we restrict the method to $u > 0, v > 0$, then we also have $x > 0, y > 0$. The orthogonality conditions (9) now read

$$u - x = tx/a^2 \quad \text{and} \quad v - y = -ty/b^2, \tag{23}$$

from which

$$x = \frac{a^2 u}{t + a^2} \quad \text{and} \quad y = \frac{b^2 v}{-t + b^2} \tag{24}$$

Since $x, y > 0$, we have constraints $-a^2 < t < b^2$. Substituting (24) into (22) we obtain a function

$$F(t) = \frac{a^2 u^2}{(t + a^2)^2} - \frac{b^2 v^2}{(-t + b^2)^2} - 1, \tag{25}$$

whose root we need to find. Note that

$$\lim_{t \to -a^2+} F(t) = +\infty \quad \text{and} \quad \lim_{t \to b^2-} F(t) = -\infty.$$

Taking the derivatives of F we see that

$$F'(t) = -\frac{2a^2 u^2}{(t + a^2)^3} - \frac{2b^2 v^2}{(-t + b^2)^3} \tag{26}$$

hence $F' < 0$ for all $t \in (-a^2, b^2)$. Next,

$$F''(t) = \frac{6a^2 u^2}{(t + a^2)^4} - \frac{6b^2 v^2}{(-t + b^2)^4}. \tag{27}$$

Now F'' decreases from $+\infty$ (near $-a^2$) to $-\infty$ (near b^2), and it is monotonic (because $F''' < 0$, as one can easily verify). Thus F has a unique inflection point, t_*, within the interval $(-a^2, b^2)$. See Fig. 3, where two possible cases are shown: (a) the inflection point lies above the x axis, i.e., $F(t_*) > 0$ and (b) the inflection point lies below the x axis. The inflection point is found by solving $F'' = 0$, hence

$$t_* = \frac{b^2\sqrt{au} - a^2\sqrt{bv}}{\sqrt{au} + \sqrt{bv}}.$$

Now by computing $F(t_*)$ we can determine which case, (a) or (b), we have at hand. Standard Newton's method will converge to the root of $F(t) = 0$, but the starting point t_0 must be selected wisely. In the case (a) we need to choose t_0 such that $F(t_0) < 0$, and in the case (b) we need $F(t_0) > 0$. In the case (a) we can try points $t_k = b^2 - (b^2 - t_*)/2^k$ for $k = 1, 2, \ldots$ until we find one where F is negative. In the case (b) we can try points $t_k = -a^2 + (t_* + a^2)/2^k$ for $k = 1, 2, \ldots$ until we find one where F is positive. This process of choosing t_0 is relatively inexpensive and it does not involve the derivatives of F. This completes our projection algorithm for hyperbolas.

In practice, it works about 1.5 longer than the projection algorithm for ellipses, due to a more elaborate choice of t_0, so its speed is close to that of heuristic schemes [4, 7]. But it is guaranteed to converge, according to our analysis.

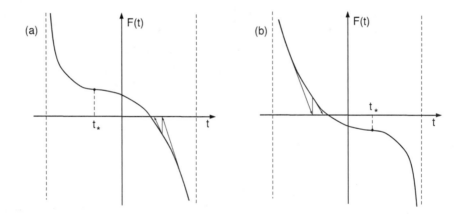

Figure 3. Two possible appearances of $F(t)$ on the interval $-a^2 < t < -b^2$. Arrows show the progress of Newton's iterations toward the root.

The MATLAB code for this method is posted on our web page [29].

Parabolas. Next let us project a point (u, v) onto a parabola. Again, the latter can be defined in its canonical coordinates:

$$y^2 - 2px = 0, \tag{28}$$

where $p > 0$ is the distance from the focus to the directrix. Due to symmetry, we restrict the method to $v > 0$, then we also have $y > 0$. The orthogonality conditions (9) now give

$$u - x = -pt \qquad \text{and} \qquad v - y = yt \tag{29}$$

from which

$$x = u + pt \qquad \text{and} \qquad y = \frac{v}{t + 1} \tag{30}$$

Since $y > 0$, we have constraint $t > -1$. Substituting (30) into (28) we obtain a function

$$F(t) = \frac{v^2}{(t+1)^2} - 2pu - 2p^2 t, \tag{31}$$

whose root we need to find. Note that

$$\lim_{t \to -1+} F(t) = +\infty \qquad \text{and} \qquad \lim_{t \to \infty} F(t) = -\infty.$$

Taking the derivatives of F we see that $F'(t) = -\frac{2v^2}{(t+1)^3} - 2p^2$ and $F''(t) = \frac{6v^2}{(t+1)^4}$. Thus on the interval $(-1, \infty)$ we have $F' < 0$ and $F'' > 0$, i.e., the function F is monotonically decreasing and concave. Now standard Newton's method starting at any point t_0 where $F(t_0) > 0$ will converge to the unique root of F. We can try points $t_k = -1 + 2^{-k}$ for $k = 1, 2, \ldots$ until we find one where F is positive. The MATLAB code for this method is posted on our web page [29].

4. Projection onto Quadrics

Here we describe the projection of a spacial point (u, v, w) onto quadratic surfaces of various kinds.

Ellipsoids. An ellipsoid is defined its canonical coordinates as follows:

$$\frac{x^2}{a^2} + \frac{y^2}{b^2} + \frac{z^2}{c^2} - 1 = 0, \tag{32}$$

where $a \geq b \geq c > 0$ are its semiaxes. (Other ellipsoids case be translated and rotated to the canonical form (32), and then the projection point can be translated and rotated back to the original ellipsoid.) Due to symmetry, we restrict the method to $u > 0, v > 0, w > 0$, then we also have $x > 0, y > 0, z > 0$. The orthogonality conditions now give

$$u - x = tx/a^2, \qquad v - y = ty/b^2, \qquad w - z = tz/c^2 \tag{33}$$

for some scalar t, from which

$$x = \frac{a^2 u}{t + a^2}, \qquad y = \frac{b^2 v}{t + b^2} \qquad z = \frac{c^2 w}{t + c^2} \tag{34}$$

Since $x, y, z > 0$, we have constraint $t > \max\{-a^2, -b^2 - c^2\} = -c^2$. Substituting (34) into (32) we obtain a function

$$F(t) = \frac{a^2 u^2}{(t + a^2)^2} + \frac{b^2 v^2}{(t + b^2)^2} + \frac{c^2 w^2}{(t + c^2)^2} - 1, \tag{35}$$

whose root we need to find. Note that

$$\lim_{t \to -c^2+} F(t) = +\infty \qquad \text{and} \qquad \lim_{t \to \infty} F(t) = -1.$$

Taking the derivatives of F we see that

$$F'(t) = -\frac{2a^2u^2}{(t+a^2)^3} - \frac{2b^2v^2}{(t+b^2)^3} - \frac{2c^2w^2}{(t+c^2)^3} \tag{36}$$

and

$$F''(t) = \frac{6a^2u^2}{(t+a^2)^4} + \frac{6b^2v^2}{(t+b^2)^4} + \frac{6c^2w^2}{(t+c^2)^4}. \tag{37}$$

Thus on the interval $(-c^2, \infty)$ we have $F' < 0$ and $F'' > 0$, i.e., the function F is monotonically decreasing and concave, just as in Fig. 2. Thus standard Newton's method starting at any point t_0 where $F(t_0) > 0$ will converge to the unique root of F, and we choose (see (21))

$$t_0 = \max\{au - a^2, bv - b^2, cw - c^2\}.$$

Hyperbolic paraboloids. Now let us project a point (u, v, w) onto a hyperbolic paraboloid ("saddle") defined in its canonical coordinates as

$$\frac{x^2}{a^2} - \frac{y^2}{b^2} - z = 0. \tag{38}$$

Due to symmetry, we restrict the method to $u > 0, v > 0$, then we also have $x > 0, y > 0$. The orthogonality conditions now give

$$u - x = tx/a^2, \qquad v - y = -ty/b^2, \qquad w - z = -t/2 \tag{39}$$

for some scalar t, from which

$$x = \frac{a^2u}{t+a^2}, \qquad y = \frac{b^2v}{-t+b^2}, \qquad z = w + \frac{t}{2}. \tag{40}$$

Since $x, y > 0$, we have constraints $-a^2 < t < b^2$. Substituting (40) into (38) we obtain a function

$$F(t) = \frac{a^2u^2}{(t+a^2)^2} - \frac{b^2v^2}{(-t+b^2)^2} - w - \frac{t}{2}, \tag{41}$$

whose root we need to find. Note that

$$\lim_{t \to -a^2+} F(t) = +\infty \qquad \text{and} \qquad \lim_{t \to b^2-} F(t) = -\infty.$$

Taking the derivatives of F we see that

$$F'(t) = -\frac{2a^2u^2}{(t+a^2)^3} - \frac{2b^2v^2}{(-t+b^2)^3} - \frac{1}{2} \tag{42}$$

hence $F' < 0$ for all $t \in (-a^2, b^2)$. Next,

$$F''(t) = \frac{6a^2u^2}{(t+a^2)^4} - \frac{6b^2v^2}{(-t+b^2)^4}. \tag{43}$$

Now F'' decreases from $+\infty$ (near $-a^2$) to $-\infty$ (near b^2), and it is monotonic (because $F''' < 0$, as one can easily verify). Thus F has a unique inflection point, t_*, within the interval $(-a^2, b^2)$. Our further analysis repeats that done for hyperbolas in the previous section.

Hyperboloids. Now let us project a point (u, v, w) onto a hyperboloid (one sheet) defined in its canonical coordinates as

$$\frac{x^2}{a^2} + \frac{y^2}{b^2} - \frac{z^2}{c^2} - 1 = 0, \tag{44}$$

where we can assume $a \geq b$. Due to symmetry, we restrict the method to $u > 0, v > 0, w > 0$, then we also have $x > 0, y > 0, z > 0$. The orthogonality conditions now give

$$u - x = tx/a^2, \qquad v - y = ty/b^2, \qquad w - z = -tz/c^2 \tag{45}$$

for some scalar t, from which

$$x = \frac{a^2 u}{t + a^2}, \qquad y = \frac{b^2 v}{t + b^2}, \qquad z = \frac{c^2 w}{-t + c^2}. \tag{46}$$

Since $x, y, z > 0$, we have constraints $-b^2 < t < c^2$. Substituting (46) into (44) we obtain a function

$$F(t) = \frac{a^2 u^2}{(t + a^2)^2} + \frac{b^2 v^2}{(t + b^2)^2} - \frac{c^2 w^2}{(-t + c^2)^2} - 1, \tag{47}$$

whose root we need to find. Note that

$$\lim_{t \to -b^2+} F(t) = +\infty \qquad \text{and} \qquad \lim_{t \to c^2-} F(t) = -\infty.$$

Taking the derivatives of F we see that

$$F'(t) = -\frac{2a^2 u^2}{(t + a^2)^3} - \frac{2b^2 v^2}{(t + b^2)^3} - \frac{2c^2 w^2}{(-t + c^2)^3} \tag{48}$$

hence $F' < 0$ for all $t \in (-b^2, c^2)$. Next,

$$F''(t) = \frac{6a^2 u^2}{(t + a^2)^4} + \frac{6b^2 v^2}{(t + b^2)^4} - \frac{6c^2 w^2}{(-t + c^2)^4}. \tag{49}$$

Again, as before, F'' decreases from $+\infty$ (near $-b^2$) to $-\infty$ (near c^2), and it is monotonic (because $F''' < 0$, as one can easily verify). Thus F has a unique inflection point, t_*, within the interval $(-b^2, c^2)$. Its graph looks like one of those shown in Fig. 3.

But now it is not easy to determine which case we have at hand – the one shown in part (a) or in part (b) of Fig. 3 (because we cannot solve equation $F'' = 0$). However, one of the two iterative procedures described in the case of hyperbolas (i.e., Newton's method working from the left and another one – from the right), must work.

Thus we simply can choose one of these two procedures at random and follow it hoping that it converges. But if it fails, i.e., if an iteration lands outside the interval $(-b^2, c^2)$, then we switch to the other procedure, and it will surely converge. We note that even if we start on the wrong side, Newton's iteration may land on the right side and then converge.

As there is a 50% chance of choosing one of the two sides correctly at random, the current projection method is perhaps about 1.5 times slower, on average, than the previous one (a moderate price to pay for extra complications). We emphasize that our analysis still guarantees that the method converges to the correct projection point in all cases.

Other quadrics. We have covered three major types of quadratic surfaces in 3D. There are two others – elliptic paraboloid and hyperboloid of two sheets, which are treated very similarly, with small variations in each case that we leave out.

5. Conclusion

The main goal of our chapter is to put a strong argument against the customary presumption that fitting ellipses and other quadratic curves/surfaces by minimizing geometric distances is a prohibitively difficult task. It is no longer so! Three major breakthroughs have occurred in the last decade:

- Ahn et al. have designed a general fitting scheme for implicit curves and surfaces that is surprisingly simple and fast. Its most time-consuming part is the projection of data points onto the curve/surface.

- Eberly discovered a remarkably fast and totally reliable projection algorithm for ellipses (which we generalize here to other conics and quadrics).

- Taubin's algebraic fit gained the reputation of being able to provide a balanced (nearly unbiased) initialization for the subsequent iterative procedure.

Combining these three advances together gives a complete fitting scheme for fitting quadratic curves and surfaces of all kinds. This scheme is reliable and efficient.

Acknowledgment. N.C. was partially supported by National Science Foundation, grant DMS-0969187.

Appendix

Here we review non-geometric (algebraic) fits that are used to provide an initial guess, i.e., a curve that initializes an iterative procedure solving the geometric fitting problem (4).

Suppose again that one fits an implicit curve $P(x, y; \Theta) = 0$ to observed points (x_1, y_1), ..., (x_n, y_n). Perhaps the simplest non-geometric fit is the one minimizing

$$\mathcal{F}_1(\Theta) = \sum_{i=1}^{n} [P(x_i, y_i; \Theta)]^2. \tag{50}$$

To justify this method one usually notes that $P(x_i, y_i; \Theta) = 0$ if and only if the point (x_i, y_i) lies on the curve, and $[P(x_i, y_i; \Theta)]^2$ is small when the point lies near the curve. The minimization of (50) is called *algebraic fit* and $|P(x_i, y_i; \Theta)|$ is called the corresponding *algebraic distance*.

When the curve is defined by an algebraic equation, such as

$$Ax^2 + Bxy + Cy^2 + Dx + Ey + F = 0, \qquad (51)$$

then an unconstrained minimization of (50) produces the unwanted degenerate solution: $A = B = C = D = E = F = 0$. To avoid it, one can impose a constraint, such as $A^2 + B^2 + C^2 + D^2 + E^2 + F^2 = 1$. The resulting fit would not be invariant under rotations or translations of the data set, i.e., the resulting curve would depend on the choice of the coordinate system, which is hardly acceptable; see [8, 19].

Better constraints (i.e., those that are invariant under translations and rotations) are $A + C = 1$ (see [19]), or $A^2 + B^2/2 + C^2 = 1$ (see [8]), or $4AC - B^2 = 1$ (see [18]). The last constraint guarantees that the resulting curve will be an ellipse (rather than a hyperbola or parabola).

But practical experience shows that all algebraic fits, with or without constraints, are statistically inaccurate and biased, in one way or another. The main reason is that algebraic distances may be substantially different from geometric distances [28].

This defect can be compensated for by using linear approximation

$$\frac{|P(x_i, y_i; \Theta)|}{\|\nabla P(x_i, y_i; \Theta)\|} = d_i + \mathcal{O}(d_i^2)$$

where $\nabla P = \left(\partial P / \partial x, \partial P / \partial y \right)$ denotes the gradient vector. This leads to an 'approximate geometric fit', which minimizes

$$\mathcal{F}_2(\Theta) = \sum_{i=1}^{n} \frac{[P(x_i, y_i; \Theta)]^2}{\|\nabla P(x_i, y_i; \Theta)\|^2}. \qquad (52)$$

This method is called *gradient weighted algebraic fit*. It was applied to quadratic curves by Sampson [24] and popularized by Taubin [26].

If the curve is defined by an algebraic equation, such as (51), then both numerator and denominator of each fraction in (52) are homogeneous quadratic polynomials of the parameters. As a result, $\mathcal{F}_2$ is invariant under scalings of the parameter vector (A, B, C, D, E, F), hence no additional constraints are needed anymore. The minimization of (52) produces a more accurate fit than the simple algebraic fits (50) do; see statistical analysis in [12].

But the problem of minimizing (52) has no closed form solution and must be solved by iterations. Various iterative schemes for the minimization of (52) have been developed (see [16, 17, 21]); some of them have become standard in computer vision industry. They are all too complex to be used for an initialization of the geometric fit (4) (besides, each of them needs its own initialization to get started...). In this sense, the minimization of (52) and that of (4) can be regarded as two independent approaches to the task of fitting curves to data. While (4) is called Maximum Likelihood Estimation (MLE), that of (52) is called Approximate Maximum Likelihood Estimation (AMLE); see [16, 17].

One may wonder if the AMLE (52) can be used *instead of* the MLE (4), as the minimization of (52) is technically simpler than that of (4). Most researchers, however, agree that the answer is NO, i.e., the minimization of (4) would produce a better fit than that of (52); see comments in [7, p. 12]. (Though a complete statistical analysis has yet to be done.)

Taubin [26] simplified (52) and converted it into a non-iterative fit that minimizes

$$\mathcal{F}_3(\Theta) = \frac{\sum [P(x_i, y_i; \Theta)]^2}{\sum \|\nabla P(x_i, y_i; \Theta)\|^2}. \tag{53}$$

Note that Taubin simply summed up all the numerators and all the denominators in (52) separately.

If one fits conics defined by algebraic equation (51), then both numerator and denominator of (53) are homogeneous quadratic polynomials of the components of the parameter vector $\mathbf{A} = (A, B, C, D, E, F)^T$. Thus one can rewrite (53) as

$$\mathcal{F}_4(\mathbf{A}) = \frac{\mathbf{A}^T \mathbf{M} \mathbf{A}}{\mathbf{A}^T \mathbf{N} \mathbf{A}} \ \rightarrow \ \min, \tag{54}$$

where $\mathbf{M}$ and $\mathbf{N}$ are some 6×6 symmetric positive semi-definite matrices. Since $\mathcal{F}_4(\mathbf{A})$ is invariant under scalings of the vector $\mathbf{A}$, one can solve (54) by minimizing $\mathcal{F}_5(\mathbf{A}) = \mathbf{A}^T \mathbf{M} \mathbf{A}$ under the constraint $\mathbf{A}^T \mathbf{N} \mathbf{A} = 1$. Introducing a Lagrange multiplier η we can minimize the function

$$\mathcal{F}_6(\mathbf{A}, \eta) = \mathbf{A}^T \mathbf{M} \mathbf{A} - \eta(\mathbf{A}^T \mathbf{N} \mathbf{A} - 1).$$

Differentiating with respect to $\mathbf{A}$ gives the first order necessary condition

$$\mathbf{M} \mathbf{A} = \eta \mathbf{N} \mathbf{A}, \tag{55}$$

thus $\mathbf{A}$ must be a generalized eigenvector of the matrix pair $(\mathbf{M}, \mathbf{N})$. Moreover, premultiplying (55) by $\mathbf{A}$ we see that $\mathbf{A}^T \mathbf{M} \mathbf{A} = \eta$, and because we are minimizing $\mathbf{A}^T \mathbf{M} \mathbf{A}$, the desired vector $\mathbf{A}$ must correspond to the *smallest* (non-negative) eigenvalue η. (We note that $\mathbf{N}$ here is singular; one usually eliminates F to reduce $\mathbf{A}$ to a 5-vector $\mathbf{A}' = (A, B, C, D, E)^T$ and the 6×6 problem (55) to a 5×5 problem $\mathbf{M}'\mathbf{A}' = \eta'\mathbf{N}'\mathbf{A}'$, where the 5×5 matrix $\mathbf{N}'$ is positive definite; see details in [22].)

Solving a generalized eigenvalue problem takes just one call of a standard matrix function (such functions are included in most modern software packages, e.g., in MATLAB). Thus Taubin's fit is regarded as a fast non-iterative procedure. In practice the Taubin's fit is only marginally slower than the simple algebraic fit minimizing (50).

Its advantage is that Taubin's fit is more balanced than any algebraic fit. It has a much smaller bias; see statistical analysis in [22]. Its disadvantage is that it produces a conic that may be of any kind – an ellipse, a hyperbola, or a parabola. If one fits conics of a certain type (e.g., ellipses), then Taubin's fit must be supplemented with another simple fit whenever it gives the wrong curve. Experimental tests show that Taubin's fit provides a better initialization of iterative procedures than simple algebraic fits do [14].

References

[1] *3D Game Engine Design*, 2nd ed., Morgan Kaufmann Publishers, San Francisco, CA, 2007. See also Internet article *Distance from a point to an ellipse in 2D*, Geometric Tools, LLC, www.geometrictools.com

[2] Aigner, M. & Jüttler, B. (2005). Robust computation of foot points on implicitly defined curves, In: Editors Daehlen, M. et al., *Mathematical Methods for Curves and Surfaces*, Tromso 2004, Nashboro Press, pp. 1–10.

[3] Aigner, M. & Jüttler, B. (2008). Gauss-Newton type techniques for robustly fitting implicitly defined curves and surfaces to unorganized data points, In: *Shape Modeling International*, pp. 121–130.

[4] Ahn, S. J., Rauh, W. & Warnecke, H. J. (2001). Least-squares orthogonal distances fitting of circle, sphere, ellipse, hyperbola, and parabola, *Pattern Recog.*, **34**, 2283–2303.

[5] Ahn, S. J., Rauh, W. & Recknagel, M. (2001). Least squares orthogonal distances fitting of implicit curves and surfaces, In: LNCS **2191**, 398–405.

[6] Ahn, S. J., Rauh, W. & Cho, H. S. (2002). Orthogonal distances fitting of implicit curves and surfaces, *IEEE trans. PAMI*, **24**, 620–638.

[7] Ahn, S. J. (2004). Least Squares Orthogonal Distance Fitting of Curves and Surfaces in Space, In: LNCS **3151**, Springer, Berlin.

[8] Bookstein, F. L. (1979). Fitting conic sections to scattered data, *Comp. Graph. Image Proc.* **9**, 56–71.

[9] Chan, N. N. (1965). On circular functional relationships, *J. R. Statist. Soc. B*, **27**, 45–56.

[10] Cheng, C.-L. & Van Ness, J. W. (1999). *Statistical Regression with Measurement Error*, Arnold, London.

[11] Chernov, N., Ososkov, G. & Silin, I. (2000). Robust fitting of ellipses to non-complete and contaminated data, *Czech. J. Phys.* **50**, 347–354.

[12] Chernov, N. & Lesort, C. (2004). Statistical efficiency of curve fitting algorithms, *Comp. Stat. Data Anal.*, **47**, pp. 713–728.

[13] Chernov, N. & Lesort, C. (2005). Least squares fitting of circles, *J. Math. Imag. Vision* **23**, 239–251.

[14] Chernov, N. (2007). On the convergence of fitting algorithms in computer vision, *J. Math. Imag. Vision* **27**, 231–239.

[15] Chernov, N. (2010). *Circular and linear regression: Fitting circles and lines by least squares*, Chapman & Hall/CRC Monographs on Statistics and Applied Probability **117**.

[16] Chojnacki, W., Brooks, M. J. & van den Hengel, A. (2001). Rationalising the renormalisation method of Kanatani, *J. Math. Imag. Vision*, **14**, 21–38.

[17] Chojnacki, W., Brooks, M. J., van den Hengel, A. & Gawley, D. (2005). FNS, CFNS and HEIV: A unifying approach, *J. Math. Imag. Vision*, **23**, 175–183.

[18] Fitzgibbon, A. W., Pilu, M. & Fisher, R. B. (1999). Direct Least Squares Fitting of Ellipses, *IEEE Trans. PAMI* **21**, 476–480.

[19] Gander, W., Golub, G. H. & Strebel, R. (1994). Least squares fitting of circles and ellipses, *BIT*, **34**, 558–578.

[20] Geometric Product Specification (GPS) – Acceptance and representation test for co-ordinate measuring machines (CMM) – Part 6: Estimation of errors in computing Gaussian associated features. Int'l Standard ISO 10360-6. IS, Geneva, Switzerland (2001).

[21] Kanatani, K. (1994). Statistical bias of conic fitting and renormalization, *IEEE Trans. PAMI*, **16**, 320–326.

[22] Kanatani, K. (2008). Statistical optimization for geometric fitting: Theoretical accuracy bound and high order error analysis, *Int. J. Computer Vision* **80**, 167–188.

[23] Leedan, Y. & Meer, P. (2000). Heteroscedastic regression in computer vision: Problems with bilinear constraint, *Intern. J. Comp. Vision*, **37**, 127–150.

[24] Sampson, P. D. (1982). Fitting conic sections to very scattered data: an iterative refinement of the Bookstein algorithm, *Comp. Graphics Image Proc.* **18**, 97–108.

[25] Sturm, P., & Gargallo, P. (2007). Conic fitting using the geometric distance, *Proc. Asian Conf. Comp. Vision*, Tokyo, Japan, **2**, pp. 784–795.

[26] Taubin, G. (1991). Estimation of planar curves, surfaces and nonplanar space curves defined by implicit equations, with applications to edge and range image segmentation, *IEEE Trans. PAMI*, **13**, 1115–1138.

[27] Wijewickrema, S., Papliński, A. & Esson, Ch. (2006). Orthogonal distance fitting revisited, *Tech. report, Clayton School Inf. Technol.*, Monash U., Melbourne, 2006/205.

[28] Zhang, Z. (1997). Parameter Estimation Techniques: A Tutorial with Application to Conic Fitting, *Intern. J. Image Vision Comput.*, **15**, 59–76.

[29] http://www.math.uab.edu/ chernov/cl

In: Computer Vision
Editor: Sota R. Yoshida

ISBN: 978-1-61209-399-4
© 2011 Nova Science Publishers, Inc.

Chapter 8

ONTOLOGY BASED IMAGE AND VIDEO ANALYSIS

Christopher Town[*]
University of Cambridge Computer Laboratory
15 JJ Thomson Avenue, Cambridge CB3 0FD, UK

Abstract

This chapter shows how ontologies can be used as the basis for an effective computational and representational framework for computer vision. A particular focus is on the role of ontologies as a means of representing structured prior information and integrating different kinds of information in an inference framework. Ontologies are presented as an effective means of relating semantic descriptors to their parametric representations in terms of the underlying data primitives.

The efficacy of the proposed approach is demonstrated through the development and analysis of solutions to a range of challenging visual analysis tasks. Firstly, we consider the problem of content based image retrieval (CBIR). We present a CBIR system that allows users to search image databases using an ontological query language. Queries are parsed using a probabilistic grammar and Bayesian networks to map high level concepts onto low level image descriptors, thereby bridging the semantic gap between users and the retrieval system.

We then extend the notion of ontological languages to video event detection. It is shown how effective high-level state and event recognition mechanisms can be learned from a set of annotated training sequences by incorporating syntactic and semantic constraints represented by an ontology.

Keywords: Ontologies; Perceptual inference; Content-based image retrieval; Video analysis; Knowledge-based computer vision.

PACS 05.45-a, 52.35.Mw, 96.50.Fm.

1. Introduction

Visual information is inherently ambiguous and semantically impoverished. There consequently exists a wide semantic gap between human interpretations of image and video data

---

[*]E-mail address: cpt23@cam.ac.uk

and that currently derivable by means of a computer. This chapter demonstrates how this gap can be narrowed by means of ontologies. Ontology is the theory of objects in terms of the criteria which allow one to distinguish between different types of objects and their relationships, dependencies, and properties. Ontologies encode the relational structure of concepts which one can use to describe and reason about aspects of the world. This makes them eminently suitable for many problems in computer vision which require prior knowledge to be modelled and utilised in both a descriptive and prescriptive capacity.

In the work presented here, terms in the ontology are grounded in the data and therefore carry meaning directly related to the appearance of real world objects. Tasks such as image retrieval and automated visual surveillance can then be carried out by processing sentences in a visual language defined over the ontology. Such sentences are not purely symbolic since they retain a linkage between the symbol and signal levels. They can therefore serve as a computational vehicle for active knowledge representation which permits incremental refinement of alternate hypotheses through the fusion of multiple sources of information and goal-directed feedback.

This approach is broadly motivated by two notions of how visual information processing may be achieved in biological and artificial systems. Firstly, vision can be posed as knowledge-driven probabilistic inference. Deductive and inductive reasoning can be applied to deal with two key problems that make vision difficult, namely complexity and uncertainty. Recognition is thus posed as a joint inference problem relying on the integration of multiple (weak) clues to disambiguate and combine evidence in the most suitable context as defined by the top level model structure.

Secondly, vision may be regarded as closely related to (and perhaps an evolutionary precursor of) language processing. In both cases one ultimately seeks to find symbolic interpretations of underlying signal data. Such an analysis needs to incorporate a notion of the syntax and semantics that is seen as governing the domain of interest so that the most likely explanation of the observed data can be found. A visual language can also serve as an important mechanism for attentional control by constraining the range of plausible feature configurations that need to be considered when performing a visual task such as recognition. Processing may then be performed selectively in response to queries formulated in terms of the structure of the domain, i.e. relating high-level symbolic representations to extracted visual and temporal features in the signal.

This chapter presents two concrete implementations of the approach discussed above which demonstrate its utility for solving relevant research problems for both image and video analysis.

2.   Related Work

An increasing number of research efforts in medium and high level video analysis can be viewed as following the emerging trend that object recognition and the recognition of temporal events are best approached in terms of generalised language processing which attempts a machine translation [2, 3] from information in the visual domain to symbols and strings composed of predicates, objects, and relations. While this approach has shown great promise for applications ranging from image retrieval to face detection to visual surveillance, a number of problems remain to be solved. The nature of visual information poses hard challenges which hinder the extent to which mechanisms such as Hidden Markov models and stochastic parsing techniques popular in the speech and language processing community can be applied to information extraction from images and video. Consequently there remains some lack of understanding as to which mechanisms are most suitable for representing and utilising the syntactic and semantic structure of visual information and how such frameworks can best be instantiated.

The role of machine learning in computer vision continues to grow and recently there has been a very strong trend towards using Bayesian techniques for learning and inference, especially factorised graphical models such as Dynamic Belief networks (DBN). While finding the right structural assumptions and prior probability distributions needed to instantiate such models requires some domain specific insights, Bayesian graphs generally offer greater conceptual transparency than e.g. neural network models since the underlying causal links and prior beliefs are made more explicit.

Many methods for representing and matching ontological knowledge in artificial intelligence (description logics, frame-based representations, semantic nets) are coming back into vogue [1], not least because of the "semantic web" initiative. However, many problems remain when such approaches are applied to highly uncertain and ambiguous data of the sort that one is confronted with in computer vision and language processing. Much research remains to be done in fusing classical syntactic approaches to knowledge representation with modern factorised probabilistic modelling and inference frameworks.

[12] introduces an evidence driven probabilistic image analysis framework using ontologies and Bayesian networks. It is shown how this framework can yield superior performance through the integration of contextual constraints and prior domain knowledge.

This linkage between visual and linguistic information is made explicit in [18], which discusses an image parsing to text description (I2T) framework to generate text descriptions of image and video content. The mapping from extracted visual primitives to textual descriptions is facilitated by an and-or-graph (AoG) to represent a stochastic image grammar to define goal-directed top-down hypotheses during image parsing.

Similar approaches were applied to traffic surveillance problems in [8]. The authors present a spatio-temporal query language that can be used for analysing traffic surveillance scenarios. The language features unary and binary relations over attributes such as distances, orientations, velocities, and temporal intervals. Queries consisting of trees of such relations are matched to the output of a tracking framework by considering all possible ways of binding tracked objects to leaf nodes in the tree and evaluating relations to assess whether all constraints are matched.

[11] describes an event recognition language for video. Events can be hierarchical composites of simpler primitive events defined by various temporal relationships over object movements, and the authors present a standardised taxonomy for video event recognition consisting of a video event representation language (VERL) and a video event markup language (VEML) for annotation. A similar problem is given a more explicitly ontology-based solution in [13], where both domain knowledge (entities and events of interest) and system knowledge (capabilities of the visual recognition system) are modelled to facilitate video event classification.

In the domain of image analysis, [10] introduces an ontology framework to contain both visual and contextual knowledge. Probabilistic inference is used to compute high-level retrieval queries over a natural scene database from the "LabelMe" data set. The problem of semantic image interpretation is also considered in [6]. An ontology of spatial relations and fuzzy representations of visual concepts is constructed and applied to knowledge-based recognition of brain structures in 3D magnetic resonance images. To overcome the inherent user interface challenge of query formulation, [7] present a visual query language to reduce the gap between image features and high-level semantics.

The concept of an ontological query language as presented in section 4. in this chapter has recently been scaled up to a collection of some 25 million high resolution commercial images. [16] discusses how modern advances in grid computing allow efficient distributed processing and content-based analysis of such large image data sets without compromising the semantic richness of the image descriptors defined by means of an ontology.

3.   Self-referential Perceptual Inference

Our approach is based on a self-referential probabilistic framework for multi-modal integration of evidence and context-dependent inference given a set of representational or derivational goals. This means that the system maintains an internal representation of its current hypotheses and goals and relates these to available detection and recognition modules. For example, a surveillance application may be concerned with recording and analysing movements of people by using motion estimators, edge trackers, region classifiers, face detectors, shape models, and perceptual grouping operators. The system is capable of maintaining multiple hypotheses at different levels of semantic granularity and can generate a consistent interpretation by evaluating a query expressed in an ontological language. This language gives a probabilistic hierarchical representation incorporating domain specific syntactic and semantic constraints from a visual language specification tailored to a particular application.

However, there is a need to improve on this methodology when the complexity of the desired analysis increases, particularly as one considers hierarchical and interacting object and behavioural descriptions best defined in terms of a syntax at the symbolic level. The sheer number of possible candidate interpretations and potential derivations soon requires a means of greatly limiting the system's focus of attention. A useful analogy is selective processing in response to queries. Visual search guided by a query posed in a language embodying an ontological representation of a domain allows adaptive processing strategies to be utilised and gives an effective attentional control mechanism.

From an artificial intelligence point of view, this can be regarded as an approach to the *symbol grounding problem* [4] since sentences in the ontological language have an explicit foundation of evidence in the feature domain, so there is a way of bridging the semantic gap between the signal and symbol level. It also addresses the *frame problem* since there is no need to exhaustively analyse everything that is going on. One only needs to consider the subset of the state space required to make a decision given a query which implicitly narrows down the focus of attention.

The nature of such queries is task specific. They may either be explicitly stated by the user (e.g. in an image retrieval task) or implicitly derived from some notion of the system's goals. For example, a surveillance task may require the system to register the presence of people who enter a scene, track their movements, and trigger an event if they are seen to behave in a manner deemed "suspicious" such as lingering within the camera's

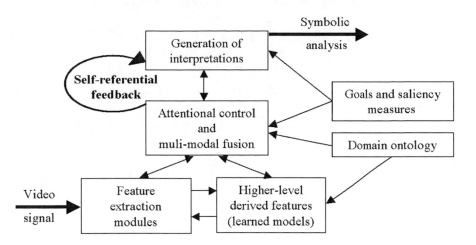

Figure 1. Sketch of the proposed approach to goal-directed fusion of content extraction modules and inference guided by an attentional control mechanism. The fusion process and selective visual processing are carried out in response to a task and domain definition expressed in terms of an ontological language. Interpretations are generated and refined by deriving queries from the goals and current internal state.

field of view or repeatedly returning to the scene over a short time scale. Internally the system could perform these functions by generating and processing queries of the kind "does the observed region movement correspond to a person entering the scene?", "has a person of similar appearance been observed recently?", or "is the person emerging from behind the occluding background object the same person who could no longer be tracked a short while ago?". These queries would be phrased in a language which relates them to the corresponding feature extraction modules (e.g. a Bayesian network for fusing various cues to track people-shaped objects) and internal descriptions (e.g. a log of events relating to people entering or leaving the scene at certain locations and times, along with parameterised models of their visual appearance). Formulating and refining interpretations then amounts to selectively parsing such queries.

This chapter demonstrates that an ontological content representation and query language is an effective vehicle for hierarchical representation and goal-directed inference in high-level visual analysis tasks. As sketched in figure 1, such a language can serve as a means of guiding the fusion of multiple sources of visual evidence and refining symbolic interpretations of dynamic scenes in the context of a particular problem. By maintaining representations of both the current internal state and derivational goals expressed in terms of the same language framework, such a system could be seen as performing self-referential feedback based control of the way in which information is processed over time. Visual recognition then amounts to selecting a parsing strategy that determines how elements of the current string set are to be processed further given a stream of lower level tokens generated by feature detectors. The overall structure of the interpretative module is not limited to a particular probabilistic framework and allows context-sensitive parsing strategies to be employed where appropriate.

4.   Content-Based Image Retrieval Using OQUEL

This section presents a system which allows users to search image databases by posing queries over desired visual content. A query and retrieval method called OQUEL (onto-logical query language) is introduced to facilitate formulation and evaluation of queries consisting of (typically very short) sentences expressed in a language designed for general purpose retrieval of photographic images. The language is based on an extensible ontology which encompasses both high-level and low-level concepts and relations. Further details on OQUEL are available in [17].

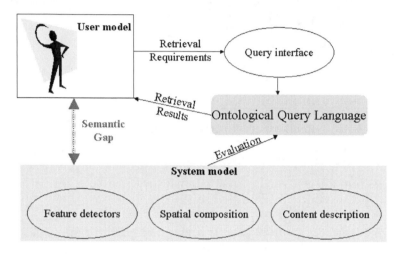

Figure 2. Model of the retrieval process using an ontological query language to bridge the semantic gap between user and system notions of content and similarity.

The retrieval process takes place entirely within the ontological domain defined by the syntax and semantics of the user query. It utilises automatically extracted image segmenta-tion and classification information, as well as Bayesian networks to infer higher level and composite terms. The OQUEL language provides an effective mechanism of addressing key problems of content based image retrieval, namely the ambiguity of image content and user intention and the semantic gap which exists between user and system notions of relevance (see figure 2). By basing such a language on an extensible ontology, one can explicitly state ontological commitments about categories, objects, attributes, and relations without having to pre-define any particular method of query evaluation or image interpretation.

4.1.   Syntax and Semantics

OQUEL queries (sentences) are prescriptive rather than descriptive, i.e. the focus is on making it easy to formulate desired image characteristics as concisely as possible. It is therefore neither necessary nor desirable to provide an exhaustive description of the visual features and semantic content of particular images. Instead a query represents only as much information as is required to discriminate relevant from non-relevant images. In order to al-low users to enter both simple keyword phrases and arbitrarily complex compound queries, the language grammar features constructs such as predicates, relations, conjunctions, and a specification syntax for image content. The latter includes adjectives for image region properties (i.e. shape, colour, and texture) and both relative and absolute object location. Desired image content can be denoted by nouns such as labels for automatically recognised visual categories of stuff ("grass", "cloth", "sky", etc.) and through the use of derived higher level terms for composite objects and scene description. The latter includes a distinction between singular and plural, hence "people" will be evaluated differently from "person". The following gives a somewhat simplified high level context free EBNF-style grammar G of a reference implementation of the OQUEL language [17]:

$$
\begin{aligned}
G : \{ & \\
S \;\rightarrow\; & R \\
R \;\rightarrow\; & modifier?\;(metacategory \mid SB \mid BR) \\
& \mid not?\,R\;(CB\,R)? \\
BR \;\rightarrow\; & SB\;binaryrelation\;SB \\
SB \;\rightarrow\; & (CS \mid PS) + LS* \\
CS \;\rightarrow\; & visualcategory \mid semanticcategory \mid \\
& not?\,CS\;(CB\,CS)? \\
LS \;\rightarrow\; & location \mid not?\,LS\;(CB\,LS)? \\
PS \;\rightarrow\; & shapedescriptor \mid colourdescriptor \mid \\
& sizedescriptor \mid not?\,PS\;(CB\,PS)? \\
CB \;\rightarrow\; & and \mid or \mid xor; \\
\}
\end{aligned}
$$

The major syntactic categories are: S: Start symbol of the sentence (text query).

R: Requirement (a query consists of one or more requirements which are evaluated separately, the probabilities of relevance then being combined according to the logical operators).

BR: Binary relation on SBs.

SB: Specification block consisting of at least one CS or PS and 0 or more LS.

CS: Image content specifier.

LS: Location specifier for regions meeting the CS/PS.

PS: Region property specifier (visual properties of regions such as colour, shape, texture, and size).

CB: Binary (fuzzy) logical connective (conjunction, disjunction, and exclusive-OR).

Tokens (terminals) belong to the following sets:

modifier: Quantifiers such as "a lot of", "none", "as much as possible".

scene descriptor: Categories of image content characterising an entire image, e.g. "countryside", "city", "indoors".

binaryrelation: Relationships which are to hold between clusters of target content denoted by specification blocks. The current implementation includes spatial relationships such as "larger than", "close to", "above", and some more abstract relations such as "similar content".

visualcategory: Categories of stuff, e.g. "water", "skin", "cloud".

semanticcategory: Higher semantic categories such as "people", "vehicles", "animals". *location*: Desired location of image content matching the content or shape specification, e.g. "background", "lower half", "top right corner".

shapedescriptor: Region shape properties, for example "straight line", "blob shaped".

colourdescriptor: Region colour specified either numerically or through the use of adjectives and nouns, e.g. "bright red", "dark green", "vivid colours".

sizedescriptor: Desired size of regions matching the other criteria in a requirement, e.g. "at least 10%" (of image area), "largest region".

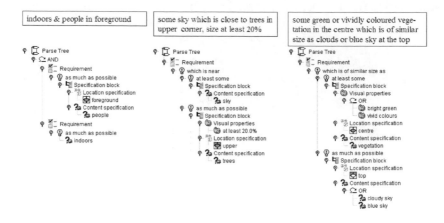

Figure 3. Examples of OQUEL query sentences and their syntax trees.

The precise semantics of these constructs are dependent upon the way in which the query language is implemented, the parsing algorithm, and the user query itself, as will be described in the following sections. Figure 3 shows some additional query sentences and their resulting abstract syntax trees.

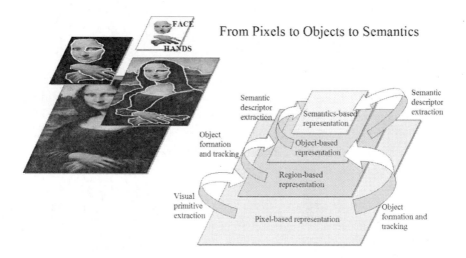

Figure 4. Hierarchical representation of visual information at different conceptual levels and example illustrating these concepts as applied to an image of the "Mona Lisa" (original copyright: Musee de Louvre).

4.2. Visual Content Analysis

Image segmentation

Images are segmented into non-overlapping regions and sets of properties for size, colour, shape, and texture are computed for each region using the approach of [14]. Initially full RGB edge detection is performed followed by non-max suppression and hysteresis edge-following steps. Regions are then grown agglomeratively from Voronoi seed points. A texture model based on discrete ridge features is also used to describe regions in terms of texture feature orientation and density. The internal brightness structure of "smooth" (largely untextured) regions in terms of their isobrightness contours and intensity gradients is used to derive a parameterisation of brightness variation which allows shading phenomena such as bowls, ridges, folds, and slopes to be identified.

Image region classification

Region descriptors computed from the segmentation algorithm are fed into artificial neural network classifiers which have been trained to label regions with class membership probabilities for a set of 12 semantically meaningful visual categories of "stuff" ("Brick", "Blue sky", "Cloth", "Cloudy sky", "Grass", "Internal walls", "Skin", "Snow", "Tarmac", "Trees", "Water", and "Wood"). The classifiers are MLP (multi layer perceptron) and RBF (radial basis function) networks trained over a large (over 40000 exemplars) corpus of manually labelled image regions.

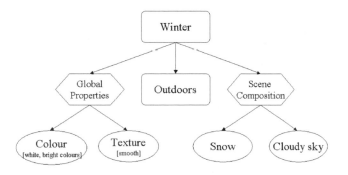

Figure 5. Simplified Bayesian network for the scene descriptor "winter".

Colour descriptors

Nearest-neighbour colour classifiers were built from the region colour representation. These use the Earth-mover distance measure applied to Euclidean distances in RGB space to compare region colour profiles with cluster templates learned from a training set. Colour classifiers were constructed for each of twelve "basic" colours ("black", "blue", "cyan", "grey", "green", "magenta", "orange", "pink", "red", "white", "yellow", "brown"). Each region is associated with the colour labels which best describe it.

Face detection

Face detection relies on identifying elliptical regions (or clusters of regions) classified as human skin. A nearest-neighbour shape classifier was trained to recognise eyes. Adjacent image regions classified as human skin in which eye candidates have been identified are then labelled as containing (or being part of) one or more human faces subject to the scale factor implied by the separation of the eyes.

Content representation

After performing the image segmentation and other analysis stages as outlined above, image content is represented at the following levels:

Region mask: Canonical representation of the segmented image giving the absolute location of each region by mapping pixel locations onto region identifiers. *Region graph*: Graph of the relative spatial relationships of the regions (distance, adjacency, joint boundary, and containment). *Grid pyramid*: The proportion of image content which has been positively classified with each particular label (visual category, colour, and presence of faces) at different levels of an image pyramid (whole image, image fifths, 8x8 grid).

Through the relationship graph representation, matching of clusters of regions is made invariant with respect to displacement and rotation using standard matching algorithms. The grid pyramid and region mask representations allow an efficient comparison of absolute position and size.

Figure 6. Search results for example OQUEL queries.

4.3.   Grounding the Vocabulary

An important aspect of OQUEL language implementation concerns the way in which sentences in the languages are *grounded* in the image domain. This section discusses those elements of the token set which might be regarded as being statically grounded, i.e. there exists a straightforward mapping from OQUEL words to extracted image properties as described above. Other terminals (modifiers, scene descriptors, binary relations, and semantic categories) and syntactic constructs are evaluated by the query parser as will be discussed in section 4.4..

visualcategory: The 12 categories of stuff which have been assigned to segmented image regions by the neural net classifiers.

location: Location specifiers which are simply mapped onto the grid pyramid representation. For example, when searching for "grass" in the "bottom left" part of an image, only content in the lower left image quadrant considered.

shapedescriptor: The current terms include "straight line", "vertical", "stripe", "top edge", "left edge", "right edge", "polygonal", and "blobs". They are defined as predicates over region properties and aspects of the region graph representation derived from the image segmentation.

colourdescriptor: Region colour specified either numerically in the RGB or HSV colour space or through the colour labels assigned by the nearest-neighbour classifiers. By assessing the overall brightness and contrast properties of a region using fixed thresholds, colours identified by each classifier can be further described by a set of three "colour modifiers" ("bright", "dark", "faded").

sizedescriptor: The size of image content matching other aspects of a query is assessed by adding the areas of the corresponding regions. Size may be defined as a percentage value of image area ("at least x%", "at most x%", "between x% and y%") or relative to other image parts (e.g. "largest", "bigger than").

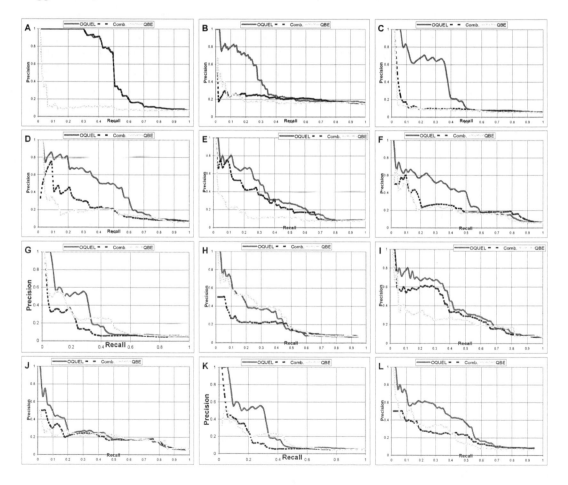

Figure 7. Plots of relative percentages for precision versus recall for the retrieval experiments. As can be seen, results obtained using OQUEL generally outperform those achieved using query-by-example or a combination of sketch and feature based retrieval.

4.4. Query Evaluation and Retrieval

OQUEL queries are parsed to yield a canonical abstract syntax tree (AST) representation of their syntactic structure. Figures 3 and 6 show sample queries and their ASTs. The structure of the syntax trees follows that of the grammar, i.e. the root node is the start symbol whose children represent particular requirements over image features and content. The leaf nodes of the tree correspond to the terminal symbols representing particular requirements such as shape descriptors and visual categories. Intermediate nodes are syntactic categories instantiated with the relevant token (i.e. "and", "which is larger than") which represent the relationships that are to be applied when evaluating the query.

In the first stage, the syntax tree derived from the query is parsed top-down and the leaf nodes are evaluated in light of their predecessors and siblings. Information then propagates back up the tree until one arrives at a single probability of relevance for the entire image. At the lowest level, tokens map directly or very simply onto the content descriptors via SQL queries. Higher level terms are either expanded into sentence representations or evaluated using Bayesian graphs. Matching image content is retrieved and the initial list of results is sorted in descending order of a probability of relevance score. Next, nodes denoting visual properties (e.g. size or colour) are assessed in order to filter the initial results and modify relevance scores according to the location, content, and property specifications which occur in the syntax tree. Finally, relationships (logical, geometric, or semantic, e.g. similarity) are assessed and probability scores are propagated up the AST until each potentially relevant image has one associated relevance score. Relations are evaluated by considering matching candidate image content (evidence) . A closure consisting of a pointer to the identified content (e.g. a region identifier or grid coordinate) together with the probability of relevance is passed as a message to higher levels in the tree for evaluation and fusion. Query sentences consist of requirements which yield matching probabilities that are further modified and combined according to the top level syntax.

At the leaf nodes of the AST, derived terms such as object labels and scene descriptions are either expanded into equivalent OQUEL sentence structures or evaluated by Bayesian networks integrating image content descriptors with additional sources of evidence (e.g. a face detector). Bayesian networks tend to be context dependent in their applicability and may therefore give rise to brittle performance when applied to very general content labelling tasks. In the absence of additional information in the query sentence itself, it was therefore found useful to evaluate mutually exclusive scene descriptors for additional disambiguation. For example, the concepts "winter" and "summer" are not merely negations of one another but correspond to Bayesian nets evaluating different sources of evidence. If both were to assign high probabilities to a particular image then the labelling is considered ambiguous and consequently assigned a lower relevance weight. Figure 5 shows a simplified Bayesian network for the scene descriptor "winter". Arrows denote conditional dependencies and terminal nodes correspond to sources of evidence or, in the case of the term "outdoors", other Bayesian nets.

Due to the inherent uncertainty and complexity of the task, query evaluation is performed in a way that limits the requirement for runtime inference by quickly ruling out irrelevant images given the query. The overall approach relies on passing messages (image structures labelled with probabilities of relevance), assigning weights to these messages according to higher level structural nodes (modifiers and relations), and integrating these at the topmost levels (specification blocks) in order to compute a belief state for the relevance of the evidence extracted from the given image for the given query. The approach adopted here is related to that of [9] in that it applies notions of weighting akin to the Dempster-Shafer theory of evidence to construct an information retrieval model which captures structure, significance, uncertainty, and partiality in the evaluation process. Image regions which match the target content requirements can then be used to assess any other specifications (shape, size, colour) which appear in the same requirement subtree within the query. Groups of regions which are deemed salient with respect to the query can be compared for the purpose of evaluating relations as mentioned above. As long as one maintains a notion of uncertainty, borderline false detections will simply result in lowly ranked retrieved images. Top query results correspond to those image where the confidence of having found evidence for the presence of people is high relative to the other images.

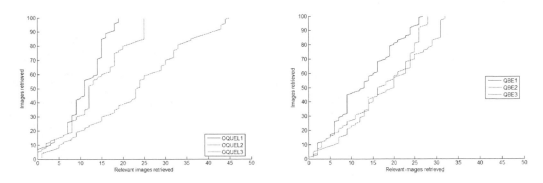

Figure 8. Plots of total number of images retrieved versus number of relevant images retrieved for *left*: OQUEL queries, *right*: query-by-example (QBE). In each case, results are shown for an initial query and two iterations of query refinement (top line: OQUEL1 query; middle line: OQUEL2 query; bottom line: OQUEL3 query).

4.5. Qualitative and Quantitative Evaluation

While most evaluation of CBIR systems is performed on commercial image collections such as the Corel image sets, their usefulness is limited by the fact that they consist of very high quality photographic images and that the associated ground truth (category labels such as "China", "Mountains", "Food") are frequently too high-level and sparse to be of use in performance analysis. Therefore a set of images consisting of 670 Corel images augmented with 412 amateur digital pictures of highly variable quality and content were chosen. Manual relevance assessments in terms of relevant vs non-relevant were carried out for all 1082 images over the test queries described below. Twelve retrieval requirements were chosen, which have the following expressions in the OQUEL language:

Query A "bright red and stripy"

Query B "people in centre"

Query C "some water in the bottom half which is surrounded by trees and grass, size at least 10%"

Query D "winter"

Query E "artificial stuff, vivid colours and straight lines"

Query F "indoors & people in foreground"

Query G "some vividly coloured vegetation in the centre which is of similar size as clouds or blue sky at the top"

Query H "city or countryside"

Query I "artificial stuff and tarmac"

Query J "people or animals"

Query K "[blue sky at top] and [trees centre] and grass lower"

Query L "some sky which is close to buildings above"

For the first four OQUEL queries, top ranked search results are shown in figure 6. For each OQUEL query a further two queries embodying the same retrieval need were composed using the other search facilities of the retrieval system:

- Combined query ("Comb."): a query which may combine a sketch with feature constraints as appropriate to yield best performance in reasonable time.

- Query-by-example ("QBE"): the single image maximising the normalised average rank metric was chosen as the query. This type of query is commonly used to assess baseline performance.

To quantify performance, graphs of precision versus recall were computed using manual relevance assessments for each test query as shown in figure 7. In each case, OQUEL query results are shown together with results for the two other query modalities described above, i.e. a combined query ("Comb.") and a query-by-example ("QBE") designed and optimised to meet the same user search requirements. It can be seen that OQUEL queries generally yield better results, especially for the top ranked images. In the case of query A, results are essentially the same as those for a query consisting of feature predicates for the region properties "stripy" and "red". In general OQUEL queries are more robust to errors in the segmentation and region classification due to their ontological structure. Query-by-example in particular is usually insufficient to express more advanced concepts relating to spatial composition, feature invariances, or object level constraints.

In order to investigate the scalability of the OQUEL retrieval technology, an image collection consisting of over 12000 high-resolution photographic images was compiled. The images were taken by 11 different amateur photographers and represent a very diverse range of subject matter, focal lengths, lighting conditions, and picture quality. An important goal of CBIR is to allow users to identify sets of images which are semantically related yet disparate in their visual properties and composition. The sample retrieval requirements were translated into an initial OQUEL query which was subsequently modified twice in light of search results. This allows the ease and effectiveness of query refinement within the OQUEL framework to be assessed. In order to avoid the prohibitive effort of manually assessing and ranking every image in the collection, only the top 100 images returned by each query were analysed and rated as being either relevant or not relevant with respect to the task of finding pictures of archaeological sites. Most users are unlikely to view more than the top 100 results and this method is sufficient for quantitative comparison of the relative merits of different approaches. The following OQUEL queries were analysed:

OQUEL1 (initial query): "brick and (grass or trees)"

OQUEL2 (first refinement): "[outdoors] and brick"

OQUEL3 (second refinement): "[outdoors] and [summer] and brick"

In order to quantify precision by means of the cumulative frequency of relevant images returned by each query, figure 8 shows results in terms of the number of images retrieved versus number of relevant images retrieved for the top 100 search results. It can be seen that even simple refinement of the OQUEL queries leads to improvements in performance without requiring complicated queries. In order to contrast the performance of OQUEL on this task with another retrieval method, queries were also composed by selecting example images. Results for these are also shown in figure 8. After some manual browsing, a relevant image was found and used as a single positive example forming the first query (QBE1). Subsequently one non-relevant image was selected from the QBE1 retrieval results and added to the query to form a new query (QBE2). Finally, an additional relevant image was added to the query set to form QBE3. As can be seen, absolute performance is significantly lower and even the refined QBE queries fail to adequately capture the semantics behind the retrieval requirement, even though all queries have access to the same set of image descriptors.

5. Ontology-Guided Dynamic Scene Understanding

Figure 9. Tracking results (from left to right): Original frame; Model of the background variances; Results of background subtraction; Detected blobs after morphological operations; Resulting tracked objects (with bounding box).

Video sequences and ground truth from the CAVIAR project[1] were used to define an ontology of visual content descriptors arranged in a hierarchy of scenarios, situations, roles, states, and visual properties. The latter properties were defined by choosing object attributes such as translational speed and appearance change which could easily be computed by means of a visual tracking and appearance modelling framework. The CAVIAR training data was then automatically re-labelled with this extended set of descriptors by instantiating the tracking framework with the individual objects in the ground truth and computing the selected visual attributes for all frames in the sequences. The resulting data was then used to learn both the structure and parameters of Bayesian networks for high-level analysis. Evaluations were performed to assess how easily the categories of the ontology could be inferred on the basis of the chosen visual features and on the basis of preceding layers in the hierarchy. The former allows one to assess the (in)adequacies of a set of given visual content extraction and representation methods, which is an important tool in designing the computer

[1]EC Funded CAVIAR project/IST 2001 37540, *http://homepages.inf.ed.ac.uk/rbf/CAVIAR/*.

vision components of a surveillance system in order to maximise their utility for high-level inference in light of the domain ontology. Conversely, one can use the probabilistic scoring methods applicable to Bayesian networks to evaluate how well-defined e.g. the pre-defined set of situation descriptors are in terms of the labels for object roles and states which appear in the ground truth. Further implementation details can be found in [15].

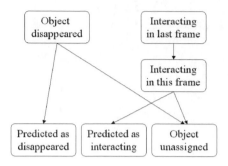

Figure 10. Bayesian network for occlusion reasoning and prediction of object interactions.

5.1. Visual Analysis and Tracking

The tracking system maintains a background model and foreground motion history (obtained by frame differencing) which are adapted over time using an exponential rate of decay to determine the decreasing influence of previous frames im_{i-1} in the history. The motion history M_i is used to identify a background image bim_i of pixels undergoing sufficiently slow change which can then be used to reliably update the background model B_i and estimate its variance:

$$B_i = \alpha * bim_i + (1 - \alpha) * B_{i-1}; \quad B_0 = im_0 \tag{1}$$

$$where\ bim_i = |im_i - M_i| < \tau; \quad \alpha = 1 - e^{-1/\lambda_B} \tag{2}$$

Pixels are deemed to be part of the dynamic foreground if they exceed a difference threshold which is a multiple of the background variance σ_i^B and if they are not deemed to be part of a shadow as determined by a simple test over luminance vs hue and saturation changes.

After performing some morphological clean-up operations, foreground pixels are clustered using connected components analysis to identify moving regions ("blobs"). Blob positions are tracked using a Kalman or particle filter with a second order motion model. Tracked objects are matched to detected blobs using a weighted dissimilarity metric which takes into account differences in predicted object location vs blob location and changes in object appearance. Colour appearance is modelled by histograms in RGB space and Gaussian Mixture models in HSV space, with distance metric computed through the Earth Mover's distance and likelihood computation respectively. Object arrivals, departures and occlusions are inferred using a Bayesian network (see figure 10). Figure 9 illustrates the approach.

In order to model and track the shape of objects in terms of their closed boundaries, approaches based on active contours have been very prominent in the vision community.

We have adapted Gradient Vector flow (GVF) in order to make the transition from tracked edges to closed boundary contours. The snake's external force is computed as a diffusion of the gradient vectors of an edge map derived using our edge detector. After fitting a motion model to the edges of each object by means of the edge tracker and also fitting the GVF active contour to the object's outer boundary, the shape of that boundary is parameterised. The approach chosen here uses the first four of the seven affine invariant moments ϕ_i proposed by Hu [5]. In the present case, the invariant moments are calculated over object boundary pixels only, i.e. $f(x,y)$ is an indicator function which is 1 for a given object's boundary pixels and 0 elsewhere. All x, y values are transformed such that they lie in the range $[0; 1]$ by normalising with respect to the object's bounding box. In order to reduce the range of the ϕ_i, the logarithms $log(\phi_i)$ of the actual values are used.

Scenario	A description of an individual's overall context.
scBSC	Browsing scenario
scIM	Immobile scenario
scWG	Walking scenario
scDD	Drop-down scenario
Situation	The situation in which the individual is participating.
siM	Moving situation
siIS	Inactive situation
siBSI	Browsing situation
Role	The individual's role in the current situation.
rF	Fighter role
rBR	Browser role
rLV	Left victim role
rLG	Leaving group role
rWK	Walker role
rLO	Left object role
State	The individual's current attributes.
tAP	Appear
tDI	Disappear
tO	Occluded
tIN	Inactive: visible but not moving
tAC	Active: visible, moving but not translating across the image
tWK	Walking: visible, moving, translating across the image slowly
tR	Running: visible, moving, translating across the image quickly

Name	Explanation
CVx	Relative x-position
CVy	Relative y-position
CVv	Speed
CVa	Absolute acceleration
CVm	Relative mass
CVn	Relative change in mass
CVt	Major axis orientation
CVrx	Direction of movement relative to positive x-axis
CVry	Direction of movement relative to positive y-axis
CVf	Motion flow (exponentially smoothed history of the object's motion)
CVl	Object lifetime
CVs	Combined appearance measure difference score
CVo	Occlusion status
CVbm	Six element (CVbm1..CVbm6) vector of motion model parameters corresponding to the projective deformations of x- and y-translation, rotation, dilation, pure shear, and shear at 45°
CVbs	Four element (CVbs1..CVbs4) vector of shape model parameters corresponding to the invariant moments ($\phi_1, \phi_2, \phi_3, \phi_4$)

Figure 11. Left: CAVIAR ontology; Right: Extended set of concepts derived through visual analysis.

5.2. Ground Truth and Domain Ontology

Video sequences and ground truth from the CAVIAR project comprise 28 annotated sequences taken by a surveillance camera in the entrance lobby of the INRIA Rhone-Alpes research laboratory in France. They consist of six scenarios of actors performing different activities such as walking around, browsing information displays, sitting down, meeting one another and splitting apart, abandoning objects, fighting and running away. The CAVIAR annotations can naturally be organised into a hierarchical ontology as shown in figure 11. This arrangement offers guidance for the design of Bayesian inference networks. For example, one would expect an individual's state to depend primarily on their current role, their current role to depend on the situation they are facing, and their situation to depend on the scenario in which they are participating. These relationships can be used as a structural prior for the training of Bayesian networks as described below. In order to ground the terms of the ontology, we extend it with appropriate descriptors computed from the tracking and appearance modelling framework described in section 5.1.. These visual descriptors (see table 11) are not claimed to constitute the best choice for the analysis task at hand. They are merely properties of tracked objects which can be simply and robustly defined using the techniques described in section 5.1. and offer a reasonable basis for studying the requirements for low-level analysis mechanisms which result from the pre-defined ontology of higher-level terms.

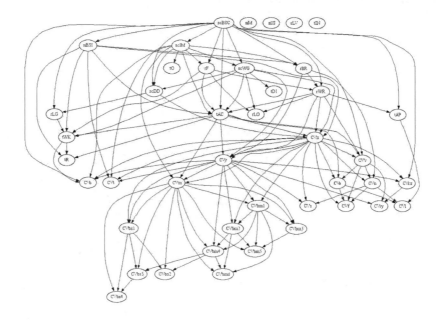

Figure 12. Bayesian network structure trained using the K2 algorithm from the extended ontology.

5.3. Learning Bayesian Network Structure and Parameters

In this chapter, the goal was to learn the structure and parameters of a static directed Bayesian network given fully observed data, i.e. the values of all nodes are known in each case from the ground truth (augmented as required with the information gathered by the computer vision techniques). The variables were discretised by choosing a number of quantisation levels (usually 3 or 4) and quantising by sub-dividing the range $[\mu - 2\sigma; \mu + 2\sigma]$ (where μ and σ are the mean and standard deviation respectively of the observed values of the variable as computed over the entire data set) into the corresponding number of subranges. Each value of the variable in the data set is then quantised by assigning it one of the quantisation values according to the subrange which it occupies. Making the reasonable assumption that the values are approximately normally distributed, this quantisation method

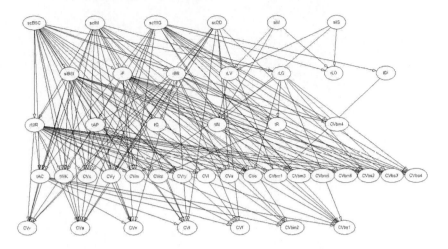

Figure 13. Bayesian network structure trained using the K2 algorithm with a structural prior from the extended ontology.

accounts for about 95.5% of the variation in the data while reducing the effect of outliers that may occur due to discontinuities caused by imperfect visual analysis.

Learning the network structure requires a means of searching the space of all possible DAGs over the set of nodes X and a scoring function to evaluate a given structure over the training data D. The K2 algorithm is a greedy search technique which starts from an empty network but with an initial ordering of the nodes. A Bayesian network is then created iteratively by adding a directed arc to a given node from that parent node whose addition most increases the score of the resulting graph structure. This process terminates as soon as none of the possible additions result in an increased score.

Markov Chain Monte Carlo (MCMC) can be applied to Bayesian network structure learning without the need for a prior node ordering (although such orderings can be employed to speed up convergence). The Metropolis-Hastings sampling technique is applied to search the space of all graphs G by defining a Markov Chain over it whose stationary distribution is the posterior probability distribution $P(G|D)$. Following Bayes' rule, $P(G|D) = P(D|G)P(G)$. The marginal likelihood of the data $P(D|G)$ can be computed by means of an appropriate scoring function (see below) and the prior $P(G)$ may be left uninformative (i.e. a uniform distribution over the set of possible DAGs G). Candidate structures are then sampled by performing a random walk over the Markov chain. The highest scoring network structure can then be inferred by averaging over a sufficiently large number of samples.

In order to compute the score of a candidate network over the training data while avoiding overfitting, two scoring functions were considered:

- The marginal likelihood of the model

$$P(D|G) = \int_{\theta} P(D|G, \theta)P(\theta|G)$$

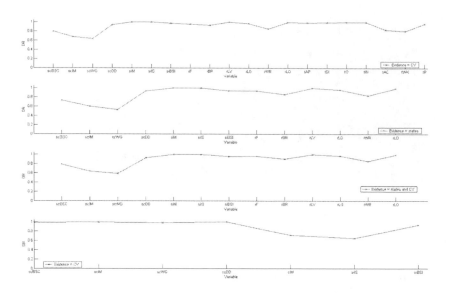

Figure 14. Plot of recognition rates achieved by the Bayesian network shown in figure 13 for the variables in the CAVIAR ontology given different evidence. *Top*: given only the computer vision derived nodes as evidence; *2nd from top*: given only the states (tAP, tDI, tO, tIN, tAC, tWK, tR); *3rd from top*: given both the states and computer vision information; *Bottom*: recognition rates for the states given the computer vision derived nodes as evidence. It can be seen that some nodes in the ontology are insufficiently grounded using the computer vision components alone but that embedding them in an ontology derived structure improves recognition.

where D is the training data, G is the graph structure, and θ are the network parameters.

- The Bayesian Information Criterion (BIC), which approximates the marginal likelihood using a Minimum Description Length (MDL) approach. The Laplace approximation to the parameter posterior can be written in terms of the likelihood and a penalty term $\frac{d}{2}\log M$ to explicitly penalise model complexity:

$$\log P(D|G) \approx \log P(D|G, \hat{\theta}_G) - \frac{d}{2}\log M = \mathrm{BIC}(D, G)$$

where M is the number of training cases in D, d is the number of free parameters, and $\hat{\theta}_G$ is their maximum likelihood estimate.

MCMC was largely found to provide inferior results and required many thousands of iterations to converge to a solution. Furthermore, the K2 method directly benefits from the prior structural information contained in the ontology. Although the BIC score is a more crude approximation than that inherent in the computation of the marginal likelihood shown above, there was very little difference in resulting network performance using the two scoring methods. Once the network structure has been trained, parameters can be estimated easily using maximum likelihood estimation using Dirichlet priors (pseudo-counts).

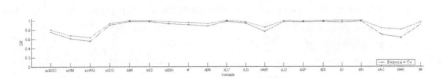

Figure 15. Plot of Bayesian network recognition rates for the variables in the CAVIAR ontology given only the computer vision derived nodes as evidence. The rates achieved by the network in figure 13 are shown in red (top line), those for the network in figure 12 are shown in blue (bottom line). It can be seen that the use of an ontological prior improves accuracy.

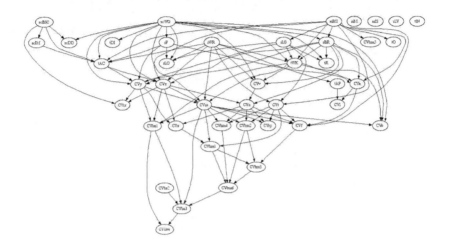

Figure 16. Bayesian network structure trained using the K2 algorithm with random initial ordering of the nodes.

5.4. Results

Figure 12 shows a Bayesian network trained in the manner described in section 5.3. using the K2 algorithm without a structural prior. The network structure looks somewhat erratic but captures some of the hierarchical relationships between variables that one would expect from their semantics. Some nodes in the network (siM, siIS, rLV, tIN) remain unconnected. That is because their values are almost constant in the data set and hence can in most cases be inferred trivially through a purely deterministic prior.

The network shown in figure 13 was trained using K2 and a structural prior specifying that nodes which are part of the same semantic level in the ontology (e.g. all situation labels) should be treated as equivalent in terms of the ordering of nodes. The resulting network structure encompasses many of the causal relationships one would expect from the semantics and shows that there are strong dependencies between the computer vision derived terms and the states and roles in particular. Figure 14 shows classification rates achieved by this network given different sets of evidence. As shown in figure 15, this network achieves better recognition rates than the one trained without a structural prior.

The average recognition rates (computed over an independent testing set) over all elements of the CAVIAR ontology are now 0.911 and 0.882 respectively for the Bayesian network with and without a structural prior.

Even without the structural prior (which groups variables in the same level of the ontology into an equivalence class), the ontology has thus far still been used to define an ordering of the nodes in the Bayesian network. Figure 16 shows an example of a Bayesian network which was trained using K2 without any such ontological information, i.e. with a random initial ordering of the nodes. The performance of this network is worse than the two discussed before, with the average recognition rate now being 0.865. This implies that the use of an ontological prior has reduced the expected error rate from about 14% to about 9% (i.e. a 36% reduction) even though the same data set, image processing, and learning method are being used.

It is also possible to provide a structural prior for MCMC learning by initialising the search with a particular network structure. The resulting average recognition rates for the CAVIAR ontology are 0.642 (MCMC without ontological prior) and 0.659 (search initialised with a prior).

6.   Conclusion

This chapter presents research in the area of high-level computer vision which shows how ontologies can be used as effective computational and representational mechanisms that allow one to relate semantic descriptors to their parametric representations in terms of the underlying data primitives. A particular focus of this work is on the role of ontologies as a means of representing structured prior information and of fusing different kinds of information in an inference framework.

Section 4. presents a novel approach to content-based image retrieval founded on an ontological query language, OQUEL. The problems of expressing, representing, and matching user queries are thus solved through a *prescriptive* ontology of image content descriptors which is hierarchically decomposed using a language which embodies a general syntax and semantics for query composition and representation of target image content. It is shown how the ontological query language provides a way of narrowing the *semantic gap* between users and the retrieval system by providing a shared language and hierarchy of concepts for both. Rather than attempting to describe image content in terms of the language, this approach recognises that the meaning attributed to a given image by a user relative to some current retrieval need (and therefore its relevance to a given query) is only discernable through the composition of the query itself which defines the ontological domain over which relevance assessment is carried out. Inference of image content thus occurs only directly in response to the user query and terminates as soon as the relevance or irrelevance of each image has been established. Comparisons with other query composition and retrieval paradigms (sketch, sample images, property thresholds) show that the OQUEL query language constitutes a more efficient and flexible retrieval tool. Few prior interpretative constraints are imposed and relevance assessments are carried out solely on the basis of the syntax and semantics of the query itself. Such queries have also generally proven to be more efficient to evaluate since one only needs to analyse those aspects of the image content representation that are relevant to nodes in the corresponding syntax tree and because of various possible optimisations in the order of evaluation to quickly rule out non-relevant images.

In section 5., the problem of building reliable high-level recognition systems for dynamic scene analysis (in particular that of surveillance video) is addressed by a combination of pre-annotated training data, a set of automatically derived visual descriptors, and an extended ontology incorporating both of these. The section describes how Bayesian networks can be trained from this data to perform inference over the terms of the ontology. Moreover, an analysis of the composition and performance of different Bayesian recognition networks can lead to insights into the coherence, utility, and groundedness of the ontology itself in terms of the basis vocabulary derived by the visual analysis.

A central problem in the development and application of ontologies is that of grounding their terms and relations in the underlying data. One way in which this may be achieved is to hierarchically decompose and re-express the terms of the ontology until they are all defined in terms of primitives which the system can readily recognise. Another way is to provide sufficient training data such that the system can be made to internalise an appropriate definition of the concept by means of machine learning. Both of these approaches are investigated in this work.

The general idea is that recognising an object or event requires one to relate loosely defined symbolic representations of concepts to concrete instances of the referenced object or behaviour pattern. This is best approached in a hierarchical manner by associating individual parts at each level of the hierarchy according to rules governing which configurations of the underlying primitives give rise to meaningful patterns at the higher semantic level. Thus syntactic rules can be used to drive the recognition of compound objects or events based on the detection of individual components corresponding to detected features in time and space. Visual analysis then amounts to parsing a stream of basic symbols according to prior probabilities to find the most likely interpretation of the observed data in light of the top-level starting symbols in order to establish correspondence between numerical and symbolic descriptions of information.

References

[1] Dasiopoulou, S., Kompatsiaris, I.: Trends and issues in description logics frameworks for image interpretation. In: S. Konstantopoulos, S. Perantonis, V. Karkaletsis, C. Spyropoulos, G. Vouros (eds.) Artificial Intelligence: Theories, Models and Applications, *Lecture Notes in Computer Science*, vol. 6040, pp. 61–70. Springer Berlin / Heidelberg (2010)

[2] Duygulu, P., Barnard, K., De Freitas, J., Forsyth, D.: Object recognition as machine translation: Learning a lexicon for a fixed image vocabulary. In: *Proc. European Conference on Computer Vision* (2002)

[3] Duygulu, P., Bastan, M.: Multimedia translation for linking visual data to semantics in videos. *Machine Vision and Applications* pp. 1–17 (2009)

[4] Harnad, S.: The symbol grounding problem. *Physica D* **42**, 335–346 (1990)

[5] Hu, M.: Visual pattern recognition by moment invariants. *IRA Transactions on Information Theory* **17**(2), 179–187 (1962)

[6] Hudelot, C., Atif, J., Bloch, I.: Fuzzy spatial relation ontology for image interpretation. *Fuzzy Sets and Systems* **159**(15), 1929 – 1951 (2008). From Knowledge Representation to Information Processing and Management - Selected papers from the French Fuzzy Days (LFA 2006)

[7] Iskandar, D.: Visual ontology query language. In: *Networked Digital Technologies, 2009. NDT '09. First International Conference on,* pp. 65 –70 (2009)

[8] Kohler, C.: Selecting ghosts and queues from a car trackers output using a spatio-temporal query language. In: *Proc. Conference on Computer Vision and Pattern Recognition* (2004)

[9] Lalmas, M.: *Applications of Uncertainty Formalisms, chap. Information retrieval and Dempster-Shafer's theory of evidence,* pp. 157–177. Springer (1998)

[10] Liu, Y., Zhang, J., Li, Z., Tjondronegoro, D.: High-level concept annotation using ontology and probabilistic inference. In: *Proceedings of the First International Conference on Internet Multimedia Computing and Service, ICIMCS '09,* pp. 97–101. ACM, New York, NY, USA (2009)

[11] Nevatia, R., Hobbs, J., Bolles, B.: An ontology for video event representation. In: *Proc. Int. Workshop on Detection and Recognition of Events in Video (at CVPR04)* (2004)

[12] Nikolopoulos, S., Papadopoulos, G., Kompatsiaris, I., Patras, I.: An evidence-driven probabilistic inference framework for semantic image understanding. In: P. Perner (ed.) Machine Learning and Data Mining in Pattern Recognition, *Lecture Notes in Computer Science,* vol. 5632, pp. 525–539. Springer Berlin / Heidelberg (2009)

[13] SanMiguel, J., Martinez, J., Garcia, A.: An ontology for event detection and its application in surveillance video. In: Advanced Video and Signal Based Surveillance, 2009. *AVSS '09. Sixth IEEE International Conference on,* pp. 220 –225 (2009)

[14] Sinclair, D.: Smooth region structure: folds, domes, bowls, ridges, valleys and slopes. In: *Proc. Conference on Computer Vision and Pattern Recognition,* pp. 389–394 (2000)

[15] Town, C.: Ontology-driven Bayesian networks for dynamic scene understanding. In: *Proc. Int. Workshop on Detection and Recognition of Events in Video (at CVPR04)* (2004)

[16] Town, C., Harrison, K.: Large-scale grid computing for content-based image retrieval. *Aslib Proceedings* **62**(4/5), 438–446 (2010)

[17] Town, C., Sinclair, D.: Language-based querying of image collections on the basis of an extensible ontology. *International Journal of Image and Vision Computing* **22(3)**, 251–267 (2004)

[18] Yao, B., Yang, X., Lin, L., Lee, M.W., Zhu, S.C.: I2t: Image parsing to text description. *Proceedings of the IEEE* **98**(8), 1485 –1508 (2010)

In: Computer Vision
Editor: Sota R. Yoshida

ISBN: 978-1-61209-399-4
© 2011 Nova Science Publishers, Inc.

Chapter 9

COMPUTER VISION BY LASER METROLOGY AND ALGORITHMS OF ARTIFICIAL INTELLIGENCE

J. A. Muñoz-Rodríguez[*]

Centro de Investigaciones en Optica, A. C. Leon, Gto, Mexico

ABSTRACT

We present a review of our algorithms for computer vision based on laser metrology and artificial intelligence. This chapter includes laser metrology, image processing, contouring by neural networks, modelling of mobile setup and vision parameters. To achieve the computer vision, the object shape is reconstructed by a laser metrology method. To carry it out, the object is scanned by a laser line. Based on the deformation of the laser line, a network provides object dimension. The behavior of the laser line is obtained by image processing. The modelling of the relationship between the laser line and the object shape is performed b approximation networks. The architecture of the networks is built using data of images of a laser line projected on objects, whose dimensions are known. The approach of the neural networks is to perform the contouring without measurements on the optical setup. Also, the network provides the camera parameters and the setup parameters. Thus, the performance and accuracy are improved. It is because the errors of the measurement are not passed to the contouring system. To describe the accuracy a root mean square of error is calculated using data produced by the networks and data provided by a contact method. This technique is tested with real objects and its experimental results are presented.

1. INTRODUCTION

The computer vision largely deals with the analysis of the images in order to achieve results similar to those obtained by the man. This matter is directed towards the recovery the object contour in a scene. The optical metrology is a valuable tool in computer vision,

---

[*] E-mail address: munoza@foton.cio.mx; Tel: (477) 441 42 00

especially for object contouring. Application areas such as: object modelling, distance measurements, position of obstacles, shape inspection and navigation are performed by computer vision [1]. In optical metrology, the object contouring is treated by image processing to achieve the vision. Based on a light pattern image, the contour data are computed to reproduce object shape. The optical sensors provide the contouring without contact to achieve the computer vision [2]. The use of structured light generally makes the system more reliable and the acquired data are easier to interpret. Lighting methods have been implemented to perform the object contouring. Optical methods such as: fringe patter projection, laser line projection and light spot projection have been developed to extract three-dimensional data [3-5]. In these methods, the contouring is performed by triangulation using the geometry of the optical setup [6-8]. In the triangulation procedure, the distances of the geometry are obtained by an external procedure to the contouring system. This kind of performance involves a high level of position location of the components of the optical setup.

In this chapter, the computer vision includes automatic contouring by networks to avoid measurements on the optical setup. In this procedure, the object is scanned by a laser line. From this step, images of the laser line are captured and digitized. By means of a neural network, the object contour is computed based on the laser line deformation. This network generates a mathematical function, which contains the relationship between the object dimension and the laser line position. Thus, contour dimension is deduced computationally and the measurements on the optical setup are avoided. In this manner, the performance and the accuracy are improved. It is because the errors of measurement on the setup are not passed to the computer vision system. Also, a modelling of the mobile setup is performed by the network, which computes the contour dimension. In this case, the devices of the setup can be moved to detect the occluded areas and little details, which are not detected by a static setup. The network computes the contour dimension based on the laser line deformation at any camera position. In this manner, the object dimension is deduced for the mobile setup. Also, the parameters of the imaging system are deduced from the network and by image processing. The viability of computer vision is examined based on the root mean squared error. This analysis is carried out based on a contact method used as reference. The setup used in this technique consists of an electromechanical device, a laser projector, a CCD camera and a computer. In this arrangement, object is moved on an axis and scanned by a laser line. In the scanning procedure, images of laser line are captured by a CCD camera. These images are processed to detect the laser line position by measuring the maximum intensity. This position is processed by the neural network to determine the object dimension.

The content of this chapter is organized as follow. In section 2, the optical setup for object contouring is described. In section 3, neural networks are implemented to perform the object contouring. In section 4, modelling of mobile setup is presented. In section 5, the computer vision parameters are determined. In section 6, experimental results of computer vision by optical metrology are presented. Finally, a conclusion is presented.

2. DESCRIPTION OF THE OPTICAL SETUP

In optical metrology, lighting methods have been implemented for object depth recovery. A particular technique is the laser line projection [9]. The approach of this technique is to detect the laser line deformation. When a laser line is projected on an object, the line is deformed at the image plane. This is due to the surface depth variation and the viewer direction. From the laser line position and the geometry of the optical setup, the contour data are recovered [10]. The proposed technique for object contouring is the laser line projection. The setup includes an electromechanical device, a CCD camera, a laser line projector and a computer. The experimental setup is shown in Figure 1. In this setup, the object is fixed on a platform of the electromechanical device. A laser line is projected perpendicularly to the object surface and a camera is aligned at an oblique angle. To perform the scanning, the object is moved by the electromechanical device based on computer procedure. In each step of the scanning, the laser line is deformed in x-axis according to the object surface. Every deformed line is captured and digitized by a CCD camera and a frame grabber, respectively. By detecting the position of the line deformation, the contouring is performed. A neural network computes the object dimensions by mean of the laser line position. The contour data extracted from a laser line image corresponds to a transverse section of the object. The data of all transverse sections produce the complete object shape.

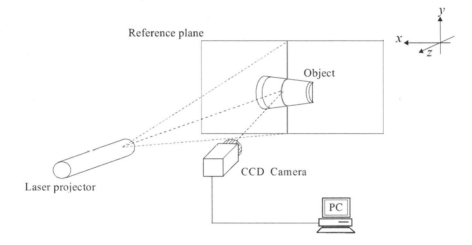

Figure 1. Optical setup for scanning by means of a laser line.

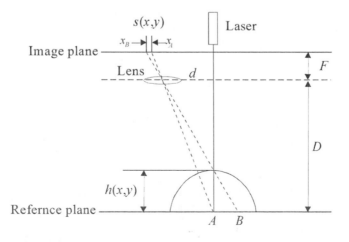

Figure 2. Geometry of the optical setup.

The relationship between the laser line position and the object depth is described by the geometry shown in Figure 2. In this figure, on the reference plane are located the x-axis and y-axis, and the object depth is indicated by $h(x, y)$. The points A and B correspond to laser line projected on the reference plane and the object surface, respectively. When a laser line is projected on the target, the line position in the image is moved from x_A to x_B. This displacement can be represented as:

$$s(x,y) = x_A - x_B. \tag{1}$$

This line displacement $s(x, y)$ is directly proportional object depth $h(x, y)$. A network performs the model that describes this relation-ship. Therefore, the network computes the depth $h(x, y)$ for each displacement $s(x,y)$ detected in the image.

To detect the line displacement, the position of the intensity maximum is measured in the image. The intensity projected by a laser diode is a Gaussian distribution in lateral direction (x-axis) [11]. The pixel intensity of every row of the laser line image is represented by (x_0, z_0), (x_1, z_1), ..., (x_n, z_n), where x_i is the pixel position and z_i is the pixel intensity and n is the pixel number. A simple way for representing the pixel intensity is a Gaussian function. The equation of a Gaussian function is

$$f(x) = \frac{Ni}{\sqrt{2\pi\sigma}} e^{-\frac{1}{2}\left(\frac{x-\mu}{\sigma}\right)^2}, \tag{2}$$

where Ni is the area under the curve, μ is the mean of the function, and σ is the standard deviation [12]. To determine the position of the laser line, Eq.(2) is computed for each row of the image. It is because the μ represents the position of the intensity maximum of the Gaussian function. The mean for a Gaussian function is described by

$$\mu = \frac{\sum_{i=0}^{n} z_i x_i}{\sum_{i=0}^{n} z_i}. \tag{3}$$

In this equation x_i represents the pixel position and z_i the pixel intensity. To detect the laser line position, the maximum position is calculated for every row of the image via Eq.(3). To describe this procedure, the maximum position is calculated for the pixels shown in Figure 3. These pixels correspond to a row of a laser line image. To compute the maximum position, the pixel position x_i and intensity pixel z_i are substituted into Eq.(3). In this case, the result is $\mu = 34.184$, which corresponds to the maximum position. Therefore, the laser line position is $x_B = 34.184$ pixels. Also, Ni and the standard deviation σ are calculated to fit the Gaussian function $f(x)$ shown in Figure 3.

Also, Bezier Curves are used to detect the position of the laser line. The nth-degree Bezier function is determined by $n+1$ pixels [13]. The nth-degree Bezier function is determined by two parametric equations, which are described by

$$x(u) = \binom{n}{0} (1-u)^n u^0 x_0 + \binom{n}{1} (1-u)^{n-1} u x_1 + \dots\dots + \binom{n}{n} (1-u)^0 u^n x_n, \quad 0 \le u \le 1. \quad (4)$$

$$z(u) = \binom{n}{0} (1-u)^n u^0 z_0 + \binom{n}{1} (1-u)^{n-1} u z_1 + \dots\dots + \binom{n}{n} (1-u)^0 u^n z_n, \quad 0 \le u \le 1. \quad (5)$$

Eq.(4) represents the pixel position and Eq.(5) represents the pixel intensity. To fit the Bezier curve shown in Figure 3, $x_0, x_1, x_2,\dots,x_n$, are substituted into Eq. (4) and $z_0, z_1, z_2,\dots,z_n$, are substituted into Eq. (5). Then, these equations are evaluated in the interval $0 \le u \le 1$ to fit the curve shown in Figure 3. Then, the first and the second derivative are applied to determine the local maximum or minimum. In this case, the second derivative $z''(u) > 0$ in the interval $0 \le u \le 1$. Therefore, the maximum is detected by the first derivative equal to zero $z'(u)=0$ via bisection method [14]. Beginning with a pair of values $u_i = 0$ and $u_s = 1$, because $z(u)$ is defined for the interval $0 \le u \le 1$, u^* is halfway between u_i and u_s. If $z'(u)$ evaluated at $u = u^*$ is positive, then $u_i = u^*$. If $z'(u)$ evaluated at $u = u^*$ is negative, then $u_s=u^*$. Next, u^* is taken as the mid point of the last pair values that converges to the root. The value u^* where $z'(u) = 0$ is substituted into Eq.(5) to obtain maximum position x^*. The result is $x^* = 34.274$ and the stripe position is $x_B = 34.274$ pixels, which is shown in Figure 3. The examination of these methods is based on the best accuracy provided by the laser line detection. According to the root mean square of error (*rms*), the laser line detection by Bezier curves provides the best accuracy for object contouring. A laser line image is shown in Figure 4(a), which is processed to detect the line displacement. To carry it out, the maximum position is computed for every row of the image via Bezier curves. Then, the maximum position is substituted in Eq.(1) to calculate the displacement $s(x,y)$, which represents the depth profile shown in Figure 4(b). These depth data are used to compute the object dimension by means of a network, which is described in section 3.

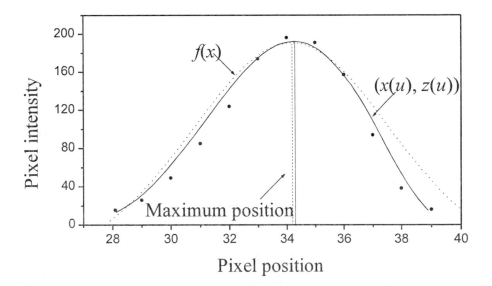

Figure 3. Maximum position from a Gaussian function and Bezier curves.

Figure 4 (a). Image of a laser line.

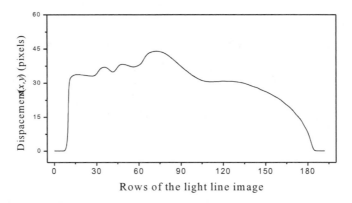

Figure 4 (b). Displacement corresponding to laser line of Figure 4(a).

3. APPROXIMATION NETWORKS FOR OBJECT CONTOURING

3.1. Structure of a Radial Basis Function Neural Network

Radial basis function neural networks (RBFNN) is an artificial network applied to solve problems of supervised learning, regression, classification, shape identification, object detection and time series prediction [15-19]. The structure of an RBFNN includes an input vector, a hidden layer and output layer [20]. This structure is shown in Figure 5. The input vector is only a fan-out to connect the input data with the hidden layer. The hidden layer is constructed by radial basis function. The output layer is obtained by the summation of the neurons of the hidden layer, which are multiplied by a weight. Each layer of the network is defined as follow. The input vector s_1, s_2, s_3,....,s_n are obtained by measuring the laser line position by image processing described in section 2. The radial basis function of the hidden layer is a Gaussian neuron, which is described by the next equation

$$\phi_i = \exp\left(-\frac{\|s - s_i\|^2}{2\sigma^2}\right),$$

(6)

where s_i is the neuron centre and σ is the neuron width, which is calculated as

$$\sigma = \sqrt{\frac{1}{q}\sum_{i=1}^{q}(s - s_i)^2},$$

(7)

where $q = 2$, $s - s_i$ is de distance between each couple of nearest neurons. The output layer is computed by the summation of the weighted neurons, which is represented by

$$h(s) = \sum_{i=1}^{m} w_i \phi\left(\|s - s_i\|\right),$$

(8)

where m is the number of neurons. To construct the complete network architecture, the parameters of the Eq.(8) should be determined. These parameters include: the neuron shape, neuron centre, neuron width, number of neurons and the weights.

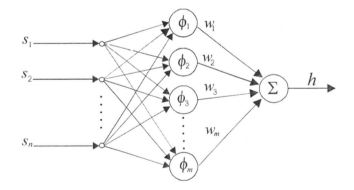

Figure 5. Structure of a RBFNN.

The first parameter to be determined is the neuron shape. Some functions can be used to construct the neuron shape, such as: cubic, inverse quadratic, inverse multi-quadratic and Gaussian [18]. Using these functions, four RBFNN are constructed. Then, a mean squared error (*MSE*) [18] is calculated to determine the best network according to the neuron shape. The *MSE* is defined by

$$MSE = \frac{1}{n}\sum_{i=1}^{n}(hc_i - h_i)^2,$$

(9)

where hc_i is the output calculated by the RBFNN, h_i is the desired output and n is the number of analyzed data. Based on the *MSE*, the best output response is given by the Gaussian function. Therefore, the Gaussian function Eq.(6) is used to built the hidden layer. The second parameter is the neuron centre s_i, which is given by each data of the input vector. The third parameter to be determined is the number of neurons of the hidden layer. Again, the *MSE* criterion is used. This criterion, also, provides the error according to the number of neurons. To define neuron number, the network is constructed with different neuron number. Then, the neuron number that provides the best *MSE* is selected. The parameter sigma, which corresponds to the neuron width is calculated by Eq.(7). Finally, the training process is applied to determine the weights. This training is supervised, because the outputs are known and the network is being forced to produce the correct outputs. To carry it out, the input data $s_1, s_2, s_3,...,s_n$ are connected to the hidden layer. Therefore, for each input s_i an output h_i is produced and the next equation system is generated

$$h_1 = w_1 \exp\left(-\frac{\|s_1 - s_1\|^2}{2\sigma^2}\right) + w_2 \exp\left(-\frac{\|s_1 - s_2\|^2}{2\sigma^2}\right) +..........+ w_m \exp\left(-\frac{\|s_1 - s_m\|^2}{2\sigma^2}\right)$$

$$h_2 = w_1 \exp\left(-\frac{\|s_2 - s_1\|^2}{2\sigma^2}\right) + w_2 \exp\left(-\frac{\|s_2 - s_2\|^2}{2\sigma^2}\right) +..........+ w_m \exp\left(-\frac{\|s_2 - s_m\|^2}{2\sigma^2}\right) \qquad (10)$$

$$\vdots \qquad\qquad \vdots \qquad\qquad \vdots \qquad\qquad \vdots$$

$$h_n = w_1 \exp\left(-\frac{\|s_n - s_1\|^2}{2\sigma^2}\right) + w_2 \exp\left(-\frac{\|s_n - s_2\|^2}{2\sigma^2}\right) +..........+ w_m \exp\left(-\frac{\|s_n - s_m\|^2}{2\sigma^2}\right)$$

The linear system of Eq.(10) can be represented as

$$h_1 = w_1\phi_{1,1} + w_2\phi_{1,2} +..........+ w_m\phi_{1,m}$$

$$h_2 = w_1\phi_{2,1} + w_2\phi_{2,2} +..........+ w_m\phi_{2,m} \qquad (11)$$

$$\vdots \qquad \vdots \qquad \vdots \qquad\qquad \vdots$$

$$h_n = w_1\phi_{n,1} + w_2\phi_{n,2} +..........+ w_m\phi_{n,m}$$

Eq.(11) can be rewritten in matrix form as $\phi\mathbf{W} = \mathbf{H}$, which is represented as

$$\begin{bmatrix} \phi_{1,1} & \phi_{1,2} & \phi_{1,3} & .... & \phi_{1,m} \\ \phi_{2,1} & \phi_{2,2} & \phi_{2,3} & .... & \phi_{2,m} \\ \vdots & \vdots & \vdots & & \vdots \\ \phi_{n,1} & \phi_{n,2} & \phi_{n,3} & .... & \phi_{n,m} \end{bmatrix} \begin{bmatrix} w_1 \\ w_2 \\ \vdots \\ w_m \end{bmatrix} = \begin{bmatrix} h_1 \\ h_2 \\ \vdots \\ h_n \end{bmatrix}.$$

$$(12)$$

By solving the linear equation system Eq.(12), the weights w_i are determined. This system can be solved by the Chelosky method [21]. This method uses a Lower and Upper (LU) decomposition to transform the matrix system. By using the lower and upper triangular matrix, linear system Eq.(17) $\mathbf{H}=\phi\mathbf{W}$ is transformed into $LU\mathbf{W}=\mathbf{H}$. In this LU decomposition $\phi = LU$ is determined as

$$
\begin{bmatrix}
\phi_{1,1} & \phi_{1,2} & \phi_{1,3} & \cdots & \phi_{1,m} \\
\phi_{2,1} & \phi_{2,2} & \phi_{2,3} & \cdots & \phi_{2,m} \\
\vdots & \vdots & \vdots & \vdots \\
\phi_{n,1} & \phi_{n,2} & \phi_{n,3} & \cdots & \phi_{n,m}
\end{bmatrix}
=
\begin{bmatrix}
L_{1,1} & 0 & 0 & \cdots & 0 \\
L_{2,1} & L_{2,2} & 0 & \cdots & 0 \\
\vdots & \vdots & \vdots & \vdots \\
L_{n,1} & L_{n,2} & L_{n,3} & \cdots & L_{n,m}
\end{bmatrix}
\begin{bmatrix}
U_{1,1} & U_{1,2} & U_{1,3} & \cdots & U_{1,m} \\
0 & U_{2,2} & U_{2,3} & \cdots & U_{2,m} \\
\vdots & \vdots & \vdots & \vdots \\
0 & 0 & 0 & \cdots & U_{n,m}
\end{bmatrix},
\tag{13}
$$

Then, triangular system is solved as $LY=H$ and $UW=Y$. In this manner, Y is calculated using L and H. Then, W is solved with Y and U. With this step the weight values w_1, w_2, $w_3,...,w_n$ are determined. With these calculated weights, the RBFNN has been completed. In this manner, for a particular given s_i a h_i is calculated by the RBFNN.

3.2. Structure of a General Regression Neural Network

The GRNN was developed by D. Specht in 1991 for systems modeling and identification [22]. The GRNN is an architecture that can solve any approximation problem. The basic idea of a GRNN is that a data set can be approximated by a continuous function. Assuming that a function has x inputs from x_1 to x_n and one output y, the expected mean value of the output for a particular input x can be found using the next equation:

$$
\overline{y} = \frac{\displaystyle\int_{-\infty}^{\infty} y\, f(x,y)dy}{\displaystyle\int_{-\infty}^{\infty} f(x,y)dy}.
\tag{14}
$$

In this equation, $f(x,y)$ is a joint probability density function (PDF), the probability of the output being y and input being x. The PDF can be approximated by a sum of Gaussians [22]. This process is done by placing the center of Gaussian over the input data and multiplying the Gausian by the corresponding output. The Eq.(14) can be approximated by the next equation

$$
\hat{y} = \frac{\displaystyle\sum_{i=1}^{n} w_i \exp(-d_i^2/2\sigma^2)}{\displaystyle\sum_{i=1}^{n} \exp(-d_i^2/2\sigma^2)}.
\tag{15}
$$

From this equation d_i is the distance between each input, n is the number of input/output, σ is the width of the Gaussian function, and w_i is a weight that multiplies at Gaussian function. The architecture to construct a GRNN to obtain the Eq.(15) is shown in Figure 6. In this structure, the output h is the object dimension and s_i is its corresponding laser line displacement. This GRNN is formed by an input vector, a hidden layer, two nodes of summation and output layer.

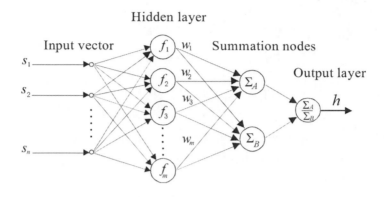

Figure 6. Structure of a GRNN.

The data of input vector s_1, s_2, s_3,....,s_n are the laser line displacement measured by image processing. The hidden layer is constructed by neurons, whose shape is a Gaussian function centered at the input data. The effective range of the Gaussian function is determined by the values allocated to the center and width of it. The function used to obtain each neuron is determined by the next equation

$$f_i = \exp\left(-\frac{\|s - s_i\|^2}{2\sigma^2}\right),$$ (16)

where $\|s\text{-}s_i\|$ is the distance d_i used in Eq.(15), s_i and σ are center and the width of the Gaussian function respectively. The two nodes contain the summation of the neurons of the hidden layer, which are multiplied by a weight. The output layer is determined with the division of the two summation nodes. In this manner, the network output is defined by the next equation

$$h = \frac{\sum_{i=1}^{n} w_i f_i}{\sum_{i=1}^{n} f_i}.$$ (17)

To construct the GRNN via Eq.(17), neuron width, and weights should be determined. The width of the Gausian neuron is the smother parameter σ, which is calculated via Eq.(7). To determine the weights, also, the supervised learning is applied. It is because the outputs are known and the network should be forced to produce the correct outputs. To carry it out, the input vector s_1, s_2, s_3, ...,s_n are connected to hidden layer to produce the outputs h_1, h_2, h_3,.....,h_n. The output of this GRNN is defined by the division of two summations nodes. Therefore, for each input s_i an output is generated as a linear equation system:

$$h_1 = \frac{w_1}{k_1} \exp\left(-\frac{\|s_1 - s_1\|^2}{2\sigma^2}\right) + \frac{w_2}{k_1} \exp\left(-\frac{\|s_1 - s_2\|^2}{2\sigma^2}\right) +,\ldots\ldots,+ \frac{w_m}{k_1} \exp\left(-\frac{\|s_1 - s_m\|^2}{2\sigma^2}\right)$$

$$h_2 = \frac{w_1}{k_2} \exp\left(-\frac{\|s_2 - s_1\|^2}{2\sigma^2}\right) + \frac{w_2}{k_2} \exp\left(-\frac{\|s_2 - s_2\|^2}{2\sigma^2}\right) +,\ldots\ldots,+ \frac{w_n}{k_2} \exp\left(-\frac{\|s_2 - s_n\|^2}{2\sigma^2}\right) \qquad (18)$$

$$\vdots \qquad\qquad \vdots \qquad\qquad \vdots \qquad\qquad \vdots$$

$$h_n = \frac{w_1}{k_n} \exp\left(-\frac{\|s_m - s_1\|^2}{2\sigma^2}\right) + \frac{w_2}{k_n} \exp\left(-\frac{\|s_m - s_2\|^2}{2\sigma^2}\right) +,\ldots\ldots,+ \frac{w_m}{k_n} \exp\left(-\frac{\|s_n - s_m\|^2}{2\sigma^2}\right)$$

where

$$k_1 = \exp\left(-\frac{\|s_1 - s_1\|^2}{2\sigma^2}\right) + \exp\left(-\frac{\|s_1 - s_2\|^2}{2\sigma^2}\right) +,\ldots\ldots,+ \exp\left(-\frac{\|s_1 - s_m\|^2}{2\sigma^2}\right)$$

$$k_2 = \exp\left(-\frac{\|s_2 - s_1\|^2}{2\sigma^2}\right) + \exp\left(-\frac{\|s_2 - s_2\|^2}{2\sigma^2}\right) +,\ldots\ldots,+ \exp\left(-\frac{\|s_2 - s_m\|^2}{2\sigma^2}\right)$$

$$\vdots \qquad\qquad \vdots \qquad\qquad \vdots \qquad\qquad \vdots$$

$$k_n = \exp\left(-\frac{\|s_n - s_1\|^2}{2\sigma^2}\right) + \exp\left(-\frac{\|s_n - s_2\|^2}{2\sigma^2}\right) +,\ldots\ldots,+ \exp\left(-\frac{\|s_n - s_m\|^2}{2\sigma^2}\right)$$

The linear system of Eq.(18) can be represented as

$$h_1 = w_1 f_{1,1} + w_2 f_{1,2} +\ldots\ldots+ w_n f_{1,m}$$
$$h_2 = w_1 f_{2,1} + w_2 f_{2,2} +\ldots\ldots+ w_n f_{2,m} \qquad (19)$$
$$\vdots \qquad \vdots \qquad \vdots \qquad\qquad \vdots$$
$$h_n = w_1 f_{n,1} + w_2 f_{n,2} +\ldots\ldots+ w_m f_{n,m}$$

This equation system can be rewritten in matrix form as the product $\mathbf{H} = \mathbf{FW}$ by

$$\begin{bmatrix} f_{1,1} & f_{1,2} & f_{1,3} & \cdots & f_{1,m} \\ f_{2,1} & f_{2,2} & f_{2,3} & \cdots & f_{2,m} \\ \vdots & \vdots & \vdots & & \vdots \\ f_{n,1} & f_{n,2} & f_{n,3} & \cdots & f_{n,m} \end{bmatrix} \begin{bmatrix} w_1 \\ w_2 \\ \vdots \\ w_m \end{bmatrix} = \begin{bmatrix} h_1 \\ h_2 \\ \vdots \\ h_n \end{bmatrix} \qquad (20)$$

By solving linear system Eq.(20), the weights w_i are obtained. This system is solved by Chelosky method. With this step the weights w_1, w_2, w_3,....,w_m are calculated. In this manner, the GRNN has been constructed. The result of this GRNN is a continuous function, which describes the object dimension according to the laser line displacement. In this manner, for a particular given s_i an h_i is calculated by the GRNN. Based on *MSE*, the neuron that provides the best approximation respect to desired output is the Gaussian function. Therefore, the Gaussian function Eq.(16) is used to construct the hidden layer of this GRNN. The number of neurons used in the hidden layer for this GRNN is determined again by the *MSE* criterion.

3.3. Structure of a Bezier Neural Network

The Bezier basis function has been used to represent curves and surfaces [23-26]. This is the main aim to propose a network of Bezier basis function. The structure proposed for this Bezier neural network (BNN) consists of an input vector, a parametric input, a hidden layer and an output layer. The structure of this BNN is shown in Figure 7. This network includes an input vector, a parametric input, a hidden layer and an output layer. The input includes: object dimensions h_i and its corresponding laser line displacement s_i. The parametric input u is a value proportional to the displacement s_i. This value u is computed by a weighted linear input combination (WLIC) [27]. The hidden layer is constructed by Bezier basis function. The output layer is formed by the summation of the neurons of the hidden layer, which are multiplied by a weight. Each layer of the network is performed as follow. The input data s_0, s_1, s_2,....,s_n are line displacements computed by the image processing described in section 2. By means of these displacements, the parametric u value is determined via WLIC.

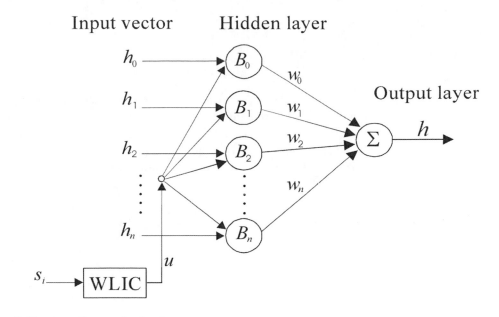

Figure 7. Structure of a neural network.

The relationship between the displacement and the parametric u value is described by

$$u = a_0 + a_1 s, \tag{21}$$

where a_i are the unknown constants, s is position of the stripe displacement $s(x,y)$. Using the position s and its respective u, the Eq.(21) can be determined. The Bezier curves are defined in the interval $0 \leq u \leq 1$ [28]. Therefore, $u = 0$ for the first displacement s_0, and $u=1$ for the last displacement s_n. Substituting the values (s_0, $u=0$) and (s_n, $u=1$) in Eq.(21), two equation with two unknown constants are obtained. Solving these equations, a_0 and a_1 are determined. Thus, the WLIC Eq.(21) is completed. Thus, for a particular displacement s_i a value u is computed. The input data h_0, h_1, h_2,...,h_n are obtained measuring pattern objects by a contact method. The neurons of the hidden layer are defined by the Bezier basis function, which are described by

$$B_i(u) = \binom{n}{i} u^i (1-u)^{n-i}, \qquad 0 \leq u \leq 1, \tag{22}$$

and
$$\binom{n}{i} = \frac{n!}{i!(n-i)!},$$

denotes the binomial distribution from probability and statistics [29]. The output layer is obtained by the summation of the weighted neurons. The output response is the object dimension $h(u)$ given by

$$h(u) = \sum_{i=0}^{n} w_i B_i(u) h_i, \qquad\qquad 0 \le u \le 1, \qquad\qquad (23)$$

where w_i are the weights, h_i is the known dimension of the object and B_i is the Bezier basis function represented by Eq.(22). To compute the weights w_0, w_1, w_2,.....,w_n, the network is being forced to produce the correct outputs h_0, h_1, h_2,......,h_n. To carry it out, an adjustment mechanism is applied. This is performed substituting the values u_i and h_i in Eq.(23). For each input u_i, an output h_i is obtained. In this manner, the next equation system is obtained

$$h_0 = w_0 \binom{n}{0}(1-u)^n u^0 h_0 + w_1 \binom{n}{1}(1-u)^{n-1} u h_1 +,.....,+ w_n \binom{n}{n}(1-u)^0 u^n h_n, \quad 0 \le u \le 1.$$

$$h_1 = w_0 \binom{n}{0}(1-u)^n u^0 h_0 + w_1 \binom{n}{1}(1-u)^{n-1} u h_1 +,.....,+ w_n \binom{n}{n}(1-u)^0 u^n h_n, \quad 0 \le u \le 1. \quad (24)$$

$$\vdots \qquad \vdots \qquad\qquad \vdots \qquad\qquad\qquad \vdots$$

$$h_n = w_0 \binom{n}{0}(1-u)^n u^0 h_0 + w_1 \binom{n}{1}(1-u)^{n-1} u h_1 +,.....,+ w_n \binom{n}{n}(1-u)^0 u^n h_n, \quad 0 \le u \le 1.$$

This linear system of Eq.(24) can be represented as

$$h_0 = w_0\beta_{0,0} + w_1\beta_{0,1}+..........+w_n\beta_{0,n}$$

$$h_1 = w_0\beta_{1,0} + w_1\beta_{1,1}+..........+w_n\beta_{1,n} \qquad\qquad (25)$$

$$\vdots \qquad \vdots \qquad \vdots \qquad\qquad \vdots$$

$$h_n = w_0\beta_{n,0} + w_1\beta_{n,1}+..........+w_n\beta_{n,n}$$

This equation can be rewritten in matrix form as the product between the matrix of the input data and the matrix of the corresponding output values: $\boldsymbol{\beta}\mathbf{W} = \mathbf{H}$. The linear system represented by the next matrix

$$\begin{bmatrix} \beta_{0,0} & \beta_{0,1} & \beta_{0,2} & \cdots & \beta_{0,n} \\ \beta_{101} & \beta_{1,1} & \beta_{1,2} & \cdots & \beta_{1,n} \\ \vdots & \vdots & \vdots & \vdots & \vdots \\ \beta_{n,0} & \beta_{n,1} & \beta_{n,2} & \cdots & \beta_{n,n} \end{bmatrix} \begin{bmatrix} w_0 \\ w_1 \\ \vdots \\ w_n \end{bmatrix} = \begin{bmatrix} h_0 \\ h_1 \\ \vdots \\ h_n \end{bmatrix}. \qquad (26)$$

By solving the linear system Eq.(26), the weights w_i are obtained. This system is solved by the Chelosky method. With this step the weights w_0, w_1, w_2,....,w_n are calculated. In this manner, the network has been completed. The result of this network is a continuous function, which provides the object dimension according to the laser line displacement. Thus, for a s_i given an h_i is computed by the network Eq.(23). Figure 8(a) shows the surface of a dummy bell. Figure 8(b) shows the surface extrated by means of the laser line and the network. In this procedure the measurement of the setup parameter are not passed to vision system. Thus, computational process provides a better performance and the accuracy is improved.

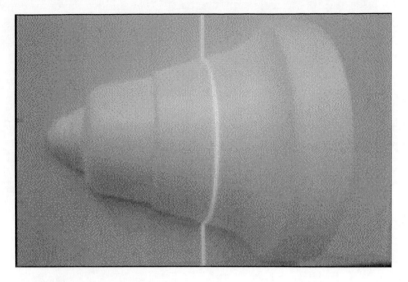

Figure 8 (a). A dummy bell to be profiled.

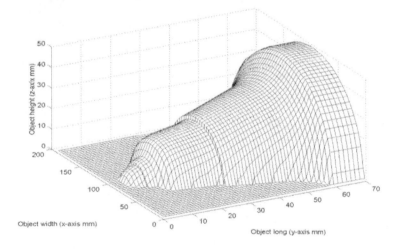

Figure 8(b). Shape of dummy bell.

4. MODELLING OF MOBILE SETUP BY APPROXIMATION NETWORKS

For the mobile setup, the laser line displacement $s(x,y)$ is proportional to the object dimension. Based on this relationship, an approximation network is constructed to compute the object dimension. This network generates an equation, which performs the relationship between the laser line deformation, camera position and the object dimension. The proposed network consists of an input vector, two parametric inputs, a hidden layer and an output layer.

The structure of this network is shown in Figure 9. The input includes: the object dimension h_i and the parametric values u and v. The value v is directly proportional to laser line position x_A at each camera position in the x-axis, which is shown in Figure 10. The value u corresponds to laser line displacement in the x-axis. The hidden layer is constructed by neurons, whose shape is represented by the Bezier basis function. The output layer is formed by the summation of the neurons of the hidden layer, which are multiplied by a weight. Each layer of the network is performed as follow. The input data h_0, h_1, h_2,...,h_n are the known dimensions of the pattern objects. The input data s_{00}, s_{01}, s_{02},..., s_{0n}, s_{10}, s_{11}, s_{12},..., s_{1n},..., s_{m0}, s_{m1}, s_{m2},....,s_{mn} are the laser line displacements, which are computed by image processing described in section 2. The n-index corresponds to the displacement for each pattern dimension. The m-index corresponds to the displacement at each camera position x_A in the x-axis. The displacements at different camera position are shown in Figure 10.

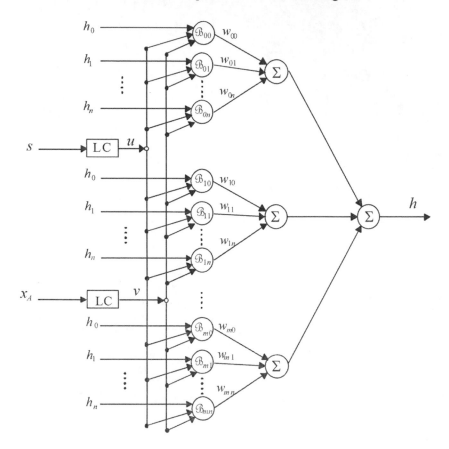

Figure 9. Bezier network for modelling of the mobile setup.

Using the position x_A, the parametric v is determined by a linear combination (LC). The relationship between x_A of the camera position and the parametric value v is represented by

$$v = a_0 + a_1 x_A \tag{27}$$

where a_i are the unknown constants and x_A is laser line position at each camera position. Using x_A of the camera position and its respective v, the Eq.(27) can be determined. The Bezier curves are defined in the interval $0 \leq v \leq 1$. Therefore, the value $v = 0$ for the first x_A and the value $v = 1$ for the last camera position x_A. Substituting these two x_A positions and its corresponding values v in Eq.(27), two equation with two unknown constants are obtained. Solving these equations a_0 and a_1 are determined and Eq.(27) is completed. In this manner, for each x_A of the camera position, a parametric v valued is computed via Eq.(27). In the same manner, the displacement $s(x,y)$ is represented by a parametric value u. The relationship between the displacement and the parametric u value is represented by

$$u = b_0 + b_1 s,$$

(28)

where b_i are the unknown constants, s the laser line displacement. Based on the displacement s and its respective u, the Eq.(28) can be determined. The Bezier curves are defined in the interval $0 \leq u \leq 1$. Thus, $u=0$ for the first displacement s_{00} and $u=1$ for the last displacement s_{mn}. Substituting these values and its corresponding values u in Eq.(28), two equation with two unknown constants are obtained. Solving these equations b_0 and b_1 are determined and Eq.(28) is completed. In this manner, a parametric value u is computed via Eq.(28) for a each displacement s_{ij}.

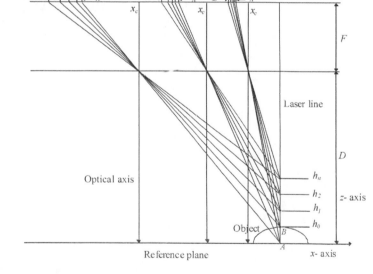

Figure 10. Displacements at different camera position.

The hidden layer is built by means of the Bezier basis function. The expression for a two-dimensional Bezier basis function is described by

$$\mathcal{B}_{ij} = B_i(u)B_j(v), \qquad (29)$$

where

$$B_i(u) = \binom{n}{i} u^i (1-u)^{n-i} \quad , \quad B_j(v) = \binom{m}{j} u^j (1-v)^{m-j},$$

and

$$\binom{n}{i} = \frac{n!}{i!(n-i)!} \, , \quad \binom{m}{j} = \frac{m!}{j!(m-j)!} \cdot$$

The output layer is generated by the summation of the neurons, which are multiplied by a weight. The output response is the object dimension $\mathcal{H}(u, v)$, which is given by

$$\mathcal{H}(u, v) = \sum_{i=0}^{n} \sum_{j=0}^{m} w_{ij} h_i \, B_i(u) B_j(v), \quad 0 \le u \le 1, \ 0 \le v \le 1, \quad (30)$$

where w_{ij} are the weights, h_i is the object dimension, $B_i(u)$ and $B_j(v)$ are the Bezier basis function represented by Eq.(29). To construct the complete network Eq.(30), the suitable weights w_{ij} should be determined. To carry it out, the network is being forced to produce the correct object dimension h_i. To do this, for each h_i, the x_A of the camera position and displacement s_{ij} are converted to values (u, v) via Eq.(27) and Eq.(28) respectively. Then, the object dimension h_i and its corresponding (u, v) are substituted in Eq.(30). Thus, for each pair (u, v) an output $\mathcal{H}_{ij}(u, v)$ is generated and the next equation system is obtained

$$\mathcal{H}_{00}(u, v) = h_0 = w_{00} \, h_0 \, B_0(u)B_0(v) + w_{01} \, h_1 \, B_0(u)B_1(v) + ,\dots , + w_{0n} \, h_n \, B_0(u)B_n(v) +$$
$$,\dots, + \quad w_{m0} \, h_0 \, B_m(u)B_0(v) + ,\dots, + w_{mn} \, h_n \, B_m(u)B_n(v)$$

$$\mathcal{H}_{01}(u, v) = h_1 = w_{00} \, h_0 \, B_0(u)B_0(v) + w_{01} \, h_1 \, B_0(u)B_1(v) + ,\dots , + w_{0n} \, h_n \, B_0(u)B_n(v) +$$
$$,\dots, + \quad w_{m0} \, h_0 \, B_m(u)B_0(v) + ,\dots, + w_{mn} \, h_n \, B_m(u)B_n(v)$$

$$\vdots \qquad\qquad \vdots \qquad\qquad\qquad \vdots \qquad\qquad\qquad \vdots$$

$$\mathcal{H}_{0n}(u, v) = h_n = w_{00} \, h_0 \, B_0(u)B_0(v) + w_{01} \, h_1 \, B_0(u)B_1(v) + ,\dots , + w_{0n} \, h_n \, B_0(u)B_n(v) +$$
$$,\dots, + \quad w_{m0} \, h_0 \, B_m(u)B_0(v) + ,\dots, + w_{mn} \, h_n \, B_m(u)B_n(v) \qquad (31)$$

$$\vdots \qquad\qquad \vdots \qquad\qquad\qquad \vdots \qquad\qquad\qquad \vdots$$

$$\mathcal{H}_{m0}(u, v) = h_0 = w_{00} \, h_0 \, B_0(u)B_0(v) + w_{01} \, h_1 \, B_0(u)B_1(v) + ,\dots , + w_{0n} \, h_n \, B_0(u)B_n(v) +$$
$$,\dots, + \quad w_{m0} \, h_0 \, B_m(u)B_0(v) + ,\dots, + w_{mn} \, h_n \, B_m(u)B_n(v)$$

$$\vdots \qquad\qquad \vdots \qquad\qquad\qquad \vdots \qquad\qquad\qquad \vdots$$

$$\mathcal{H}_{mn}(u, v) = h_n = w_{00} \, h_0 \, B_0(u)B_0(v) + w_{01} \, h_1 \, B_0(u)B_1(v) + ,\dots , + w_{0n} \, h_n \, B_0(u)B_n(v) +$$
$$,\dots, + \quad w_{m0} \, h_0 \, B_m(u)B_0(v) + ,\dots, + w_{mn} \, h_n \, B_m(u)B_n(v)$$

This linear system of Eq.(31) can be represented as

$$H_{00} = w_{00}\beta_{0,0} + w_{01}\beta_{0,1} + ,\dots, + \ w_{mn}\beta_{0,mn}$$

$$H_{01} = w_{00} \, \beta_{1,0} + w_{01}\beta_{1,1} + ,\dots, + w_{mn}\beta_{1,mn} \qquad (32)$$

$$\vdots \qquad \vdots \qquad \vdots \qquad \vdots$$

$$H_{mn} = w_{00}\beta_{mn,0} + w_{01}\beta_{mn,1} + \ldots\ldots, + w_{mn}\beta_{mn,mn}$$

This equation can be rewritten in matrix form as $\boldsymbol{\beta}\mathbf{W} = \boldsymbol{H}$. The linear system is represented by the next matrix

$$\begin{bmatrix} \beta_{0,0} & \beta_{0,1} & \beta_{0,2} & \cdots & \beta_{0,mn} \\ \beta_{1,0} & \beta_{1,1} & \beta_{1,2} & \cdots & \beta_{1,mn} \\ \vdots & \vdots & \vdots & & \vdots \\ \beta_{mn,0} & \beta_{mn,1} & \beta_{mn,2} & \cdots & \beta_{mn,nn} \end{bmatrix} \begin{bmatrix} w_{00} \\ w_{01} \\ \vdots \\ w_{mn} \end{bmatrix} = \begin{bmatrix} H_{00} \\ H_{01} \\ \vdots \\ H_{mn} \end{bmatrix} \qquad (33)$$

By solving the linear system Eq.(33), the weights w_{ij} are obtained. This system is solved by the Chelosky method. In this manner, the network $\mathcal{H}(u, v)$ Eq.(30) has been completed. The result of this network is a two-dimensional model, which computes the object dimension. Thus, for a particular diplacement s_{ij} and its respective x_A of the camera position an h_{ij} is computed by the network Eq.(30). The displacement s_{ij} and the x_A of the camera position are detected by image processing described in section 2.

5. PARAMETERS OF THE VISION SYSTEM

In optical metrology, the object dimension is determined based on the camera parameters and the geometry of the setup. Usually, these parameters are determined by an external procedure to the reconstruction system. Then, these parameters are given to the contouring model to reconstruct the object shape. The camera parameters include focal distance, camera orientation, image center, scale factor of the pixel and distortion. In this system, the camera parameters are computed in the contouring system by means of the network and image processing. Based on the pinhole camera model Fg.11(a), the camera parameters are determined. The camera orientation is determined based on the optical axis of the camera. In this case, the optical axis is perpendicular to the reference plane as shown Figure 11(b). In this geometry, the laser line projected on the reference plane and on the object is indicated by x_A and x_B at the image plane, respectively. The distance between the image center and the laser line in the x-axis is indicated by ℓ_a. The object dimension is indicated by h_i and $D = z_i + h_i$. In this case, the reference plane is a platform, which moves the object in the x-axis. Based on the displacement s_{ij} and dimension h_i produced by the network, the camera orientation is computed. According to the perpendicular optical axis, the object dimension h_i has a projection k_i at the reference plane. From Figure 11(b), the displacement is defined as $s_{ij} = (x_c - x_B) - (x_c - x_A)$. Thus, the projection k_i at the reference plane is computed by

$$k_i = \frac{F h_i}{s_{ij} + x_c - x_A}$$

(34)

From Eq.(12) F, x_c, x_A are constants and h_i is computed by the network according to s_{ij}. In this case, k_i is a linear function and the derivative k_i respect to s_{ij} dk/ds is a constant.

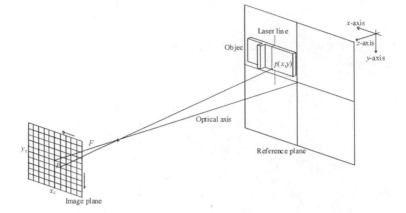

Figure 11(a) Geometry of the pinhole camera model.

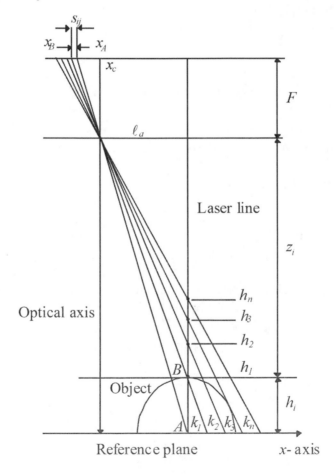

Figure 11(b). Geometry of an optical axis perpendicular to the reference plane x-axis.

Other camera orientation is an optical axis not perpendicular to the reference plane, which is shown in Figure 11(c). For this geometry, the distance between the image center and the laser line position is defined by $x_c - x_B = F \tan \theta$. Thus the laser line displacement is defined by $s_{ij} = F \tan \theta - (x_c - x_A)$. The angles of this geometry are defined by $\theta + \delta + \alpha = 180$, $\alpha + \gamma = 90$ and $k_i = h_i \tan \gamma$. Therefore, the projection k_i is given by

$$k_i = h_i \tan\left[\tan^{-1}\left(\frac{s_{ij} + x_c - x_A}{F} \right) + \delta - 90° \right] \qquad (35)$$

From Eq.(34) F, x_c, x_A and δ are constants and h_i is computed by $h_i = D - \ell_a \tan \alpha$. Where δ is an angle minor than 90° and D is constant. In this case, s_{ij} of Eq.(35) does not produce a linear function k_i and the derivative dk/ds is not a constant.

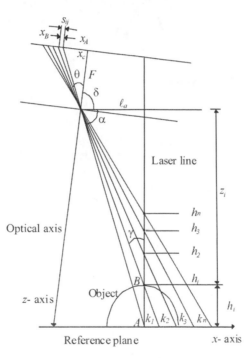

Figure 11(c). Geometry of an optical axis not perpendicular to the reference plane x-axis.

The orientation of the camera in y-axis is performed based on the geometry of Figure 11(d). In this case, the object is moved in y-axis over the laser line. When the object is moved, the object pattern changes from y_p to y_i in the laser line. In this case, $t = (y_c - y_p) - (y_c - y_i)$. For an optical axis perpendicular to the reference plane y-axis, a linear q_i produces a linear t_i at the image plane. Therefore, the derivative dt/dq is a constant. Thus, the orientation camera is performed by means of dk/ds = constant for the x-axis and dt/dq = constant for the y-axis. Based on these criterions, the optical axis of the camera is aligned perpendicular to x-axis and y-axis. The orientation in x-axis, k_i is computed from h_i provided by the network. Due to the distortion, the derivative dk/ds is slightly different to a constant. But, this derivative is the more similar to a constant, which is shown in Figure 11(e). In this figure, the dash line is dk/ds for δ minor than 90° and the dot line is dk/ds for δ major than 90°. Thus, the generated network corresponds to an optical axis aligned perpendicularly along the x-axis. For the orientation in y-axis, q_i is provided by the electromechanical device, the object position y_i and t_i are obtained by image processing in each movement. Due to the distortion, the derivative dt/dq is not exactly a constant. But, this derivative is the more similar to a constant. Thus, the optical axis is aligned perpendicular to the y-axis. In this manner, the network and image processing provide an optical axis aligned perpendicularly to the reference plane.

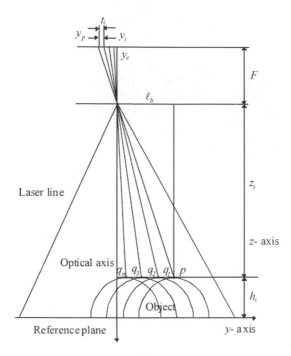

Figure 11(d). Geometry of an optical axis perpendicular to reference plane y-axis.

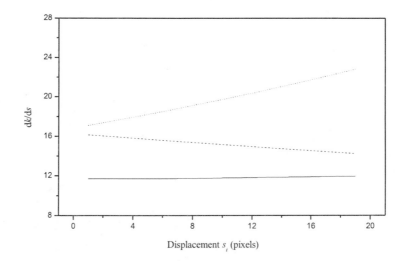

Figure 11(e). Derivative dk/ds for an optical axis perpendicular and not perpendicular to x-axis.

Based on the optical axis perpendicular to reference plane Figure 11(b), the camera parameters are deduced. To carry it out, the network produces the object depth h_i according to the displacement s_{ij} and x_A of the camera position. The geometry of the setup Figure 11(b) is described by

$$\frac{z_i}{\ell_a} = \frac{z_i + F}{\eta(x_c - x_B) + \ell_a} , \qquad (36)$$

From this equation η is the scale factor to convert the pixels to millimeters. Using $D = z_i + h_i$ and $\eta s_{ij} = \eta(x_c - x_B) - \eta(x_c - x_A)$, Eq.(36) is rewritten as

$$\frac{D - h_i}{\ell_a} = \frac{D - h_i + F}{\eta(s_{ij} + x_c - x_A) + \ell_a} \qquad (37)$$

Where D is the distance from the lens to the reference plane. From Eq.(37) the constants D, ℓ_a, F, η, x_c should be determined. To carry it out, Eq.(37) is rewritten as equation system

$$h_0 = D - \frac{F \ell_a}{\eta(s_{00} + x_c - x_A)}$$

$$h_1 = D - \frac{F \ell_a}{\eta(s_{01} + x_c - x_A)}$$

$$h_2 = D - \frac{F \ell_a}{\eta(s_{02} + x_c - x_A)} \qquad (38)$$

$$h_3 = D - \frac{F \ell_a}{\eta(s_{03} + x_c - x_A)}$$

$$h_4 = D - \frac{F \ell_a}{\eta(s_{04} + x_c - x_A)}$$

$$h_5 = D - \frac{F \ell_a}{\eta(s_{05} + x_c - x_A)}$$

The values $h_1, h_2,....,h_5$, are computed by the network according to $s_{01}, s_{02},....,s_{06}$ at any camera position. These values are substituted in Eq.(38) and the equation system is solved. Thus, the constants D, ℓ_a, F, η, and x_c are determined for the initial camera position. The coordinate y_c is computed from the geometry Figure 11(c) described by

$$t_i = (y_c - y_p) - \frac{F(D - h_i)}{\eta(\ell_b - q_{i-1})},$$

(39)

From Eq.(39) the constants D, F, η, q_i, t_i, h_i are known and y_c, ℓ_b, y_p should be determined. To carry it out, Eq.(39) is rewritten as equation system for an h_i constant by

$$t_1 = (y_c - y_p) - \frac{F(D - h_1)}{\eta(\ell_b - q_0)}$$

$$t_2 = (y_c - y_p) - \frac{F(D - h_1)}{\eta(\ell_b - q_1)} \qquad (40)$$

$$t_3 = (ay_c - ay_p) - \frac{F(D - h_1)}{\eta(\ell_b - q_2)}$$

The values t_1, t_2, t_3, are taken from the orientation in y-axis, $q_0 = 0$ and the values q_1, q_2, are provided by the electromechanical device. These values are substituted in Eq.(40) to solve the equation system. Thus, the constants y_c, y_p and ℓ_b are determined. In this manner, the camera parameters and the setup geometry are determined based on the network and image processing. The distortion is observed by means of the laser line position x_B in the image plane, which is described by

$$x_B = \frac{F \ell_a}{D - h_i} + x_c$$

(41)

Based on Eq.(41), the behavior of x_B respect to h_i is a linear function. However, due to the distortion, the real data x_B are not linear. The network is constructed by means of the real data using the displacement $s_{ij} = (x_c - x_B) - (x_c - x_A)$ at each camera position. Therefore, the network produces a non linear data h_i, which is shown in Figure 11(f). Thus, the distortion is included in the network, which computes the object dimension in the imaging system. This network computes a transverse section of the object from each laser line. By means of the information of all laser line images, the complete object is constructed.

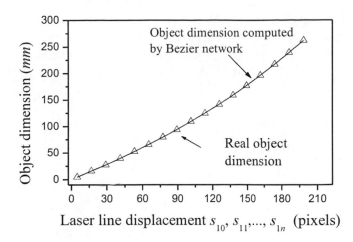

Laser line displacement s_{10}, s_{11},..., s_{1n} (pixels)

Figure 11(f). Object dimension produced by the Bezier network at the firs camera position.

6. EXPERIMENTAL RESULTS OF COMPUTER VISION

The optical setup to perform the three-dimensional vision is shown in Figure 1. In this arrangement, the object is moved in the x-axis by the electromechanical device in steps of a fraction of millimeter. To perform the scanning, a laser line is projected on the surface target by a 15 mW laser diode. This laser line is deformed according to the object surface at the image plane. Each deformed line is digitized a CCD camera and a frame grabber with 320 x 200 pixels and 256 gray levels. To perform the contouring, the line displacement $s(x,y)$ is detected via Bezier curves Eq.(4), Eq.(5) and Eq.(1). The Bezier network computes the object dimension based on the laser line displacement. The produced data by the network is stored in array memory to obtain the complete object shape. Thus, the computer vision process is achieved.

The computer vision is performed with four objects. The first object is a glass, which is shown in Figure 12(a). To carry it out, this object is scanned along x-axis in steps of 1.27 mm. From the scanning, a set of laser line images are digitized. From each image, the laser line displacement is detected. This is carried out by computing the maximum position via Bezier curves in each row of the image. The result of this step is the displacements s_0, s_1, s_2, ..., s_n. Then, a value u is computed for each s_i via Eq.(21). The value u is processed by the network Eq.(23) to determine the contour dimension h_i. All data produced by the network is stored in an array memory to obtain the shape of the glass shown in Figure 12(b). To know the accuracy provided the two-dimensional network, the root mean squared error (*rms*) [30] is calculated. To carry it out, contour data given the network and data measured by a coordinate measure machine (**CMM**) are used. The *rms* is described by the next equation

$$rms = \sqrt{\frac{1}{n}\sum_{i=1}^{n}(ho_i - hc_i)^2} \, , \qquad (42)$$

where ho_i is the data measured by the CMM, hc_i is the computed by the network and n is the data number. For the glass the n was 480 data, which was measured by the **CMM** and computed by the two-dimensional network. The error calculated for the glass shape is a $rms = 0.162$ mm. Based on the average dimension the rms value can be represented in percentage terms. The average of the glass dimensions is 22.00 mm. Therefore, the error is 0.0073 based on the rms, which represents a 0.73 % of error.

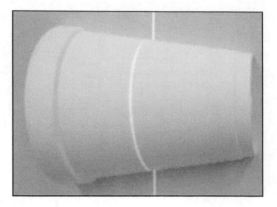

Figure 12 (a). Surface of a glass for computer vision.

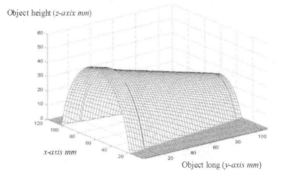

Figure 12(b) Three-dimensional shape of the glass.

To determine if the value n is according to the desired precision of the error, the confidence level is calculated [31]. The value n based on the confidence desired is described by the next relation

$$n = \left(z_\alpha \frac{\sigma_x}{e} \right)^2, \tag{43}$$

where z_α is the confidence desired, e is the error expressed in percentage, and σ_x is standard deviation. Therefore, the confidence level according to the data n can be calculated by

$$z_\alpha = \frac{e}{\sigma_x}\sqrt{n} \ . \tag{44}$$

To know if the value n is right according to the desired confidence level, Eq.(42) is applied. The confidence level desired is 95 %, which corresponds to z_α=1.96 based on the confidence table [32]. The error is e = 0.73% and standard deviation is 7.62. Substituting these values in Eq.(42), the result is a n = 418.57. This value indicates that value n chosen is right to produce a confidence level of 95 %. Therefore, the values $z_\alpha >$ 1.96, provide a confidence level greater than 95%. The confidence level for the n=480 is z_α=2.09. It indicates a confidence level over 95%.

The second object to be profiled is a dummy face shown in Figure 13(a) and Figure 13(b). In the initial sequence, the laser line occlusion appears due to the surface variation Figure 13(b). The camera is moved toward the laser projector to obtain Figure 13(c), which provides the occluded region of the laser line. Thus, the contouring can be performed completely. To carry it out, the dummy face is scanned in x-axis in steps of 1.27 mm. From each image produced in the scanning, the x_A of the camera position and the laser line displacement s_{ij} are computed via image processing. Then, these values are converted to values v and u are deduced via Eq.(27) and Eq.(28), respectively. Based on u and v, the object dimension is computed by means of the network Eq.(30). All data produced by the network are stored in array memory to construct the complete object shape. In this case, sixty eight images of the mobile setup are processed to determine the complete object shape shown in Figure 13(d). The scale of this figure is mm. To determine the accuracy of the data provided by the modelling of the mobile setup, the dummy face is measured by the CMM. The rms is computed using n=1122 data, which were provided by the network and by the CCM as reference. The rms calculated for this object is a rms = 0.155 mm. The precision of this error produces a confidence level over 95%. The result of the contouring using a static setup is a not completed object shape. This is because some regions are not profiled due to the occlusions.

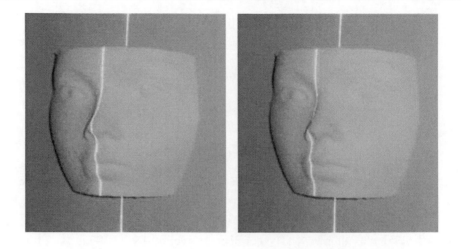

Figure 13(a). Image of a dummy face. Figure 13(b). Dummy face with laser line occlusion.

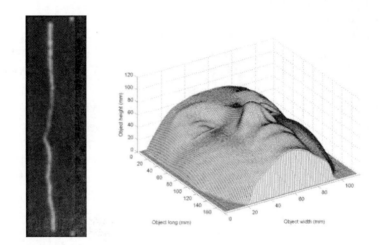

Figure 13(c). Laser line with out occlusions. Figure 13(d). Three-dimensional shape of the dummy face.

The third object to be profiled is a plastic fruit shown in Figure 14(a). The contouring is performed by scanning the fruit in steps of 1.27 *mm*. In this case, forty laser lines were processed to determine the complete object shape shown in Figure 14(b). To determine accuracy of the model provided by the network, the plastic fruit was measured by the CMM. The *rms* was computed using $n=420$ data, which were provided by the two-dimensional network and by the CMM as reference. The *rms* is calculated for this object is a *rms* = 0.142 *mm*. The precision of this error produces a confidence level over 95%.

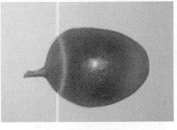

Figure 14(a). Image of the plastic fruit with out stripe occlusion.

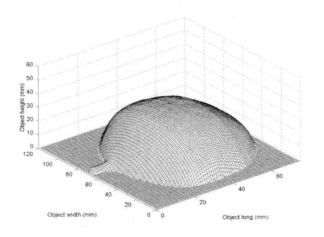

Figure 14(b) Three-dimensional shape of the plastic fruit.

The fourth object to be profiled is an hippopotamus shown in Figure 15(a). An occlusion appears due to the surface variation. In this image, the pixels of high intensity is minor than three in the occluded region. Thus, a laser line occlusion is detected in the image. The result of the displacement detection by image processing is a broken contour. In this case, the camera is moved toward the laser projector. The result of this process is a complete laser line shown in Figure 15(b). From this image, the displacement of laser line is detected. Based on this displacement and the camera position, the network produces a complete object contour. Thus, the object contouring is achieved by the modelling of the mobile setup. In this system, the scanning is performed in steps of 1.27 mm in the x-axis. From each image produced in the scanning, the camera position x_A and the laser line displacement s_{ij} are computed by image processing. Then, these are converted to values v and u via Eq.(27) and Eq.(28), respectively. By means of the network Eq.(30), the object dimension is computed based on u and v. Thus, the network produces a transverse section from each image of the laser line. All data produced by the network are stored in array memory to construct the complete object shape. For the hippopotamus, the rms is computed using the number data $n = 480$. The error calculated for the hippopotamus is a $rms = 0.132$ mm. Sixty two images of the mobile setup are processed to obtain the complete object shape, which is shown in Figure 15(c). In this Figure, the scale of the axis is in mm.

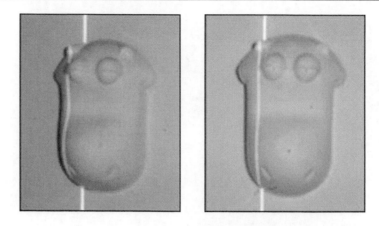

Figure 15 (a). Object with laser line occlusion.   Figure 15(c). Laser line with out occlusions.

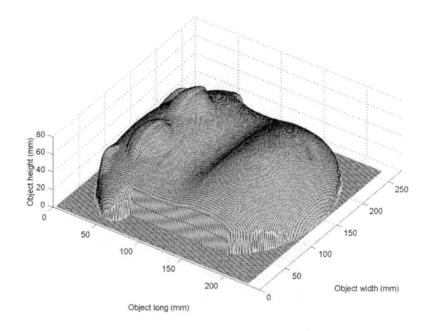

Figure 15(c). Three-dimensional shape of the hippopotamus.

The employed computer in this process is a PC to 1 GHz. Each light line image is processed in 0.022 sec. The capture velocity of the camera used in this camera is 34 fps. Also, the electromechanical device is programmed to moving the object at 34 steps per second. In this computer vision procedure, the parameters such as projection angle, distances of the geometry are not used to determine the shape representation. Therefore, the automatic procedure provides an easier performance than those techniques that use distances of the components of optical setup. In this manner, the computer vision is performed by computational process and measurements on optical step are avoided. Therefore, a good repeatability is achieved in each computer vision process.

CONCLUSION

A review of the shape detection technique based on a laser line and approximation networks has been presented. The described technique here provides a valuable tool for inspection industrial and reverse engineering. The automatic technique avoids the physical measurements of the setup, as is common in the methods of laser line projection. In this technique, the parameters of the setup are obtained automatically by computational process via image processing and Bezier networks. This procedure improves the accuracy of the results, because measurement errors are not passed to the contouring system. In this technique, the ability to detect the laser line with a sub-pixel resolution has been achieved by Bezier curves. This step is achieved with few operations. By using this computational-optical setup a good repeatability is achieved in every measurement. Therefore, this technique is performed in good manner.

ACKNOWLEDGMENTS

J. Apolinar Muñoz Rodríguez would like to thank to CONCYTEG of Guanajuato and CONACYT of Mexico, for the partial support of this research.

REFERENCES

[1]   W. R. Uttal, R. Kakarala, S. Dayanand, T. Shepherd, J. Kalki, C. F. Lunskis and N. Liu, (1999), Computational modeling of vision: The role of combination, Marcel Dekker, U.S.A..

[2]   G. Sansoni, R. Rodella, M. Carocci and V. Carbone, (2000), "Machine vision: Optical digitization of free-form complex surface using the projection of structured light," *Optics and Photonics News*, 23-29.

[3]   C. Lulie, Q. Chenggen, T. Cho-Jui and F. Yu, , (2005), "Shape measurement using one frame projected sawtooth fringe pattern", Opt. Comm., Vol. 246, Issue 4-6, p. 275-284.

[4]   J. A. Muñoz Rodríguez and R. Rodríguez-Vera, (2003). "Evaluation of the light line displacement location for object shape detection", Journal of Modern Optics, Vol. 50 No. 1 p. 137-154.

[5]   R. Klette, K. Schluns and A. Koschan, (1998), Computer vision: Three-dimensional data from images, Springer-Verlag, Singapore.

[6]   W. Guanghui, H. Zhanyi, W. Fuchao and T. Hung-Tat, (2004), "Implementation and experimental study on fast object modeling based on multiple structured stripes", Optics and Laser in Eng. Vol. 42 No. 6, p. 627-638.

[7]   F. Remondino, A. Guarnieri and A. Vettore, (2004), "3D modeling of close-range objects: photogrammetry or laser scanning?", SPIE Proc. Vol. 5665, p. 216-225.

[8] Z. Wei, G. Zhang and Y. Xu, (2003), "Calibration approach for structured–light-stripe vision sensor based on invariance of double cross-ratio," Opt. Eng. Vol. 42 No. 10, p. 2956-2966.

[9] M. Mclvor, (2002), "Nonlinear calibration of a laser profiler," Opt. Eng. Vol. 42 No.1, p. 205-212.

[10] L. Zagorchev and A. Goshtasby, (2006), "A paintbrush laser range scanner", Computer vision and image understating, Vol. 10, p. 65-86.

[11] F. Causa and J. Sarma, (2003), "Realistic model for the output beam profile of stripe and tapered superluminescent light–emitting diodes," Appl. Optics, Vol. 42 No.21, p. 4341-4348.

[12] J. S. Milton and J. C. Arnold, (2003), Introduction to probability and statistics: principles and applications for engineering and the computing science, McGraw-Hill, U.S.A.

[13] M. E. Mortenson, Geometric Modeling, (1997), Willey, Second edition, U.S.A. .

[14] C. F. Gerald and P. O. Wheatley, (1992), Applied numerical analysis, Addison Wesley, Fifth edition, U.S.A.

[15] M. Neifeld and D. Psaltis, (1993), "Optical implementations of radial basis classifiers," Appl. Optics Vol. 32 No.8, 1370-1379.

[16] E. W. Foor and A. M. Neifeld, (1995), "Adaptive optical radial basis function neural network for handwritten digit recognition," Appl. Optics Vol. 34 No.32, 7545-7555.

[17] T. Sabisch, A. Ferguson, H. Bolouri, (2000), "*Identification of complex shapes using a self organizing neural system*," IEEE Transactions on Neural Networks, Vol. 11 Issue: 4, 921 -934.

[18] Rojas, H. Pomares, J. Gonzalez, J. L.Bernier, E. Ros, F. J. Pelayo, A.Prieto, (2000), "*Analysis of the functional block involved in the design of Radial basic Functions*," Neural Processing Letters , Vol.12 No.1, 1-17.

[19] J.A. Muñoz Rodríguez, R. Rodríguez-Vera and A. Asundi, (2003), "*Shape detection of moving objects based on a neural network of a light line*". Optics communication Vol. 221, 73-86.

[20] P. Picton, (1998), *Neural networks*, Polgrave, U.S.A.

[21] W.H. Press, B. P. Flannery, S. A. Teukolsky, W. T. Vetterling, (1993), *Numerical Recipes in C*, U.S.A. Cambridge Press.

[22] Specht, D. F. (1991), "A general regression neural network," IEEE Trans. Neural Networks, vol. 2, 568-576.

[23] L. Shao and H. Zhou, (1996), "Curve Fitting with Bezier cubics", Graphical models and image processing Vol. 58 No.3, 223-232.

[24] Zhang, (1999), "C- Bezier Curves and Surface*"*, Graphical models and Image processing Vol. 61, 2-15.

[25] Mohamed, N. Horoshi and A. Takeshi, (1993) "Bezier and polynomial methods of making curves," SPIE Vol. 2644, 290-295.

[26] A. Muñoz Rodríguez, Miguel Rosales Ciseña and R. Rodriguez-Vera, (2005), "3D shape detection based on a Bezier neural network of a light line," SPIE Proc. Vol. 5776, 630-639.

[27] Robert J. Schalkoff, (1997), Artificial Neural Networks, Mc Graw Hill. U.S.A.

[28] E. Mortenson, (1997), Geometric Modeling, Willey, Second edition, U.S.A.

[29] J. Zhang, (1999), *"C- Bezier Curves and Surface"*, Graphical models and Image processing Vol. 61, p. 2-15.

[30] T. Masters, (1993), Practical Neural Networks Recipes in C++, Academic Press, U.S.A.

[31] J. E. Freund, (1979), Modern Elementary Statistics, Prentice Hall, U.S.A.

INDEX

A

access, viii
actuators, viii
adaptability, 3
adaptation, 5, 17
ADC, 275
adjustment, 341
aerospace, 21
algebraic topology, vii, ix, 239, 240, 241, 265
algorithm, vii, viii, x, 29, 32, 33, 38, 41, 42, 44, 49, 54, 55
artificial intelligence, vii, x, 329
Artificial Neural Networks, 360
Austria, 55, 239
automate, 3
automation, vii, 2, 12, 13, 21, 24, 39

B

base, viii, 2, 13, 24, 25, 26, 30, 32, 35, 36, 37
bias, 10
brain, viii, 15, 283

C

C++, 55, 360
calibration, 359
CCR, 2, 38
ceramic, 2
cerebral cortex, 11, 18
chemical, 278
China, 41, 54
chlorophyll, 278
chromosome, 44, 45, 53

classes, 4, 5, 6, 10, 16, 18, 20, 24, 26, 29, 30, 32, 33, 35, 36
classification, 3, 12, 20, 37, 38, 334
coding, 6, 8, 9, 11, 18, 27
color, 272, 278
commercial, 22
communication, 21, 359
compensation, ix
competitors, 269
complexity, viii
compliance, ix
computation, 23, 42
computer, vii, ix, x, 1, 10, 13, 14, 21, 24, 28, 35, 36, 42, 329, 330, 331, 352, 353, 358
computer numerical control (CNC), vii, 1
computing, 24, 353, 359
conference, 42
construction, 2, 13
consumption, viii, 41
content based image retrieval (CBIR), x, 303
contour, 22, 23, 24, 31, 32, 329, 330, 331, 353, 356
convergence, x, 6, 12, 17
correlation, 2, 3, 23
cost, vii, 2, 12, 13, 22, 38
cycles, 9, 11, 17, 28, 31, 32

D

data set, 337
database, 3, 4, 8, 10, 12, 18, 20, 23, 24, 28, 29, 30, 31, 32, 33, 36, 38
decision trees, 20
decoding, 42, 44, 45
decomposition, 337
defects, 2, 3, 4, 13, 38, 283
deficiencies, 278
deformation, x, 329, 330, 331, 343

denoising, ix
depth, 330, 332, 333, 350
depth recovery, 330
detection, vii, viii, x, 2, 3, 21, 22, 23, 24, 36, 37, 38, 41, 42, 55, 280, 281, 329, 333, 334, 356, 358, 359, 360
detection system, 55
diodes, 359
discretization, 270
dispersion, 283
displacement, 34, 332, 333, 338, 340, 341, 342, 343, 344, 346, 347, 348, 350, 352, 353, 354, 356, 358
distortions, 10, 11, 18, 28, 31, 32, 36
distribution, 2, 332, 341
distribution function, 2

E

electronic circuits, 275
encoding, 42, 43
energy, 3, 13
engineering, ix, 21, 38, 55, 358, 359
environment, viii, ix, 3, 4, 42
environmental control, 21
equipment, 13, 21, 270
error detection, 14
evolution, 42, 53
excitation, 9, 10, 17, 18, 27
execution, 8, 46
extraction, 2, 5, 24, 55, 278, 280
extracts, 29

F

facial expression, 54
factories, 13
FFT, 282
fires, 272
fitness, 3, 44, 45, 49, 50, 54
flaws, 3, 37
flexibility, viii, 13
forest fire, 272
formula, 9
Fourier analysis, 37
fractures, 283
freedom, 22
fusion, viii

G

genes, 44
genetic algorithm (GA), viii, 41, 42

genetics, 53
geometrical parameters, 24
geometry, 29, 330, 331, 332, 347, 348, 349, 350, 351, 352, 358
Germany, 1, 39, 57
graph, 22
guidelines, 42

H

hair, 37
Hawaii, 39
height, 3, 6, 10, 15, 27, 29, 45, 46
histogram, 3
human, viii, ix, 14, 269, 283
human information processing, ix
human machine interface (HMI), viii, 57
hybrid, 39

I

identification, 334, 337
illumination, ix, 26, 29, 35
image analysis, 278
image recognition systems, vii, 1, 2
imaging systems, 269, 275
indexing, 282
individuality, 14
individuals, 44
industry, 2, 21
input, 334, 336, 337, 340
intelligence, 42
interface, viii, 25, 28, 29
Israel, 239

J

Japan, 13, 39, 41

L

landscape, 272
languages, x
laser metrology, vii, x, 329
lead, viii
learning, 13, 16, 17, 18, 23, 24, 37, 334, 338
learning process, 17, 18
lens, 351
light, 24, 269, 272, 275, 276, 277, 283, 330, 358, 359, 360
linear function, 347, 348, 352

LIRA classifier, vii, 1, 6

M

machine learning, 55
machinery, ix
magnitude, 9, 18
man, 272, 329
manipulation, 22
manufacturing, 13, 14, 15, 20, 21, 24, 38
materials, 37
mathematics, ix
matrix, 2, 270, 272, 278, 281, 336, 337, 339, 342, 346
matter, 329
measurement, x, 329, 330, 342, 358
measurements, ix, x, 329, 330, 358
mechanical metal treatment, vii, 1
media, 275
median, 279
medical, 21
memory, 15, 23, 38, 353, 355, 357
Mexico, 13, 21, 329, 358
micro mechanics, vii, 1
micromanipulator, vii, 2
micromechanical components, vii, 2
milled surface, vii, 1
miniaturization, 21
modeling, 337
modelling, x, 329, 330, 344, 355, 356
models, ix, 38, 47, 359, 360
modifications, 5
modules, viii, 24, 28, 29
moisture, 272
moisture content, 272
morphology, viii, 282
Moscow, 38
motion control, 39
multiplication, 12, 278, 281
mutation, 44, 53

N

network, 334, 335, 340
neural classifiers, vii, 1, 8, 15
neural network, viii, x, 2, 3, 13, 14, 15, 16, 17, 24, 26, 35, 38, 39, 41, 329, 330, 331, 334, 340, 359, 360
neural networks, x, 2, 14, 24, 39, 329, 330, 334
neurons, 5, 6, 7, 8, 9, 11, 15, 16, 17, 18, 27, 31, 334, 335, 336, 338, 340, 341, 343, 345
neuroscience, 14, 38

next generation, 13
nodes, 338, 339
null, 27
numerical analysis, 359
nutrients, 278

O

object trajectories, viii, 58
observable behavior, viii
obstacles, 42, 330
occlusion, 354, 355, 356, 357
operations, 12, 42, 49, 50, 52, 53, 358
opportunities, ix, 269
optimization, 42, 49, 55
output, 334, 335, 336, 337, 340

P

Pairwise Coding Classifier, vii, 1
parallel, 12, 24
parameter, 335, 336
parents, 44
pattern recognition, 42, 54
permission, 37
permit, vii, 2, 24
photographs, 270
photons, 276
plants, 278
platform, 331, 347
playing, viii, 41
polished with file, vii, 1
polished with sandpaper, vii, 1
ponds, 272
population, 53
prediction, 334
preparation, 24
principal component analysis, 22
principles, viii, 15, 26, 359
probability, 337, 341, 359
probability density function, 337
programming, 39, 54
project, 36
propagation, 3
prototype, ix
prototypes, 37

Q

quadratic curve, x
quantization, 270
query, x

R

radio, 270
random numbers, 6
real time, 24
recognition, vii, viii, x, 1, 2, 3, 4, 5, 7, 8, 9, 10, 11,
    12, 13, 14, 15, 17, 18, 19, 20, 21, 22, 23, 24, 26,
    29, 31, 32, 33, 34, 35, 36, 37, 38, 39, 41, 42, 43,
    46, 48, 49, 50, 52, 53, 54, 55, 278, 359
recognition test, 38
reconstruction, 347
recovery, 329
redundancy, 35
regression, 278, 334, 359
reinforcement, 17
relationship, x, 329
reliability, 42
remote sensing, 272
requirements, 9
researchers, ix, 37, 42
resolution, 18, 29, 31, 272, 274, 275, 276, 358
resources, 24
response, 42, 336, 341, 345
retina, 5, 6, 7, 26
rings, 3
RNA, 28, 29
robot hand, 24
robotic vision, 39
root, x, 329, 330, 333, 353
rotations, 18, 29, 282
roughness, 3
rules, 13
Russia, 38

S

saturation, 280, 282
scaling, 23
science, vii, ix, 270, 359
security, 21
sensing, 38, 272, 275, 277, 283
sensitivity, 272
sensors, viii, 42, 330
Serbia, 39
shape, vii, ix, x, 1, 13, 14, 20, 24, 32, 38, 329, 330,
    331, 334, 335, 336, 338, 343, 347, 353, 354, 355,
    356, 357, 358, 360
showing, 15
signals, 3, 278
signs, viii, 42
simulation, 14
Singapore, 359

software, 21, 28, 29, 275, 278
soil type, 278
solution, x, 53, 54
Spain, 187
specifications, 276
spectroscopy, 272
stability, 23
standard deviation, 332, 354
state, x, 5, 7, 15, 16, 38
statistics, ix, 2, 341, 359
stimulus, 15
storage, 275, 277
storage media, 275, 277
stress, 278
stretching, 280
structure, viii, 5, 7, 12, 25, 26, 28, 334, 337, 340, 343
subtraction, 278, 281
Sun, 39, 276
surface properties, 37
systems, 337

T

target, 14, 54, 332, 352
techniques, ix, 24, 42, 53, 269, 278, 280, 281, 282,
    358
technologies, 2, 14, 21, 24, 270, 283
technology, vii, ix, 2, 13, 14, 21, 42, 269, 270
temperature, 278
terminals, 34
testing, vii, 1, 3, 12, 19, 28
texture, vii, 1, 2, 3, 4, 10, 12, 23, 36, 37, 38, 282
texture recognition problem, vii, 1, 2
time, 334
time series, 334
tones, 272
topology, vii, ix
training, vii, viii, x, 1, 4, 5, 8, 9, 10, 11, 12, 16, 17,
    18, 19, 20, 27, 28, 30, 31, 32, 33, 36, 41, 48, 336
trajectory, 33
transformation, 6, 23
transformations, 18, 19, 20
translation, 45, 54
transport, 21
transportation, vii, 2
transverse section, 331, 352, 357
treatment, vii, 1, 2
triangulation, 330
turned with lathe, vii, 1

U

UK, 303
Ukraine, 39
universality, 20
USA, 1, 39, 272, 273, 274, 277, 283, 284, 285

V

values, 337
variables, ix
varieties, 269, 275
vector, 6, 8, 15, 23, 24, 27, 38, 334, 336, 338, 340, 343
vegetation, 272

vehicles, viii, ix
velocity, 3, 358
vibration, 3
vision, vii, viii, ix, x, 1, 13, 14, 15, 21, 22, 38, 39, 41, 42, 329, 330, 342, 347, 352, 353, 358, 359
visions, 38
visual environment, viii
vocabulary, 2

W

water, 272, 277, 278
water structure, 272
wavelengths, 272, 275, 276, 277, 278, 283
web, 24, 42
workpiece treatment, vii, 1